A Harmony of the Gospels
# MATTHEW, MARK AND LUKE
## VOLUME II

## CALVIN'S COMMENTARIES

# CALVIN'S COMMENTARIES

A Harmony of the Gospels

# MATTHEW, MARK AND LUKE

## VOLUME II

Translator

## T. H. L. PARKER

Editors
DAVID W. TORRANCE
THOMAS F. TORRANCE

WILLIAM B. EERDMANS PUBLISHING COMPANY
GRAND RAPIDS, MICHIGAN

THE PATERNOSTER PRESS
CARLISLE

Translation © 1972 The Saint Andrews Press

Published jointly in the United States
by Wm. B. Eerdmans Publishing Co.
255 Jefferson Ave. S.E., Grand Rapids, Michigan 49503
and in the U.K. by The Paternoster Press
P.O. Box 300, Carlisle, Cumbria CA3 0QS

First paperback edition published 1995

Printed in the United States of America

00 99 98 97 96 95      7 6 5 4 3 2 1


Eerdmans ISBN 0-8028-0802-6


**British Library Cataloguing in Publication Data**

Calvin, Jean
Harmony of the Gospels — Matthew, Mark and Luke
Vol. 2. - New ed.
(Calvin's New Testament Commentaries; Vol. 2)
I. Title   II. Parker, T. H. L.   III. Series
226.07

Paternoster ISBN 0-85364-681-3

# A COMMENTARY ON THE HARMONY
# OF THE GOSPELS

*And they went out, and preached that men should repent. And they cast out many devils, and anointed with oil many that were sick, and healed them.* (Mark 6.12-14)

*And they departed, and went throughout the villages, preaching the gospel, and healing everywhere.* (Luke 9.6)

Luke 12. *And they went out and preached.* Matthew makes no mention of what the apostles did. Mark and Luke relate that they executed the charge laid on them. From what they say it becomes clear, as I have said, that the duty then committed to them by Christ was temporary—in fact, for a few days. For they say that they went through towns and villages, and there is no doubt that they soon returned to the Master, as it is said elsewhere.

In Mark's account only one thing requires explanation: 'Many that were sick were anointed with oil.' Why did they use oil when they had been given the ability to heal by Christ? Some learned men think that it was a kind of medicine, and I grant that in those lands oil was often used as a medicine. But it will not do to say that the apostles used ordinary and natural remedies, for this would obscure the miraculous quality of Christ's work. The Lord did not teach them the art and practice of medicine, but commanded them to perform miracles which would stir up all Judaea. Therefore I consider this to have been a visible symbol of spiritual grace which testified that the healing of which they were the ministers came from the secret power of God. For it was usual under the Law for the grace of the Spirit to be signified (*figurari*) by oil. But what a perverted aping of the apostles it is to invent in the Church a ceremony of anointing the sick! This is quite clear from the fact that the gift of healing that Christ bestowed on the apostles was not an inheritance for them to hand down to their descendants, but a seal of the preaching of the Gospel for that occasion. And today the ignorance of the Papists is too ridiculous: they claim that their stinking unction, which precipitates the half-dead into their graves, is a sacrament.

*And it came to pass, when Jesus had made an end of commanding his twelve disciples, he departed thence to teach and preach in their cities.*

*Now when John heard in the prison the works of the Christ, he sent by his disciples, and said unto him, Art thou he that cometh, or look we for another? And Jesus answered, and said unto them, Go your way and tell John the things which ye do hear and see: the blind receive their sight, and the lame walk, the lepers are cleansed, and the deaf hear, the dead are raised up, and the poor have good tidings preached to them.* (Matt. 11.1-6)

*And the disciples of John told him of all these things. And John calling unto him two of his disciples sent them to Jesus, saying, Art thou he that cometh, or look we for another? . . . In that hour he cured many of diseases and plagues and evil spirits; and on many that were blind he bestowed sight. And he answered and said unto them, Go your way, and tell John what things ye have heard and seen; the blind receive their sight, the lame walk, the lepers are cleansed, and the deaf hear, the dead are raised up, the poor have good tidings preached to them. And blessed is he, whosoever shall find none occasion of stumbling in me.* (Luke 7.18-19, 21-23)

Matt. 11.1. *And it came to pass.* Matthew here simply means that Christ did not discontinue His own work while the apostles were active elsewhere. At the same time as He sent them with His commission to go throughout Judaea, He Himself engaged in teaching in Galilee. The word *commanding* is significant. Matthew does not mean that He gave them free hands as ambassadors, but that He commanded and laid down what they were to put forward and how they should bear themselves.

Matt. 11.2. *Now when John heard in the prison.* The Evangelists do not interpret this situation as meaning that John is persuaded by the miracles to recognize at last that He is the Mediator, but that he sees from Christ's celebrity that the time is fit and ripe for confirming the truth of his witness to Him. He therefore sends disciples to Him. Some think he sent them for his own sake. But it is quite absurd to imagine that he had not a firm conviction and clear knowledge that Jesus was the Christ. Some also hold the silly idea that the Baptist, soon to die, enquired of Christ what word he should bear from Him to the dead fathers. But it is plain that this holy herald of Christ, seeing he was not far from the end of his course, was looking for the crowning remedy to heal the weakness of his disciples, who were still undecided in spite of all the teaching he had given them. As I said, he devoted himself faithfully to seeing that his disciples embraced Christ forthwith. His efforts met with so little success that he was afraid that after he was dead his disciples would fall away altogether. Hence his intention

2

when he sent them to Christ was to awaken them from their dullness.

Moreover, this passage warns pastors of the Church about their duty, not to aim at making and keeping disciples for themselves, but at directing them to Christ, the unique Master. Right at the beginning John had confessed that he was not the bridegroom. Therefore as the faithful attendant of the bride [*paranymphus*], he presents her chaste and pure to Christ Himself, the unique Bridegroom of the Church. Paul too declares that this was his whole care, and puts it forward as an example for all ministers of the Gospel to imitate.

Matt. 11.3. *Art thou he that cometh?* John takes for granted what his disciples had known all their lives. For it was a religious axiom common to all the Jews that the Christ would come as the author of salvation and perfect blessedness. His question did not touch on this point. He was only asking whether Jesus was the promised Redeemer. Already convinced about the redemption promised in the Law and Prophets, they must now embrace it revealed in the person of Christ.

When he adds, *Or look we for another?*, it is an implied reproof of their stupidity in still being undecided when they had been taught so certainly for a long time. At the same time also he shows the nature and power of faith, that it is founded on the truth of God and therefore does not vary or go searching here and there. Content with Christ alone, it is not deflected to another.

Matt. 11.4. *Go your way and tell John.* John had, so to say, put on a disguise. And so Christ tells his disciples to report to him what really was addressed to themselves. He does not answer directly, first because He considers it better that the facts should speak for themselves, and secondly He is giving His herald the material to use for a more open teaching. Yet it is not that He merely supplied him with the raw material of the miracles. Rather He adapted the miracles to their genuine purpose by means of the oracles of the prophets. In particular He refers to one place in Isaiah 35, and to another in Isaiah 61. And this so that John's disciples may know that what the prophets testified concerning the Kingdom of Christ has been completed and fulfilled. The former passage contains a description of the Kingdom of Christ, under which God promises that He will be so generous and kind as to give help and remedy to all the sick. This refers, without doubt, to a spiritual liberation from all ills and miseries. But, as was said before, Christ shows by outward symbols that He came as a spiritual physician to heal souls. So it happened that the disciples could depart without any confusion when they had such a clear and unambiguous reply. The second passage resembles the first. It teaches that the treasures of God's grace are exhibited to the world in Christ, and in particular that Christ is for the poor and afflicted. Christ deliberately refers to this

3

prophecy, partly to instil in all His people the elements of humility, partly to remove the stumbling block which the carnal mind might feel at His contemptible little flock. For as we are by nature proud, we reckon hardly anything precious unless it is adorned with great splendour. But the Church of Christ is a collection of poor little human beings; nothing lies further from superb and splendid beauty. The reason why many despise the Gospel is because it is not accepted by some of the great and important ones. How perverse and wrong this reckoning is Christ teaches us from the nature of the Gospel itself, that it is intended only for the poor and lowly. From this it follows that it is nothing new or disturbing if it is despised by all the great. They are so filled with their riches that they leave no place vacant for God's grace. Indeed, even if it is rejected by the greater part of mankind, this is not surprising, for there is scarcely one in a hundred who is not puffed up with a depraved confidence. But in the way He vindicates His Gospel from contempt, Christ shows who are fit to receive the grace of salvation offered in it. In this way He sweetly invites wretched sinners to the hope of salvation and raises them to assured trust. For it is certain that the poor are called, those whose state is wretched and low and who count for nothing. Poverty, even of the meanest kind, is no reason for hopelessness; rather it should make a man pull himself together and seek Christ. But we must remember that only those are to be reckoned poor who are such to themselves—that is, who are cast down and oppressed with the sense of their own poverty.

Matt. 11.6. *And blessed.* In this verse Christ intends to warn us that anyone who wants to stand fast in the faith of the Gospel must strive against the offences which hinder the course of faith. And by this fore-warning He also fore-arms us against offences. For we shall never lack opportunities of denying Him until we lift our minds above every offence. Therefore the first thing to grasp is that, to persevere in the faith of Christ, we must fight against offences. For Christ truly called Himself a Rock of scandal and a Stone of offence, against which many fall. This certainly happens through our own fault; but He corrects our error when He says that they are blessed who are not offended in Him. From this also we gather that there is no excuse for unbelievers, however many the offences they may claim put them off. For what prevents them coming to Christ? Or what forces them to desert Christ? Just that He is revealed with His cross, despised and degraded, exposed to the reproaches of the world; that He calls us to share in His afflictions; that the world overlooks His glory and majesty, because they are spiritual; that His teaching is completely contrary to our minds; that by his cunning Satan raises up many troubles which defame and make

4

detestable the Gospel and the name of Christ; finally, that everyone, as if deliberately, fabricates for himself a mass of offences, because all withdraw from Christ no less by malice than by desire.

*And as these went their way, Jesus began to say unto the multitudes concerning John, What went ye out into the wilderness to behold? a reed shaken with the wind? But what went ye out for to see? a man clothed in soft raiment? Behold, they that wear soft raiment are in kings' houses. But what went ye out to see? a prophet? Yea, I say unto you, and much more than a prophet. This is he, of whom it is written,*
*Behold, I send my messenger before thy face,*
*Who shall prepare thy way before thee.*
*Verily I say unto you, Among them that are born of women there hath not arisen a greater than John the Baptist: yet he that is but little in the kingdom of heaven is greater than he. And from the days of John the Baptist until now the kingdom of heaven suffereth violence, and men of violence take it by force. For all the prophets and the law prophesied until John. And if ye are willing to receive it, this is Elijah, which is to come. He that hath ears to hear, let him hear.* (Matt. 11.7-15)

*And when the messengers of John were departed, he began to say unto the multitudes concerning John, What went ye out into the wilderness to behold? a reed shaken with the wind? But what went ye out to see? a man clothed in soft raiment? Behold, they which are gorgeously apparelled, and live delicately, are in kings' courts. But what went ye out to see? a prophet? Yea, I say unto you, and much more than a prophet. This is he of whom it is written,*
*Behold, I send my messenger before thy face,*
*Who shall prepare thy way before thee.*
*I say unto you, Among them that are born of women there is not a greater prophet than John the Baptist: yet he that is least in the kingdom of God is greater than he. The law and the prophets were until John: from that time the kingdom of God is preached, and every man entereth violently into it.* (Luke 7.24-28 and Luke 16.16)

Matt. 11.7. *Jesus began to say.* Christ commends John to the people, so that they might remember what they heard from him and believe in his witness. For his name was well known to the people and they spoke highly of him. But his teaching was little prized; in fact, there were very few who paid heed to his ministry. But Christ tells them that they would have wasted their time in going out into the desert to see him unless they reverently applied their minds and study to his teaching.

5

Thus the meaning of the words is: 'You went out into the desert. But your journey would have been quite foolish and ridiculous if you had not had a definite purpose. You were not seeking worldly pomp, nor any sort of show. Your aim was to hear God's voice from the mouth of His prophet. Therefore, that your purpose may bear fruit, let his words remain fixed in your memory.'

Matt. 11.8. *Those that wear soft raiment.* They are in error who think that Christ here is condemning the splendour of courts. There are many other places where luxurious dress and lavish style are reproved. But the meaning of this place is simpler—that there was nothing like this in the desert to draw the crowds. For there everything was uncivilized, squalid and completely disgusting. Those who delight to gaze on elegance and culture will have to do their sight-seeing in the courts of kings.

Matt. 11.11. *Verily I say unto you.* With these words He not only confirms John's authority, but puts his teaching on a higher level than that of the old prophets, so that the people may perceive the true significance of his ministry. It was because they did not reckon why he was sent that hardly any profited from his word. Christ praises him and raises him above the order of prophets, so that they may learn that a certain peculiar and more excellent mandate had been given to him. The fact that elsewhere John denies that he is a prophet is not inconsistent with this title that Christ gives him. He was not a prophet in the same way as those others, whom God had once set over His Church both as interpreters of the Law and messengers carrying His will. But he was greater than the prophets because his proclamation that the time of redemption was present was made plainly and openly, not, like theirs, from afar and obscurely under shadows. The sub-joined prophecy of Malachi refers to this also: John's pre-eminence lies in his being the herald and attendant [*apparitor*] of Christ. For although the old prophets spoke of his kingdom, they were not, like John, set before His face to show Him as present. The rest readers may discover in the first chapter of Luke.

*There hath not arisen a greater prophet.* The Lord goes further. To the extent that John surpasses the prophets, the ministers of the Gospel will surpass him. They were quite ignorant and deceived who thought that Christ was comparing Himself with John. For here He is not treating of the dignity of the person but praising the excellence of the office. This comes out more clearly in Luke's words (7.28): *There has arisen none greater than John.* For his greatness is referred particularly to the office of teaching. In brief, John is adorned with such a splendid title that the Jews may look more closely at the embassy he represented. Then there are placed above him the teachers who followed soon after,

6

so that the majesty of the Gospel might transcend the Law and the teaching which came between them. But just as Christ wanted to prepare the Jews for receiving the Gospel, so we today ought to be aroused to listen with reverence to Christ speaking from the lofty throne of his Heavenly glory. Else will our contempt be avenged with that terrifying curse pronounced against unbelievers by Malachi in the same passage.

'The kingdom of heaven' and 'of God' are put for the new state of the Church, as in earlier verses, because the restoration of all things was promised in the coming of Christ.

Where I have translated it 'least' (Luke 7.28), the Greek has the comparative 'less'. But 'least' makes the sense clearer, since all the ministers of the Church are included. Now in that many have been given a small measure of faith, they are far beneath John. Yet this does not prevent their preaching being more excellent than his so far as it sets forth Christ the conqueror of death and Lord of life, who has made a perfect and eternal expiation for sin by His one sacrifice. This preaching removes the veil and raises disciples to the heavenly sanctuary.

Matt. 11.12. *And from the days of John the Baptist.* I have no doubt that Christ is commending the majesty of the Gospel from the fact that so many sought it with burning zeal. For as God had raised up John as the herald of the kingdom of His Son, so He added to his teaching the efficacy of the Spirit, that it might penetrate men's hearts and kindle their zeal. Therefore it becomes clear that it proceeded from God, for it came forth so suddenly and unusually and made such a great disturbance.

But in the second clause a limitation is added: *Men of violence take it by force.* Because the greater part are as little moved as if Christ's voice had never been sent by the prophets, or as if John His witness had never come, Christ tells them that the violence He is speaking of exists only in a certain sort of man. The meaning therefore is: There is now taking place a great popular uprising, as if men were violently storming and occupying the kingdom of God. For when one man uplifts his voice they turn out in their regiments and snatch at the proffered grace, not merely greedily but violently. And although very many slumber and are no more touched than if John had been telling them fairy-stories in the wilderness, yet many hasten with a violent zeal. The intention of Christ's statement is: They are inexcusable who contemptuously shut their eyes to the revealed power of God which shines both in the teacher and in the hearers. And we learn from these words what is the true nature and way of faith—that men assent to God when He speaks, not coldly and out of mere duty, but aspiring after Him with burning affection and so to say breaking through by a vehement effort.

7

Luke 16.16. *The Law and the Prophets.* The Lord had said that the people's zeal was the foretaste of what the prophets had predicted concerning the future renewing of the Church. And now He compares John's ministry with the Law and the prophets, as if He were saying: 'It is not surprising if God now acts so powerfully in men's souls, for He does not, as before, work His way in from afar under obscure shadows, but is openly at hand to set up His kingdom. Hence it follows that those who stubbornly rejected John's teaching were less excusable than the despisers of the Law and prophets'. The word 'prophesying' is important, because the Law and the prophets did not set God before men's eyes but represented Him in figures as absent.

Thus we see the intention of the comparison. It is all wrong that men should now be so cool when God reveals Himself to them whereas He kept the old people waiting with prophesies. The fact that Christ here numbers John among the ministers of the Gospel, when He had earlier placed him between them and the prophets, is quite consistent. Although his preaching was a part of the Gospel, yet it was only a rudimentary part of it.

Matt. 11.14. *And if ye are willing to receive.* He starts to explain more distinctly how John began to proclaim the kingdom of God—that he was that Elijah who was to be sent before the face of God. Christ therefore wants the Jews to recognize the great and terrible coming of God declared by Malachi, since the Elijah there promised is fulfilling his office of attendant [*apparitor*].

By this condition *If ye are willing to receive*, He reproves their hardness, for they are maliciously blind in clear light. But would he cease to be Elijah if they did not receive him? Christ does not mean that John's office depends on their approval. He is just accusing them of apathy and ingratitude if they do not give him the authority he deserves.

Matt. 11.15. *He that hath ears to hear.* We know that this was a customary expression of Christ when He was dealing with a particularly important and noteworthy matter. But at the same time the things He declares are mysteries, not grasped by all, since many of the hearers are deaf or at least have their ears blocked. Now because some are hampered by their own unbelief and some are hindered by other people, Christ exhorts the elect of God, whose ears have been pierced, to be diligent in considering this unique secret of God and not to be deaf, like unbelievers.

*But whereunto shall I liken this generation? It is like unto children sitting in the marketplaces, which call unto their fellows, and say, We*

8

*piped unto you, and ye did not dance; we wailed, and ye did not mourn. For John came neither eating nor drinking, and they say, He hath a devil. The Son of man came eating and drinking, and they say, Behold a gluttonous man, and a winebibber, a friend of publicans and sinners! And wisdom is justified by her children.* (Matt. 11.16-19)

*And all the people when they heard, and the publicans, justified God, being baptized with the baptism of John. But the Pharisees and the lawyers rejected in themselves the counsel of God, being not baptized of him. And the Lord said, Whereunto then shall I liken the men of this generation, and to what are they like? They are like unto children that sit in the marketplace, and call one to another; which say, We piped unto you, and ye did not dance; we wailed, and ye did not weep. For John the Baptist is come eating no bread nor drinking wine; and ye say, He hath a devil. The son of man is come eating and drinking; and ye say, Behold, a gluttonous man, and a winebibber, a friend of publicans and sinners! And wisdom is justified of all her children.* (Luke 7.29-35)

Luke 7.29. *And all the people when they heard.* Matthew omits the whole of this section, although it throws no little light on the context; for it creates the situation when Christ reproves the Scribes, whom He sees so obstinately contemptuous of God. The sum of the passage is that the common people and the publicans gave glory to God, but the scribes, who flattered themselves with their confidence that they knew everything, regarded Christ's teaching as worthless. At first sight it quite obscures, or even disfigures, the glory of the Gospel, that Christ can gather disciples only from the dregs and refuse of the people, while the eminent saints and doctors reject Him. But the Lord wanted to lay down a pattern right at the outset, so that neither in that nor in any succeeding age men might assess the Gospel by human values—a thing we are nearly all prone to do by nature. But there is nothing more perverse than to subject the truth of God to man's judgment, whose whole acuteness and perspicacity is mere emptiness. Therefore, as Paul says, God chooses the weak and foolish part according to the world, so as to cast down from its loftiness whatever seems strong and wise (I Cor. 1.27). But, as Paul teaches in the same place, we must put this foolishness of God before all the magnificence of human wisdom (I Cor. 1.21).

*Justified God.* A noteworthy saying, that they are said to attribute righteousness to God who embrace and honour His Son and assent to the teaching that He brought. It is not surprising that the Holy Spirit everywhere specially praises faith and puts it first in the worship of God and declares it to be the obedience most acceptable to Him. For what

9

more holy duty can be imagined than to ascribe to God His righteousness? But the word justify refers in general to the whole praise of God,
as if it were said that God was approved and honoured by the people
who assented to the teaching He put forth. But as faith justifies God,
so on the other hand it must be that unbelief is blasphemy against Him
and despitefully deprives Him of His praise. This saying also teaches us
that men are only compelled to believe when they forsake the prompt-
ing and mind of the flesh and decide that all that comes from Him is
right and pure and do not let themselves grumble at His word or works.

*Being baptized.* Luke means that the fruit of the baptism which they
had received was now visible, in that it was the right preparation for
receiving Christ's teaching. Their coming forward for baptism had
already been a sign of godliness. But now the Lord leads them from
that lowly beginning to higher things. The Scribes had in their pride
shut the gate of faith against themselves by despising the baptism of
John. Therefore if we desire to ascend to complete perfection, we
must first take care not to despise even the slightest invitations of God,
and must be ready to start humbly from the very rudiments. And
secondly, we must take pains to ensure that our faith, weak as its
beginnings may have been, shall gradually progress more and more.

Luke 7.30. *They despised in themselves the counsel of God.* He contrasts the counsel of God in all its honour with the ungodly pride of the
Scribes. For there lies in the word 'counsel' an excellence that puts
God's doctrine beyond the reach of all human contempt. Moreover,
Luke's words literally mean: *They despised against themselves.* I do not
reject the sense that some prefer, that their rebellion would lead to their
destruction. But because Luke's statement is straightforward, and
because the preposition εἰς is often taken for ἐν, I have preferred to
translate it 'In themselves', as if he said: 'Although they do not proclaim it openly and in so many words, yet they are puffed up inwardly
with a hidden pride and thus despise it within themselves.'

Luke 7.31. *Whereunto then shall I liken?* He does not include all men
of His generation but is really speaking of the Scribes and their associ-
ates. And He blames them because when the Lord tried in various
ways to draw them to Himself they repulsed His grace with unbending
stubbornness. He uses a similitude, taken apparently from a common
children's game (for the conjecture that boys sang this antiphonally is
not improbable). And indeed I think that Christ deliberately, to cast
down the pride of the Scribes, took the substance of His rebuke from
children playing together, meaning that, however great they were, a
song sung by boys playing in the market-place was sufficient to condemn them.

Luke 7.33. *For John the Baptist is come.* He lived an austere life; he thundered repentance and harsh reproofs; and it was as if he were singing a mournful song. But the Lord Himself had as His whole aim to draw them sweetly to the Father with a pleasant and gay song. Yet neither way profited them at all, and what was there to blame but their iron obstinacy? Moreover, this place teaches why there was such a great external difference between the lives of Christ and the Baptist, although they both did the same thing. By taking on this, so to say, variety of roles, the Lord wanted the better to convict unbelievers; for if He adapted and transformed Himself to their characters, He would not turn them. If He takes away all excuse from the men of that age, who rejected the twofold invitation of God harshly and maliciously, we also are brought to trial in their examples, for God neglects no gay melody, no sad and grave strain, to draw us to Himself: but we are static, stone-like. They called John a demoniac, just as now men who are mentally sick or unsettled in their brains are commonly called madmen.

Luke 7.34. *The Son of man is come.* 'Eating and drinking' here is equivalent to living an ordinary sort of life. When Christ said that John did not eat or drink He meant that his way of life was peculiar to him, in that he abstained from common foods. Luke's words express it more clearly: *Eating no bread, nor drinking wine.* This is a passage which they should note who place the height of perfection in outward austerity of life and define the angelic life as abstemiousness or self-mortification in fasting. By this rule, John is better than the Son of God. Rather should we hold that bodily discipline is moderately helpful but godliness is useful for all things (I Tim. 4.8). Yet this is no pretext for indiscipline of the body, for a man to indulge himself in delights and effeminacy. We must just beware of the superstition that foolish men invent when they think that perfection lies in the physical elements and neglect the spiritual worship of God. Besides this, Christ accommodated Himself to the common way of life in such a manner as to maintain a truly divine temperance; He did not countenance the luxury of others either by dissembling or by example.

Luke 7.35. *And wisdom is justified.* Interpreters expound this verse variously. Some say that wisdom was absolved by the Jews because, with bad consciences and being judges of their own unbelief, they were forced to acknowledge that what they were rejecting was holy and godly doctrine. So they take 'sons of wisdom' to mean the Jews, who claimed this title to themselves. Others think it was spoken ironically: 'You who boast of being the sons of wisdom, is this how you approve the wisdom of God?' But because the Greek preposition ἀπό is not strictly used with the agent, some expound it thus: Wisdom is absolved by her children, so that now she is not legally bound to them— as if an inheritance were being transferred to another. And so Paul says that

Christ is justified from sin because the curse of sin no longer has any rights over Him (Rom. 6.7). Some make it more difficult by their free rendering, that wisdom is alienated by her children. But on the strength of the Greek preposition another meaning seems more apt to me: Wisdom, although her own children may irreligiously detract from her, loses nothing of her dignity and excellence, but remains entire. The Jews, and especially the Scribes, boasted they were the nurselings of God's wisdom. Yet when they trampled their mother beneath their feet, they not only congratulated themselves on their sacrilege, but wanted to slay Christ for His criticism. And Christ replies: 'Although wisdom has evil and degenerate children, yet she herself remains sound; nor does the malice of those who wickedly and malignantly slander her take aught from her right.' Yet I have still not brought out the meaning which, in my judgment, is most fitting and genuine. First, there is an implied antithesis in Christ's words between genuine children and illegitimate, who claim an empty title without cause. It is as if Christ were saying: 'Let those who fiercely claim to be children of wisdom continue in their obstinacy; she will still keep her praise and authority with her true children.' Hence a universal expression is added in Luke: *Of all her children.* By it he means that the rejection by the Scribes will not prevent all God's elect from remaining in the faith of the Gospel. As to the Greek word, there is no doubt that ὑπό sometimes means the same as ἀπό—I need refer only to Christ's words in Luke 17.25: 'The Son of man must suffer many things καὶ ἀποδοκιμασθῆναι ἀπὸ τῆς γενεᾶς ταύτης.' None will deny that the syntax is the same as in the other clause. Chrysostom (and Greek was his mother tongue) exchanges the words without more ado. But apart from the fact that this sentence fits in better, it also corresponds with the previous clause, where it is said that the people justified God. Therefore, although many apostates defected from the Church of God, yet the faith of the Gospel ever continued safe in all the elect, the true members of the flock.

*Now after these things the Lord appointed seventy others, and sent them two and two before his face into every city and place, whither he himself was about to come. And he said unto them, The harvest is plenteous, but the labourers are few: pray ye therefore the Lord of the harvest, that he send forth labourers into his harvest. Go your ways: behold, I send you forth as lambs in the midst of wolves. Carry no purse, no wallet, no shoes: and salute no man on the way. And into whatsoever house ye shall enter, first say, Peace be to this house. And if a son of peace be there, your peace shall rest upon him: but if not, it shall turn to you again. And in that same house remain, eating and drinking such things as they give: for the labourer is worthy of his hire. Go not from house to house. And into whatsoever city ye enter, and they receive you, eat such things as are set before you: and heal the sick that are therein, and say unto them, The kingdom of God is come nigh unto you. But into whatsoever city ye shall enter, and they receive you not, go out into the streets thereof and say, Even the dust from your city, that cleaveth to our feet, we do wipe off against you: howbeit know this, that the kingdom of God is come nigh to you. I say unto you, It shall be more tolerable in that day for Sodom, than for that city.* (Luke 10.1-12)

Luke 10.1. *Now after these things.* We can gather from many details that the Apostles had returned to Christ before the Seventy were sent out as their substitutes. Hence the Twelve were sent to raise the Jews to the hope of the salvation that was nigh. After they had returned and there was need for the work to be extended, more were sent out as secondary heralds to spread the news of Christ's coming into every place. Strictly speaking, they were not commissioned as ambassadors of Christ. Christ simply sent them out as messengers to prepare peoples' minds for receiving His teaching. The number seventy seems to have been chosen as at one time well known among the people. It will be remembered that we said in regard to the twelve Apostles that there were twelve tribes in the flourishing age of the nation, and that He chose twelve Apostles as if they were the Patriarchs to collect into one the members of the torn body, and so bring in the complete restoration of the Church. The reason for the Seventy was not very different. We know that when Moses could not carry all the work alone, he co-opted seventy judges to rule the people along with himself. And when the Jews returned from the Babylonian exile, they had a council or *synedrion* (which word they corrupted to *Sanhedrim,*) composed of seventy-two judges. But as usually happens with such numbers, when they were speaking of the council, they called them only the seventy judges. Philo tells us that they were chosen from the descendants of David, so that some power might still remain in the royal line. After various disasters, the final catastrophe came when Herod dissolved the assembly and deprived the people of a legitimate government. And, just as the return from Babylon was the prelude to a true and genuine redemption, it seems that the Lord now chose the Seventy as heralds of His coming, to promise the restoration of the ruined state. Yet, since the people were to be recalled to one Head, He did not appoint them as judges, with power, but only bade them go before Him, that He alone might have the glory. That He sent them in twos seems to have been because of their weakness. He feared that alone they might lack the necessary courage to carry out their work energetically. They were sent out by twos for their mutual encouragement.

Luke 10.2. *The harvest is plenteous.* I have expounded this sentence in Matthew 9: but it must be treated here also because it refers to a different occasion. For, to stir His disciples up to diligent efforts, Christ declares that the harvest is plenteous, and therefore by implication that their labour will not be in vain but that they will find abundant opportunities for effectual work to undertake. Afterwards He warns them of dangers, struggles and assaults and tells them to go girded and to cover the whole of Judaea swiftly. Finally, He repeats the command that He had given to the Apostles. There is no point in burdening readers with many words here, since they can find the full exposition in the other passage.

But we must briefly advise on the meaning of the saying: *Salute no man on the way.* It is a sign of extreme haste when we meet someone on a journey and hurry on without speaking to him lest he should delay us even for a moment. Thus in II Kings 4.29, when Elisha sent his servant to the Shunamite, he forbade him to speak to anyone on the way. Christ does not mean that His disciples should be so inhumane as to disdain to salute anyone they meet. He does, however, command them so to haste as to take no notice of any obstacles.

Luke alone says that the disciples shall eat and drink what is put before them. By which words Christ not only bids His people to be content with common and poor food, but He also allows them to live on charity. The straightforward and plain meaning is: You are free to live at the expense of another while you are on your journey; for it is only fair that they for whose sake you labour should supply your food. Some think that He was removing any scruple that the disciples might have in eating food they thought was unclean. But Christ meant nothing like this nor was it His intention to prescribe frugality. He was simply permitting them, in lieu of wages, to partake of hospitality in their mission.

*Then began he to upbraid the cities wherein most of his mighty works were done, because they repented not. Woe unto thee, Chorazin! woe unto thee, Bethsaida! for if the mighty works had been done in Tyre and Sidon which were done in you, they would have repented long ago in sackcloth and ashes. Howbeit I say unto you, it shall be more tolerable for Tyre and Sidon in the day of judgment, than for you. And thou, Capernaum, who art exalted unto heaven, thou shalt be dragged down to hell: for if the mighty works had been done in Sodom which were done.in thee, it would have remained until this day. Howbeit I say unto you, that it shall be more tolerable for the land of Sodom in the day of judgment, than for thee.* (Matt. 11.20-24)

*Woe unto thee, Chorazin! woe unto thee, Bethsaida! for if the mighty works had been done in Tyre and Sidon, which were done in you, they would have repented long ago, sitting in sackcloth and ashes. Howbeit it shall be more tolerable for Tyre and Sidon in the judgment, than for you. And thou, Capernaum, who art exalted unto heaven, thou shalt be dragged down to hell. He that heareth you heareth me; and he that rejecteth you rejecteth me: and he that rejecteth me rejecteth him that sent me.* (Luke 10.13-16)

Matt. 11.20. *Then began he to upbraid.* Luke explains why and when Christ inveighed against those cities. It was when He sent out His disciples into the various parts of Judaea to go about and announce that the Kingdom of God was come. He was thinking of the ingratitude of those among whom He had for a long time fruitlessly performed the office of Prophet and done many wonderful works, and He broke out into these words, as if He were saying that the time had come for Him to turn to other cities, now that He had found the inhabitants of that shore, where he had begun to preach the Gospel and to do miracles, so unteachable and terribly malicious. Without mentioning His teaching, however, He blames them that His miracles had not led them to repentance. For it is certain that the Lord put forth signs of His power to invite men to Himself. But since by nature all are turned from Him, it is necessary to start at repentance. Chorazin and Bethsaida are known to be cities on the shore of the lake of Gennesareth.

Matt. 11.21. *In the city of Tyre and Sidon.* The neighbourhood of Tyre and Sidon was notorious for ungodliness, pride, extravagance and other vices. Christ chose this comparison carefully, to touch His own people the Jews to the quick. For they all regarded the Tyrians and Sidonians as wicked despisers of God. Therefore Christ does not a little intensify His curse when He says that those places in which there was no religion were more likely to correct their ways than was Jewry herself. Now, lest anyone should raise difficult questions about the secret judgments of God, we must take it that this saying of the Lord's was accommodated to the ordinary grasp of the human mind. In comparing the city of Bethsaida and its neighbourhood with Tyre and Sidon, He is not concerned with what God will foresee as the future of the one or the other, but just what the facts show Him these others would have done. For the corruption and unbridled dissoluteness of those towns could be imputed to ignorance, in that no voice of God had been heard there, no miracles done to call them to repentance. But the cities of Galilee which Christ reproves had an iron-like obstinacy in despising the miracles, for they had seen so many without any profit. The sum of it is that Christ's words mean that in malice and insane contempt of God, Tyre and Sidon were only surpassed by Chorazin and Bethsaida. And yet we have no just quarrel with God that He should pass over those whose case was more hopeful and show His power to the worst and most lamentable. Whomsoever He does not deem worthy of His mercy He justly appoints to destruction. If He takes His Word away from some, He allows them to perish. But to make others more inexcusable, He invites and exhorts them in one way or another to repentance. Who can charge Him with evil for this? Therefore, conscious of our weakness, let us learn to reverence this sublime truth. For their arrogant captiousness is quite unbearable who will only give God the praise of righteousness when their own opinions assent to Him. They contemptuously reject those mysteries which they ought to adore, because the reason for them is not plain.

*If the mighty works had been done.* We have said that these words teach us the right use of miracles. Yet they refer also to teaching; for Christ was not dumb while He was showing them the power of the Father. In fact, the miracles were joined to the Gospel so as to draw attention to the voice of Christ.

*In sack-cloth and ashes.* Penitence is here sketched under its outward signs, which were then in ceremonial use in the Church of God. It was not that Christ insisted on the signs but that He was adapting himself to the capacity of ordinary people. We know that penitence is not demanded of believers for a few days only, but that they shall zealously occupy themselves in practising it to their life's end. But it is not necessary to put on sack-cloth and scatter one's self with ashes every day. Hence the outward profession of penitence is only called for when men turn to God from some serious defection. And indeed, sack-cloth and ashes are signs of guiltiness, for appeasing the anger of the judge. Therefore they properly apply to the beginning of conversion. Now since by this outward ceremony men bear witness to their regret and sorrow, there must first be a hatred of sin, the fear of God and mortification of the flesh; as Joel says: 'Rend your hearts and not your garments' (2.13). We now see why sack-cloth and ashes are joined to repentance when Christ mentions Tyre and Sidon, to whose inhabitants the Gospel could not be preached without a condemnation of their previous life; and then there was nothing left for them but to supplicate for pardon in the sad attire of the guilty. Luke's word 'sitting' has the same reference, and means that they lie prostrate on the earth, as befitting the wretched, testifying to their sorrow. This appears from very many passages in the prophets.

Matt. 11.23. *And thou, Capernaum.* He addresses by name Capernaum, where He spent so much time that people thought He was a native of the town. It was an incomparable dignity that the Son of God as He first set up His kingdom and priesthood should choose it as the place for his palace and His sanctuary. But the city was as sunk in its filth as if no drop of divine grace had ever fallen upon it. Christ therefore declares that their punishment would be the more dreadful in proportion to the blessings of God given to them. In this passage we should carefully note that the contempt of God's gifts is sacrilege and never goes unpunished. Therefore the higher a man's position the harsher his punishment if he unworthily defiles the gifts divinely bestowed on him. Specially does a terrible vengeance hang over us if we are furnished with Christ's spiritual gifts and yet despise Him and His Gospel.

*If the mighty works had been done in Sodom.* We have already said that Christ was speaking in a human way and was not revealing the heavenly secret of what would have happened if a prophet had been sent to Sodom. If this explanation does not satisfy the contentious, there is one thing that will deprive them of any opportunity for cavil, that, although a remedy for the saving of the Sodomites lay in God's hands, yet His vengeance in destroying them was righteous.

Luke 10.16. *He that heareth you.* They are in error who think that this is merely a repetition of what we have in Matthew 10.40: 'He that receiveth you, receiveth me.' There Christ was concerned with persons, here with doctrine. That receiving related to the duties of love commends the faith which receives God in His Word. The sum of it is that a man's godliness is testified by the obedience of his faith. Those who reject the Gospel, however devout they may claim to be as worshippers of God, simply betray their ungodly contempt. Moreover, we must take Christ's purpose into account. A large part of the world perversely assesses the Gospel according to human worth and therefore disparages it when it is carried by a humble and mean sort of man. It is this perverse judgment that Christ is attacking. Then again, nearly all have the pride that will not willingly submit to equals or supposed inferiors. But God has determined to rule His Church by the ministry of men, and indeed chooses the ministers of His Word from the low off-scourings of the people. It was necessary that He should assert the majesty of the Gospel lest the fact that it was preached by men should lower its estimation. It is therefore a notable commendation of the outward ministry when Christ declares that any honour and reverence paid to the preaching of men (granting it be faithful preaching), God acknowledges as paid to Himself. Moreover, this commendation is useful in two ways. There is nothing that should stir us up to embrace the teaching of the Gospel more than to learn that the pre-eminent worship of God, the sacrifice of a sweet odour, is to hear Him speaking by the mouth of men and to submit ourselves to His Word as it is brought by men no less than if He himself had come down from heaven or had revealed His purpose by an angel. And secondly, trust is confirmed and doubting removed when we hear that the witness to our salvation is no less when declared by men sent of God than if His voice sounded from heaven. On the other hand, to warn us of contempt of the Gospel, He adds the strong threat that those who refuse to hear ministers, however humble, are not insulting men but Himself and God the Father. Here Christ splendidly extols the dignity of pastors who exercise their ministry sincerely and faithfully. But the Pope and his followers are ridiculous when they hide their tyranny under this excuse. For Christ certainly did not mean that He was resigning to men the right given Him by His Father. He was only clearing His Gospel from contempt. He was not transferring to men the honour due to Himself but only striving to keep it united to His Word. If the Pope therefore wants to be received, let him be the bearer of the doctrine by which Christ's minister can be known. But so long as he continues like himself, he is the chief enemy of Christ and has nothing in common with the Apostles. Let him then put off his borrowed plumes!

*And the seventy returned with joy, saying, Lord, even the devils are subject unto us in thy name. And he said unto them, I beheld Satan fallen as lightning from heaven. Behold, I have given you authority to tread upon serpents and scorpions, and over all the power of the enemy: and nothing shall in any wise hurt you. Howbeit in this rejoice not, that the spirits are subject unto you; but rejoice that your names are written in heaven. (Luke 10.17-20)*

Luke 10.17. *And the seventy returned.* It would seem that the seventy disciples did not have a full and firm faith in Christ's words when on their return they were exulting that by Christ's power they had cast out devils, as if this were new and unexpected, although the power and commission to do just this had been given to them. But I have no doubt that when they went out they were sure that nothing their Master had said would be in vain. Afterwards, however, they were overcome by what they had seen, for the greatness of the events

18

exceeded their expectation. And it mostly happens that believers conceive from the Word only a certain taste of God's power, but experience ravishes them with wonder. But what their rejoicing was appears more clearly from Christ's reply.

Luke 10.18. *I beheld Satan.* Christ leads them from the particular to the general. He had commanded that His Gospel should be proclaimed in order that it might overturn the kingdom of Satan. When the disciples took the phenomena they had experienced only at their face value, Christ explained that the force and efficacy of the doctrine was more far-reaching in that it would overthrow the tyranny which Satan exercised over the whole of mankind. We now have the sense of the words: When Christ commanded them to preach His Gospel He was undertaking no doubtful task, for He foresaw the downfall of Satan. Since the Son of God cannot be deceived and His foreknowledge applies to the whole course of the Gospel, we cannot doubt that whenever He raises up faithful teachers He will give success to their work. From this we gather, that we are rescued from slavery to Satan only by the Gospel, and also that only they profit aright in the Gospel in whom Satan's power is destroyed and sin is extinguished, so that they begin to live to the righteousness of God. The metaphor He uses must also be noted, that at the thunder of the Gospel Satan fell down like a lightning flash. By this He expresses the Divine and incredible power of the teaching, that it could so suddenly and with such violence cast down the prince of the world equipped with all his forces. He expresses also the wretched state of men, over whom Satan triumphs, he who rules in the air and holds the world subject under his feet until Christ the Redeemer comes.

Luke 10.19. *Behold, I have given you authority.* This is a concession. Christ does not deny that what they are glorying in is a wonderful gift; but He tells them to look higher and not stay on the level of outward miracles. As their rejoicing was not baseless, He does not entirely condemn it; but He does show its weakness, in that they were too pleased with the temporal and did not raise their minds on high. This is a disease that nearly all the godly suffer from. Although they remember God's goodness and thank Him for it, they are not helped as they should be by His benefits, which are like ladders for them to climb up to heaven. Therefore they need to be raised up by the Lord stretching out His hand, so to say, that they may not sink down on earth but aspire to heavenly newness. He calls all evils 'the power of the enemy', because the devil hurls at us whatever is against us. Not that the power to wound men lies in his will, but because he is armed with the curse of God and tries to turn all his scourges to our destruction and snatches them up as weapons to wound us.

19

Luke 10.20. *Your names are written.* Since Christ wanted to draw His disciples away from passing joy to glorying in eternal life, He leads them to its origin and fount—that they have been chosen by God and adopted as His children. He could have told them to rejoice in being born anew by God's Spirit, to be new creatures in Christ, illuminated in the hope of salvation and possessing the seal of it. But He wishes them to observe the beginning from which all these blessings flow, the free election of God, lest they should ascribe anything to themselves. True, His blessings, which we feel in ourselves, give us matter for praising God; but eternal election, which is outside ourselves, demonstrates more clearly that our salvation is grounded in the sheer goodness of God. He says in a metaphor that their names were written in heaven, which means that they were reckoned before God as His sons and heirs, as if they were written down in a catalogue.

*At that season Jesus answered and said, I thank thee, O Father, Lord of heaven and earth, that thou didst hide these things from the wise and understanding, and didst reveal them unto babes: yea, Father, for so it was well-pleasing in thy sight. All things have been delivered unto me of my Father: and no one knoweth the Son, save the Father; neither doth any know the Father, save the Son, and he to whom the Son will reveal him. Come unto me, all ye that labour and are heavy laden, and I will give you rest. Take my yoke upon you, and learn of me; for I am meek and lowly in heart: and ye shall find rest unto your souls. For my yoke is easy, and my burden is light.* (Matt. 11.25-30)

*In that same hour Jesus rejoiced in the Spirit, and said, I thank thee, O Father, Lord of heaven and earth, that thou didst hide these things from the wise and understanding, and didst reveal them unto babes: yea, Father; for so it was well-pleasing in thy sight. All things have been delivered unto me of my Father: and no one knoweth who the Son is, save the Father; and who the Father is, save the Son, and he to whomsoever the Son willeth to reveal him.* (Luke 10.21-22)

Matt. 11.25. *Jesus answered and said.* Although the word 'answer' is a common Hebraism to mark the beginning of speech, yet in this verse I regard it as emphatic, in that Christ was speaking in response to the present situation. This is confirmed by Luke's words, that in that hour Christ was exalted in the Spirit. Now what was the cause of this exulting but that He held the Church, composed as it was of weak and lowly men, no less dear and precious than if it had shone with all the nobility and excellence of the world? Because they were addressed to the Father His words have more fervour than if He had spoken them to the disciples. Yet it was indeed in response to them and for their sake that He gave thanks to the Father, lest the lowly and ignoble form of the Church should offend them. For we always seek what is brilliant; and nothing seems more incongruous than that the heavenly kingdom of the Son of God, its glory so magnificently extolled by the Prophets, should consist of the offscourings and refuse of the people. And yet it is of God's wonderful purpose, that with the whole world in His hands, He prefers to choose His people from the humble masses than from the leaders who might adorn Christ's name with their excellence. But here Christ withdraws His disciples from such a proud highmindedness, lest they should dare to despise the low and obscure state of the Church in which He is pleased and delights. Moreover, to restrain more effectually the curiosity that sometimes possesses the human mind, He raises Himself above the world and surveys the secret judgments of God, so that He may carry His disciples with Him in wonder at them. And indeed although this appointment of God is alien to our thinking, yet our arrogance is altogether too blind and wild if we clamour against what Christ our Head reverently adores. But now we must consider the words He uses.

*I thank thee, O Father.* With these words He confesses that He assents to the Father's decree, so different from human ideas. There is a tacit antithesis between the praise He ascribes to the Father and the malevolent detraction—or impudent yapping—of the world. We must now see in what He glorifies the Father. It is because He, who is Lord of the whole universe, chooses the little and unlearned rather than the wise. His calling the Father 'Lord of heaven and earth' adds weight to His meaning. For in this way He declares that the reason why the wise are blind but the ignorant and unlearned grasp the mysteries of the Gospel depends only on the will of God. There are many other places like this, where the Lord shows that all who come to salvation have been freely chosen by Him, the framer and creator of the world, to whom belong all the nations. This clause therefore has a twofold force. First, it is not due to any impotence in God that not all obey the Gospel, for it is easy for Him to subject all creatures to His rule. Secondly, the fact that some arrive at faith and others remain dull and obstinate happens by His free election; for, in drawing some and passing over others, He alone distinguishes between men whose state is equal by nature. But in choosing the simple rather than the wise He had respect to His own glory. For as the flesh is too greedy in self-praise, if the clever and learned were put first, the idea would soon hold sway that men acquired faith by their own skill or industry or learning. Therefore God's mercy could not appear so clearly as it deserves except in such a choice as makes it plain that men contribute nothing of their own. The reason why human wisdom is cast down is that it may not obscure the praise of the divine grace.

But we may ask whom Christ calls wise and whom simple. For experience plainly teaches that not all the unlearned and ignorant are enlightened to believe, nor all the wise and lettered left in their blindness. The prudent and wise are to be defined as those who are swollen with devilish pride and cannot bear to listen to Christ speaking to them from a higher level. But Paul's example, of savagery tamed by Christ, shows us that this is not necessarily perpetual, that those who are more than self-satisfied are not necessarily reprobate by God. For if we come to the ignorant masses, the majority of them show a virulent antagonism and we see them left, along with the princes and the great, to destruction. I agree that all unbelievers are puffed up with a perverse self-confidence, whether in their wisdom, or in their good name, or their honours, or in their wealth; but I consider that here Christ was merely and without thought of blame including all the great in mind and learning—and similarly that He was not calling them simple in regard to virtue. For although Christ is the Master of the humble, and the first lesson of faith is: 'Be not wise in your own conceits', yet this verse is not concerned with voluntary simpleness, but Christ is magnifying the grace of the Father in that He does not shrink from descending to the lowest of the low to raise the poor from their squalor.

But now arises a problem. How can wisdom, which is the gift of God, be an obstacle to us and prevent us seeing the light of God, shining in the Gospel? We must remember what I have already said, that unbelievers corrupt whatever wisdom is given them, and brilliant minds are often so hindered that they cannot allow themselves to be taught. But in particular reference to the present verse, I reply that although their perspicacity may be no drawback to the wise, yet they can be deprived of the light of the Gospel. For since the condition of all was the same or alike, why should not God choose these or those at His will? But Paul teaches in I Cor. 1.27 why the wise and great are passed over—that God chose the weak and foolish things of the world to put to shame the glory of the flesh. But from this we also gather that Christ's saying that the mysteries of the Gospel are hid from the wise is not general. For it is fulfilled if four out of five wise reject the Gospel and the other one embraces it, while of the same number of the unlearned two or three become Christ's disciples. And the passage from Paul just quoted confirms this, for he does not exclude all the wise, noble and powerful from the kingdom of God but only warns us that they will be few. The problem is now solved. Wisdom, so far as it is the gift of God, is not condemned. Christ simply declares that it is to no importance in obtaining faith. And on the other hand, He does not commend ignorance, as if it reconciled men to God, but says that it will not prevent Him in His mercy enlightening ignorant and foolish men with heavenly wisdom.

Now it remains to say what 'reveal' and 'hide' mean. That Christ is not speaking of outward preaching we can gather from the fact that He offered Himself as a teacher indiscriminately to all, and gave the same mandate to His Apostles. Therefore His meaning is that none can reach faith by his own intelligence but only by the secret illumination of the Spirit.

Matt. 11.26. *Yea, Father.* This phrase denies us any occasion for the frivolous curiosity that sometimes titillates our mind. For there is nothing more difficult for God to wring out of us than the acknowledgment that His will is highest reason and righteousness. He often says most earnestly that His judgment is a profound abyss; but we charge wildly into that profundity. And if there is anything that does not please us, we chafe or murmur against Him. Many even break out into open blasphemies. But the Lord lays down for us the rule that we must regard as right whatever is pleasing to God. This alone is serious wisdom, to reckon one decision of God worth a thousand reasons. Christ could certainly have given the reasons for the discrimination, if there were any. Because He is satisfied with God's good pleasure He does not trace any further why He calls the simple to salvation rather than others and forms His kingdom out of the common herd. Hence those who stir up trouble when they hear that God of His free will chooses some and rejects others are raging against Christ, for they hate to yield to God.

Matt. 11.27. *All things have been delivered unto me.* Some interpreters have mistakenly linked this verse with the last, for they think it merely means that Christ confirms His disciples in stronger faith so that they may preach the Gospel. But I consider that Christ spoke like this for another reason and to another end. Just as He had asserted before that the Gospel flows from the secret well of God's free election, so now He shows how the grace of salvation comes to men. For many, when they hear that none are heirs of eternal life save those whom God chose before the foundation of the world, ask anxiously how they can know about the secret counsel of God. And so they enter into a labyrinth and can find no way out. But Christ tells them to come straight to Him and seek assurance of salvation in Him. The meaning therefore is that life is opened up to us in Christ Himself, so that none will be partaker of it but he who enters by the gate of faith. And so we see that He joins faith and the eternal predestination of God. Foolish people contrast

23

these two as if they were contraries. Although our salvation is always hidden in God, yet Christ is the conduit through whom it flows to us and is received by our faith, so that it is firm and certain in our hearts. Therefore we must not swerve from Christ if we do not want to reject the salvation offered to us.

*No-one knoweth the Son.* He says this in case His majesty should be wrongly estimated according to human judgment. The meaning therefore is that, if we would know what Christ is we must accept the testimony of the Father who alone truly and really can show us what He has given us in Him. By imagining Him such as our mind in its limitations can grasp, we strip Him of a great part of His power. He is therefore only known aright by the account [*voce*] of His Father. Yet the account [*vox*] alone is not sufficient without the guidance of the Spirit, for Christ's power is too sublime and hidden for men to reach it until they are enlightened by the Father. Understand it as meaning that the Father knows Him, not for Himself but for us, to reveal Him to us. The sentence seems incomplete, in that the two clauses do not correspond. It is said of the Son that no-one knows the Father apart from Himself and he to whom He wishes to reveal Him; but of the Father it says only that the Son alone knows Him—no mention occurs here of revelation. I reply that there was no point in His repeating what He had already said, for does not His earlier thanksgiving also mean that the Father reveals the Son to whom He will? Therefore when He now adds that the Father is known only by the Son, it is like a reason for what He had said. For some might think: 'What need is there for the Son to be manifested by the Father, since He openly reveals Himself to our sight?'

Now that we have grasped the meaning of 'the Son is known only by the Father', there remains the next clause, that 'none knows the Father except the Son.' This knowledge is different from the former, for the Son is said to know the Father, not because He manifests Him by His Spirit, but because as His lively image He reveals Him visibly, so to say, in His person. Yet I do not leave out the Spirit. It is simply that I refer the revelation treated here to the mode of knowledge. And in this way the words are connected best, for Christ confirms what He had said before: 'All things are delivered to me by my Father', so that we may know that the fulness of the Godhead dwells in Him. It all comes back to this: It is the Father's gift that the Son is known, for by His Spirit He opens the eyes of our minds and we perceive the glory of Christ which otherwise would be hidden from us. But the Father, who dwells in light inaccessible and is in Himself incomprehensible, is revealed to us by the Son, His lively image, and in vain do we seek Him elsewhere.

24

Matt. 11.28. *Come unto me.* With kindness He had already invited to Himself those whom He knew were fit to be His disciples. For although He was ready to manifest the Father to all, yet a great part did not trouble to respond because they were not moved by any feeling of necessity. Hypocrites do not care for Christ. Drunk with their own righteousness, they are not hungry and thirsty for His grace. Those who are devoted to the world, think nothing of the heavenly life. Both types Christ called to Himself in vain; and so He turned to the wretched and afflicted. Now He calls them 'ye that labour', those who are oppressed under a burden—but not simply those laden with sorrow and suffering in general, but who sink under the burden of being confounded by their sins and stricken with the fear of God's wrath. God humbles His chosen in many ways; but because many who are laden with miseries nevertheless remain stubborn and obstinate, Christ means by 'ye that labour and are heavy laden' those whose consciences are afflicted by the guiltiness of eternal death and are inwardly so moved by their wretchedness that they faint. For this failure makes us fit to receive His grace. It is as if He said that His grace was despised by the greater part because few feel their need. Yet there is no reason why their pride or dullness should hold back afflicted souls which yearn for help. Therefore let us leave all those who are bewitched by the wiles of Satan or imagine they can have righteousness outside Christ or think they are blessed in this world. Our ills drive us to desiring Christ.

And because Christ admits to the enjoyment of peace only those who faint under their burden, let us learn that there is no more virulent poison than the indolence which begets in us a false and vain idea either of earthly happiness or righteousness and virtue. Therefore let each of us continually bestir himself and be zealous first in shaking off the delights of the world and then in clearing himself of all perverse confidence. Now although this preparation for receiving the grace of Christ takes all the heart out of men, yet we must note that it is the gift of the Holy Spirit, for it is the beginning of repentance, to which none can attain by his own efforts. For Christ did not mean to teach what a man can do on his own, but only how they must be affected who come to Him. Those who restrict being laden and labouring to ceremonies of the Law weaken Christ's statement. I allow that the burden of the Law was intolerable and crushed men's souls. But we must remember what I said, that Christ stretched His hand to all the afflicted in such a way that He made a distinction between the disciples and the despisers of the Gospel.

But the particle 'all' is to be noted. For Christ included all without exception who labour and are heavy laden, lest anyone should shut the door on himself by a perverted doubt. And yet the 'all' in this number are few; for, of the innumerable host of those who really are perishing, only a few feel that they are perishing. The reviving that He promises is the free forgiveness of sins which alone gives us peace.

Matt. 11.29. *Take my yoke.* We see that many abuse the grace of Christ by making it an excuse for indulging the flesh. Therefore, when Christ has promised peaceful joy to those labouring wretchedly in their consciences, He tells them that He is the Deliverer on condition that they take His yoke upon them. It is as if He said that He did not absolve from sins in order that those who have God on their side may use it as a licence for sinning, but in order that, raised by His grace, they may at the same time take up His yoke and as free in the spirit restrain the wantonness of their flesh. From this we can infer the definition of the rest He had spoken of—that it does not release Christ's disciples from fighting under the Cross to enjoy a smooth life, but it exercises them under the burden of discipline and keeps them under the yoke.

*Learn of me.* To my mind they are in error who think that Christ is here bearing witness to His gentleness, lest the disciples should flee from Him because of His Divine glory—as intercourse with the mighty is frightening. Rather does He form us to the imitation of Him, since we, in the obstinacy of our flesh, fly from His yoke as something harsh and difficult. A little after He says that His yoke is easy. But how does it come about that anyone freely and quietly submits to the yoke, unless by putting on meekness and being conformed to Christ? It is certain that this is the meaning of the words; for, having exhorted His disciples to bear their Cross, Christ at once goes on, in case the difficulty should frighten them: 'Learn of me'. He means that the yoke will not be troublesome to them when they have become used to meekness and humility by His example.

When he adds *ye shall find rest*, it relates to the same thing. For so long as the flesh is mutinous we raise an uproar; and those who refuse Christ's yoke and try to please God in some other way exhaust and weary themselves in vain. We see how the Papists wretchedly torment themselves and bear in silence the harsh tyranny under which they are tortured, rather than submit to Christ's yoke.

*At that season Jesus went on the sabbath day through the cornfields; and his disciples were an hungred, and began to pluck ears of corn, and to eat. But the Pharisees, when they saw it, said unto him, Behold, thy disciples do that which it is not lawful to do upon the sabbath. But he said unto them, Have you not read what David did, when he was an hungred, and*

26

*they that were with him; how he entered into the house of God, and did eat the shewbread, which it was not lawful for him to eat, neither for them that were with him, but only for the priests? Or have ye not read in the law, how that on the sabbath day the priests in the temple profane the sabbath, and are guiltless? But I say unto you, that one greater than the temple is here. But if ye had known what this meaneth, I desire mercy, and not sacrifice, ye would not have condemned the guiltless. For the Son of man is lord of the sabbath.* (Matt. 12.1-8)

*And it came to pass, that he was going on the sabbath day through the cornfields; and his disciples began, as they went, to pluck the ears of corn. And the Pharisees said unto him, Behold, why do they on the sabbath day that which is not lawful? And he said unto them, Did ye never read what David did, when he had need, and was an hungred, he, and they that were with him? How he entered into the house of God when Abiathar was high priest, and did eat the shewbread, which it is not lawful to eat save for the priests, and gave also to them that were with him? And he said unto them, The sabbath was made for man, and not man for the sabbath: so that the Son of man is lord even of the sabbath.* (Mark 2.23-28)

*Now it came to pass on the second sabbath after the first, that he was going through the cornfields; and his disciples plucked the ears of corn, and did eat, rubbing them in their hands. But certain of the Pharisees said to them, Why do ye that which is not lawful to do on the sabbath day? And Jesus answering them said, Have ye not read even this, what David did, when he was an hungred, he, and they that were with him? How he entered into the house of God, and did take and eat the shewbread, and gave also to them that were with him; which it is not lawful to eat save for the priests alone? And he said unto them, The Son of man is lord of the sabbath.* (Luke 6.1-5)

Matt. 12.1. *Jesus went on the sabbath day.* In this narrative the aim of the Evangelists is to show up partly the malevolent spirit of the Pharisees, partly their superstition in placing the whole of sanctity in outward and trivial things. They accuse Christ's disciples because, when they are hungry, they pluck ears of corn on their journey, as if this were a violation of the Sabbath. The keeping of the Sabbath was certainly holy, but not in the way they thought, making it scarcely lawful to move a finger with a clear conscience. It is hypocrisy that makes them so scrupulous in trivialities while they forgive themselves gross superstitions. Christ elsewhere accuses them of tithing mint and anise but despising the precepts of the Law (Matt. 23.23). And it is always the way of hypocrites to take licence in important matters and to be very

27

devout in ceremonies. This is also why those who want to offer to God only a carnal worship demand a stricter observation of external rites. But it is malevolence and malice rather than superstition that drives them to this censure, or they would not be so acrimonious against others. And it is useful for us to see how they were affected, for it might disturb some that the doctors of the Law themselves should be such enemies to Christ.

Luke 6.1. *A second-first Sabbath.* There is no doubt at all that this Sabbath belonged to one of the feast days which the Law ordered to be celebrated once a year. Therefore some think that it continued for two days. But this opinion is refuted by the fact that after the Babylonian exile the Jewish feasts were so distributed that there was always one day in between them. They have more reason on their side who say that it was the last day of the festivity, which was celebrated equally with the first. But I prefer the view of those who understand it as the second feast of the year. The name fits in very well—it was called the second-first Sabbath because in order of time it was the second of the chief and yearly feasts. The first was the Passover, and so this was probably that of Firstfruits.

Mark 2.24. *Why do they on the sabbath day?* The Pharisees did not rebuke Christ's disciples for plucking corn in someone else's field but for breaking the Sabbath. As if this were ordained so that hungry men should perish sooner than relieve their hunger. The only purpose of the Sabbath was that the people might sanctify God to themselves and practice a true, spiritual worship, and that they might be released from all earthly business and join together in a holy assembly. This legitimate observation should be referred to the purpose, for the interpretation of the Law is to be sought from the mind of the Legislator. From this appears how malicious and implacable superstition is, and especially how arrogantly and cruelly hypocrites behave when ambition and personal hatred concur in them. It was not merely the affectation of pretended holiness, as I have said, that made the Pharisees so strict and unbending; but they deliberately set out to criticise all Christ's sayings and actions, and therefore they could not fail to interpret unfavourably perfectly innocent things, as unfair critics usually do. There is no contradiction between Matthew and Mark saying that it was the Lord who was blamed and Luke saying that it was the disciples. For it is possible that the disciples were so upset that the accusation moved the Master Himself. It may also be that the rebuke began at the disciples and then was shifted on to Christ, and that the exasperated Pharisees in their malice imputed to Him the blame for tacitly allowing His disciples to break the Sabbath.

Matt. 12.3. *Have ye not read what David did?* Christ refutes the

28

false accusation with five arguments. First, He pleads David's example to excuse the disciples. When David was fleeing from the wrath of Saul he asked the high priest Ahimelech for provisions on his journey. No ordinary food was available, but he was given the sacred bread. If necessity absolved David from blame, it absolves others as well. Whence it follows that the ceremonies of the Law are not violated so long as godliness is unharmed. But Christ takes for granted that David was guiltless, for the high priest who allowed him to take the sacred bread is praised by the Holy Spirit. When he says that it was lawful only for the priests to eat the bread, we may understand it by the ordinary situation in law, for if David had attempted anything unlawfully Christ would have pleaded his example in vain. But what was forbidden for a certain purpose necessity made lawful.

Matt. 12.5. *On the sabbath day the priests.* This is the second argument by which Christ proves that the breaking of the Sabbath of which the Pharisees complained was innocent. Sacrifices were offered on the Sabbath days, children were circumcised, and whatever else belonged to the worship of God took place. It follows that the duties of religion do not conflict with one another. If the Temple sanctifies the manual work involved in sacrificing and all the outward cult, the holiness of the true and spiritual temple is more excellent and purges its worshippers from all fault when they perform the duties of godliness. Moreover, the disciples were intent on their work of offering up consecrated souls to God by the Gospel. Matthew alone mentions this argument. When He says that the sabbath was profaned by the priests, it was imprecise language; Christ was adapting Himself to His hearers. For when the Law commands men to abstain from their works it does not forbid holy work. For Christ grants the truth of what ordinary people might superficially believe; it is enough for Him that the works of the Temple do not offend God.

Matt. 12.7. *But if ye had known.* This third argument also occurs only in Matthew. Christ reproaches the Pharisees for not considering for what purpose and intent the ceremonies were commended. And this is indeed a common fault in nearly all ages. The Prophet Hosea chided his contemporaries because they were wedded to ceremonies and cared nothing for the duties of love. But God cries out that He will have mercy rather than sacrifices (Hos. 6.6). This word 'mercy' signifies by synecdoche the duties of love, just as the outward cult of the Law is comprehended under 'sacrifices'. Christ accommodates this verse to His own time and accuses the Pharisees of twisting God's Law into an alien meaning, in that they neglected the second table and were devoted to ceremonies.

But it may be asked why God says that He cares nothing for sacrifices when there is a strict command in the Law to observe them. The solution is easy. Outward ceremonies have no importance, nor are they demanded by God, except so far as they are directed to their proper end. God does not reject them absolutely, but tells us that He prizes them less in comparison with the works of love. This is so despite the fact that the worship of God holds the highest place in perfection of righteousness and that the duties paid to men come second. For although godliness is deservedly thought more precious than love so far as God excels men, yet because believers show that they truly worship God by the righteousness which they maintain within their society, it is not without cause that God recalls hypocrites to the duties of love, for they counterfeit godliness in external signs and pervert it, clinging painfully to a carnal cult alone. From the prophet's testimony Christ rightly concludes that His disciples are guiltless, because when God exercises His people in the elements of the Law it is not His aim to kill poor men with hunger.

Matt. 12.8. *For the Son of man is Lord.* Some connect this verse with the previous one—that one greater than the Temple is present. But I judge them to be distinct. Previously Christ was referring to the Temple and said that the duties connected with its holiness were not a transgression of the Law. But here He says that power is given to Him to free His people from the necessity of keeping the sabbath. 'The Son of man', He says, 'because He is Lord, has the power to regulate the sabbath and other legal ceremonies.' And indeed, outside Christ the Law is a wretched slavery from which He alone releases those to whom He grants the free Spirit of adoption.

Mark 2.27. *The sabbath was made for man.* The fifth argument is narrated by Mark alone. The point of it is that it is wrong to turn the Sabbath to man's destruction, since God instituted it for his sake. The Pharisees saw Christ's disciples busy in a holy work, they saw them exhausted and famished by their journey, yet they are angry that these hungry men should refresh their weary bodies with a few grains of corn. Is it not an ignorant perversion of God's will to demand the observance of the Sabbath to man's hurt when God intended it to help him? Those who think that Christ was here abrogating the Sabbath for good are, as I think, mistaken. He is simply teaching its proper use. For although He had asserted just before that He was Lord of the Sabbath the full time of its abrogation was not yet come, for the veil of the Temple had not yet been rent.

*And he departed thence, and came into their synagogue: and behold there was a man having a withered hand. And they asked him, saying, Is it lawful to heal on the sabbath day? that they might accuse him. And he said unto them, What man shall there be of you, that shall have one sheep, and if this fall into a pit on the sabbath day, will he not lay hold on it, and lift it out? How much then is a man of more value than a sheep! Wherefore it is lawful to do good on the sabbath day. Then saith he to the man, Stretch forth thy hand. And he stretched it forth; and it was restored whole, as the other.* (Matt. 12.9-13)

*And he entered again into the synagogue; and there was a man there which had his hand withered. And they watched him, whether he would heal him on the sabbath day; that they might accuse him. And he saith unto the man that had his hand withered, Rise up in the midst. And he saith unto them, Is it lawful on the sabbath day to do good, or to do harm? to save a life, or to kill? But they held their peace. And when he had looked round about on them with anger, being grieved at the blindness of their heart, he saith unto the man, Stretch forth thy hand. And he stretched it forth: and his hand was restored whole as the other.* (Mark 3.1-5)

*And it came to pass on another sabbath, that he entered into the synagogue and taught: and there was a man there, and his right hand was withered. And the scribes and Pharisees watched him, whether he would heal on the sabbath; that they might find how to accuse him. But he knew their thoughts; and he said to the man that had his hand withered, Rise up, and stand forth in the midst. And he arose and stood forth. And Jesus said unto them, I ask you, Is it lawful on the sabbath to do good, or to do harm, to save life, or to destroy it? And he looked round about on them all, and said unto the man, Stretch forth they hand. And he did so: and his hand was restored whole, as the other.* (Luke 6.6-10)

Matt. 12.9. *And he departed thence.* This story has the same purpose as the one before—to narrate how the scribes in their malice were intent on criticising everything that Christ did, and that it was no wonder that they were His implacable foes when their minds were so vicious. We see that it is usual with hypocrites to chase the shadowy righteousness of the Law and, as the phrase goes, to stick to the form instead of the substance. We first learn from it that when we have to judge any matter we must bring to it minds pure and free from any touch of malice. For if we are ruled by hatred, or pride, or anything of that sort, not only shall we be harming men but we shall affront God Himself by turning light into darkness. No-one unbiassed by malice would have denied that what those good doctors do not hesitate to condemn was a divine work. Why all the fury, except because their minds were completely filled with an ungodly hatred of Christ, so that they stand blind

31

in the full shine of the sun? We are also cautioned lest by attributing too much to ceremonies we let slip what is far more important to God and what Christ elsewhere calls the chief points of the Law (Matt. 23.23). Such is our propensity to outward rites that we shall never keep a balance in this matter unless we remember what is commanded about the worship of God: first, that it is spiritual, and secondly that it should be measured by the rule that Christ lays down here.

Matt. 12.10. *And they asked him.* Mark and Luke say only that they watched what the Lord would do. Matthew declares more clearly that they provoked Him with words. It is probable that He had healed some others on previous Sabbaths. This gives them the opportunity to ask if He thinks it right to do once more what He had done before. But they ought to have been considering whether that work was divine or human which healed a withered hand, be it by touch or by word. For when God instituted the Sabbath He was not laying a Law down for Himself or binding Himself to any sort of servitude; He would work on Sabbaths like any other day, as it seemed good to Him. It was quite insane to raise this question and to force God Himself under rules and cut down the free course of His actions.

Matt. 12.11. *What man shall there be of you.* Christ again shows what is the true keeping of the Sabbath. But at the same time He accuses them of calumny because they censured Him alone for something which was in fact common practice. If a man's sheep falls into a pit, no-one will tell him he should not pull it out. But as a man is more than a beast, so he should be helped the more. Therefore if anyone succours his brethren in need, he is not violating the rest commanded by the Lord. This analogy is not found in Mark and Luke, who say only that Christ demanded whether it was lawful to do good or to do evil. For he who takes a man's life is guilty of doing evil, but those who do not trouble to help the needy are little different from murderers. Christ therefore rebukes them for wanting, under pretext of the sacred rest, to make Him do evil. For, as it is said, not only is he delinquent who intends anything against the law but also he who neglects his duty. From this we see that Christ did not always use the same arguments against this slander. For here He does not discuss His Divinity, as in John. There was no need, for this one defence was more than sufficient to confute the Pharisees—that it was quite inconceivable that He who followed the pattern of God should be a Sabbath-breaker.

Luke 6.8. *But he knew their thoughts.* If Matthew is right, they betrayed their thoughts in words. In which case Christ replied to expressed words and not to unspoken thoughts. But both may be true: they spoke openly, and Christ judged of their secret opinions. In their deceit they did not speak frankly; and Matthew also says that their question was captious.  Hence all that Luke means is that Christ noticed their trap, even though they hid it by their words.  Mark adds that Christ looked at them with anger; and He was right to be angry at their ungodly stubbornness.  To show us that it was a just and holy anger he says that He was grieved at the blindness of their hearts.  First, then, Christ is sad because men brought up in the Law are so grossly blind.  But then, because it was malice that blinded them He is angry as well as sad.  It is a true moderation of zeal when we are sorry for the perdition of ungodly men and get heated about their ungodliness.  But as this verse says that Christ was not immune from human passions, so we also gather that those passions are not in themselves vicious so long as they are not intemperate.  Because we with our corrupt nature do not hold the mean, we are never sinlessly angry, even when the reason is just.  It was different with Christ; not only did integrity of nature flourish with Him, but also there shone in Him a perfect example of righteousness.  Therefore we ought to seek from heaven God's Spirit, to correct our excesses.

*But the Pharisees went out, and took counsel against him, how they might destroy him.  And Jesus perceiving it withdrew from thence: and great multitudes followed him; and he healed them all, and charged them that they should not make him known: that it might be fulfilled which was spoken by Isaiah the prophet, saying,*
*Behold, my servant whom I have chosen;*
*My beloved in whom my soul is well pleased:*
*I will put my Spirit upon him,*
*And he shall declare judgment to the Gentiles.*
*He shall not strive, nor cry aloud;*
*Neither shall any one hear his voice in the streets,*
*A bruised reed shall he not break, and smoking flax shall he not quench,*
*Till he send forth judgment unto victory.*
*And in his name shall the Gentiles hope.*  (Matt. 12.14-21)

*And the Pharisees went out, and straightway with the Herodians took counsel against him, how they might destroy him.  And Jesus with his disciples withdrew to the sea: and a great multitude from Galilee followed him, and from Judaea, and from Jerusalem, and from Idumaea, and beyond Jordan, and they who lived about Tyre and Sidon, a great multitude of men, hearing what great things he did, came unto him.  And he spake to his disciples, that a little boat should wait on him because of the*

33

*crowd, lest they should throng him: for he had healed many; inasmuch that as many as had plagues pressed upon him that they might touch him. And the unclean spirits, whensoever they beheld him, fell down before him, and cried, Saying, Thou art the Son of God. And he charged them much that they should not make him known.* (Mark 3.6–12)

*But they were filled with madness; and communed one with another what they might do to Jesus.* (Luke 6.11)

Matt. 12.14. *But the Pharisees.* What a stubborn rage it is that drives the reprobate to resist God! Let them be convicted, and their poison will only pour out the more. It is a fearful monstrosity that the leading doctors of the Law, at the helm of the Church, should act like bandits ready for murder. But this is bound to happen when men's malice breaks out; they want to kill whatever thwarts their desires, even if it is of God.

We must not put it down to fear that Christ slipped secretly away. He did not increase in courage as time went on, but He was endued with the same fortitude of spirit when He fled as when afterwards He offered Himself voluntarily to death. And this was a part of that emptying which Paul extols in Phil. 2.7. It would have been easy for Him to have preserved His life by a miracle, but He preferred to submit to our infirmity by fleeing. Moreover, He did not defer dying for any other reason than because the fit time decreed by the Father was not yet come. Yet it is clear that heavenly power rather than flight preserved Him. For it would not have been difficult for His enemies to find their way to the place He went to. He did not hide in obscurity, but drew a great company along with Him and made the place well-known. All He did was to get out of their sight in case He should inflame their fury.

Mark adds that they took counsel with the Herodians, even though they hated them bitterly. When they wanted to seem the public guardians and champions of liberty, they had to practice deadly and deliberate opposition to the servants of the tyrant. But their furious hatred of Christ forced them not only to conspire with foreigners but even to become friendly with them while all the time they hated their presence. For although ungodliness scatters men and drives them into different factions, yet it unites them in a common cause to fight against God. No animosities prevent men from joining hands to attack the truth of God.

Matt. 12.16. *And he charged them.* Mark adds the particular, that He restrained the evil spirits who cried out that He was the Son of God. We have shown elsewhere why He should not allow witnesses of this

34

sort. Yet there is no doubt that this confession was divinely extorted from the demons. After Christ had shown that they were subject to His rule, He at once deservedly rejected their testimony. But Matthew's saying has a wider scope—that Christ commanded that the news of the signs which He did should not be spread abroad. Elsewhere we have said that He did not want to suppress it altogether. He wanted His signs to take root and then bear fruit in due season. For we know that miracles were not some game that Christ was playing but had the deliberate purpose of proving Him to be the Son of God and the Redeemer given to the world. Little by little, and by steady degrees, He came out into the light. And He was only revealed as the one He was to the extent that the time ordained of the Father allowed. Yet it is worth noting that when the ungodly try their hardest to obscure the glory of God, things do not turn out as they plan, but God drives their perverted attempts backwards. For although Christ left a well-known place, yet even in His hiding place His glory did not cease to shine; rather it broke splendidly forth into its own righteous splendour.

Matt. 12.17. *That it might be fulfilled.* Matthew does not mean that the prophesy was completely fulfilled when Christ forbade reports of His power being noised abroad. But that this matter also showed an example of His meekness as it is revealed in Isaiah's portrayal of the Messiah. Those mighty works, which were performed among a few and which Christ did not wish to be grandly published, could shake heaven and earth. Therefore He shows by no common proof, how far He was from the ostentation and pomp of the world.

But it will be worthwhile to examine Matthew's purpose more closely. By this circumstance he wanted to show that the glory of Christ's divinity is to be estimated none the less because it is revealed under the phenomenon of weakness. And it is to this end that the Holy Spirit directed the eyes of the prophets. For as the flesh always desires outward display, the Spirit of God, to stop believers seeking it in the Messiah, declared that He would be quite unlike earthly kings, who want to win admiration, and wherever they go excite great cheers and fill cities and towns with wild enthusiasm. Now we can see how apt is Matthew's use of this prophesy in the present situation. God laid on His Son a humble and lowly role. But the simple might be offended at His contemptible and obscure life; and so the prophets and Matthew agree that this was no accident but came to pass by the decree of heaven. From this it follows that all those are acting wickedly who reject Christ because His outward state does not match up to their wishes. For we must not imagine a Christ who corresponds to our ideas, but must simply embrace Him as He is set forth by the Father. He is unworthy of salvation who vilipends the lowliness of Christ, which the Father

35

declared was well pleasing to Him. Now let us come to the prophets' words.

Mark 12.18. *Behold, my servant.* To bind us to His purpose, God points, so to say, to the one whom He would send. And this is the point of the exclamation 'Behold'. A similar reason underlies the following epithets: He calls Him His 'servant' and His 'chosen', in whom His soul delights. For how does it come about that men dare to measure Christ by their own sense, save because they do not consider that their redemption depends on the sheer grace of God? When God offers us this incomparable treasure it is a wicked licence to assess its value by our fleshly standards. 'Servant' is a title of honour, not making Him one of the common herd but the one on whom God laid the function and office of ransoming the Church. No-one may usurp this honour to himself, but he who is called is deservedly reckoned in the order. God therefore declares that He who comes forward in this way is chosen by His decree. From this it follows that it is not right for men to reject Him, for this would be an injury and sacrilege against God. And indeed it is quite absurd that God's calling, which ought to be holy and inviolable, should be frustrated by our desire or pride. The statement is more far-reaching, however. In the prophet God adds that His soul is well pleased with Christ. For although our calling flows to each of us from the favour of God, the one well-spring, what is unique in Christ is that in His person God the Father embraces the whole Church in His love. For since we are all by nature enemies of God, His love never reaches us unless it begins first at the Head, as we have seen elsewhere and will see again in Matt. 17.

*He shall declare judgment to the Gentiles.* When he foretells His coming, the prophet briefly points to the office of Christ: He shall bring judgment to the Gentiles. By the word 'judgment' is understood a state with a good and orderly constitution, where equity and uprightness flourish. Hence it is as if the prophet said that He would come who would restore the justice which had collapsed and be indeed the governor not of one people only but add to God's Kingdom the Gentiles too, dominated as they were by a vast disintegration. And this is the meaning of the words 'lead forth' which the prophet uses. The office of Christ was to extend God's Kingdom, then confined to a corner of Judea, into all the world; as it is said elsewhere: 'The Lord shall send forth the sceptre of thy strength out of Zion' (Ps. 110.2). At the same time he expresses the manner of putting forth judgment—God shall place His Spirit in Christ. It is indeed true that there was never any uprightness in the world which did not proceed from the Spirit of God and remain in being by His heavenly power. In the same way no king can either set up or maintain a legitimate order save in so far as he is equipped by the same Spirit. But Christ in bringing judgment far excels all others, for He receives from His Father the Spirit whom He pours out on all His people. For He does not teach [*dictat*] what is right just by voice or by writing, but by the grace of His Spirit He inwardly forms men's hearts to observe the rule of righteousness.

Matt. 12.19. *He shall not strive*. The whole point of this is, as I suggested a little earlier, that Christ's coming would not create a big stir, for it would lack regal trappings and spendour. But he quickly adds that it will be for men's good if His gentleness, despised everywhere in the world, is lovely to them. And it is an incredible foolishness in men to set less store by Christ because He lowers Himself kindly and unasked to their level. If Christ appeared in His glory we should think that it would engulf us. How depraved it is, then, to welcome Him less cordially when for our sakes He descends from His sublimity! Therefore Isaiah tells us how useful, in fact necessary, Christ's gentleness is, to evoke reverence from believers. Because each of us is aware of his weakness, we should consider how much we all need to be cherished tenderly by Christ. I am not talking about unbelievers, who are completely empty of any grace of the Spirit, but of those who have already been called by the Lord and in whom He will in due course kindle a fuller light, supply a firmer strength. Are they not all like half-broken reeds and smoking lamp-wicks? When Christ accommodates Himself to our weakness, let us learn to return the embrace of His infinite goodness. Yet let none indulge himself in his faults; rather let him endeavour to march forward, so that we are not tossed about all our life or swayed like a reed at every breeze. Let us grow up into full adulthood, so as to stand fast against the various assaults of Satan and that our faith may not just glimmer with weak sparks in the midst of thick smoke but may send out shining rays. But now all Christ's ministers are taught by His example how they should act.

Because some mistakenly and absurdly argue on the basis of this verse that we must be gentle with all indiscriminately, we must note the distinction that the prophet expressly makes between the weak and the wicked. For those who are strong enough and to spare must have their hardness beaten violently with a hammer. Those who try to spread darkness all abroad or are like incendiaries must have their black smoke scattered and their fire put out. Therefore just as faithful ministers of the Word must take care to spare the weak and cherish and increase God's grace, yet weak in them, so on the other hand they must beware not to indulge the obstinate malice of those who are far from being a smoking wick or a shaking reed.

Matt. 12.20. *Till he send forth judgment unto victory*. The prophet's words are a little different—that He will bring forth or lead forth

37

judgment in truth. But the phrase which Matthew uses is very emphatic, to teach us that righteousness is not set up in the world without a great fight and struggle. For the devil heaps up against us all possible difficulties, so that we cannot break out without a struggle—which is confirmed by the word 'victory', which is won only by fighting. For the next clause the prophet has 'the isles shall wait for his law'. But although Matthew has changed the words, the sense still stands, that Christ's grace will be common to the Gentiles.

*Then was brought unto him one possessed with a devil, blind and dumb; and he healed him, inasmuch that the dumb man spoke and saw. And all the multitudes were amazed, and said, Is this the son of David? But when the Pharisees heard it, they said, This man doth not cast out devils, but by Beelzebub the prince of the devils.* (Matt. 12.22-24)

*And they come into a house. And the multitude cometh together again, so that they could not so much as eat bread. And when his friends heard it, they went out to lay hold on him: for they said, He is beside himself. And the scribes which came down from Jerusalem said, He hath Beelzebub, and, by the prince of the devils casteth he out the devils.* (Mark 3.20-22)

*And he was casting out a devil which was dumb. And it came to pass, when the devil was gone out, the dumb man spake; and the multitudes marvelled. But some of them said, By Beelzebub the prince of the devils casteth he out devils.* (Luke 11.14-15)

Mark 3.20. *And they come into a house.* There is no doubt that Mark makes quite a long space of time elapse when he moves on from the miracles to this ungodly conspiracy among Christ's relatives to put Him under restraint as a madman. In Matthew and Luke there is express mention of only one miracle to give the Pharisees a chance to revile Him. But since the three agree in this last clause, it will be well to treat here what Mark relates. It is surprising that Christ's relatives should be so wicked, those who ought to have been the first to help in forwarding the kingdom of God. When they see that He has already made a name for Himself, their ambition is awakened to become famous in Jerusalem. They exhort Him to go there, just so that He may display Himself. Now, however, that they see Him on the one hand hated by the rulers, on the other the target of many slanders, even despised by the most part, they do not want any of the condemnation or hatred or shame to rub off on the family as a whole; and so they make up their minds to lay hands on Him and to restrain Him at home as a lunatic. And they were, in fact, convinced of this, as the evangelist's words show.

From this we learn first of all how blind is the human mind, that it can make such a perverse judgment on the revealed glory of God. Surely the power of the Holy Spirit shines splendidly in all Christ's words and deeds. And even if this was obscure to others, how could it have been hidden to His kinsfolk, who knew Him so well? But because Christ's method of working did not please the world or win its approval but exposed Him to the hatred of many, they think He is raving.

In the second place we learn that the light of faith comes not from flesh and blood, but from heavenly grace, lest any should glory in any other birth than that of the Spirit; as Paul says: 'If any man wishes to be thought to be in Christ, let him be a new creature' (II Cor. 5.17).

Matt. 12.22. *Then was brought unto him.* Luke calls the demon that possessed the man 'dumb' from the effect it had. But Matthew says that the man was afflicted with a twofold plague. It is, of course, true that many are blind and dumb from natural causes. But this man seems to have gone blind and been deprived of the use of speech without anything being wrong with his optical nerves or the shape of his tongue. But it is not surprising that there is permitted to Satan such licence in harming the physical senses when all the faculties of our soul are corrupted or perverted by the righteous permission of God.

Matt. 12.23. *And all the multitudes were amazed.* From this we gather that God's display of power was obvious, for it swung the crowd round from their malicious attitude to a pure and sound admiration of Him. For how did it happen that they were all amazed, except because the event itself was compulsive? And indeed there is not one of us who does not perceive in this story, as in a mirror, the extraordinary power of God. From which we infer that the minds of the scribes were infected with a devilish venom, when they did not hesitate to speak ill of such a wonderful work of God. We must also observe the result of this miracle. Those who saw it were touched with wonder and asked among themselves whether Jesus could be the Christ. When they knew the power of God, they were led as it were by the hand to faith. Not that they all at once got as much out of it as they should have done (for they speak with doubt), but it was no small advance when they bestirred themselves to look more closely at Christ's glory. To some it seems to be a complete assent; but the words do not say this, and what happened shows that they were struck by this unexpected event and did not judge perfectly but only entertained the thought that He might possibly be the Christ.

Matt. 12.24. *But when the Pharisees heard it they said.* The event is so open and evidential that the scribes cannot get out of it. So they maliciously disparage it—Christ did not do it by divine power. They not only obscure the praise of the miracle but try to turn it into a disgrace, that He had performed it by some magical exorcism; and so they suggest that, as His work cannot be attributed to human agency, the devil must be its author. I spoke in Matthew 10 on the word 'Beelzebub'. And the leadership among the devils we touched on in chapter 9. For it was not from vulgar error or superstition that the scribes attributed a leader to the evil spirits, but from the received opinion among the godly, that the reprobate have a head just as Christ is the Head of the Church.

*And knowing their thoughts he said unto them, Every kingdom divided against itself is brought to desolation; and every city or house divided against itself shall not stand: and if Satan casteth out Satan, he is divided against himself; how then shall his kingdom stand? And if I by the help of Beelzebub cast out devils, by whose help do your sons cast them out? therefore shall they be your judges. But if I by the Spirit of God cast out devils, then is the kingdom of God come upon you. Or how can one enter into the house of the strong man, and spoil his goods, except he first bind the strong man? and then he will spoil his house. He that is not with me is against me; and he that gathereth not with me scattereth. Therefore, I say unto you, Every sin and blasphemy shall be forgiven unto men; but the blasphemy against the Spirit shall not be forgiven. And whosoever shall speak a word against the Son of man, it shall be forgiven him; but whosoever shall speak against the Holy Spirit, it shall not be forgiven him, neither in this world, nor in that which is to come.* (Matt. 12.25-32)

*And he called them unto him, and said unto them in parables, How can Satan cast out Satan? And if a kingdom be divided against itself, that kingdom cannot stand. And if a house be divided against itself, that house will not be able to stand. And if Satan hath risen up against himself, and is divided, he cannot stand, but hath an end. But no-one can enter into the house of the strong man, and spoil his goods, except he first bind the strong man, and then he will spoil his house. Verily I say unto you, All their sins shall be forgiven unto the sons of men; and their blasphemies wherewith soever they shall blaspheme: but whosoever shall blaspheme against the Holy Spirit hath never forgiveness, but is guilty of an eternal sin: because they said, He hath an unclean spirit.* (Mark 3.23-30)

*And others, tempting him, sought of him a sign from heaven. But he, knowing their thoughts, said unto them, Every kingdom divided against itself is brought to desolation; and a house divided against a house falleth. And if Satan also is divided against himself, how shall his kingdom stand? because ye say that I cast out devils by Beelzebub. But if I by Beelzebub cast out devils, by whom do your sons cast them out? therefore shall they be your judges. But if I by the finger of God cast out devils, then is the kingdom of God come upon you. When the strong man fully armed guardeth his own court, his goods are in peace: but when a stronger than he shall come upon him, and overcome him, he taketh from him his whole armour wherein he trusted, and divideth his spoils. He that is not with me is against me; and he that gathereth not with me scattereth.* (Luke 11.16-32)

*And everyone who shall speak a word against the Son of man, it shall be forgiven him: but unto him that blasphemeth against the Holy Spirit it shall not be forgiven.* (Luke 12.10)

Matt. 12.25. *And Jesus, knowing their thoughts.* Although Christ knew well enough (and frequently indeed by experience), that in their malevolence the scribes were for ever taking what He did in the worst part, I have no doubt that Matthew and Luke mean that Christ possessed a knowledge of their hearts. And it is probable that they spoke against Christ openly and that their slanders reached Him; but by His divine Spirit He knew the thoughts which lay behind their calumnies. It often happens that men judge perversely, not because they are deliberately attacking what is right but because they are ignorantly mistaken; or they do not nurse a hidden and secret poison, but are carried away by impulsiveness. The meaning therefore is that Christ castigates them so fiercely because He was witness and judge of their inwardly conceived malice.

*Every kingdom.* He rebuts the first calumny levelled against Him with a proverb. Yet His refutation does not seem at all solid. We know what tricks Satan sometimes uses to deceive men, presenting an appearance of dissension to ensnare their minds in superstitions. Thus the exorcisms in the Papacy are nothing but counterfeit fights of Satan against himself. But no such suspicion rests on Christ. He casts out the demons from men to restore them sane and whole to God. When the devil enters into this conspiracy with himself, he pretends to be overcome, but in such a way that he emerges victorious. But Christ attacked the devil in open battle, and cast him completely down and left him with nothing. He did not strike him down in one respect

41

and set him up on his feet in another, but destroyed his weapons of war everywhere. Therefore Christ rightly argues that He has nothing in common with him; for the father of lies has one purpose only, to keep his kingdom. If any object that the devils are often carried away by dizziness and blindness to self-destruction, the reply is easy—Christ's words merely say that it is absurd for the scribes to claim that the devil of his own free will should demolish his power over men when his whole aim is to keep them his slaves. We must also remember that Christ was using popular proverbs, which were probable conjectures rather than solid arguments. Add to this that, because He is speaking of something well-known and attested, He accuses the conscience of His enemies more surely. It was plain to everyone that Satan has been driven from his possession by Christ, and it was also quite clear that all the miracles pointed in this direction. From this it was easy to assert that His power, so opposed to Satan, was divine.

Matt. 12.27. *By whom do your sons cast them out?* He accuses them of unjust and malicious judgment, because respect for persons caused them to cast different judgments in the same case. This inequality shows that equity and right did not prevail but they were ruled by blind love or hatred. This depraved and invidious φιλαυτίας was a sign that they condemned in Christ what they praised in themselves.

Some take 'your sons' to mean the children of the whole nation. Some think it was the apostles, in that they were acknowledged to be sons whereas Christ was regarded as a foreigner. Others refer it to the prophets of old. I have no doubt that He means the exorcists, whose art was then commonly practised among the Jews, as appears from Acts 19.13ff. For it is probable that they thought no more kindly of Christ's disciples than of the Master. And it does violence to the text to transfer it to the dead when the words clearly convey a comparison of that present time. The Jewish exorcists had no standing under the Law, but we know that God, to keep the people in the faith and pure worship of His covenant, sometimes bore witness to His presence among them by various miracles. So it could happen that they put demons to flight by the invocation of God's name. Then when the people had experienced such a power of God they rashly instituted an ordinary office. Afterwards the Papists, not to be outdone, aped them by creating exorcists, thus becoming the apes of apes. There was, moreover, no point in Christ approving those exorcisms, for He rebuked the malice of those who wanted them to be regarded as holy and marked with the name of God. Yet they pretended that Christ was the minister of Beelzebub. The objection was directed against Him personally (as one says).

What follows just after, *your sons shall be your judges*, is an imprecise

42

saying which means: 'Your condemnation does not take much looking for. You ascribe to Beelzebub the miracles that I do while you praise similar ones in your own sons. There is sufficient to condemn you in your own household.' If anyone would prefer to take it in the sense that He was blaming them for forgetting the grace of God which was sometimes shown through the exorcists, I shall not much argue the point. For although they were degenerate, the Lord did not want them to be completely deprived of His power, but adorned the priestly line and the worship of the Temple with a certain testimony. For it was very much to the purpose that this should be distinguished by clear marks from Gentile superstitions. But the former sense seems to me the genuine one.

Matt. 12.28. *But if I by the Spirit of God.* Luke uses the metaphor 'finger' for Spirit. Since God works and puts forth His power through His Spirit, the name 'finger' is aptly ascribed to Him. It was a common expression among the Jews. Moses, for example, relates that Pharaoh's wise men said: 'This is the finger of God' (Exod. 8.19). Now Christ sums up from what He had said that the scribes were ungrateful to God, for they did not want Him to reign over them. Hitherto He had been refuting their empty calumny. Now He orders them, as men defeated in argument, not to set themselves impiously against the Kingdom of God. He is not taking His stand on this one single miracle but using it as an occasion to treat of the reason for His coming. He means that they should not consider this one particular event but something far more wonderful—that by revealing His Messiah God wished to raise up their broken down common-weal and restore His Kingdom among them. Hence we see that Christ complained of their ingratitude in that they wildly drove God's incomparable grace out of their midst.

The words 'come upon' are emphatic: God the Redeemer has appeared to them unasked, but they (so far as they can) banish Him afar and can not endure to give Him a place when He is present and equipped to save them.

Matt. 12.29. *Or how can one enter.* Although the Evangelists differ a little about the words, they agree very well on the point of the saying. Christ follows up what He has touched on about the Kingdom of God and says that it is necessary for Satan to be cast out with violence, so that God may win His Kingdom among men. Hence this sentence is simply a confirmation of the last. But, to grasp Christ's meaning the better, we must remind ourselves of the analogy that Matthew had made between the visible and spiritual graces of Christ. Whatever Christ does for bodies He wants to be referred to souls. So by setting men's physical faculties free from the tyranny of the devil, He testified that

43

He was sent by His Father to be the champion who would destroy his spiritual tyranny over their souls.

I now return to his words.

He says that domination cannot be taken from a powerful and strong tyrant until he is despoiled of his weapons. He will never yield of free will but only when opposed by a superior force. Why does He say this? First, we know that the devil is everywhere called the prince of the world. His tyrannical government is protected all round by strong defences. For there are numberless snares to entrap men, or rather, he binds men—already his slaves—in various fetters so tightly that they would rather enjoy the slavery to which they are doomed than aspire to liberty. Numberless also are the kinds of ills by which he holds down the wretched oppressed. In a word, there is neither let nor hindrance to prevent him ruling tyrannically in the world. Not, indeed, that he can do anything that God does not permit, but because Adam, when he separated himself from God's rule, brought all his posterity under this alien rod. But although the devil's rule is unnatural and men are subjected to his tyranny by the just punishment of God because of their sin, yet he possesses his kingdom in tranquility and triumphs over us at his will, until a stronger rises up against him. But there is none stronger than he on earth, for men have not the power to help themselves. Therefore the Redeemer from heaven was promised. Christ now shows that this method of redemption is necessary, that He may disarm the devil who will never give up till he is overpowered. By these words He means that men hope in vain for liberation until Satan is conquered in a violent battle. Although He deliberately rebukes the ignorance of the scribes in not grasping the principles of the Kingdom of God, yet his reproof covers nearly everyone, since they are troubled by pretty much the same foolishness. There is no-one who does not boast in words that he desires the Kingdom of God; yet we do not allow Christ to fight valiantly (as there is need) to rescue us from the hand of our tyrant. We are like a sick man begging a doctor to help him and yet shrinking from every remedy. We now see that Christ's purpose in employing this parable was to show that the scribes were anatagonistic to the Kingdom of God and were malignantly hampering its beginnings. Yet we learn that, because we are all subject to Satan God only sets up His Kingdom in us when He frees us from that ill-fated and unhappy slavery by the strong and victorious hand of Christ.

Matt. 12.30. *He that is not with me.* This place is interpreted in two ways. Some connect it with the parable He has just spoken, and so it becomes an argument from contraries—as if Christ said: 'I can reign only if the devil is overthrown. For all his endeavours have the one aim of scattering what I collect'. And, indeed, it is all too obvious that the

44

enemy devotes himself to scattering Christ's Kingdom. But I subscribe rather to the opinion of those who expound it that the scribes were called enemies of God's Kingdom in a twofold sense, because they deliberately hinder its progress. The meaning therefore is: 'It was for you to give me your support and to lend a hand in setting up God's Kingdom. For whoever does not help is in some way an opponent or at least deserves to be reckoned among the opponents. What about you, then, driven by your raging madness into open warfare?'

Moreover, from what has been said it is quite clear that Christ's next words are true: 'he that gathereth not with me, scattereth'. It comes from the propensity of our nature to evil that there is no place for God's righteousness except among those who devote themselves earnestly to it. Yet this doctrine has a wider application—they are reckoned unworthy to be in Christ's flock who do not put all their energy into it. For by their sloth the Kingdom of God will be weakened and suffer harm, and we are all called to extend it.

Matt. 12.31. *Therefore I say unto you.* This corollary should not be restricted to the last clause, but depends on the whole context. For after Christ had taught that the scribes could not condemn Him for casting out demons without opposing the Kingdom of God, He concludes that this was no light or bearable offence but a wicked crime; knowingly and deliberately they had cast slanders on God's Spirit. For we have already said that Christ did not say this of their mere words but of their irreligious and wicked thoughts.

*Every sin and blasphemy.* Since the Lord declares that blasphemy against the Spirit is the worst of all sins, it will be well to enquire what He means by this word. Those who define it to be impenitence can be refuted without more ado; for it would be meaningless and inept for Christ to say that they would not be forgiven in this age. Again, the word 'blasphemy' cannot be extended to any sort of sin indiscriminately. But we can easily get a definition from the comparison which Christ makes. Why is he said to sin more gravely who blasphemes against the Spirit than he who blasphemes against Christ? Is it because the Spirit has a more eminent majesty that He must be avenged more severely? The reason is certainly different, for the fulness of Divinity shines in Christ, and whoever blasphemes against Him overturns and destroys (so far as he can) the whole glory of God. Again, how shall Christ be divided from His Spirit so that he who speaks against the Spirit leaves Christ Himself unharmed and untouched? From this we can begin to gather that it is not because the Spirit is superior to Christ that blasphemy against him surpasses all other sins. It is that when once God's power has been revealed there is no longer any excuse on the grounds of ignorance for those who reject Him. We must also note

45

that the blasphemy spoken of here does not refer simply to the essence of the Spirit but to His grace which is given us. For those who lack the light of the Spirit, much as they may detract from His glory, are not held guilty of this crime. We do not hold that those who fight against His grace and power with determined malice are blaspheming the Spirit of God; but we do hold that such sacrilege is committed only when we strive knowingly to extinguish the Spirit dwelling within us. And the reason why the Spirit, rather than the Son or the Father Himself, is said to be blasphemed is that, in depreciating God's grace and power, we are making a direct assault on the Spirit, from whom they proceed and in whom they are manifest to us. Does some unbeliever curse God? It is as if a blind man came into collision with a wall. But he is not cursing the Spirit unless he has been enlightened by Him and is aware of his ungodly rebellion. For the distinction He makes is necessary, that all other blasphemies will be pardoned except this one, which is offered to the Spirit. If anyone straightforwardly blasphemes against God, hope of forgiveness will not be denied him; but it is declared that God will never be forgiving to those who affront the Spirit. Why is this, but because only they blaspheme against the Spirit who disparage His gifts and power in contradiction to their own understanding? This is the point also of what we read in Mark, that the Pharisees were so severely threatened by Christ because they said that He was endowed with an unclean spirit, thus deliberately and maliciously turning light into darkness. But this is to make war on God like the Titans, as they say.

Now this gives rise to a question: Do men ever really burst out into such madness as not to scruple to attack God wittingly and willingly? For this seems unbelievable and unnatural. I reply, that this audacity proceeds from a delirious blindness, in which, however, malice and poisonous frenzy predominate. What Paul says in I Tim. 1.13 is not irrelevant. He was a blasphemer, but he obtained pardon, because he did it ignorantly in his unbelief. By this word he distinguished his sin from a willing obstinacy. And also this verse refutes the error of those who imagine that any sort of voluntary sin and what is committed in opposition to one's conscience, is unforgivable. But Paul expressly restricts that sin to the first table of the Law, and the Lord no less clearly indicates by the word 'blasphemy' one particular sort and shows at the same time that it is a direct attack on the glory of God.

From all these things we can now gather that they sin against the Holy Spirit and are blasphemers who maliciously turn God's powers, revealed to them by the Spirit and in which His glory should be celebrated, to dishonour and with Satan as their leader are the professed enemies of God's glory. It is not surprising, then, if Christ denies hope of pardon to such sacrilege, for they are past weeping for who change the one medicine of salvation into a deadly poison. To some this seems too harsh, and so they take refuge in the childish quibble that it is called unforgiveable because its pardon is rare and difficult to obtain. But Christ spoke too clearly for His words to be evaded so easily. They argue very foolishly that God would be cruel if He never remitted this sin—a sin whose wickedness should shock us all with amazement. They do not sufficiently consider how great is the crime of not only deliberately profaning God's holy Name, but spitting in His face when He appears transplendent before us. Equally ignorant is their cavil who say that it would be absurd if penitence could not beg for forgiveness. For blasphemy against the Spirit is a certain sign of reprobation. Hence it follows that whoever fall into it have been given a reprobate spirit. For just as we deny that it is possible for anyone truly born again of the Spirit to cast himself into such a horrifying crime, so on the contrary we must hold that those who do fall into it never rise again. In this way God avenges contempt of His grace: He hardens the hearts of the reprobate so that they never desire to repent.

Matt. 12.32. *Neither in this world.* Mark briefly explains the sense of these words when he says that he who has spoken against the Spirit is guilty of eternal judgment. Daily we pray for forgiveness of sins from God, and He reconciles us to Himself. And at last in death He wipes out all our sins and declares that He is propitious to us. The fruit of His mercy will appear at the last day. The meaning therefore is that we can have no hope that those who blaspheme against the Spirit will beg forgiveness in this life or be absolved at the last judgment. From this the Papists infer that sins are forgiven men after they are dead. But this misrepresentation can easily be refuted. In the first place they are stupid to twist the term 'in that which is to come' into an intermediate time when it is plain to anyone that the last day is meant. But they also betray their insincerity, for their objection contradicts their own theology. They make the well-known distinction that sins are freely forgiven in respect of their guilt, but that punishment and satisfaction are also demanded. They have already confessed in this that there is no hope of salvation unless the guilt is remitted before death. Therefore there remains no remission to the dead except that of punishment. But they dare not deny that the subject here is guilt. Let them go and try to light the fire of their purgatory with this cold stuff, if they can coax a flame out of ice.

*Either make the tree good, and its fruit good; or make the tree corrupt, and its fruit corrupt: for the tree is known by its fruit. Ye offspring of*

47

*vipers, how can ye, being evil, speak good things? for out of the abundance of the heart the mouth speaketh. The good man out of his good treasure bringeth forth good things: and the evil man out of his evil treasure bringeth forth evil things. And I say unto you, that every idle word that men shall speak, they shall give account thereof in the day of judgment. For by thy words thou shalt be justified, and by thy words thou shalt be condemned.* (Matt. 12.33-37)

Matt. 12.33. *Either make the tree good.* It may seem absurd that a choice is given to men to be good or evil; but if we consider the kind of men Christ is talking to, the solution is easy. We know what people thought of the Pharisees. Common minds were so dazzled by their imagined holiness that no-one dared to criticize their faults. Christ wants to unmask them, and so He bids them be either good or bad—as if He said that there was nothing more foreign to uprightness than dissimulation, and that it was empty for them to boast of being righteous if they were not sincere and honest. He is not allowing anything to their will or relaxing the bridle, but only telling them that their hollow mask would avail them nothing while they were so two-faced, for men must of necessity be either good or bad.

When He says *make the tree good*, some ignorantly infer that men have the ability to regulate their life and their morals. It is an imprecise expression, with which Christ dispels the scribes' hypocrisy like smoke and summons them back to a solid and sound righteousness. He afterwards expresses the manner and way in which trees show whether they are good or bad—if they bear good fruit or bad. There is nothing ambiguous in this meaning. The life of the scribes was not notorious for gross wickedness; yet their slanders were the symptoms of the poison of their pride, ambition and envy. Because all this was hidden from the ordinary folk, Christ draws the inner evil out of darkness into light. If anyone objects that in the corruption of our nature there is none who is inwardly sound and free from any fault, the answer is easy. What Christ requires is not a precise and complete perfection, but only a simple and sincere affection; and from this the Pharisees He was addressing had wandered very far. For as Scripture calls those who are devoted to Satan evil and wicked, so it calls the sincere worshippers of God good, even though they are encompassed by the weakness of their flesh and by many faults. And it is by God's free kindness that those who aspire after goodness are given such an honourable title.

Matt. 12.34. *Ye offspring of vipers.* Christ here refers this metaphor of the tree and the fruit only to language; and this uncovers the inward and hidden malice of the scribes—which is why He keeps to this one

48

sort of sin. Because they betrayed by their false slanders what was less obvious in the rest of their life, Christ assails them severely. 'No wonder', He says, 'if you spew out evil words when your heart is stuffed with malice.' Nor could He have treated them more gently to make His reproof seem less immoderate. Other sins deserve harsh rebukes; but when equivocal men deprave what is right, or throw a disguise over vices, their depravity deserves a far more vehement condemnation from God than other sins. Christ's intention was, as the situation demanded, to condemn that ungodly cleverness that turns light into darkness. Hence this verse teaches how precious truth is to the Lord, its strict defender and champion. I wish that those people would give good heed to this who are too ready to lend their intelligence to defending any cause and who sell their tongue for disguising deceit. But particularly is Christ angry with those who are driven to reviling by ambition or envy or other crooked desire, even where there is naught for their disapproval. In His usual way, Christ was rougher against the Pharisees, because they were so bewitched by their faulty idea of righteousness that a milder admonition would do little good. And indeed, unless hypocrites are pricked sharply they proudly despise anything that is said to them.

*How can ye, being evil.* We have already mentioned elsewhere that proverbial statements ought not to be taken as a constant norm, since they only teach what generally happens. It sometimes occurs that the cruel man will deceive simple folk by his smooth charm, that the trickster will gain his ends by pretence of simplicity, that the evil-thinker will breathe an almost angelic purity of speech. Yet what Christ says here is proved true by common use: 'out of the abundance of the heart the mouth speaks'. Another old proverb calls the tongue the expression [*character*] of the mind. And indeed, although man's mind has hidden and tortuous coverts and each may hide his faults with wonderful skill, the Lord extorts a certain confession from everyone so that his tongue betrays his mind and inward feelings.

We must also note the end to which Christ turns these parables: He blames the Pharisees that what they declare in words is an inwardly conceived malice. Moreover, knowing them to be sworn enemies, He uses one false accusation to lay bare their whole life and destroys their credit with the people, who were too much deceived and harmed by the weight of their authority. Moreover, although good words do not always flow from the inward being but are just born on the tip of the tongue, as they say, yet it is on the other hand true that evil words are always witnesses to an evil heart.

Matt. 12.36. *Every idle word.* This is an argument from the lesser

49

to the greater. For if every useless word is called into account, how shall God spare the open blasphemies and irreligious impudences of those who snarl against His glory? An 'idle word' is taken to be a useless word, one which produces no edification or fruit. To many this seems too strict. But if we consider the use for which our tongues were formed we shall agree that they are justly guilty who devote their tongues recklessly to trifling nonsense and so prostitute them. It is a serious fault to abuse with frivolities the time which Paul bids us anxiously to redeem (Col. 4.5). But since no-one is so sparing in speech and so wise and temperate that he does not sometimes sink into some idle words, nothing would remain for us all but desperation if God acted towards us with strict Law. But since our trust in our salvation is founded on God not entering into judgment with us but freely burying in oblivion our sins which deserve unnumbered deaths, let us not doubt that when He wipes out the guilt of our whole life He therewith pardons the sin of empty speaking. For when Scripture speaks of God's judgment it is not at all overturning the forgiveness of sins. Nobody should be permissive to himself, however, but should be careful to keep a tight reign on his tongue. First so that we may speak reverently and soberly about the holy mysteries of God, and then that we may abstain from buffoonery and empty witticisms, and much more from hostile vituperation, and lastly that we may ensure that our word is seasoned with salt (Col. 4.6).

Matt. 12.37. *For by thy words thou shalt be justified.* He turns a common proverb to the present case. For I have no doubt that the saying was common among the people that a man would be condemned or absolved by his own confession. But Christ changes its meaning somewhat—that a perverse word is enough to condemn a man, since it is a pointer to hidden malice. The Papists are childish in twisting it in an endeavour to weaken the righteousness of faith. A man is justified by his own words, not because a word is the cause of righteousness (for we receive God's grace reckoning us as righteous by faith) but in that a pure word saves us from being found un-righteous in language. Is it not absurd to deduce that men deserve even a drop of righteousness before God? On the contrary, this verse confirms our teaching, for although Christ is not speaking of the cause of our salvation, the antithesis between the two words shows what the word 'justified' means. To the Papists it is absurd when we say a man is justified by faith, because they explain righteousness as becoming and being righteous. But we understand it as being reckoned righteous and being absolved before the judgment of God, as is clear from very many testimonies of Scripture. Does not Christ confirm this, when He opposes 'to justify' and 'to condemn'?

*But the unclean spirit, when he is gone out of the man, passeth through waterless places, seeking rest, and findeth it not. Then he saith, I will return into my house whence I came out; and when he is come, he findeth it empty, swept, and garnished. Then goeth he, and taketh to himself seven other spirits more evil than himself, and they enter in and dwell there: and the last state of that man becometh worse than the first. Even so shall it be also unto this evil generation.* (Matt. 12.43-45)

*The unclean spirit when he is gone out of the man, passeth through waterless places, seeking rest; and finding none, he saith, I will turn back unto my house whence I came out. And when he is come, he findeth it swept and garnished. Then goeth he, and taketh seven other spirits more evil than himself; and they enter in and dwell there: and the last state of that man becometh worse than the first.* (Luke 11.24-26)

Matt. 12.43. *But the unclean spirit.* He threatens the punishment their ingratitude deserves to the scribes and such like hypocrites who spurn God's grace and conspire with the devil. But to extend the usefulness of His teaching He tells them in general the sort of judgment they will face who spurn grace offered and re-open the gate to the devil. But because almost every phrase is very weighty, we must consider some things in order before coming to the meaning of the parable.

When Christ speaks of the devil going out, He is praising the power and effect that God's grace has when it comes to us. But especially when God draws near to us in the person of His own Son, His aim is to rescue us from the tyranny of the devil and receive us to Himself—which thing Christ plainly testified by the miracle He had just wrought. Since, therefore, it is His proper office to put evil spirits to flight, that they may no longer reign in men, the devil is truly said to go out from the men to whom Christ offers Himself as Redeemer. Although Christ's presence was not efficacious to all (for the unbelievers made it unavailing for themselves), He wanted to show why He visited us, what power lay in His very coming, and what it means to the evil spirits. For He never works in men without the devils being forced to fight and to yield to His power. Therefore we must hold that the devil is cast out of us when Christ shines upon us and gives us some evidence of His grace.

Then there is described the wretched state of all mankind; for it follows that the devil had his dwelling place in men, if he is cast out of them by the Son of God. This is not spoken of one or another individual but of the whole of Adam's offspring. Here lies the glory of our nature—the devil has his throne within us, inhabits us body and soul! This makes God's mercy the more wonderful, that He converts us from Satan's stinking stables to His own temple and consecrates us as a spiritual habitation for himself.

Thirdly, He portrays Satan's character, that he never ceases from evil but is incessantly busy, everlastingly on the move. All his attempts are to work our destruction. But especially, when he has been conquered and degraded by Christ, his rage and lust to hurt are only sharpened the more. Before Christ gives us a share in His power, the enemy rules in us as easy as a game. But when he is cast out, he grieves at the loss of his prey, gathers his strength together and stirs up all his faculties to attack us afresh. He is therefore said metaphorically 'to pass through waterless places', because it is like a sad exile for him and a wild desert, to have his dwelling outside men. In the same sense it is said that 'he seeks rest' so long as he lives outside men, for then he is unhappy and tortured; and he does not cease from trying this way and that to recover what he has lost. Hence we learn that when Christ calls us we must be ready to fight more strongly and fiercely. For although he is set on the destruction of us all (and what Peter said is true of all without exception, that he goes about as a roaring lion, seeking whom he may devour), yet these words of Christ warn us that he has a greater hatred for us who are rescued from his snares and attacks us with the greater hostility. But this admonition should not frighten us but rather arouse us to keep careful watch and, clad in spiritual armour, to be bold in our resistance.

Matt. 12.44. *He findeth it empty.* Without doubt Christ means that they are ready to receive the devil who are empty of God's Spirit. For believers, in whom God's Spirit dwells secure, are everywhere so garrisoned that no chink is left for Satan. 'A house swept and garnished' is a metaphor from people delighting in the cleanness and brightness of their homes. To Satan, deformity alone is beautiful, stink and filth alone savoury. And the meaning is that no place in us is more convenient for Satan than when we bid Christ farewell and make him our guest. The height of his joy is that emptiness which follows upon the neglect of divine grace.

Matt. 12.45. *And taketh with himself.* As in many places, the number seven is indefinite. Christ is telling us by these words that if we cut ourselves off from His grace, we are twice bound to Satan and he attacks us more freely than before. And this is the just penalty for our laziness. We must not think the devil is overcome in one battle, when he has gone out of us once; but we should remember that since he had his lodging in us from of old, from our birth, all the entrances by which he can enter into us are well-known and understood. And if there is no straightforward entrance, he is cunning enough to worm his way in secretly by underground shafts and thwart adits. We must therefore ensure that Christ's Kingdom may be established within us and so shut up all entrances against His enemy. For although Satan's attempts are violent and dangerous, they need not weaken God's children, for the unconquerable power of the Holy Spirit keeps them safe. And we know that this punishment is threatened only to those who despise God's grace, who become utterly godless by quenching the light of faith and suppressing any desire for godliness.

*While he was yet speaking to the multitudes, behold, his mother and his brethren stood without, seeking to speak to him. And one said unto him, Behold, thy mother and thy brethren stand without, seeking to speak to thee. But he answered and said unto him that told him, Who is my mother? and who are my brethren? And he stretched forth his hand towards his disciples, and said, Behold my mother and my brethren! For whosoever shall do the will of my Father which is in heaven, he is my brother, and sister, and mother.* (Matt. 12.46-50)

*And there come his mother and his brethren; and, standing without, they sent unto him, calling him. And a multitude was sitting about him; and they say unto him, Behold, thy mother and thy brethren without seek for thee. And he answereth them, and saith, Who is my mother, and my brethren? And looking round on them which sat round about him, he saith, Behold, my mother and my brethren! For whosoever shall do the will of God, the same is my brother, and sister, and mother.* (Mark 3.31-35)

*And it came to pass, as he said these things, a certain woman out of the multitude lifted up her voice, and said unto him, Blessed is the womb that bare thee, and the breasts which thou didst suck. But he said, Yea rather, blessed are they that hear the word of God and keep it.*
    *And there came to him his mother and brethren, and they could not come at him for the crowd. And it was told him and said, Thy mother and thy brethren stand without, desiring to see thee. But he answered and said unto them, My mother and my brethren are these which hear the word of God, and do it.* (Luke 11.27-28; 8.19-21)

Luke 11.27. *Blessed is the womb.* By this homage the woman intended to praise Christ's excellence. It was not Mary that she was thinking of—maybe she had never seen her—but she magnified Christ's glory by lauding and blessing the womb in which He was carried. There is nothing absurd in the way this blessing of God is celebrated; it is after the usual Scriptural manner. For we know that offspring, especially if endowed with excellent qualities, were regarded as the best of God's gifts. Nor can it be denied that in choosing and appointing Mary to be the mother of His own Son God was bestowing upon her the highest honour. Yet Christ's reply does not accord with this good soul's saying. Rather, it contains a hint of reproof: 'No', He says, 'blessed are they who hear God's Word'. We see that Christ thought next to nothing of what the woman praised. And surely what she thought was Mary's special glory was far inferior to her other graces. For it was a better thing to be born again by the Spirit of Christ than to conceive the flesh of Christ in her womb, to have Christ spiritually living in her than to suckle Him at her breast. The height of the holy Virgin's bliss and glory was to be a member of her own Son and to be numbered by His heavenly Father among the new creatures.

Yet I think that He corrected the woman for another reason, for a different purpose. Men are wont to neglect wickedly God's gifts which they admire in astonishment and proclaim at the top of their voices. For when this woman praised Christ, she left out the most important thing, that in Him salvation is set forth for all. Her homage was therefore weak; it made no mention of His grace and power which are poured out to all. And so Christ rightly claims for Himself another ground for praise, lest His mother alone should be accounted blessed—and that merely in a physical regard. It is that He bestows solid and eternal blessedness on us all. We only estimate the dignity of Christ aright when we consider why He was given to us by the Father and perceive what benefits He has brought us, and this in such a way that we who are wretched in ourselves are blessed in Him. But why is He silent about Himself and mentions only God's Word? Because in this way He opens to us all His treasures, and He has no commerce with us, nor we with Him, apart from His Word. When therefore He communicates Himself to us by His Word He rightly and properly calls us to hear and keep it, that He may become ours by faith. Now we see the difference between Christ's reply and the woman's praise. She confines the grace of blessedness to His family; He offers it freely to all. Then He teaches us not to think of Him in the common way, for He possesses hidden within Himself all the treasures of the heavenly life, of blessedness and of glory, which He dispenses by His Word and apportions to all who embrace the Word by faith. For the key to the Kingdom of heaven is God's free adoption which we receive from the Word.

And we must note the conjunction here: it is necessary first to hear and then to keep. For since faith comes from hearing, this is also the beginning of the spiritual life. Again, because hearing on its own is like an evanescent look at a mirror, as James puts it (1.23), He adds the keeping of the Word, which is equivalent to an efficacious reception, when it strikes root in the heart and bears fruit. The hearer on whose ears beats only the outward teaching retains nothing and gains nothing. But those who boast that they are satisfied with secret inspiration and for this cause neglect the outward preaching withdraw from the heavenly life. What therefore the Son of God joins together, let not men put asunder by an ungodly rashness. But the stupidity of the Papacy is incredible when they sing in honour of Mary words which expressly refute their superstition. In their thanksgiving they single out the woman's saying and omit Christ's correction. But it behoved them to become senseless in every way, for they deliberately profane God's holy Word as they wish.

Luke 8.19. *And there came to him.* There seems to be some discrepancy between Luke and the other two evangelists. The order of the story as they put it makes Christ's mother and family come when He had taught about the unclean spirit. But Luke refers it to a different occasion, and he alone mentions the woman's exclamation which we have already expounded. But it is well-known that the Evangelists were not scrupulous in their time sequences, nor even in keeping to details of words and actions. And so the difficulty is easily resolved. Luke does not say precisely when Christ's mother arrived, but he places it after the parable of the sower instead of before, like the other two.

The woman's cry out of the crowd is not unrelated to his narrative, for it may have been that with thoughtless warmth she praised to the heights what she thought Christ had too much debased. They all agree that while Christ was preaching in the midst of a crowd of people, His brothers and mother came to Him—either, no doubt, because they were worried about Him or because they wanted to learn. For they had some purpose in coming to Him; nor is it likely that those who accompanied His holy mother were unbelievers. To accuse Mary of ambition, as Ambrose and Chrysostom do, is baseless. What need is there for this charge when her piety and modesty are everywhere commended by the testimony of the Spirit? Perhaps they were motivated by a strong human affection and went too far. I do not deny this; but I also do not doubt that they were led by a godly zeal to be with Him.

Matthew relates that one man brought news of their coming; but Mark and Luke say it was many. There is nothing inconsistent in this. As often happens, the message which His mother gave to call Him was taken by many in turn until in the end it reached Him.

Matt. 12, 48. *Who is my mother?* Without doubt these words rebuked Mary's importunity. It was quite wrong for her to interrupt Him while He was teaching. But by diminishing the physical relationship He teaches a very useful lesson. He receives all His disciples and believers into the same rank of honour as if they were His closest relatives; more, He substitutes them for His mother and brothers. But this statement is based on Christ's office; for it means that he was given, not just to a few but to all the godly, who by faith compose with Him one body. Moreover, there is no bond of relationship more holy than the spiritual; for He ought not to be considered according to the flesh but by the power of His Spirit in which the Father gave Him to renew men, that those who were by nature the impure and accursed seed of Adam [for *Abrahae*] might begin by grace to be the holy and heavenly sons of God. Paul says that Christ is not truly known according to the flesh but that what is to be considered in Him is that restoration of the world which far surpasses human power when by His Spirit He reforms us to the image of God. The point of this saying therefore is that we should learn to look at Christ with the eyes of faith. We should know also that every man who is born again of the Spirit should devote himself entirely to God in true righteousness and should be so conjoined with Christ as to be made one with Him. Moreover, by 'doing the will of the Father' He does not intend a precise fulfilling of all the righteousness of the Law (for if this were so the name of brothers which He gives to His disciples would belong to no-one). But in particular He commends faith, the well-spring and origin of holy obedience, and also covers up the defects and faults of the flesh so that they may not be imputed. Christ's saying is well known: 'This is the will of my Father, that whosoever beholds the Son, and believes on Him, shall not perish but have eternal life' (John 6.40).

Christ seems here to have no respect for blood relationship. But we know that He did in fact cherish as holy the human order and that He paid His lawful duties to His parents; but He tells us that physical relationship is of little or no importance in comparison with the spiritual. This comparison should rule our thinking. We should pay nature its just debts but not be overmuch devoted to flesh and blood. Moreover, since Christ gives the disciples of His Gospel the incomparable honour of regarding them as His brothers, our ingratitude must be held accursed if we do not disregard all the desires of the flesh and bend every effort to this aim.

*Then certain of the scribes and Pharisees asked him, saying, Master, we would see a sign from thee. But he answered and said unto them,*

*An evil and adulterous generation seeketh after a sign; and there shall*
*no sign be given to it but the sign of Jonah the prophet: for as Jonah*
*was three days and three nights in the belly of the whale; so shall the*
*Son of man be three days and three nights in the heart of the earth.*
*The men of Nineveh shall rise up in the judgment with this generation,*
*and shall condemn it: for they repented at the preaching of Jonah; and*
*behold, a greater than Jonah is here. The queen of the south shall rise*
*up in the judgment with this generation, and shall condemn it: for she*
*came from the ends of the earth to hear the wisdom of Solomon; and*
*behold, a greater than Solomon is here.* (Matt. 12.38-42)

*And others, tempting him, sought of him a sign from heaven. And*
*when the multitudes were gathering together unto him, he began to*
*say, This generation is evil: it seeketh after a sign; and there shall no*
*sign be given to it but the sign of Jonah. For even as Jonah became a*
*sign unto the Ninevites, so shall also the Son of man be to this generation.*
*The queen of the south shall rise up in judgment with the men of this*
*generation, and shall condemn them: for she came from the ends of the*
*earth to hear the wisdom of Solomon; and behold, a greater than Solomon*
*is here. The men of Nineveh shall rise up in the judgment with this*
*generation, and shall condemn it: for they repented at the preaching of*
*Jonah; and behold, a greater than Jonah is here.* (Luke 11.16; 29-3 2)

Luke 11.16. *And others, tempting him.* Matthew (chapter 16) and
Mark (chapter 8) repeat something similar to this; which shows that
they quite often argued with Christ about this matter—the dishonesty
of those who have once determined to resist the truth is endless. And
it is certain that they were seeking a sign to make a plausible excuse
for their refusal to believe that Christ's calling was legitimately
attested. They are unwilling to be taught. They would not submit
if they saw three or four miracles, let alone one. But, as I have just
said, they make it an excuse for their lack of faith in the Gospel that
Christ shows no sign from heaven. He had already performed a
number of manifest miracles, before their eyes, but these failed to
confirm His teaching. What they wanted to see was some heavenly
phenomenon in which God should in some way visibly appear.
They greet him as 'Master' in the usual way of addressing scribes and
interpreters of the Law, but they will not acknowledge that He is
God's prophet until He produces witness from heaven. The meaning
therefore is: 'you profess to be a doctor and master. If you want us
to be your disciples, cause God to testify from heaven that He is the
author of your ministry, and confirm your vocation with a miracle.'

Matt. 12.39. *An evil and adulterous generation.* He is not only attacking
the malice of that particular age, but is calling the Jews a perverse race

—or at least the scribes and their like—meaning that they had an hereditary disease of stubbornness. For γενεὰ sometimes signifies one age, sometimes a race or nation. He said 'adulterous' as meaning 'born in adultery' or 'illegitimate', in that they had degenerated from the holy patriarchs. In the same way the prophets reproached the unbelievers in their day with not being descendants of Abraham but the profane seed of Canaan.

It may now be asked whether Christ addresses them so harshly because they asked Him for a sign. For elsewhere God shows that He is not very displeased with this. When Gideon asked a sign (Judges 6.17), God was not angry but granted his request. And although he goes on importunately, God is kind to his infirmity. Hezekiah is offered a sign without his asking (Isa. 38.7ff.). But Ahaz is severely rebuked for refusing to seek a sign as the prophet had commanded him (Isa. 7.10ff.). Hence Christ does not directly censure the scribes for asking a sign but because in their ingratitude to God they maliciously spurn His many wonderful works and seize an excuse to be disobedient to His Word. I will not call this laziness but malice, that they shut their eyes to so many signs. Their annoyance was therefore unmeaning, since their only intention was to reject Christ as they liked. Paul condemns the same vice in the next generation when he says that the Jews seek a sign (I Cor. 1.22).

*There shall no sign be given to it.* Even after this they were to be convicted by all sorts of miracles, and Christ would not cease to exercise His power among them so as to make them inexcusable. But what He means here is that one sign is representative of all the signs; they are unworthy and He is not going to humour their ungodly wish. 'Let them be satisfied', He says, 'with this sign: As Jonah rose out of the depths of the sea and preached to Nineveh, so they themselves shall hear the voice of the prophet come back to life.'

I know that this verse has been expounded more subtly by many, but since the likeness between Christ and Jonah does not hold in the details, we must see how Christ does compare Himself with Jonah. I will leave out the speculations of others. Now I think that what is indicated is (as I have already suggested) just one thing, that He would be a prophet to them after He had risen from the dead; as if He had said: 'You despise the Son of God, who came down to you from heaven. It only remains for me to die and to rise from the grave and, once more alive, to speak to you—just as Jonah came to Nineveh from the depths of the sea.' And so the Lord takes from them any palliation for their wicked request and warns them that He will be a prophet to them after His resurrection since He is not accepted when He comes in His mortal flesh. In Luke He says that He will be a sign to them as Jonah was to the Ninevites. But the word 'sign' is used imprecisely: it does not mean that which foretells something, but that which is remote from the usual order of nature; just as Jonah's mission to call Nineveh to repentance was unnatural in that he was taken out of the fish's belly as from a tomb.

'Three nights' is a synecdoche, as is well known. For night is an appendix to the day; or a day consists of two parts, light and darkness. By day and night Christ means one day and He puts a whole day for half a day.

Matt. 12.41. *The men of Nineveh shall rise up.* While He was talking about the Ninevites, Christ went on to show that the scribes and the others who rejected His teachings were far worse than they. 'Heathen men', He says, 'who never heard a word about the true God, repented at the voice of a completely unknwown necomer. But this country, the shrine of heavenly doctrine, does not listen to the Son of God, the promised Redeemer.' This antithesis underlies the comparison. It is known who the Ninevites were—men quite unaccustomed to having prophets and devoid of true doctrine. Jonah was among them without any fine title; he was just a foreigner who might well have been thrown out. The Jews boasted that the Word of the Lord had its throne and habitation among them. If they had gazed on Christ with pure eyes they would have known not only that He was the Teacher from heaven but also the Messiah and the promised author of their salvation. But if the desperate ungodliness of the people was condemned when they despised Christ speaking on the earth, we ourselves surpass the unbelievers of every age if the Son of God seated now in heaven does not compel us to obedience by His holy and heavenly voice. Whether the Ninevites were really and perfectly converted to God I pass over. It is sufficient that they were so moved by Jonah's teaching that they applied their minds to repentance.

Matt. 12.42. *The queen of the south.* Here I readily agree with Josephus and the rest in saying that this was the queen of Ethiopia, since, so far as Judea is concerned, Ethiopia lies to the south. But when she is called the queen of Sheba in the sacred histories, we should not take it as the country of Sheba, which lay rather to the east, but the city in Meroë, an island in the Nile, which was the capital of the kingdom.

It will be well to consider this antithesis. A woman, quite uneducated in the school of God, came from a distant land to learn from Solomon, an earthly king. The Jews, pupils of God's Law, reject His highest and indeed unique Teacher, the Head of all the prophets. The word 'judgment' here refers not so much to persons as to the lesson of the thing itself.

On that day Jesus went out of the house, and sat by the sea side. And there were gathered unto him great multitudes, so that he entered into a boat, and sat; and all the multitude stood on the beach. And he spake to them many things in parables, saying, Behold, the sower went forth to sow; and as he sowed, some seeds fell by the wayside, and the birds came and devoured them: and others fell upon rocky places, where they had not much earth: and straightway they sprang up, because they had no deepness of earth: and when the sun was risen, they were scorched; and because they had no root they withered away. And others fell among the thorns; and the thorns grew up, and choked them: and others fell upon the good ground, and yielded fruit, some a hundredfold, some sixty, some thirty. He that hath ears to hear, let him hear. And his disciples came, and said unto him, Why speakest thou unto them in parables? And he answered and said unto them, Unto you it is given to know the mysteries of the kingdom of heaven, but to them it is not given. For whosoever hath, to him shall be given, and he shall have abundance: but whosoever hath not, from him shall be taken away even that which he hath. Therefore speak I to them in parables; because seeing they see not, and hearing they hear not, neither do they understand. And in them is fulfilled the prophecy of Isaiah, which saith, With your ears ye shall hear, and shall not understand; and seeing ye shall see, and shall not perceive: for this people's heart is waxed gross, and their ears are dull of hearing, and their eyes they have closed; lest haply they should perceive with their eyes, and hear with their ears, and understand in their heart, and should turn again, and I should heal them. But blessed are your eyes, for they see; and your ears, for they hear. For verily I say unto you, that many prophets and righteous men desired to see the things which ye see, and saw them not; and to hear the things which ye hear, and heard them not. (Matt. 13.1-17)

And again he began to teach by the seaside. And there was gathered unto him a very great multitude, so that he entered into a boat, and sat in the sea; and all the multitude were by the sea on the land. And he taught them many things in parables, and said unto them in his teaching, Hearken: Behold, the sower went forth to sow: and it came to pass, as he sowed, some seed fell by the wayside, and the birds came and devoured it. And other fell on the rocky ground, where it had not much earth: and straightway it sprang up, because it had no deepness of earth: and when the sun was risen, it was scorched; and because it had no root, it withered away. And others fell among the thorns, and the thorns grew up, and choked it, and it yielded no fruit. And others fell into the good ground, and yielded fruit, growing up and increasing; and brought forth, thirty-fold, and sixtyfold, and a hundredfold. And he said, Who hath ears to *hear, let him hear. And when he was alone, they that were about him with the twelve asked him of the parable. And he said unto them, Unto you is given the mystery of the kingdom of God: but unto them that are without, all things are done in parables: that seeing they may see and not perceive; and hearing they may hear, and not understand; lest haply they should turn again, and their sins should be forgiven them. And he said unto them, Take heed what ye hear: with what measure ye mete it shall be measured unto you: and more shall be given unto you who hear. For he that hath, to him shall be given: and he that hath not, from him shall be taken away even that which he hath. (Mark 4.1-12; 24-25)*

*And it came to pass soon afterwards, that he went about through cities and villages, preaching and bringing the good tidings of the kingdom of God, and with him the twelve, and certain women which had been healed of evil spirits and infirmities, Mary that was called Magdalene, from whom seven devils had gone out, and Joanna the wife of Chuza, Herod's steward, and Susanna, and many others, which ministered unto them of their substance. And when a great multitude came together, and they of every city resorted unto him, he spake by a parable: The sower went forth to sow his seed: and as he sowed, some fell by the wayside; and it was trodden under foot, and the birds of the heaven devoured it. And other fell on the rock; and as soon as it grew, it withered away, because it had no moisture. And other fell amidst the thorns; and the thorns grew up with it, and choked it. And other fell into the good ground, and grew, and brought forth fruit a hundredfold. As he said these things, he cried, He that hath ears to hear, let him hear. And his disciples asked him what this parable might be. And he said to them, Unto you it is given to know the mysteries of the kingdom of God: but to the rest in parables; that seeing they may not see, and hearing they may not understand.*

*Take heed therefore how ye hear: for whosoever hath, to him shall be given; and whosoever hath not, from him shall be taken away even that which he thinketh he hath.*

*And turning to the disciples, he said privately, Blessed are the eyes which see the things that ye see: for I say unto you, that many prophets and kings desired to see the things which ye see, and saw them not; and to hear the things which ye hear, and heard them not. (Luke 8.1-10, 18; 10.23-24)*

Luke here inserts material which may belong to a different occasion. But I see no cogent reason for separating what he has joined in one passage. First he says that the twelve apostles preached the Kingdom of God along with Christ. From this we infer that although the ordinary office of teaching had not yet been laid upon them, they acted as enthusiastic public-criers to get together an audience for their Master. Hence, although their position was inferior, they were called Christ's assistants.

He then adds that Christ had among His band certain women who had been healed from evil or infirm spirits, like Mary Magdalene who had been vexed by seven devils. This company might seem something less than respectable. Surely it hardly behoved the Son of God to take round with Him women known for their unchastity? In fact, we see the better from this that the vices with which we were burdened before we believed are no hindrance to Christ's glory; rather do they magnify it. It is certainly not said that He found the Church which He chose without spot or stain; but He cleansed it with His blood that it should be pure and beautiful. The wretched and shameful state of those women brought great glory to Christ after He had freed them. They were the insignia of His power and grace. At the same time Luke praises their gratitude, for they followed their liberator, despising the ignominy of the world. No doubt everybody pointed the finger at them, and being with Christ was like being exhibited on a stage; but they allow their shame to be seen so that they may not hide Christ's grace. That He may shine more radiantly, they willingly endure to be humiliated. Mary was a singular miracle of Christ's infinite goodness. She was a woman who had been possessed by seven devils and had been, so to say, the vilest slave of Satan. And now she is given the honour not only of being a disciple but also a companion of Christ. Luke adds the surname Magdalene to distinguish her from the sister of Martha and the other Maries who are mentioned elsewhere.

Luke 8.3. *And Joanna the wife of Chuza.* It is not clear whether Luke intends what he has said of Mary to be understood of these other women. It seems likely to me that she is put first because Christ worked so mightily in her, whereas the wife of Chuza and Susanna, married women of chaste and untouched reputation, were then added as those who had been healed only of ordinary diseases. But since they were well-to-do and fashionable sort of women, their godly zeal deserves the more praise. For they supply Christ's needs from their own means, and not content with this, leave their homes and affairs and prefer to follow Him in spite of hostility and many inconveniences through all sorts of unsatisfactory shelters rather than enjoy the cultivated calm of their own drawing-rooms. It may well be that Chuza, Herod's procurator, was too like his master and was set against his wife's purpose, but that that godly woman overcame the obstacle by the warmth and strength of her zeal.

Matt. 13.2. *And there were gathered unto him.* The Evangelists have a definite reason for mentioning the huge gathering: it moved Christ to teach the parable of the seed. The crowd had come together from various places; they were all waiting to see what would happen and they were all avid to hear Him; but they did not all have the same desire to profit from it. This was the occasion for the parable, which taught them that the seed of the teaching is not everywhere fruitful when it is broadcast, since it does not always fall on fertile and well-cultivated soil. Christ therefore declares that He is there like a farmer going out to sow. But many of His hearers are like barren and un-cultivated land, others are weed-ridden land, and work and seed are wasted. But I will not deal further with the sense of the parable until we come to the explanation that the Lord Himself gives a little later. The only thing I would warn readers of at this point is that if those who came to Christ from remote places like starving men were com-pared to useless and sterile soil, what wonder is it if today the Gospel bears no fruit in many? For some are backward and slow, and some are careless hearers; some can hardly be brought to hear at all.

Matt. 13.9. *He that hath ears, let him hear.* By these words Christ partly meant that not all are given true understanding to follow what He said. But partly He was stirring up His disciples to a clear realiza-tion that the teaching is not easy and obvious to everyone. He dis-tinguishes between His hearers: some have the gift of hearing, others are deaf. And if we ask how the first get their hearing, Scripture elsewhere testifies that their ears are not adapted and formed by their own industry but perforated by the Lord (Ps. 40.6).

Matt. 13.10. *And the disciples came.* From Matthew's words it would seem that the disciples were not merely thinking of themselves but also of others. They did not grasp the parable themselves and realized it would be no less obscure to the people. They complained that Christ had spoken things from which the hearers derived no profit. Although similitudes usually cast light on the matter in hand, yet if they consist of one continual metaphor they are enigmatic. Hence when Christ put forward this similitude, He wanted to wrap up in an allegory what He could have said more clearly and fully without a figure. But when the explanation has been given, the figurative word has more power and effect than the straightforward. That is to say, it is not only more efficacious in affecting the mind but it is more perspicuous. It is important, therefore, both to consider how a thing is said and what is said.

Matt. 13.11. *Unto you it is given.* We infer from Christ's reply that God sets the teaching of salvation before men for different ends. For He declares that He had deliberately spoken obscurely so that His sermon might be enigmatic to many and only strike on their ears with a confused and ambiguous sound. The objection might be raised that

63

Isaiah says, 'I have not spoken in secret, nor in a dark corner. Not in vain have I said to the seed of Jacob, Seek me' (Isa. 45.19), and again that David praises the Law as a lantern to the feet and wisdom to the simple (Ps. 119.105 and 130). But the answer is easy. By its nature the Word of God is always light; but its light is quenched by men's darkness. For although the Law was covered, so to say, by a veil, the truth of God was nevertheless manifest in it if the eyes of many had not been blind. Paul declares truly of the Gospel that it was veiled only to the reprobate and those given over to destruction, whose minds Satan had blinded (II Cor. 4.4). We must therefore understand that the power of enlightening which David mentioned and the familiar way of teaching which Isaiah proclaimed, refer strictly to the elect people.

It is always a settled principle that God's Word is not obscure save in so far as the world darkens it by its blindness. Yet nevertheless the Lord keeps control over His mysteries so that the meaning of them may not reach the reprobate. He deprives them of the light of His teaching in two ways. Sometimes He declares in an enigma what could be said more clearly. Sometimes He opens His mind without ambiguities or figures, yet deadens their intellects and bewilders them, so that they are blind in plain daylight. This is the thought behind the terrible threats in Isaiah, where he warns them that he would be a barbarian to the people, someone speaking a strange and unknown tongue; that the prophetic visions would be a closed and sealed book to the learned so that they would be unable to read it; and then, when the book should be open, all would be unlearned, struck stupid and not knowing how to read (Isa. 28.11; 29.11-12). Now, since Christ deliberately dispensed His teaching in such a way that in only a few minds it would firmly stick and be useful while it kept the others doubtful and perplexed, it follows that God did not set the Gospel of salvation before men for one end only. In His wonderful purpose He so ordered it that it should be an odour of death to the reprobate as well as an odour of life to the elect. And if anyone should dare to quarrel with this, Paul replies that whatever the effect of the Gospel may be, its odour, even if of death, always mounts up sweetly to God.

But to be sure of the meaning of the present passage, we must look more closely at the intention and reason behind Christ's words. First, the comparison undoubtedly aims at showing that Christ was magnifying the grace bestowed on the disciples, because it was given especially to them and not indiscriminately to all. If anyone should ask why the apostles received this privilege of dignity, the cause is certainly not to be found in them; for when Christ declares that it was given to them He excludes all merit. He asserts that they are selected and chosen men, whom God peculiarly honoured by opening to them His mysteries, whereas the rest were deprived of this grace. The cause of this distinction is to be found only in the fact that God calls to Himself those whom He freely chooses.

Matt. 13.12. *For whosoever hath.* Christ carries on with the subject I have just mentioned. He reminds His disciples how liberally God dealt with them, so that they may be the more grateful and acknowledge their greater indebtedness to Him. He repeats these words in another place, but in a different sense. There He is talking about the lawful use of gifts; but here He is simply teaching them that more is given to the apostles than to ordinary people, because the heavenly Father wishes to fill to the brim His benefits towards them. He never forsakes the work of His own hands, as Ps. 138.8 puts it. Those whom He once began to form He works at more and more and improves them until at last He makes the final and perfect polishing. The sight of the liberation that He has wrought stirs God up to a continual course of bountifulness; and this is why such manifold graces flow to us from Him, this is why we progress so joyfully. And as His riches are inexhaustible, so He never tires of bestowing them on His children. Whenever He raises us higher, let us remember that all the blessings that come to us daily flow from one spring—He wishes to complete the work of salvation that He has begun in us.

And on the opposite side Christ declares that the reprobate always go from bad to worse until they are completely ruined and end up in poverty. At first sight it is a difficult saying that from the ungodly is taken away what they do not possess; but Luke smoothes it somewhat and removes the ambiguity by slightly changing the words. He says that what they seem to have is taken away. It often happens that the reprobate are endowed with excellent gifts and are apparently like the children of God. But there is nothing solid in them; their minds are void of godliness; it is all an empty show. Matthew rightly says that they have nothing, since it is as nothing in God's sight and also is only transient inwardly. But Luke aptly means that they vitiate the gifts bestowed on them, so that they only shine before men and in fact have nothing but pomp and vain show. From this also we learn to aspire after progress all our lives, for God gives us a taste of His heavenly doctrine on condition that we shall daily feed on it more and more until we are fully satisfied.

In Mark this sentence reads rather confusedly. 'Take heed', says the Lord, 'what is said to you'. Then He promises them a richer grace if they progress well: 'It shall be added to you who hear'. Finally follows the clause which agrees with Matthew's words, but it is put in the middle of the sentence. This I have expounded under Matthew 7, for it is unlikely that the words are here placed in their proper order. As I have said elsewhere, the Evangelists were not precise in the way they wove together Christ's discourses, but often assembled a variety of sayings. But Luke mixes this sentence among other scattered sayings of Christ and at the same time indicates a different purpose He had in speaking them—that men should be attentive to His teaching lest they should carelessly let slip the seed of life which ought to strike root deep within their souls. It was as if He said, 'Beware lest what has been given to you be taken from you because it proves ineffectual.'

Matt. 13.13. *Therefore speak I to them in parables.* He says that He spoke obscurely to the crowd because they were not partakers of the true light. Yet when He declared that they were covered with a veil of blindness and remained in their darkness, He was not saying that they were guilty, but commending more highly the grace given to the apostles, in that it was not common to all alike. He does not give any reason apart from the secret counsel of God, which, as we shall soon see, stands fast even if the grounds of it are hidden from us. Now although parables have another purpose besides being the vehicles of enigmas which God does not wish to reveal clearly, yet we have said that this present parable was so presented by Christ that its continuous allegory might be, as it were, a doubtful enigma.

Matt. 13.14. *And unto them is fulfilled the prophecy.* By Isaiah's prediction He confirms that it is not at all new if many derive no profit from the Word of God. For in olden days the Word had been appointed for the greater blinding of the people. This passage in the prophet is quoted variously in the New Testament. Paul rebukes the Jews for their obstinate malice and says that they are blinded by the light of the Gospel because they are bitter rebels against God (Acts 28.26ff). Thus he points out a cause which lay in the men themselves. In Romans 11.7ff. he traces the distinction down from its sublime and more hidden springs. 'The remnant is saved according to the grace of election', he says, 'and the rest are blinded, even as it is said by Isaiah, etc.' The antithesis there must be noted. If God's election alone, and that gratuitous, saves a certain remnant of the people, it follows that all others perish by the hidden but just judgment of God. Who are the rest, whom Paul contrasts to the elect, save those whom God does not honour with a special salvation? There is a similar reasoning in John 12.38ff. It says that there were many unbelievers, since none believes save he to whom God reveals His arm. And it at once adds that they are not able to believe, for it is written again, 'Blind the heart of this people' (Isa. 6.10). Christ has the same purpose when He attributes it to the secret counsel of God that the truth of the Gospel is not revealed indiscriminately to all but is put forward under enigmas and remotely so that thicker darkness will cover the minds of the people. I agree it is always true that those whom God blinds deserve this punishment. But the immediate cause is not always evident in the person and therefore it remains an axiom that those whom God freely chooses are enlightened by Him to salvation, and that by a unique gift. But all the reprobate are deprived of the light of life, by God either withdrawing His Word from them or keeping their eyes and ears blocked up so that they may not hear and see.

Now we can understand how Christ accommodates the prophecy to the present occasion.

*With your ears ye shall hear.* These are not the *ipsissima verba* of the prophet; but it does not matter, for all Christ wanted to show was that there was nothing novel or unusual in many people being struck senseless at God's Word. The prophet's saying, 'Go blind minds and hard hearts', is applied by Matthew to the hearers, that their blindness and hardness make them guilty. The two things cannot be separated. However much learning is urged on the minds of the reprobate, they just blind and harden themselves deliberately and from inward malice. It can never be any different where God's Spirit does not reign, and it is the elect alone who are ruled by Him. Therefore we must keep to the logic of this, that those whom God does not enlighten by the Spirit of adoption are out of their minds and therefore are only the more blinded by the Word of God; and yet the guilt is theirs, for their blinding is voluntary.

But from this ministers of the Word should seek consolation if their work is often less successful than they could hope. Their teaching will not help many but in fact make them worse. It will happen to them as it did to the best of all the prophets. Certainly we should desire to bring all into submission to God; this should be our aim and this we should strive after. But it must not surprise us that the God who once exercised His judgment through the ministry of the prophet should today fulfil it. Nevertheless, we must be very careful lest our laziness should prevent the Gospel bearing fruit.

Mark 4.12. *That seeing they may not see.* Here it is enough to note briefly what I have explained more fully elsewhere. The Gospel (*doctrina*) is not the cause of blindness properly speaking or in itself or in its nature, but only in the event (*per accidens*). It is like the dim-sighted going out in the sunshine. It only makes their eyes weaker still. Yet the fault lies, not in the sun, but in their eyes. When the Word of God blinds and hardens the reprobate, it is through their own native depravity; so far as the Word is concerned, it is accidental.

*Lest haply they should turn again.* This clause shows the value of seeing and hearing. Men who are converted to God return to His favour and in His grace live well and happily. And the real reason why God wishes His Word to be proclaimed is to renew men's minds and hearts and to reconcile them to Himself. But on the other hand Isaiah says that the reprobate remain in their hardness lest they should obtain mercy, and the Word is deprived of any effect on them lest it should soften their hearts to penitence. Under the word 'heal' Matthew, like the prophet, comprehends liberation from all ills. They are comparing a people afflicted by the hand of God to a sick man. Hence they say that when the Lord frees from punishment it is like a gift of health. But since this healing depends on the forgiveness of sins, Mark very aptly and cleverly calls it the cause and fount. For why are our punishments softened but because the Lord is reconciled to us and gives us His blessings? Yet even when our guilt is abolished, He does not cease to punish us, either to humble us the more or to make us more careful in future. Nevertheless, by showing signs of His favour He quickens and restores us; and as punishments mostly cease along with the guilt, healing is rightly joined with pardon. But we must certainly not infer from this that penitence is the cause of pardon, as if God receives men into favour because they deserve it by turning to Him. For conversion itself is a sign of God's free favour. This is just an indication of the order and sequence: God remits sins only when men are displeased at them.

Matt. 13.16. *But blessed are your eyes.* Luke seems to transpose this saying to a different occasion. But the solution is easy. He is there assembling a number of sayings irrespective of when they were spoken. We shall therefore follow Matthew, who expresses more clearly the occasion when this was said. Earlier He had told them of the extraordinary grace they had been given, that the Lord had separated them out and admitted them as intimates into the mysteries of the Kingdom. Now He lauds the same grace in another comparison—they surpass the prophets of old and the holy kings. And this is much finer than being preferred to the multitudes of unbelievers.

Moreover, Christ did not mean any sort of hearing or ordinary human sight. He says their eyes are blessed because they perceive the glory worthy of the only begotten Son of God and acknowledge that He is their Redeemer, because the lively image of God shines upon them and in it they perceive their salvation and full blessedness, and because there is fulfilled in them what was spoken by the prophets, that those who have been fully and perfectly taught by God shall not learn each one from his neighbour. This therefore explains the objection that could arise from Christ's other saying that they are blessed who have not seen and yet believe (John 20.29). It was a quite different

68

matter there, when Thomas was desiring to see for the sake of his gross understanding. The sight which Christ is speaking of here is common to believers of every age along with the apostles. For we see Christ without seeing and hear Him without hearing. In the Gospel, as Paul says (II Cor. 3.18) He appears to us face to face, so that we are transformed into His image, and the perfection of wisdom, righteousness and life which was once revealed in Him shines constantly in the Gospel.

Luke 10.24. *And kings desired to see.* The state of the present Church is deservedly said to be better than that of the holy fathers who lived under the Law. What is now revealed in the shining appearance of Christ was shown to them only under shadows and veils. Now that the veil of the Temple has been rent we enter by faith into the heavenly sanctuary, and an intimate access to God is opened. For although the fathers were content with their lot and cherished a blessed peace in their minds, yet this did prevent them having far greater hopes. Thus Abraham saw Christ's day from afar and rejoiced (John 8.56): yet he longed to enjoy a closer sight without having his wish granted. Simeon spoke for them all when he said, 'Now thou lettest thy servant depart in peace' (Luke 2.29). It had to be like this. Under the weight of the curse with which the human race was oppressed, they burned with desire for the promised liberation. Therefore let us know that they yearned for Christ like famished men and yet their faith was quiet, they did not argue with God; they just waited patiently for the perfect time of revelation.

*Hear then ye the parable of the sower. When any one heareth the word of the kingdom, and understandeth it not, then cometh the evil one, and snatcheth away that which hath been sown in his heart. This is he that was sown by the way side. And he that was sown upon the rocky places, this is he that heareth the word, and straightway with joy receiveth it; yet hath he not root in himself, but is temporary; and when tribulation or persecution ariseth because of the word, straightway he stumbleth. And he that was sown among thorns, this is he that heareth the word; and the care of the world, and the deceitfulness of riches, choke the word, and he becometh unfruitful. And he that was sown upon the good ground, this is he that heareth the word, and understandeth it; who verily beareth fruit, and bringeth forth, some a hundredfold, some sixty, some thirty.* (Matt. 13.18-23)

*And he saith unto them, Know ye not this parable? and how shall ye know all the parables? The sower soweth the word. And these are*

*they by the wayside, wherethe, word, is, sown; and whenthey have heard,
straightway cometh Satan, and taken away the word which hath been
sown in their hearts. And these in like manner are they that are sown
upon the rocky places, who, when they have heard the word, straightway
receive it with joy; and they have no root in themselves, but are temporary; then, when tribulation or persecution ariseth because of the word,
straightway they stumble. And others are they that are sown among
the thorns; these are they that have heard the word, and the cares of the
world, and the deceitfulness of riches, and the lusts of other things entering
in, choke the word, and it becometh unfruitful. And those are they that
were sown upon the good ground; such as hear the word, and accept it,
and bear fruit thirtyfold, and sixtyfold, and a hundredfold. (Mark 4.13-20)*

*Now the parable is this: The seed is the word of God. And those by
the way side are they that have heard; then cometh the devil, and taketh
away the word from their heart, that they may not believe, and be saved.
And those on the rock are they which, when they have heard, receive
the word with joy; and these have no root, which for a while believe, and
in time of temptation fall away. And that which fell among the thorns,
these are they that have heard, and as they go on their way they are
choked with cares and riches and pleasures of this life, and bear no fruit.
And that in the good ground, these are such as in an honest and good
heart, having heard the word, hold it fast, and bring forth fruit with
patience. (Luke 8.11-15)*

In Matthew and Luke, Christ simply and without any rebuke ex-
pounds the parable to His disciples. But in Mark He idnirectly reproves their slowness in not being the first to understand—they who
were to be the teachers of all the rest. The sum of it all is that the
preaching of the Gospel is like seed broadcast and is not fruitful everywhere, for it does not always fall on fertile and well tilled soil. .He
enumerates four sorts of hearer. The first do not receive the seed into
themselves (*semen non concipiunt*). The second seem to receive it, but
in such a way that it strikes no root. In the third it is choked by weeds.
Thus there remains the fourth part, which bears fruit. It is not a case
of only one in four hearers, or ten in forty, embracing the teaching
and bearing fruit. Christ was certainly not predetermining a number
nor dividing those of whom He spoke into equal parts. Where the
Word is sown the harvest of faith is not always the same; sometimes
it is more abundant, sometimes poor. Christ is only warning them
that the seed of life perishes in many on account of the various faults
by which it is either straightway corrupted, or dried up, or slowly
impaired. This warning will help us the more when we realize that

there is no mention here of the despisers who openly repulse God's Word; it is concerned only with those who seem to be teachable. Yet if the greater part of them fall away, what will become of the rest of the world, who openly repel the preaching of salvation? Now we must look at these different classes.

Matt. 13.19. *He heareth the word of the kingdom.* He first speaks of the barren and uncultivated, who do not inwardly conceive the seed, because there is no preparation for it within their hearts. Such He compares to hard and dry soil, like a footpath which gets as hard as a stone pavement. It is a pity we see so many today like this. They come to hear, but they remain bewildered and stupid and they do not even taste the Word. They are hardly different from stocks and stones, and it is no wonder if they slip away. Where Christ says that it is sown in their hearts, this is an imprecise expression; yet it is not without reason, for men's vice and depravity do not deprive the Word of its nature; it keeps its seminal power. And we should note this carefully, for we must not think that God's graces can fail in themselves, even though their effect may not reach us. For the Word is sown in their hearts in respect to God; but not all hearts receive with meekness what is implanted, as James puts it (1.21). Therefore the Gospel is always a fruitful seed in power, but not in act.

In Luke it is added that the devil takes away the seed out of their hearts, lest they should believe and be saved. From this we gather that the enemy of our salvation, like hungry birds at sowing time, comes along as soon as the Gospel is preached and rushes in to snatch it up before it can be received into the ground and germinate. It is no ordinary praise of faith to call it the cause of our salvation.

Matt. 13.20. *And he that was sown upon the rocky places.* This sort differs from the first in that temporary faith, like the reception of seed, has a promise of fruitfulness at the outset, but their hearts are not worked on well enough or deeply enough to make them soft to nourish the seed. Of this kind also we see too many today. They embrace the Gospel greedily, but soon after fall away. They lack a living feeling (*affectus*) to confirm them in steadfastness. Everyone should examine himself inwardly, lest his readiness is merely a great flash which is soon gone like a stubble fire, as they say. For unless the Word penetrates the whole heart and puts down deep roots there will be no steady flow of moisture to make faith persevere. It is indeed praiseworthy to receive the Word of God with joy as soon as it is proclaimed. But let us realize that nothing is done until faith has gained a firm strength. Otherwise it will just dry up at the first green shoots. Christ takes as an example those who are perturbed by the scandal of the cross. And, indeed, as the barrenness of the soil is

71

demonstrated when the sun gets hot, so persecution and the cross betray the emptiness of those who are lightly touched with I know not what desire but who are not filled with an earnest affection of godliness. In Matthew and Mark these are called 'temporary', not only because they fall away in temptation after being professed disciples of Christ for a time, but also because they themselves think that they have a true faith. This is why in Luke Christ says that they believe for a time, since the honour they give to the Gospel is like faith. But we must know that they are not truly born again of incorruptible seed, which does not fade away, as Peter says (I Pet. 1.4). He says that Isaiah's words, 'The word of God remains for ever' (40.8), are fulfilled in the hearts of believers. Once the truth of God is implanted there it never fails but flourishes to the end. Yet those who have an affection for God's word and who somewhat revere it do believe in a certain way. They are far removed from unbelievers, who do not believe God when He speaks or who reject His Word. The one thing we must understand is that none are partakers of true faith save those who are sealed by the Spirit of adoption and who sincerely call upon God their Father. And as the Spirit is never extinguished in the godly, it is impossible that faith should vanish and perish when once it has been engraven in their hearts.

Matt. 13.22. *And he that was sown among thorns.* In the third group He places those who would be fit to nurse the seed inwardly if they did not let it be corrupted and adulterated from elsewhere. Christ compares to thorns the pleasures of the world, or evil desires, and avarice, and other anxieties of the flesh. Matthew puts alongside avarice only the cares of the world, but his meaning is the same, for under this word are comprehended the enticements of pleasure (which Luke mentions) and every kind of cupidity. For just as the corn might have grown well but no sooner gets some stalk than it is choked by thorns and other noxious weeds, so the vicious affections of the flesh flourish in men's hearts and outgrow faith and overwhelm the immature power of heavenly doctrine. But although evil desires rule a man's heart before the Word of the Lord shows green, they are not seen to dominate in the early stages, but then they gradually overtake the corn when it has come up and promises to be fruitful. Therefore everyone must take care to weed the thorns out of their hearts if they do not want God's Word to be choked. There is no-one who has not a huge crop, a veritable forest, of thorns. And indeed we see how few reach maturity. Hardly one in ten will take the trouble to cut back the thorns, let alone root them out. It is precisely their manifold abundance (which should shake us out of our torpor) that is the cause why so many give up exhausted.

72

Christ puts *the deceitfulness of riches* for avarice. He deliberately calls riches false or deceptive so that men may learn to beware of its snares. But we must remember that the affections of our flesh are very many and varied and that they are weeds which will choke the seed of life.

Matt. 13.23. *And the seed that was sown upon the good ground.* Christ compares to good and fertile soil only those in whom the Word of the Lord does not merely make roots, deep and strong roots, but also overcomes all opposition to its being fruitful. If anyone objects that no-one exists who is pure and free from thorns, the solution is easy. Christ was not speaking here about the perfection of faith but was only showing in whom the Word is fruitful. Therefore, although his progress may be only middling, anyone who does not degenerate from the true worship of God is reckoned to be good and fertile soil. We ought to be intent on getting the thorns out by the root; but we never keep on steadily at this task and there are always some left. So at least let each of us try hard to put paid to them, so that they do not hinder the Word.

This sentence is confirmed by what follows. Christ teaches that not all bear the same measure of fruit. For although the soil where the thirty-fold grows is less fertile than where the hundred-fold grows, yet we see that Christ lumps together all the land which does not downright balk the farmer's work and hope. By this we are taught that the less excellent are in no way to be despised. The husbandman himself, granted he prefers the one for its abundance, praises the less good along with it.

Jerome foolishly applies these three grades to virgins, widows, and wives, as if the harvest the Lord demands of us related only to celibacy and the godliness of the married were not often more richly fruitful in virtue. It should also be understood by the way that Christ was not exaggerating when He spoke of a hundred-fold fruit, for many regions were then very fertile, as we learn from several historians and eye-witnesses.

*Another parable set he before them, saying, The kingdom of heaven is likened unto a man that sowed good seed in his field: but while men slept, his enemy came and sowed tares also among the wheat, and went away. But when the blade sprang up, and brought forth fruit, then appeared the tares also. And the servants of the householder came and said unto him, Sir, didst thou not sow good seed in thy field? whence then hath it tares? And he said unto them, An enemy hath done this. And the servants say unto him, Wilt thou then that we go and gather them up? But he saith, Nay, lest haply while ye gather up the tares, ye root up the wheat with them. Let both grow together until the harvest: and in the time of the harvest I will say to the reapers, Gather up first the tares, and bind them in bundles to burn them: but gather the wheat into my barn.*

*Then Jesus left the multitudes, and went into the house: and his disciples came unto him, saying, Explain unto us the parable of the tares of the field. And he answered and said to them, He that soweth the good seed is the Son of man; and the field is the world; and the good seed, these are the sons of the kingdom; and the tares are the sons of the evil one; and the enemy that sowed them is the devil: and the harvest is the end of the world; and the reapers are the angels. As therefore the tares are gathered up and burned with fire; so shall it be in the end of this world. The Son of man shall send forth his angels, and they shall gather out of his kingdom all things that cause stumbling, and them that do iniquity, and shall cast them into the furnace of fire: there shall be weeping and gnashing of teeth. Then shall the righteous shine forth as the sun in the kingdom of their Father. He that hath ears to hear, let him hear.* (Matt. 13.24-30; 36-43)

To determine the usefulness of this parable it is necessary to grasp Christ's intention. Some think that it was because He wanted to stop the mass of the people from being satisfied with an outward profession of the Gospel that He said that in His field the bad seed was often mingled with the good and that the day would come when the tares should be separated from the wheat. They therefore join this parable with the former, as if they were both saying the same thing. But to me it seems quite different. He mentions separation so that the godly may not get weary and fed-up when they see a confused mingling of the good and the bad. For although Christ cleanses the Church with His own blood so that it is without wrinkle or stain, yet He allows it still to labour under many faults. I am not speaking of remaining weaknesses of the flesh, which all believers must endure after they are regenerate by God's Spirit; but as soon as Christ collects His little flock, many hypocrites creep in, many perverse men infiltrate, even many wicked men find an entrance. And so it happens that the holy assembly which Christ separated to Himself is defiled by much filth. It seems quite inconsistent to many that the Church should nurse in her bosom the ungodly, or the irreligious, or the wicked. Add that, under a pretence of zeal, many are more awkward than they need be if everything is not settled according to their wishes (for nowhere is an absolute purity seen) and they go mad and leave the Church or upset and ruin everything with their harsh strictness. Hence, to my mind, the intention of the parable is simple. So long as the Church is

74

on pilgrimage in this world, the good and the sincere will be mixed in it with the bad and the hypocrites. So the children of God must arm themselves with patience and maintain an unbroken constancy of faith among all the offences which can trouble them.

And it is a most apt comparison when the Lord calls the Church His field, for believers are His seed. Although Christ afterwards adds that the field is the world, there can be no doubt that He really wants to apply this name to the Church, about which, after all, He was speaking. But because His plough would be driven through all the world and He would break in fields everywhere and sow the seed of life, He transfers by synecdoche to the world what is more apt of a part of it.

We must now see what He means by 'wheat' and by 'tares'. This cannot be expounded of preaching, as if He had said that where the Gospel was sown it was at once corrupted and adulterated by depraved ideas. For Christ would never have forbidden them to work hard in purging such a corruption. For the situation is not like that in morality, where vices which cannot be mended have to be endured. But ungodly errors which infect the purity of the faith must certainly not be endured. Then Christ expressly settles the matter by saying that the tares are the children of the evil one. Again we must note that this cannot be understood simply of men in themselves, as if God had sown good men at the creation and the devil evil men. I make this point because the Manichees misused this text to give some colour to their figment of the two principles. But we know that all vice, whether in the devil or in men, is nothing but the corruption of sound nature. God does not make His elect good seed at the creation, but, since they are infected with original sin, regenerates them by the grace of His spirit. In the same way the devil did not create evil men but depraves what God created and sows in the Lord's field what will harm the pure seed.

Matt. 13.37. *He that soweth the good seed.* He had said that the Kingdom of heaven was like a man sowing; but this was imprecise. The meaning is plain, however. The same thing happens in the preaching of the Gospel as in the sowing of a field—tares grow up with the wheat. But He mentions as one special feature that an enemy secretly sowed the field with tares. We know that it is not accidentally or naturally that many wicked men mingle with the faithful, as if they too were corn. But we learn to impute the blame for this evil to the devil. Not that his condemnation absolves men from guilt, but first that God may not be besmirched on account of this adventitious fault, and secondly that we may not be surprised if tares sometimes shoot up in the Lord's field, for Satan is always ready for mischief.

75

Christ has a good reason for saying, not that the ministers of the Word sow the seed, but He Himself alone. For although it should not be restricted to Him as a person, yet He so uses our work and summons us to be his instruments in cultivating His field as alone to act through us and in us. And therefore He rightly claims for Himself what in a sense He shares with His ministers. We should remember that the Gospel is preached not only by the command of Christ but at His urging and leading, so that we are like His hand, but He is the one author of the book.

Matt. 13.39. *The harvest is the end of the world.* It is indeed distressing that the Church will be burdened with the reprobate until the end of the world. But Christ tells us to pass this time in patience and not deceive ourselves with empty hopes. Pastors ought, of course, to be occupied in cleansing the Church; and in this they should be helped by all the godly so far as they have a calling to do so. But even when all strive together in this common task they will not succeed in cleansing the Church completely from all defilement. We see then that Christ certainly did not mean us to be indulgent towards defilement. He only intended to exhort His believers not to give up in despair because they were forced to endure the evil. But he also wanted to rein and moderate the zeal of those who think it is wrong to associate with any who are not pure angels. Therefore the Anabaptists and their like abuse this testimony when they deny the use of the sword to the Church. The refutation is easy. They themselves admit of excommunication as a means of rooting out the evil and reprobate, at least temporarily. Why, then, may not godly magistrates use the sword against the wicked when necessary? They object that with a non-capital punishment, a chance for repentance is given. Did not the thief find salvation on the cross? However, it is sufficient to say that in this verse Christ was not speaking of pastors or of the office of magistrates, but only of removing an offence which might upset the weak when they see the Church composed not only of the elect but also of impure dregs.

*The reapers are angels.* This word should be adapted to the present case. Elsewhere the apostles are called reapers in relation to the prophets, since they have entered into their labour (John 4.38). And the commission is laid on all ministers of the Word that they shall bear fruit unto the Lord and that it should always abide (John 15.16). The saying is also relevant here that the harvest is whitening and needs reapers (John 4.35): and again, that the harvest is plentiful, but the labourers few (Matt. 9.37). But in this verse there is a different reason for the comparison, for they are said to be planted in the Lord's field who have a place in the Church. It makes nothing against this that Christ elsewhere says that when He comes forward with His Gospel

76

He has a winnowing-fan in His hand to cleanse the threshing floor (Matt. 3.12). There He is describing the beginning of the cleansing which this verse says will not take place until the last day, for then only will it be executed completely. Moreover, although He will then finally cleanse the Church by the angels, yet He begins to do it now by godly teachers. He assigns these duties to angels, because they will not stand idle by His judgment throne but will be all ready to offer themselves to perform his commands. Therefore those who hasten untimely to root out whatever they do not like, overturn, so far as in them lies, the judgment of Christ and recklessly usurp the office of the angels.

Matt. 13.41. *They shall gather out of his kingdom.* What follows is an explanation concerning all who are given up to iniquity. It is not making any different point; but it is as if He had said that the ripe and fit time would come when He would restore all things to their proper order and thus take away the ungodly who are now an offence. They are called this because they do not only live wickedly to themselves but also undermine the faith of many, delay others on their true course, turn some quite aside from it, overthrow yet others. From this may be drawn a profitable admonition against proceeding sluggishly and carelessly because we are encompassed by so many offences. Rather we should be keenly on our guard. It also corrects the weakness of those who are so delicate that they turn back from their course at the slightest offence. I agree that it is difficult not sometimes to stumble or occasionally even to fall, when the numberless scandals press upon us. But our minds should stand fast in their confidence, for there is no doubt that the Son of God, who commanded His people to proceed through the midst of scandals, will give them strength to overcome all things. He proclaims a terrible judgment upon all hypocrites and reprobates, who now seem the leading citizens in the Church, to awake them from their sleep and their dreaming boasts.

*The furnace of fire* is a metaphorical expression. For as the infinity of glory which is laid up for the children of God far transcends all our thoughts and our words, so there remains for the reprobate a punishment which is incomprehensible and is only outlined sufficiently for us to grasp. It was ignorance of this that made the Sophists twist themselves up in empty and meaningless disputations, as we have mentioned elsewhere. I know that some have investigated more subtly every minute detail. But there is a danger that these indefinite discussions may lead us into foolishness; and so I prefer to be sparing in philosophising and to be satisfied with the simple and genuine sense. If those who are led by their curiosity were asked how the devil can scatter tares among the good seed while Christ is asleep and unknowing,

77

they would have nothing to reply. But I have studied to be sober, yet in such a way that I omit nothing worthy and profitable to be known.

Matt. 13.43. *Then shall the righteous shine forth.* A wonderful consolation—the children of God, who now lie sunk in foulness or are hidden and worthless or even are covered with reproaches, will then shine truly and clearly as in a bright and cloudless sky. The adverb of time 'then' is emphatic; it carries a tacit antithesis between the present situation and the final restoration, by the hope of which Christ preserves His believers. The meaning therefore is that, although many worthless people are now shining lights in the Church, yet we may surely hope for the happy day when the Son of God will take all His own into the heights and wipe away all the darkness which now eclipses their brightness. It is indeed true that the future glory is promised only to those in whom God's image shines and who are transformed to it by successive degrees of glory. But because the life of the godly is now hidden and their salvation invisible, since it consists in hope, Christ rightly recalls the faithful to heaven, that they may appropriate the promised glory. There is no doubt that this is a reference to the passage in Daniel,[1] so that He may touch His hearers more closely. It is as if He said: 'When the prophet was preaching about the future glory, he also pointed out the temporary darkness. Therefore, if we accept the prophecy we must patiently bear the confusion in which God's elect are mixed up with the reprobate for the time being.' By comparing this glory to the light of the sun, He has certainly not set up an equality. For just as Christ apportions His gifts variously among believers now, so He will crown them at the last day. But we must remember what I said, that He is only comparing the restoration which is delayed until the final coming of Christ with the cloudy state of the world. The Kingdom of the Father, the heritage of the godly, is set over against the earth, so that they may remember that they are pilgrims in this life and therefore long for Heaven. For although elsewhere the Kingdom of God is said to be within us, we shall not enjoy its fruition until God is all in all.

*Another parable set he before them, saying, The kingdom of heaven is like unto a grain of mustard seed, which a man took, and sowed in his field: which indeed is the least of all seeds; but when it is grown, it is greatest among the herbs, and becometh a tree, so that the birds of the heaven come and lodge in the branches thereof. Another parable spake he unto them; The kingdom of heaven is like unto leaven which a woman*

[1] Daniel 12.3.

78

*took, and hid in three measures of meal, till it was all leavened. All
these things spake Jesus in parables unto the multitudes; and without a
parable spake he nothing unto them: that it might be fulfilled which was
spoken by the prophet, saying, I will open my mouth in parables; I will
utter things hidden from the foundation of the world.* (Matt. 13.31-35)

*And he said, So is the kingdom of God, as if a man should cast seed
upon the earth; and should sleep and rise night and day, and the seed
should spring up and grow, he knoweth not how. For the earth beareth
fruit of herself; first the blade, then the ear, then the full corn in the
ear. But when the fruit is ripe, straightway he putteth forth the sickle,
because the harvest is come. And he said, To what shall we liken the
kingdom of God? or in what parable shall we set it forth? It is like a
grain of mustard seed, which, when it is sown upon the earth, is less than
all the seeds that are upon the earth; yet when it is sown, it groweth up,
and becometh greater than all the herbs and putteth out great branches;
so that the birds of the heaven can lodge under the shadow thereof. And
with many such parables spake he the word unto them, as they were
able to hear it: and without a parable, spake he not unto them: but
privately to his own disciples he expounded all things.* (Mark 4.26-34)

*He said therefore, Unto what is the kingdom of God like? and whereunto
shall I liken it? It is like unto a grain of mustard seed, which a man
took, and cast into his own garden; and it grew, and became a great tree;
and the birds of the heaven lodged in the branches thereof. And again he
said, Whereunto shall I liken the kingdom of God? It is like unto
leaven, which a woman took and hid in three measures of meal, till it
was all leavened. And he went on his way through cities and villages,
teaching, and journeying on unto Jerusalem.* (Luke 13.18-22)

In these parables Christ encourages His disciples so that they may not
shrink back in offence at the lowly beginnings of the Gospel. We see
how irreligious men in their arrogance despise the Gospel, even laugh
at it, because it is brought by obscure and unknown ministers, and
because it is not received at once by universal applause, but has only
a few followers and those mostly insignificant and mean. And so the
weak come to despair of the outcome when they assess it by the
beginnings. But it was deliberately that the Lord started His Kingdom
from weak and lowly beginnings, so that the unlooked for progress
might glorify His power the better. Therefore the Kingdom of God
is compared to mustard seed, the smallest of seeds, which nevertheless
grows so large that it becomes a bush where birds can nest. It is
compared also to yeast, which despite its smallness so spreads its force
that a great mass of dough is leavened by it. From this we learn that

79

although Christ's kingdom appears contemptible to the eyes of the flesh, it raises our minds to the infinite and inestimable power of God, which once created all things out of nothing and now daily, transcending men's thoughts, raises up the things that are not. Let us put up with the snarls and sneers of the proud until the Lord unexpectedly strikes them dumb. Meanwhile, let us not be cast down but let us rise up in faith against the contempt of the world until the Lord shows that incredible proof of His power which He proclaims here. The word 'leaven' is used sometimes in a bad sense, as when Christ tells them to beware of the leaven of the scribes, and as when Paul says that a little leaven corrupts the whole lump (I Cor. 5.6). But here the term should simply be kept to the point at issue. I have spoken elsewhere about the Kingdom of God and the Kingdom of heaven.

Mark 4.26. *So is the kingdom of God*. Although this parable points in the same direction as the two previous ones, yet Christ seems particularly to refer to ministers of the Word, lest they should execute their office with less enthusiasm when no fruit of their labours appears immediately. Therefore He tells them to be like farmers who sow seed in the hope of harvesting it and are not worried and anxious but go to bed and get up—in other words, they get on with their daily work and are refreshed by a good night's sleep—until at last in its own time the corn is ripe. Therefore although the seed of the Word lies choked for a while, Christ bids all godly teachers to be of good cheer and not to let distrust diminish their zeal.

Matt. 13.34. *All these things spake Jesus*. Although Mark expressly says that Christ spoke as they were able to hear, yet to me it seems probable that He used a string of parables not so much for the purpose of teaching as to catch the attention of His hearers and make them more ready for another time. For why did He explain them privately to His disciples? Because they were less advanced than the common folk? Not at all; it was because He wanted to give them a private understanding of His meaning but to leave others undecided until a better opportunity should come. For this was only a sort of prelude to the Gospel, while its fuller clarity and proclamation was deferred to its own time. The apparent discrepancy between this saying of Matthew's and Isaiah's above-quoted prophecy is easily explained. Although He kept the light of the Gospel from the reprobate, this does not mean that He did not adapt Himself to their capacity, so as to make them inexcusable. Hence He used the kind of teaching that was apt and fitting for His hearers, whom He knew were not yet ready to be taught.

Matt. 13.35. *That it might be fulfilled*. Matthew does not mean that the psalm which he is quoting is a special prophecy about Christ; but just as the majesty of the Spirit shone in the prophet's words, in the same way His power was expressed in Christ's Word. In the psalm the prophet will speak of God's covenant in adopting the seed of Abraham, of His continual benefits towards the people, and of the whole government of the Church. And as a preface he uses the splendid words: 'I will open my mouth in parables' (Ps. 78.2). That is, 'I will not treat of trifles, but will declare solemnly things of great moment.' He means the same thing by 'enigmas', for repetition is very common in the psalms. The Hebrew word (מְשָׁלִים) means 'comparisons', and this is transferred to weighty statements, because similitudes usually give clarity and adornment to language. חִידוֹת sometimes means enigmas, sometimes apophthegms. But although Matthew seems to allude to the word 'parable', there is no doubt that he meant that Christ spoke figuratively, so that the very style of His speaking carried a beautiful and more than common dignity and weight. He says that what was written in the psalms was fulfilled; because He told them that He was treating of the secret mysteries of God in allegories and figures so that His teaching might not be debased. From this we gather that it was not inconsistent with this when for other reasons He spoke to the people more obscurely. For although He wanted to hide what He said from the reprobates, yet He took care that they should feel, even when they were struck with bewilderment, that something heavenly and divine lay within His words.

Luke 13.22. *Journeying on unto Jerusalem.* It is not clear whether Luke was speaking of only one journey or whether he meant that when Christ was walking through Judaea and went about teaching in different parts He was accustomed to go up to Jerusalem for the feast days. In the first clause he seems to indicate what was the continual course of Christ's life from the time He began to exercise the office laid on Him by the Father. Hence, if the second clause is to agree with this, its meaning will be that He, like the rest, celebrated the holy feasts whenever they occurred.

*Again, the kingdom of heaven is like unto a treasure hidden in a field; which a man found, and hid; and for joy thereof he goeth and selleth all that he hath, and buyeth that field. Again, the kingdom of heaven is like unto a man that is a merchant seeking goodly pearls: and having found one pearl of great price, he went and sold all that he had, and bought it. Again, the kingdom of heaven is like unto a net, that was cast into the sea, and gathered of every kind: which, when it was filled, they drew up on the beach; and they sat down, and gathered the good into vessels, but the bad they cast away. So shall it be in the end of the world; the angels shall come, and sever the wicked from among the righteous, and shall cast them into the furnace of fire: there shall be the weeping and gnashing of teeth. Jesus says to them, Have ye understood all these things? They say unto him, Yea, Lord. And he said unto them, Therefore every scribe who hath been taught in the kingdom of heaven is like unto a man that is a house-holder, which bringeth forth out of his treasure things new and old.* (Matt. 13.44-52)

The aim of the two former parables was to teach believers to put the Kingdom of heaven before the whole world and to renounce themselves and all carnal desires, so that nothing might prevent them from enjoying this great blessing. Now this admonition is very necessary for us, for the allurements of the world so bewitch us that eternal life slips away; and because we are carnal we do not prize the spiritual graces of God. Therefore Christ deservedly lauds the excellence of eternal life, so that it should not be hard for us to give up for its sake all other precious things.

He first says that the Kingdom of heaven is like hidden treasure. On the whole it is the things we can see which we prize; and so the new and spiritual life which is proclaimed in the Gospel seems too humble for us, because it is hidden, enclosed in hope. The comparison to treasure is very apt; the value of it will never depreciate, even if it is buried underground and hidden from men's eyes. By these words we learn that the riches of God's spiritual grace are not to be assessed by the perception of our flesh or by their outward beauty but as a treasure which is preferred before all desirable riches, however hidden it is. The other metaphor expresses the same thing. 'One pearl', albeit small, is so esteemed that the experienced merchant does not hesitate to sell up fields and houses to buy it. Hence, although the mind of the flesh does not understand the excellence of the heavenly life, yet we do not consider it as it deserves unless we are ready for its sake to renounce those things that shine before our eyes. Now let us get to the sum of both parables: Only those are capable of receiving the grace of the Gospel who set aside all other desires and devote themselves and their studies completely to making it their own. And we must observe that Christ does not say that the hidden treasure or the pearl are so prized by all that they would gladly give everything they have for it, but that they recognize the price of the treasure after they have found and known it, and the experienced merchant makes a similar assessment of the pearl. These words point to the knowledge of faith. It is as if Christ said that the Kingdom of heaven is not thought to be worth anything, since men have no taste for it and do not realize what an incomparable treasure the Lord offers in the Gospel.

But it may be asked whether it is necessary to renounce all possessions if we are to enjoy eternal life. I reply in brief that the straightforward meaning of the words is that the Gospel is not given its rightful honour unless we put it before all the riches, delights, honours and comforts of the world; and indeed that we should be so content with the spiritual blessings which it promises, that we neglect everything that would draw us from it. For those who aspire after heaven must be freed from all hindrances. Therefore Christ only exhorts His believers to renounce the things that are contrary to godliness. Yet He permits God's temporal benefits to be used and enjoyed as if they were not used.

Matt. 13.46. *And bought it.* By the word 'bought' Christ does not mean that men bring any payment to purchase the heavenly life. For we know how the Lord invited His faithful in Isaiah: 'Come and buy without money, etc.' (Isa. 55.1). But although the heavenly life and everything pertaining to it is God's free gift, yet we are said to pay a price when we willingly deprive ourselves of carnal desires so that nothing may prevent us obtaining it. As Paul says, for him all things were like off-scourings and dung that he might gain Christ (Phil. 3.8).

Matt. 13.47. *Like unto a net.* Christ is not here teaching something fresh but by another parable confirming what we heard before, that the Church of God, so long as it is in the world, is an admixture of good and bad and is never free from dirt and stains. But it ends up very differently. Christ not only cures the offence which troubles many who are weak when they do not find in this world the purity that is to be desired, but also He restrains His disciples in fear and modesty so that they may not be satisfied with the empty title or bare confession of faith. I readily accept both points. First, that Christ taught that the admixture of good and bad must be patiently endured to the world's end, since the true and substantial restoration of the Church will not be established before. And secondly that he warns us that it will not suffice, nay, it is no good for us, to be gathered in the sheepfold unless we are real and chosen sheep, as Paul says: 'The Lord knows who are his own. And therefore let him depart from iniquity whoever calls on the name of the Lord' (II Tim. 2.19). Moreover, He cleverly compares the preaching of the Gospel with a net sunk under the water, to teach us that the present state of the Church is confused. For although our God is the God of order and not of disorder, and therefore commends discipline to us, yet for a time He allows hypocrites a place among the faithful until He sets up perfectly His Kingdom at the last day. Therefore, so far as in us lies, let us take pains to correct our faults and be strict in cleansing ourselves of dirt. Yet the Church will not be free from all wrinkles and spots until Christ shall have separated the sheep from the goats.

Matt. 13.51. *Have ye understood all these things.* We must remember what we heard earlier, that He expounded all the parables to the disciples in private. And now that the Lord has instructed them so familiarly and kindly, He tells them that His work in teaching them was not only aimed at making them wise for themselves but that they might impart to others what had been deposited with them. And in this way He spurs and incites them the more to the task of learning. He says that teachers are like heads of families who take care not only to have enough for themselves but to have a store laid up to feed others. They do not live from hand to mouth, but have an eye to the future. The meaning is then: The doctors of the Church should be taught by long meditation, so that as need arises they may minister doctrine to the Church from God's Word as from a store-house. Many of the older writers understand 'new and old' as meaning the Law and the Gospel. But this seems forced to me. I take it more simply as the varied and manifold dispensation by which they wisely and aptly accommodate the teaching to the grasp of each individual.

*And one of the Pharisees desired him that he would eat with him. And he entered into the Pharisee's house, and sat down to meat. And behold, a woman in the city, which was a sinner, when she knew that he was sitting at meat in the Pharisee's house, brought an alabaster cruse of ointment, and standing behind at his feet, weeping, she began to wet his feet with her tears, and wiped them with the hair of her head, and kissed his feet, and anointed them with the ointment. Now when the Pharisee, which had bidden him saw it, he spake within himself, saying, This man if he were a prophet, would have perceived who and what manner of woman this is which toucheth him, that she is a sinner. And Jesus answering said unto him, Simon, I have somewhat to say unto thee. And he saith, Master, say on. A certain lender had two debtors: the one owed five hundred pence, and the other fifty. When they had not wherewith to pay, he forgave them both. Which of them therefore will love him most? Simon answered and said, He, I suppose, to whom he forgave most? And he said unto him, Thou hast rightly judged. And turning to the woman, he said unto Simon, Seest thou this woman? I entered into thine house, thou gavest me no water for my feet: but she hath wetted my feet with her tears, and wiped them with her hair. Thou gavest me no kiss: but she, since the time I came in, hath not ceased to kiss my feet. My head with oil thou didst not anoint: but she hath anointed my feet with ointment. Wherefore I say unto thee, Her sins,*

*which are many, are forgiven; for she loved much: but to whom little is*
*forgiven, the same loveth little. And he said unto her, Thy sins are*
*forgiven. And they that sat at meat with him began to say within*
*themselves, Who is this that even forgiveth sins? And he said unto the*
*woman, Thy faith hath saved thee; go in peace.* (Luke 7.36-50)

Luke 7.36. *And one of the Pharisees desired him.* This story teaches
how cross-grained, how prone to take offence, are all who do not
understand Christ's office. A Pharisee invites Christ. From this we
gather that he was not one of the hostile and violent enemies of Christ's
teaching nor a haughty despiser, but quite mild. Nevertheless, he is
at once put off when a woman who in his opinion ought to be removed from the gathering and conversation is admitted by Christ in
a friendly manner. He denies that Christ is a prophet, because he does
not know that He is the Mediator whose proper office is to bring back
unhappy sinners to favour with God. It was, of course, something
that he should honour Christ with the title of prophet. But he should
have asked himself why He was sent, what He brought, and what was
commanded Him by the Father. But he overlooked the grace of
reconciliation, which is the chief point in Christ, and therefore did not
think He was a prophet either. And certainly this woman should have
been rejected had she not received forgiveness of sins and a new
righteousness by the grace of Christ. Where Simon went wrong was
in not considering that Christ had come to save what was lost; and
hence he rashly concluded that He could not distinguish between the
worthy and the unworthy. Lest such a contempt should win a place
in us, let us know, first, that Christ was given as the liberator of
wretched and lost men, to restore them from death to life. And then
let each of us examine his own life, and then we shall not be surprised
if others are received as well as we, since none will dare to put himself
before others. For it is only hypocrisy that puffs men up and makes
them secure, so that they despise all others.

Luke 7.37. *A woman which was a sinner.* I have translated it literally.
Erasmus preferred to put it in the pluperfect, 'which had been a sinner',
so that it should not be thought that she still was a sinner. But he is
missing the genuine sense. Luke wanted to point out what the woman's state was and what everyone thought of her. For although her
sudden conversion changed her in God's sight from what she had
been, the shame of her previous life was not yet forgotten among men.
The common view therefore was that she was a sinner, that is, a
woman of wicked and shameless life. From this Simon wronlgy infers
that Christ lacks any spirit of discernment and is ignorant of her
notorious disgrace.

Luke 7.40. *And Jesus answering, etc.* By His reply Christ shows up Simon's gross error. For by putting into words his unuttered and hidden thought, He proved that He was something more excellent than a prophet. For he did not reply to what Simon had said but to what he had kept suppressed inside him—and this is not just for his sake, but so that we can all learn from it not to be afraid that He will cast out any sinners. He is no less ready to receive us all with open arms than He is to invite us sweetly and kindly.

Luke 7.41. *Two debtors.* The point of this parable is that Simon erred in condemning the woman whom the heavenly judge had forgiven. And He proves that she is righteous, not in that she satisfied God, but because her sins were forgiven. Otherwise the parallel would not hold where Christ expressly says that the debtors who were not able to pay their debts were freely remitted. It is therefore surprising that so many interpreters have been grossly deceived, making this woman receive pardon from her tears, her anointing and kissing His feet. For Christ's argument is not based on cause but on effect. The first step is to receive the benefit and then to give thanks; and free forgiveness is here indicated as the cause of mutual love. In sum, Christ shows from the fruits or after-effects that the woman was reconciled to God.

Luke 7.44. *And turning to the woman, etc.* In comparing Simon with the woman, the Lord seems to make him guilty of only light faults. But it is a concession; as if He said: 'Simon, suppose that the sin which God pardoned you had been light; and that she had been guilty of much flagrant wickedness. You can see that what she has now done bears witness to the pardon she has received. What was the meaning of her flood of tears? of her kissing my feet? of pouring the precious ointment over me? What was it but a confession that she was oppressed under a great weight of guilt? And now she has embraced God's mercy the more fervently, knowing how great need she had of it.' We cannot gather from these words of Christ's whether Simon's debt was small, or indeed that he had been forgiven it. It is more likely that he was a blind hypocrite, still sunk in the mire of his vices. All that Christ is insisting on is that, although the woman had been wicked, she manifested signs of her righteousness by doing all in her power to show by her gratitude her sense of how much she owed to God. Meanwhile Christ warned Simon that he had nothing to flatter himself about, as if he were free from all guilt, for he also needed mercy. If he himself did not please God without pardon, he ought to reckon from the woman's penitence and signs of gratitude that her sins had been forgiven. We should note the antithesis, in which the woman is preferred to Simon: she washed Christ's feet with her tears and dried them with her hair, but he had not even told his servants to give Him a cup of water; she did not cease to kiss His feet, but he had not bothered to greet Christ with the kiss of hospitality; she had poured precious ointment on His feet, but he had not anointed His head even with oil. Now the reason why the Lord, who was a remarkable pattern of thrift and frugality, allowed this expensive ointment to be used was that it was the way in which this poor sinful woman expressed that she owed everything to Him. He did not want luxury, He was not allured by sweet scents, He did not approve of colourful worship; He saw only the wonderful fervour that betrayed her penitence. And Luke makes this a pattern for us to imitate, for her tears were witnesses of sorrow, the beginning of repentance. That she fell to the ground behind Christ's feet and lay there prostrate showed that she offered herself and all she had to Christ as a sacrifice. We should imitate her in all this (but the effusion of ointment was a unique action and it would be wrong to make a rule out of it).

Luke 7.47. *Her sins are forgiven.* Some think that the verb is a hortative subjunctive: 'Let her sins be forgiven'. They therefore make the meaning: 'Because this woman shows her burning love for Christ by these wonderful actions, it would not be right for the Church to be stricter and harsher to her, but she should be treated mercifully, however gravely she has sinned.' But since in Attic Greek ἀφέωνται is put for ἀφεῖνται, that exposition proves too subtle, and is disproved by the context. For a little later Christ says the same thing to the woman herself, and there the hortative subjunctive will not fit. To the latter sentence there is also added a contrasting clause, that less is forgiven to him who loves little. The verb should be transposed from the present to the perfect tense, for Christ infers from her desire to perform all the duties of godliness that although she was overwhelmed with many sins God's mercy was so great that she should no longer be reckoned as a sinner. Moreover, her love is not said to be the cause of her forgiveness but a subsequent sign of it, as I have said. For the words mean: 'Those who see this exuberant zeal and godliness in the woman are altogether mistaken if they do not consider that God had already been propitious to her, so that the free forgiveness of her sins came first in order.' For Christ is not discussing what price men pay for the grace of God, but is saying that because God has forgiven this unhappy sinner, mortal man must not be implacable to her.

Luke 7.48. *Thy sins are forgiven.* It could be asked why Christ only now promises her the forgiveness she had already received and of which she was assured. Some say that He spoke not so much for her sake as for others. But I do not doubt that He was thinking specially of her—and this appears more clearly in what follows. It is not surprising that she should be absolved afresh by Christ's word, although she had already tasted His grace, nay, was convinced that He was her only refuge of salvation. Thus it is necessary first to have trust when daily we pray the Lord to forgive us our trespasses. Yet we do not utter this prayer in vain or superfluously, but that our heavenly Judge may more and more impress His mercy upon our hearts and in this way quieten us. Therefore, although the woman brought with her a trust conceived of the grace she had already obtained, His promise was not superfluous but was powerful to confirm her faith.

Luke 7.49. *And they began to say within themselves.* We again see how men invent new sources of offence for themselves because they are ignorant of Christ's office. And the root of the evil is that no-one investigates his own distresses—which would certainly inflame him to seek a remedy. But it is not surprising if hypocrites, who slumber in their sins, grumble when Christ forgives sins, as if it were new and strange.

Luke 7.50. *Thy faith hath saved thee.* Both to restrain their grumbling and to hearten the woman, Christ praises her faith. It is as if He said: 'However much they go on at you, you just quietly stand firm in your faith and it will bring you sure salvation.' Christ also claims the right that the Father had given Him. Because power to heal had been placed in His hands it was right to put faith in Him. And this means that the woman had not been led rashly or in error to come to Him but had been led by the Spirit and had kept to the true path of faith. From this it follows that we cannot believe in another than the Son of God without making him the judge of life and death. For if Christ is to be believed in because the heavenly Father appointed Him to remit sins, as soon as faith is transferred to another, this honour of His is of necessity stolen from Him. By this saying there is also refuted the error of those who think that sins are forgiven by love. Christ defines it very differently here: the proffered mercy is embraced by faith. The final clause notes the incomparable fruit of faith which Scripture so often commends—that it brings peace and joy to the conscience and casts out anxiety and disturbance.

*Now as they went on their way, he entered into a certain village: and a certain woman named Martha received him into her house. And she had a sister called Mary, which also sat at Jesus' feet, and heard his word. But Martha was cumbered about much serving; and she came up to him, and said, Lord, dost thou not care that my sister did leave me to serve alone? bid her therefore, that she help me. But Jesus answered and said unto her, Martha, Martha, thou art anxious and troubled about many things: but one thing is needful: Mary hath chosen the good part, which shall not be taken away from her.* (Luke 10.38-42)

Luke 10.38. *He entered into a certain village.* This story teaches us that wherever Christ went He did not treat Himself as a private person or seek His own convenience or pleasure, but bent all His energies to the one aim of helping others and executing the office laid on Him by the Father. Luke relates that as soon as He had been welcomed hospitably by Martha and had gone indoors, He set to work teaching and exhorting them.

Now this passage has been wickedly perverted to commend what is called the contemplative life. But if we aim at bringing out the genuine sense, it will appear that Christ was far from intending that His disciples should devote themselves to idle and frigid speculations. It is an ancient error that those who flee worldly affairs and engage wholly in contemplation are leading an angelic life. The nonsense that the Sorbonne theologians invent about this betrays their debt to Aristotle, who placed the highest and ultimate good of the human life in contemplation, which he calls the fruition of virtue. In fact the motive that impelled some to opt out of the community was ambition; out of pessimism others (*morosi homines*) gave themselves to solitude and idleness. But the next step was pride, and they thought that doing nothing made them like angels. For they despised the active life as if it prevented us reaching heaven. But we know that men were created to busy themselves with labour and that no sacrifice is more pleasing to God than when each one attends to his calling and studies to live well for the common good. The simple sense shows easily how ignorantly they misused Christ's words to prove their invention. Luke says that Mary took her station at Jesus' feet. Does this mean that she was doing this the whole of her life? Rather the Lord commanded that the time of a man who wishes to advance in Christ's school should be so divided up that he shall not be an attentive yet unpractising hearer but shall make use of what he has learnt. There is a time for hearing and a time for doing. Hence the monks are foolish to seize on this passage, as if Christ were comparing the speculative life with the active. It merely shows to what end and how Christ wishes to be received.

Although Martha's hospitality was praiseworthy and indeed is praised, yet Christ points out two faults in it. The first is that Martha goes too far and is extravagant. Christ preferred frugality and moderate meals, so that the godly housewife should not be put to a lot of work. The second fault was that Martha left Him and was busy with unnecessary tasks and so made Christ's coming useless so far as she was

89

concerned. For Luke indicates an excess when he mentions her much serving, whereas Christ was content with moderation. It was just as if someone received a prophet with honour but did not trouble to listen to him, but swamped his teaching by a great and superfluous preparation. The right way to receive prophets is to perceive the usefulness which God destines and offers to us through them. Now we see that Martha's business was laudable, but it was not faultless. An additional blemish was that Martha thought she was in the right in all this bustling activity and so despised her sister for her godly desire to learn. By this example we are warned to be careful when we are acting aright lest we should think we are better than others.

Luke 10.42. *But one thing is needful.* Some explain this too weakly—that only a one course meal is necessary. Others subtly and irrelevantly dispute about the 'monad'. Christ means something very different. Whatever believers undertake to do and to whatever they apply themselves, they must have one aim which should over-rule everything. The sum of it is that we shall just wander round aimlessly unless we direct all our actions to a sure end. Martha's hospitality was faulty because she neglected the chief thing and was carried away to excess. Christ does not mean that apart from this one thing everything else is nothing, but that we are to keep prudently to order, lest the accessory thing, as they call it, comes to dominate.

*Mary hath chosen the good part.* This is not a comparison, as foolish and absurd expositors imagine. Christ is only saying that Mary has occupied herself in a holy and useful study, from which she ought not to be dragged away. It was as if He said: 'You would be right to reprove your sister if she had been lazy or busy with trifles or gadding after something inconsistent with her duty, and had left you with all the domestic affairs to worry about. But when she has given herself so rightly and usefully to listening to me, it is wicked to stop her. She does not get this opportunity every day.' Some take the final clause in another sense, as if Christ said that Mary had chosen the good part in that the fruit of heavenly doctrine never decays. I do not reject this interpretation, but I have followed what I consider more accordant with Christ's meaning.

*And one out of the multitude said unto him, Master, bid my brother divide the inheritance with me. But he said unto him, Man, who made me a judge or a divider over you? And he said unto them, Take heed, and keep yourselves from all covetousness: for a man's life consisteth not in the abundance of the things which he possesseth. And he spake a parable unto them, saying, The ground of a certain rich man brought forth plentifully: and he reasoned within himself, saying, What shall I do, because I have not where to bestow my fruits? And he said, This will I do: I will pull down my barns, and build greater; and there will I bestow all my fruits and my goods. And I will say to my soul, Soul, thou hast much goods laid up for many years; take thine ease, eat, drink, be merry. But God said unto him, Thou foolish one, this night is thy soul required of thee; and the things which thou hast prepared, whose shall they be? So is he that layeth up treasure for himself, and is not rich towards God. (Luke 12.13-21)*

Luke 12.13. *Bid my brother divide.* The Lord is asked to arbitrate in a family quarrel about an inheritance; but He refuses. To have done so might have served to maintain harmony between the brothers; and Christ's office was not only to reconcile men to God but to bring men to mutual concord. We might well ask, therefore, what caused Him to refuse to intervene and stop the quarrel between the two brothers. In particular two reasons appear why He abstained from this task of arbitration. First, the Jews imagined that the Messiah's Kingdom was earthly; and therefore He wanted to be careful not to further this error by His example. If they had seen Him dividing the inheritance, rumours of it would soon have spread, and many people would have hoped for a carnal redemption, something they already wanted too much. And the wicked would have claimed that He was attempting a revolution to drive the Romans out of the kingdom. Hence it was best for Christ to give the answer He did, so that all might know that His Kingdom was spiritual. Let us therefore learn to act soberly and not to undertake anything that can be construed in a sinister sense.

The Lord also wishes to make a distinction between the political powers of this world and the government of His Kingdom. For the Father made Him a Teacher who should by the sword of the Word cut between the thinking and the thought and penetrate into men's hearts. He was not a minor court judge to divide up inheritances. This condemns the fraud of the Pope and his gang, who claim to be pastors of the Church but dare to usurp earthly and secular jurisdiction, something separate from their office. For a thing may be lawful in itself and yet not the province of every man.

To my mind there is also a third and particular reason. Christ saw this man ignoring His teaching and interested only in his personal welfare. It is a too common disease that many who profess the Gospel do not scruple to use it as a means for private gain and for hiding their greed behind Christ's authority. This may easily be inferred from the exhortation itself, for unless the man had claimed the cover of the

Gospel for his own advantage Christ would have had no cause for condemning avarice. The context shows clearly, then, that he was a false disciple, whose mind was sunk in fields and coffers.

Now the Anabaptists have been quite absurd to infer from this reply that it is not lawful for Christian men to receive inheritances, to engage in business affairs, or to undertake any civil office. For Christ's argument is not based on the thing in itself but on His own calling. Because the Father had appointed Him to another end, He denied that He was an arbitrator; He had no such mandate. The rule should therefore prevail among us that each should keep to the limits of God's calling.

Luke 12.15. *Take heed and beware.* First, Christ calls His people away from avarice; and secondly, to purge their minds completely of this disease, He says that our life does not consist in abundance. These words indicate the fount and inward origin from which flows the insane desire to possess. The common view is that the man who possesses most has the happy life. People imagine that riches bring a life of bliss. This is the source of the intemperate cupidity which throws out its heat like a burning furnace and yet still is hot within. If we are convinced that riches and a plentiful supply of good things are helps in the present life and that the Lord supplies them by His hand and blesses our use of them, then this one consideration alone will easily quieten all our cupidity—and believers find this is true in their own experience. For how does it happen that they depend on God alone with settled minds, save because they neither bind nor subject their lives to abundance but rest on God's providence, He who alone upholds us by His power and supplies as much as we should have?

Luke 12.16. *And he spake a parable.* This parable is like a mirror to show us a living image of the truth that men do not live from their abundance. For even from the richest is life taken away in a moment, and then what does it avail them to have accumulated such great wealth? All confess that this is the truth, and Christ is only saying what is ordinary and common and what everyone says. Yet nevertheless what does everyone set his heart on? Do not rather all men frame their lives and compound their purposes and intentions in such a way that they place their life in a present plenty and so stray far from God? Therefore all men need to arouse themselves against getting tied up in the snares of covetousness and thinking they are blessed because they are rich. Moreover, the parable shows us the transience and brevity of this life. And again, that riches can do nothing to lengthen life. And thirdly, something which is not expressly said, the best remedy for believers is to ask their daily bread from the Lord and rest quietly on His providence, whether they are rich or poor.

Luke 12.17. *What shall I do ?* The ungodly are perplexed in their plans because they do not understand the legitimate use of possessions, and because they drunkenly forget themselves in their perverted confidence. Thus this rich man sets his hope of life in his great harvest and completely forgets that he must die. And yet there is a distrust joined to this pride, for an insatiable cupidity disturbs these very rich men. This one, for example, enlarges his barns, as if he had not had enough when he had got his bellyful from his old barns. Christ does not, however, condemn him precisely for acting as a careful householder in setting aside a store for the future, but for wanting to swallow up and devour many barnfuls in his greedy cupidity like a bottomless pit, and therefore for not understanding the true use of plentiful possessions.

Now, when he bids himself eat and drink, he forgets that he is but man and becomes proud, trusting in his abundance. And we daily see clear examples of this arrogance among ungodly men who oppose their heaped up riches like a brazen rampart against death. When he says, 'Eat, my soul, and rejoice' it is a Hebraism with an underlying emphasis. For he urges himself in such a way that he means he can abundantly supply more than enough for the desire of his mind and all his senses.

Luke 12.20. *Thou fool, thy soul shall be required.* The word 'soul' is now used in a different sense. The rich man had addressed his soul as the seat of all his feelings. But now it is used of his very life, of his vital spirit. The expression 'shall be required' is in the third person plural: but it is indefinite and means only that, although the rich man may think that his life is in his own hand, it lies in fact in the power of another. I say this because some have irrelevantly philosophized about angels on this verse. Christ's plain intention was to teach that a man's life could be taken away in any moment, although he thinks it is well protected by his riches. And so this rich man is convicted of foolishness, for he did not know that his life depended on another.

Luke 12.21. *So is he that layeth up.* There is clearly an antithesis here, and therefore the explanation of the one sentence is to be found in the other. We must therefore define what it means 'to be rich in God, or towards God, or in respect of God'. Even those who are only moderately versed in Scripture know that the preposition εἰς is quite often used for ἐν. Here it does not much matter which way we take it, for the sum of it is that they are rich in regard to God who do not trust in earthly things but depend on His providence alone. Nor does it matter whether they abound or lack; for in both states they ask God in sincerity for their daily bread. On the opposite side 'to lay up for oneself' is as good as saying to forget God's blessing and anxiously to

93

collect many possessions and to put all one's trust in barns. It is therefore easy to gather the purpose of this parable; the plans will fail, the efforts will be ridiculous, for those who trust in the abundance of their riches and do not rest on God alone, who are not satisfied with the measure He gives nor prepared for ill or good. At the last they will receive the punishment of their futility.

*Now there were some present at that very season which told him of the Galilaeans, whose blood Pilate had mingled with their sacrifices. And Jesus answered and si id unto them, Think ye that these Galilaeans were sinners above all the Galilaeans, because they have suffered such things? I tell you, Nay: but, except ye repent, ye shall all in like manner perish. Or those eighteen, upon whom the tower in Siloam fell, and killed them, think ye that they were offenders above all the men that dwell in Jerusalem? I tell you, Nay: but except ye repent, ye shall all likewise perish. And he spake this parable; A certain man had a fig tree planted in his vineyard; and he came seeking fruit thereon, and found none. And he said unto the vinedresser, Behold, these three years I come seeking fruit on this fig tree, and find none: cut it down; why doth it cumber the ground? And he answering said unto him, Lord, let it alone this year also, till I shall dig about it, and dung it: and if it bear fruit thenceforth, well; but if not, thou shalt cut it down.* (Luke 13.1-9)

Luke 13.2. *Think ye that these Galilaeans, etc.* The chief value of this passage springs from the fact that we suffer from the almost inborn disease of being overstrict and severe critics of others while approving of our own sins. So it happens that we not only censure the sins of our brethren more harshly than we should do but also, if any affliction touches them, we condemn them as wicked and reprobate. Meanwhile, whoever is not shaken by God's hand sleeps soundly in his sins as if God were favourable and propitious to him. His fault is twofold. For as often as God chastises anyone under our eyes He is warning us of His judgments, so that each one of us may learn to examine himself and to consider what he also has deserved. And when He spares us for the time, He is inviting us by this kindness and mercy to repentance. The one thing we should not imagine is that we have been given a chance to sleep. Hence Christ corrects the wicked judgment that makes us enemies to the wretched and afflicted. And at the same time, to drive out the universal self-satisfaction, He teaches first that those who are treated more harshly than the rest are not the worst; for God executes His judgments in the order and manner He thinks best; some

94

are immediately snatched away to punishment, while others rest a long time quietly in idleness and pleasures. He then declares that all the calamities that happen in the world are testimonies of the wrath of God. Whence we gather how great is the destruction that remains for us unless we forestall it.

The occasion for this exhortation was that some of them told Him that Pilate had mingled human blood in the sacrifices—in other words, to make the sacrifices detestable by such a crime. But since it is likely that this wicked deed was committed against Samaritans, who had seceded from the pure worship of the Law, the Jews were quick to condemn these Samaritans and applaud themselves. But the Lord turns them to a different direction. Since the irreligion of that whole nation was hateful and infamous to them, He asks whether they think that those unhappy men who were slain by Pilate were worse than the rest. It is as if He said: 'It is certainly not hidden from you that that country is full of ungodly people. Yet many who deserved the same punishment are still left alive. Therefore he is a blind and unfair judge who assesses the sin of everybody from present punishment; but when God chooses to punish a few out of the many, He is in their person warning the rest that He will be their judge, so that all may fear.'

After He had spoken of the Samaritans, He came home to the Jews themselves. At that time eighteen men had been crushed when a tower fell in Jerusalem. He says that they had not been the most wicked, but that their disaster was a warning to all to fear. For if God showed an example of His judgment upon them, others shall not escape His hand even if He bears with them for the time. Christ does not forbid believers to look carefully at God's judgments, but He tells them the right way to go about it—they must begin at their own sins. This will be the best, for their voluntary repentance will anticipate the punishment of God. This is the meaning of Paul's words: 'Let no one deceive you with vain words; for because of these things cometh the wrath of God upon the rebels' (Eph. 5.6).

Luke 13.6. *And he spake this parable.* The sum of it is that many are tolerated for a time who deserve destruction; yet they will gain nothing from the delay if they go on in their obstinacy. From this arises the perverted self-flattery in which hypocrites harden themselves and make themselves more obstinate. They do not realize their sin unless they are forced, and therefore so long as God overlooks it and holds back His chastisements, they think that all is well with them. So they indulge themselves the more securely, as if they had a covenant with death and the grave, as Isaiah puts it (28.15). This is why in Romans 2.5 Paul tells them so fiercely that they accumulate for themselves the wrath of God against the last day. We know that trees are sometimes kept, not because they will be useful or fruitful to the owner, but because the careful and hardworking farmer will experiment and try various possibilities before he fells the trees in his field or vineyard. And this teaches us that when the Lord does not at once punish the wicked but delays His punishment, He has the best of reasons for His forbearance. This contrast is put between the master and the steward, not as if God's ministers were more merciful and kind than God Himself, but because the Lord not only prolongs the life of sinners but also cultivates them in various ways so as to produce better fruit.

*And he was teaching in one of the synagogues on the sabbath day. And behold, a woman which had a spirit of infirmity eighteen years; and she was bowed together, and could in no wise lift up her head. And when Jesus saw her, he called her to him, and said to her, Woman, thou art loosed from thine infirmity. And he laid his hands upon her: and immediately she was made straight, and glorified God. And the ruler of the synagogue, being moved with indignation because Jesus had healed on the sabbath, answered and said to the multitude, There are six days in which men ought to work: in them therefore come and be healed, and not on the day of the sabbath. But the Lord answered him, and said, Ye hypocrites, doth not each one of you on the sabbath loose his ox or his ass from the stall, and lead him away to watering? And ought not this woman being a daughter of Abraham, whom Satan had bound, lo, these eighteen years, to have been loosed from this bond on the day of the sabbath? And as he said these things, all his adversaries were put to shame: and all the people rejoiced for all the glorious things that were done by him.* (Luke 13.10-17)

What I have done is to bring into one connexion things that occur in Luke alone and are scattered about without being assigned to any particular period. For I have already said that the Evangelists were not at all interested in this aspect. After this it will be better for us to return to the harmony of the three.

He here relates a miracle of healing a woman and the offence that the Jews maliciously took at the Lord healing on the Sabbath. Luke says that the woman had been held by a spirit of infirmity so that her body was bent from the contraction of the sinews. From the fact that he describes it in this way it is probable that it was uncommon or that its cause was unknown to doctors. This is why he calls it 'a spirit of infirmity'. For we know that the devil afflicts men mostly with un-

usual and unnatural ills. In this Christ's divine power shone forth the
more clearly when He triumphed over Satan. Not that Satan rules in
men by his own free will, but God concedes to him an ability to hurt.
Moreover, just as the Lord, the unique Author of all good, particularly
shows His glory in individual and unusual benefits, so on the other
hand He chiefly wishes Satan's tyranny to be recognized in extraordinary afflictions, although He also employs his agency in the light
taps with which He chastises us every day.

Luke 13.12. *Woman, thou art loosed.* In this miracle, as in others,
Christ shows both His power and His grace. For He testified that He
had come to help the unhappy. His power is expressed in the words,
'Woman, thou art loosed'; for He proclaims authoritatively that
liberation lies in His hand. But He adds an external symbol, of whose
use we have treated elsewhere. The point of His saying that the people
glorified God is to teach us that this heavenly benefit was open and
plain. It was no obscure work, on which people could argue for and
against, but provided a full and sure basis for praising God. This
makes clear the wickedness of the master of the synagogue.

Luke 13.14. *There are six days.* This critic did not dare to rebuke
Christ openly, but he directed the poison of his scrupulosity to condemning Him indirectly in the person of the common folk. It was an
incredible and malicious madness. He says that six days had been set
aside for work. But how wrongly and foolishly he defines that work
which is allowed only on the six days! Why does he not drive them
away from the synagogue in case they violated the Sabbath? Why does
he not command them to cease from all the practices of religion? Since
men are only forbidden to do their own works on the Sabbath, how
wrong it is to tie down God's grace! He tells them to come on other
days to seek healing, as if God's power lay asleeping on the Sabbath
and He did not exercise it especially on that day for the salvation of His
people. What was the point of that holy assembling save that believers might beg God's aid and help? That ungodly hypocrite spoke
as if the lawful use of the Sabbath interrupted the course of God's
benefits, shut men off from praying to Him, and deprived them of any
awareness of His graciousness.

Luke 13.15. *Doth not each one of you, etc.* It would have been easy
for Christ to rebuke such gross malice with a number of arguments,
but He is content with just one: If it is lawful to show kindness on the
Sabbath to cattle, then they have invented a perverse sort of worship
if God's children may not be helped. There is a twofold comparison
in Christ's words. The cattle are compared to the daughter of Abraham, and the halter that ties the ass or ox to his manger, to the chains
of Satan that hold men bound in destruction. 'You,' He says, 'who

97

are such puritanical observers of the Sabbath, you dare to untie oxen and asses to lead them to the water-trough. Why may not I do something similar for the elect people of God, especially when a great necessity demands it and there is someone to be freed from Satan's snares?' Now, although this ungodly critic is dumb with shame, yet we see that Christ never did any such wonderful work without the wicked making it an excuse to malign Him. It is no wonder if Satan bends all his efforts to destroy the glory of Christ, for he does not cease to spread his mists everywhere to obscure the godly activities of believers.

We must note that Christ calls her a daughter of Abraham, this woman whose body Satan had bound for eighteen years. This was not only in regard to her race (all the Jews indiscriminately boasted of this title) but because she was a member of the true and genuine Church. We may also recall that Paul said that some were delivered to Satan for the destruction of their flesh so that their spirits might be saved in the day of the Lord. And this long space of time shows us that, although the Lord may not heal our miseries at once, we must not despair.

*On that same day there came certain Pharisees, saying to him, Get thee out, and go hence: for Herod would fain kill thee. And he said unto them, Go and say to that fox, Behold, I cast out devils and perform cures to-day and to-morrow, and the third day I am perfected. Howbeit I must go on my way to-day and to-morrow, and the following day: for it cannot be that a prophet perish out of Jerusalem. (Luke 13.31-33)*

It is hardly possible to conjecture when this happened, except that it is certain that Christ was living in Galilee. Throughout His ministry He stayed longer there than anywhere else. Some, who wished to be thought His friends, exhorted Him to get beyond Herod's jurisdiction if He wanted to be safe. We do not know what were the real feelings of those who gave this advice, but I am inclined to think that they were trying to get Christ out of the country because they saw the larger part of the people following Him and the preaching of the Gospel everywhere received. And it is mentioned who they were, for Luke says they were some of the Pharisees. But we know that this party was so unfavourable to Christ that it is not likely that they were solicitous for His life. What then? Their purpose was to scare Him away into some hiding place; for they were hoping that His authority would be cut short and all His teaching vanish away. But we must remember that the first teacher and framer of this purpose was Satan.

Just as he tried to break off the course of the Gospel by frightening the Son of God, so from time to time he invents and forms new terrors to dishearten Christ's ministers and force them to leave their course.

Luke 13.32. *And he said unto them.* This is certainly a reference to Herod Antipas. But although his character was foxy, no less servile than cunning, I do not think that Christ was accusing his life in general of craftiness by this word 'fox', but only the secret plots he used to undermine the teaching of the Gospel, when he did not dare to attack it openly. For Christ means that although he was crafty, his artfulness would come to nothing. 'Whatever tricks he gets up to', says Christ, 'I will fulfil my divinely appointed office today and tomorrow. When the end of the journey is reached, I shall be offered in sacrifice.'

But to bring out the meaning of the words more distinctly for us, Christ declares in the first clause that after the third day—that is, after a little while—He would have to die. In this way He shows that He could not be deflected from His duty by any fear of death, towards which He marched unafraid and determined. He then adds that this little bogey was laughable, coming as it did from false and pretended well-wishers, for it was only in Jerusalem that He was in danger of death.

With His second clause He pricks the Pharisees sharply: 'Do you bid me beware of Herod; you, whom I see shall be my executioners?' Yet the accusation goes further. He not only says that He is ready to die at Jerusalem, but that that city was like a den of thieves where nearly all the prophets had been murdered. It is true that many had been killed in other places, and especially in the days when cruel Jezebel had savaged them in her fury. But since nowhere else had the prophets been harassed more fiercely and continually, Christ brands the ungodly citizens of the holy city with this disgrace. Moreover, it was there that most of the prophets were killed, since it was the arena where God exercised His prophets. We know that the more the light of the Gospel shines and comes close to the ungodly, the more are they driven into madness. Yet it is a terrifying lesson to us that the place which was chosen as the sanctuary of the divine worship and the home of the Law and heavenly wisdom, should be polluted, not with an occasional murder, but with the common occurrence of the slaughter of the prophets. Surely from this appears the stubborn ingratitude of the world in repelling sound doctrine. The exclamation which follows immediately in Luke seems to be connected with this, as if Christ takes this occasion to inveigh against Jerusalem. But I consider rather that Luke had said that Jerusalem was in days past stained by the blood of the prophets, and in fact that it had a continuous and age-long tradition of cruel and sacrilegious slaughter of the prophets. And then, in his usual way, he at once adds the sentence which accords with what he has said. For we have very frequently seen that it was not at all unusual for him to collect together things that Christ had said on various occasions.

> *Now as he spake, a Pharisee asked him to dine with him: and he went in, and sat down to meat. And when the Pharisee saw it, he marvelled that he had not first washed before dinner. And the Lord said unto him, Now do ye Pharisees cleanse the outside of the cup and of the platter; but your inward part is full of extortion and wickedness. Ye foolish ones, did not he that made the outside make the inside also? Howbeit give for alms those things which are within; and behold, all things are clean unto you.* (Luke 11.37-41)

To some extent, but not wholly, this account agrees with the teaching in Matthew 15, that, to correct the superstition of the people and especially of the scribes, Christ deliberately neglected outward rites invented by men, in the observing of which the Jews were altogether too scrupulous. God commanded certain ablutions in His Law to exercise His people profitably in studying true purity. The Jews were not content with this modest usage and added many other washings, especially that none should take food without having washed in purificatory water, as Mark narrates more fully in chapter 7, and as appears in John 2. Moreover, a perverted trust was put in this vice. They were unmindful of the spiritual worship of God and thought they had done their duty well when they had substituted a figure in place of God. Christ knew that contempt of this ceremony would give scandal, but He omits it to show that God cares nothing for the outward cleanness of the flesh but demands the spiritual righteousness of the heart.

Luke 11.39. *Now do ye Pharisees.* In this place Christ is not reproving the Pharisees (as in Matthew and Mark) for worshipping God perversely with human inventions and breaking God's Law for the sake of their traditions. He is simply pointing out their gross hypocrisy in desiring to be pure only in men's sight, as if they were not concerned with God. And this reproof fits all hypocrites, even those who place righteousness in divinely appointed ceremonies. This is therefore more all-embracing than if Christ had said that God is worshipped in vain by the commandments of men. He condemns in general the error that God is worshipped by ceremonies and not spiritually by faith and the pure affection of the heart. And although on this matter the prophets were engaged in a continual struggle with the Jews, yet, be-

cause men's minds are prone to hypocrisy, the proud obstinacy prevailed that outward rites were pleasing to God even if they were void
of faith. But in the days of Christ especially they were so senseless that
they placed religion in mere trifles. This is why Christ attacked the
Pharisees, who were so particular about washing of cups but cherished
the foulest dirt, plundering and malice, in their hearts. He rebukes
their foolishness, for God, who created man's inward soul no less than
his body, cannot be appeased by outward show alone. Men's chief
errors are either in not reckoning that they have to do with God, or
in transforming Him, according to the emptiness of their senses, into
something no whit different from mortal man.

Luke 11.41. *Those things which are within.* In His usual way Christ
calls the Pharisees back from ceremonies to love. He declares that
both men and meats are cleansed not by water but by love. Yet by
saying this He is not weakening God's grace nor rejecting the ceremonies of the Law as empty and useless. He is speaking against those
who recklessly mock God with their naked signs; and it is as if He
said: 'It is only the lawful use of meats which sanctifies them. But
they use meats aright and legitimately who out of their own abundance
supply the poverty of the poor. Therefore it is better to give alms
from the supplies that are available than to neglect the poor while
scrupulously continuing to wash the hands and the cup.'

The Papists infer from this that alms are satisfactions which cleanse
us from sins. But this is too stupid to need much refutation. Christ is
not here discussing the price we have to pay to get remission of sins,
but is saying that they eat their food purely who give a part of it to
the poor. I take τὰ ἐνόντα to mean the present supply, and not, as
the Vulgate and Erasmus, what is left over.

We may leave till later the reproaches which directly follow this
passage, for I do not interpret it in one context, as if Christ were
attacking the scribes and Pharisees while He sat at table. But Luke
relates here what was said on another occasion, since as we have often
pointed out already, the Evangelists were not worried about the
relative time order.

*And it came to pass, when he went into the house of one of the rulers of
the Pharisees on a sabbath to eat bread, that they were watching him.
And behold, there was before him a certain man which had the dropsy.
And Jesus answering spake unto the lawyers and Pharisees, saying, Is it
lawful to heal on the sabbath, or not? But they held their peace. And
he took him, and healed him, and let him go. And he said unto them,
Which of you shall have an ass or an ox fallen into a well, and will*

*not straightway draw him up on a sabbath day? and they could not
answer again unto these things.* (Luke 14.1-6.)

This story tells only of Christ performing a miracle and correcting
the superstitious cult of the Sabbath. He did not, as some think, want
absolutely to abrogate the Sabbath, but only to show that the holy
rest commanded in the Law is not violated either by God's works or
by the offices of love. It is not clear whether the man with the dropsy
was deliberately brought there by the spokesmen. Certainly, he could
not have come by chance to the meal nor could he have gate-crashed.
It is therefore likely that they put him there as a trap for Christ.
Nevertheless they were very silly as well as wrong to attempt this,
since they had already learned what Christ would be likely to do under
similar circumstances.

Luke 14.3. *Is it lawful to heal on the sabbath, or not?* The point of the
question is whether the man's healing should be reckoned among the
activities that violate the Sabbath. If they had said that it was a breaking of the Sabbath, the objection would have been easy, that this was
a divine work. But the Law on the Sabbath merely says that men
should rest from their own works. And the reason why Christ first
puts the question to them is to forestall the offence. Therefore it was
not His fault that they were not placated, for they were imbued with
an obstinate malice. Not that He always bound Himself to this condition, for He often disregarded scandal in doing what the Father had
commanded Him. But by this example He wanted to teach us that
He was not rash in performing miracles on the Sabbath but was ready
to give a reason for doing them. By their silence they show that they
had taken occasion to blame Him and are not moved by a zeal for the
Law. Christ therefore cares nothing for their criticism of His action,
since it is clear that they were deliberately framing a scandal.

Luke 14.5. *Which of you shall have, etc.* Although they did not
deserve Christ to try to remove their offence for them, He nevertheless
shows that He had committed nothing against the Sabbath. Yet He
does this, not so much to teach them as to vindicate Himself from their
slanders. He knew that they were too blinded by their envenomed
hatred to be teachable and reasonable; but He wished to triumph over
their malice and force them to shamed silence. For if it is lawful to
give help to animals on the Sabbath day, it is too shameful not to do the
same to a man formed in God's image.

*And he spake a parable unto those which were bidden, when he marked
how they chose out the chief seats; saying unto them, When thou art*

*bidden of any man to a marriage feast, sit not down in the chief seat; lest haply a more honourable man than thou be bidden of him, and he that bade thee and him shall come and say to thee, Give this man place; and then thou shalt begin with shame to take the lowest place. But when thou art bidden, go and sit down in the lowest place; that when he that hath bidden thee cometh, he may say to thee, Friend, go up higher: then shalt thou have glory in the presence of all that sit at meat with thee. For everyone that exalteth himself shall be humbled; and he that humbleth himself shall be exalted. And he said to him also that had bidden him, When thou makest a dinner or a supper, call not thy friends, nor thy brethren, nor thy kinsmen, nor rich neighbours; lest haply they also bid thee again, and a recompense be made thee. But when thou makest a feast, bid the poor, the maimed, the lame, the blind: and thou shalt be blessed, because they have not wherewith to recompense thee; thou shalt be recompensed in the resurrection of the just.* (Luke 14.7-14)

Luke 14.7. *And he spake unto those which were bidden.* We know how all the Pharisees and scribes were swayed by ambition. But not only did they desire to domineer over everybody else; there was also a power struggle among themselves. For men have a lust for empty glory and each one envies the other and tries to get for himself what others think is due to them. Thus the Pharisees and the scribes not only claim from the people the title of a holy order, but also quarrel about rank and honour, and each appropriates the first place for their own order. Christ wittily mocks their ambition in a parable. If a man takes the first place when he is out at a meal and then has to yield to someone more important, he suffers the shame and ignominy of being relegated by the master of ceremonies to another seat. But this is the fate of all who act proudly and set themselves above others— God abases them shamefully. We must note that Christ is not preaching about external and civil modesty, for those who are proudest often seem the best behaved in this respect and show great modesty and courtesy. But in this parable taken from human intercourse He wants to tell us what we should be like inwardly before God. It was equivalent to saying: 'If a guest had foolishly taken the first seat and was debased to the lowest, he would be covered with confusion and wish that he had never done it. Therefore lest God should act in the same way to you and brand your arrogance with deepest ignominy, be voluntarily humble and modest.'

Luke 14.11. *For everyone that exalteth himself.* This clause shows that Christ was speaking about ambition. He had not declared something that happened in man's ordinary life, but set up God as our Judge, who resists the proud and humbles their pride, but gives grace to the humble. The Scriptures are full of similar testimonies, that God is the foe to all those who desire to exalt themselves, as if they who arrogate anything to themselves are forced to make war on Him. For this is pride, to glory in God's gifts as if the excellence lay in ourselves and, as our own merit, exalted us. And on the other hand, humility should be reckoned not as a mere counterfeit abasement, but as a genuine annihilation, when we are truly aware of our weakness, when we do not seek to be lifted up, knowing that we excel only in God's grace.

Luke 14.12. *When thou makest a dinner.* Those who think that He is condemning out of hand family or friendly parties are removing humanity from men. For it would be not just strict, but barbarous, to exclude relatives from one's hospitality and admit only strangers. It was not Christ's intention to stop us being neighbourly, but only to show that love is little liked in the ordinary dealings of the world. It is not liberality, but a kind of usury, to give to the rich in hope of a like return. In the same way God thinks nothing of duties done in a mercenary spirit, and they do not deserve the name of love. If I have some rich relatives or friends to a meal, this is a human way of life and is not in itself condemnable. But it is not sufficient to prove my love. For often we see those who are completely selfish treating their friends to a most extravagant dinner. What then? You may furnish a table for the rich; but do not overlook the poor. You may feast with your friends and relations; but do not reject strangers because they are poor, if you have the means to supply their need. The sum of it is that those who do good to their relations and friends but are tight-fisted to the poor, are certainly not praiseworthy, for they are not exercising love, but thinking only of their money or their ambitions. And Christ confronts His host directly, for He saw that he was over-fond of display and elegance and wanted praise and thanks from rich men, while he had small care for the poor. Hence under the person of one man, the reproof is levelled against all who are liberal out of ambition and show or for hope of mutual return, while for the poor they have nothing left—as if they were afraid that they lost what they gave freely. Christ declares that they are blessed who are liberal without any hope of earthly reward, for it is sure that they are looking to God. But those who keep their own advantage before their eyes or whose motive is popularity, should expect no reward from God.

*And Jesus answered and spake again in parables unto them, saying, The kingdom of heaven is likened unto a certain king, which made a marriage feast for his son, and sent forth his servants to call them that were bidden to the marriage feast: and they would not come. Again he sent forth other servants, saying, Tell them that are bidden, Behold, I have made ready my dinner: my oxen and my fatlings are killed, and all things are ready: come to the marriage feast. But they made light of it, and went their ways, one to his own farm, another to his merchandise: and the rest laid hold of his servants, and entreated them shamefully, and killed them. But when the king heard of it, he was wroth; and he sent his armies, and destroyed those murderers, and burned their city. Then saith he to his servants, The wedding is ready, but they that were bidden were not worthy. Go ye therefore unto the partings of the highways, and as many as ye shall find, bid to the marriage feast. And those servants went out into the highways, and gathered together all as many as they found, both bad and good: and the wedding was filled with guests. But when the king came in to behold the guests, he saw there a man which had not on a wedding garment: and he saith unto him, Friend, how camest thou in hither not having a wedding garment? And he was speechless. Then the king said to the servants, Bind him hand and foot, and cast him out into outer darkness; there shall be the weeping and gnashing of teeth. For many are called, but few are chosen.* (Matt. 22.1-14)

*And when one of them that sat at meat with him heard these things, he said unto him, Blessed is he that shall eat bread in the kingdom of God. But he said unto him, A certain man made a great supper; and he bade many: and sent forth his servant at supper time to say to them that were bidden, Come; for all things are now ready. And they all with one consent began to make excuse. The first said unto him, I have bought a field, and I must needs go out and see it: I pray thee have me excused. And another said, I have bought five yoke of oxen, and I go to prove them: I pray thee have me excused. And another said, I have married a wife, and therefore I cannot come. And the servant came, and told his lord these things. Then the master of the house being angry said to his servant, Go out quickly into the streets and lanes of the city, and bring in hither the poor and maimed and blind and lame. And the servant said, Lord, what thou didst command is done, and yet there is room. And the lord said unto the servant, Go out into the highways and hedges, and constrain them to come in, that my house may be filled. For I say unto you, that none of those men which were bidden shall taste of my supper.* (Luke 14.15-24)

Matt 22.1. *And Jesus answered.* Matthew places this parable among other discourses delivered by Christ just before His last Passover. Yet because he does not assign a time to it and Luke says definitely that

He spoke it when He sat at the Pharisee's table, I have thought it better to follow Luke's order. Moreover, Matthew's aim was to show why the scribes were incensed to such a pitch of madness, and therefore he took no notice of the time sequence but put this parable into the context of other discourses that they hated. But Luke's account must be noticed, for it is here that one of the diners said, 'Blessed are those who shall eat bread in the Kingdom of God', and Christ took this as an opportunity to reprove the Jews for their ingratitude. Although it is hardly likely that a guest and friend of a Pharisee would come out with this saying from a sincere feeling of piety, yet to me it does not seem to be mockery. Just as men imbued with a slight faith and not openly ungodly are accustomed to gossip carelessly about eternal life in their cups, I think that this man let drop his saying about future blessedness so as to draw something out of Christ. His words indicate that his only hopes were gross and earthly; for he did not use 'bread' as a metaphor for eternal glory, but seems to have dreamt I know not what condition filled with a happy richness of everything. But the meaning is that those who eat God's bread after He has gathered His children into His Kingdom will be blessed.

Matt. 22.2. *The kingdom of heaven is likened.* There was once a Spartan who said that the Athenians knew what was right but did not do it. Similarly Christ reproves the Jews that they could speak well about God's Kingdom, but when God kindly and friendly invited them to enter, they rejected His grace contemptuously. There is no doubt that it is the Jews He is aiming at, as will appear shortly.

Matthew's account differs from Luke's in that he gives many details, whereas Luke relates the story only summarily and in general. Thus Matthew says that the king made a marriage feast for his son, Luke merely mentions a feast. Matthew speaks of several servants, Luke of only one. Matthew says they were sent on several occasions, Luke on only one. Matthew says that some of the servants were badly treated or killed, Luke speaks only of contempt. Finally, Matthew tells us that one was cast out who had entered the feast without a wedding garment, and of this Luke makes no mention. In other places we can also observe a similar difference, where Matthew is richer and fuller in teaching the same thing as Luke. In sum, however, they agree very well—when God deigned to honour the Jews especially, as if He were their host preparing a table for them, they despised the honour they were offered. Many interpreters make the wedding celebrations of the king's son refer to Christ as the end of the Law, in that God's only purpose in His covenant was to set Him over His people and to join the Church to Him by a sacred bond of spiritual marriage. I agree with this. And where He says that He sent out servants to call them

that were bidden, He wants to point out the twofold grace of God—
that He preferred the Jews before all other races, and that He revealed
His adoption of them through the prophets. For it is an allusion to
the common practice of drawing up a list of guests to invite to the
wedding, and then inviting them by the servants. Thus God chose
the Jews before all others, as if they were His familiar friends. Then
He called them by the prophets to share in the promised redemption
which was to be celebrated in the marriage feast. Now although those
who were called at first did not live until the coming of Christ, yet we
know that the common salvation was set before all but that their
ingratitude and malice deprived them of it. For from the beginning
that people had an ungodly contempt of God's invitation.

Matt. 22.4. *Again he sent forth other servants.* He expresses it as if
they were the same men, because the people was one body. And the
meaning is: When the happy and joyful day of redemption was
drawing near they were given warning so that they might be ready in
time. For the time had been agreed for them long before. But now
Christ said that they were urged to come quickly at the hour itself with
fresh messages. For the first invitation that He mentions embraced all
the foregoing prophets up to the proclamation of the Gospel. And
whereas in earlier days they had raged against the prophets, their fury
increased with the time and was poured out at last in a flood on Christ
and the apostles. He therefore accuses the people of old of contempt
and pride. But He says that the last servants, who had been sent near
the hour of the supper, were treated violently or even killed. Thus
the people broke out into extreme wickedness when their mad cruelty
was added to an arrogant rejection of grace. Yet He is not accusing
them all of the same fault. In the last calling, the calling of the Gospel,
some despised God's grace carelessly and others, hypocrites, furiously
attacked it. And as usually happens, the more the ungodly were
invited to salvation, the more they raged against God.

Now we must treat that part of the discourse which is common to
Matthew and Luke, that one went to his farm, another to his merchandise; or, as Luke puts it, one excused himself because he had
married a wife, another had bought a farm and another five yoke of
oxen. By these words Christ means that the Jews were so given up to
the world and earthly things that none had the time to come to God.
For while the cares of the world bind us round they are diversions
and draw us away from God's Kingdom. It is wicked and shameful
that men who are created for the heavenly life should be completely
carried away to transitory things in a brutish manner. But this disease
is prevalent everywhere; scarcely one in a hundred puts the Kingdom
of God before fleeting riches or other pleasures. And although all do

not suffer from the same sickness, yet each one is turned off course by his cupidity and all flow away hither and thither. Moreover, we must note that ungodly men put forward honest pretexts when they want to reject God's grace, as if their laziness were excusable when they are set on affairs of this life and value little the heavenly heritage. But we see how Christ tells us that such enticements must be banished, in case anyone should think he is making progress while he is in fact being held back by earthly hindrances. And men are doubly guilty when they make hindrances out of otherwise lawful things which should be a help. What is God's purpose in our giving up the comforts of the present life, except to draw us to Himself? For God's benefits are far from being a help in aspiring for heaven; holy matrimony, fields, other riches become merely snares which bind men down to earth.

Matt. 22.7. *But when the king heard thereof.* Only Matthew mentions this punishment, for Luke has nothing about the injury done to the servants. They both say that those who did not come at the appointed time were excluded and deprived of the honour of being guests. But this teaching touches us too. The same destruction of which Christ forewarned the Jews remains for all the ungodly who rise up violently against the ministers of the Gospel. All those who are so possessed by earthly cares that they care nothing for God's invitation will wretchedly waste away at last from famine. And therefore as often as He calls us, let us be ready and swift to follow Him.

Matt. 22.9. *Go ye therefore into the highways.* After He had shown that they who contemptuously reject God's grace are unworthy, He now says that others are substituted for them, and those the meanest and most contemptible. And here He is pointing to the calling of the Gentiles which would provoke the Jews to jealousy, as it says in the Song of Moses: 'They have provoked me by those who were not gods, and I will move them to jealousy with those which are not a people; I will provoke them to anger with a foolish nation' (Deut. 32.21). Because they were the first to be chosen, they thought His grace was bound to them and that He could not do without them. It is well known how they despised all others. Therefore He makes a concession and compares the Gentiles to beggars, to the blind and lame. And He says they were called from the street-corners and lanes like outcasts and strangers, yet that they supply the place left empty by the friends and relations. Thus what the prophets foretold more obscurely of the creating of the new Church, He expressed clearly. And certainly this shaming was the consummation of the divine wrath. God cut them off and inserted new shoots in the root of the olive (Rom. 11.17). He renounced them and received the polluted and unclean Gentiles into His house. But if He did not spare the natural branches, the same

108

vengeance awaits us today if we do not respond to His call. But the supper prepared for us will not be lost; God will summon other guests.

Luke 14.23. *Compel them to come in.* This is as good as saying that the householder commands his servants to force the beggars to be his guests and not to overlook the lowest dregs of humanity. By these words Christ means that God would rather scrape together all the off-scourings of the world than admit the ungrateful to His table. Yet He seems to allude to the manner of the Gospel invitation, for He does not simply lay before us God's grace, but adds the spurs of exhortation to the teaching. And in this is seen the wonderful goodness of God: when He sees us whom He has called to Himself slow to come He importunately harasses our slothfulness and not only pierces us with exhortations but even compels us with threats to draw near to Him. But I do not think Augustine was wrong in often using this testimony against the Donatists to prove that the disobedient and rebellious might legitimately be forced by the edicts of godly princes to the worship of the true God and to unity in the faith; because, although faith is voluntary, yet we see that these are useful means to tame the obstinacy of those who will not obey unless they are forced.

Matt. 22.11. *But when the king came in.* Christ is not here reproving the Jews for irreligiously despising God's grace and calling but fore-warning those who were to be substituted for them, lest they should defile the holy wedding with their uncleanness when God had hon-oured them with participation in His feast. Hitherto He had said that the Jews would be deprived of this special privilege and honour be-cause of their ungodly disdain, and that there would be called from the heathen and rejected Gentiles those who would succeed to their place. But now He warns that even out of this number those will be expelled who bring shame to the Church. Because God calls all in-discriminately by the Gospel, many impure and filthy men break in. For a time they keep their place among the rest, but at last, when God surveys His guests, they will be thrown out and taken to be punished. The sum of it is that not all who have once entered the Church will be partakers of eternal life but only those who shall be found attired fit for the palace of heaven.

There is no point in arguing about the marriage garment, whether it is faith or a holy and godly life; for faith cannot be separated from good works and good works proceed only from faith. All Christ wants to say here is that we are called by the Lord under the condition that we be renewed in our spirits into His image, and therefore, if we are to remain always in His house, the old man with all his blemishes is to be cast off and we are to practice the new life so that our appear-ance (*vestitus*) may correspond to our honourable calling.

But we may ask why a beggar should be so harshly treated and punished because he had no wedding garment. For it is nothing new for the poor wretches who seek their living in the gutters to be in rags. I reply that the origin of the garment is not under discussion. For when the Lord invites anyone, He also at the same time clothes them. He fulfils in all of us what Ezek. 16.7 says, that when God finds in us nothing but wretched nakedness and stinking foulness, He clothes us with beautiful raiment. We know also that we are reformed into the image of God only when we put on Christ. Therefore Christ does not declare that unhappy men are cast out because they fail to bring with them a fine garment from their wardrobe, but because they will be discovered in all their uncleanness when God comes to survey his guests.

The conclusion shows the intention of the parable: few are chosen although many are called. From this we may infer that each particular phrase is not to be examined minutely. For Christ had just said that only one, and not the greater part, was expelled. But now we hear that few of a great number will be kept. And indeed, although more are gathered into the Church by the Word of the Gospel than of old by the Law, yet only a small portion of them prove their faith by newness of life. Therefore, do not let us flatter ourselves with an empty title of faith, but let each one examine himself seriously so that in the final choosing he may be reckoned among the genuine guests. For, as Paul says, the vessels in the house of the Lord are not all of one sort, therefore let him who calls on the name of the Lord depart from evil (II Tim. 2.19). I am not here entering deeply into the eternal election of God, since Christ's words merely mean that an outward profession of faith in no way suffices for God to acknowledge as His own those who seem to have enrolled at His calling.

*And he said also unto his disciples, There was a certain rich man, which had a steward; and the same was accused unto him that he was wasting his goods. And he called him, and said unto him, What is this that I hear of thee? render the account of thy stewardship; for thou canst be no longer steward. And the steward said within himself, What shall I do, seeing that my lord taketh away the stewardship from me? I have not strength to dig; to beg I am ashamed. I am resolved what to do, that, when I am put out of the stewardship, they may receive me into their houses. And calling to him each one of his lord's debtors, he said to the first, How much owest thou unto my lord? and he said, A hundred measures of oil. And he said unto him, Take thy bond, and sit down quickly and write fifty. Then said he to another, And how much owest thou? And he said, A hundred measures of wheat. He saith unto him, Take thy bond, and write fourscore. And his lord commended the unjust steward because he had done wisely: for the sons of this world are in their own generation wiser than the sons of the light. And I say unto you, Make to yourselves friends from the unrighteous mammon; that, when you shall fail, they may receive you into the eternal tabernacles. He that is faithful in a very little is faithful also in much: and he that is unrighteous in a very little is unrighteous also in much. If therefore ye have not been faithful in the unrighteous mammon, who will commit to your trust what is true? And if ye have not been faithful in that which is another's, who will give you that which is your own? . . . And the Pharisees, who were lovers of money, heard all these things; and they scoffed at him. And he said unto them, Ye are they that justify yourselves in the sight of men; but God knoweth your hearts: for that which is exalted among men is an abomination in the sight of God.* (Luke 16.1-15 omitting v.13)

The sum of this parable is that we must treat our neighbours humanely and kindly, so that when we come before God's judgment seat, we may receive the fruit of our liberality. Although the parable seems hard and far-fetched, yet the conclusion shows that this was Christ's intention. Hence we perceive that those who investigate minutely every single part of a parable are poor theologians. For Christ does not here bid us to redeem by gifts the frauds, extortions, squandering and other faults of bad administration; but since God has appointed us stewards of all the good things He bestows on us, a method is prescribed which one day, when the time of rendering account shall come, will lighten us from the extremest strictness. For those who think that alms are a compensation for a luxurious and dissolute life do not consider that we are first of all taught to live soberly and temperately, and then that the streams shall flow to us from a pure spring. It is certain that no-one is so thrifty as not to lose the goods under his keeping; and therefore even those who cultivate the utmost economy are not entirely free from maladministration. Add that God's gifts can be misused in many different ways, and some are guilty in one way, some in another. But I do not deny that our awareness of our faulty stewardship should rather stimulate us the more to the duties of love. But we should set another aim before us than that of fleeing God's judgment by paying the price of redemption; and that is that liberality well and holy disposed may bridle and correct our extravagance, and also that our humanity to our brethren may stir up God's mercy to us. Therefore the Lord is not here showing

His disciples a way of escape, to free themselves from guilt when the heavenly Judge demands a reckoning from them, but is warning them in good time that they must pay the punishment of their cruelty if they are detected in swallowing up the good things of God without troubling about being beneficent. For we must always hold to this saying: 'With what measure ye mete to others it shall be measured to you again' (Matt. 7.2).

Luke 16.8. *And his lord commended.* Here, too, we can easily see how foolish it would be to insist on the details. There is nothing laudable in giving away other men's goods; and who would put up with a dishonest rascal robbing him and letting off his debtors at will? It would be too crass altogether for a man to see part of his possessions embezzled and the rest given away by the thief, and then approve of it. But all Christ meant was, as He adds just after, that heathen and worldly men are more industrious and clever in taking care of the ways and means of this fleeting world than God's children are in caring for the heavenly and eternal life, or making it their study and exercise. By this comparison He reproves our worse than spineless laziness that we do not at least have the same eye to the future that heathen men have to feathering their nests in this world. How wicked it is that the children of light, on whom God shines by His spirit and His Word, should sleep and neglect the hope of everlasting bliss offered to them, when greedy, worldly men are so devoted to their own interests, so far-sighted and shrewd! And so we gather that this is not a comparison of the wisdom of the Spirit and of the flesh (which would mean an insult to God), but only an arousing of believers to ponder more carefully on the future life and not to close their eyes to the light of the Gospel when they perceive the blind better sighted in their darkness. And that should move them the more when they see the children of this world so far-sighted for the sake of this transitory life, which passes in a moment.

Luke 16.9. *Make to yourselves friends.* Just as in the former verse Christ had not commanded us to offer plunder to God as a sacrifice, so now He does not mean that we should look ourselves out intercessors and patrons who will hide and defend us under their protection. But He teaches us that loving gifts bring us the favour of God, who promises that He will be merciful to the merciful and humane. They are foolish and absurd who infer from this that we are helped by the prayers or suffrages of the dead. For in this way whatever was bestowed on the unworthy would be lost. But man's depravity does not prevent God from recording in His account book whatever we give to the poor. Hence the Lord is not concerned with the giver but with the gift; so that our benefits, even if made to the ungrateful, will be accounted (*respondeat*) to us before God. But this seems to suggest that eternal life is a recompense for our merits. I reply that the context makes it clear that this is spoken in a human sort of way. Just as a flourishing and rich man who makes friends during his prosperity will have them to help him when misfortune strikes, so our kindness will be like a timely refuge in that the Lord acknowledges as bestowed on Himself whatever we give liberally to our neighbour.

*When ye fail.* By this word He means the hour of death, and warns us that the time of our stewardship is brief, lest the belief that we will live a long time should make us grudging. For why is it that the most of men slumber in their riches, that many waste what they have in extravagances, that others hoard it up and so defraud themselves and others, why is it save because they are deceived by a false hope of a long life and so live in security?

He calls it 'the unrighteous mammon', so as to make riches suspect to us, for they usually involve their owners in unrighteousness. Of themselves they are not evil. But because they are rarely acquired without fraud or violence or other illegal methods, and rarely, too, possessed without pride or luxury or some other depraved attitude, Christ is right to make them suspect to us. Elsewhere He calls them thorns (Matt. 13.22). Yet there seems to be an implicit antithesis, as if He were saying: 'Riches can defile their owner if he misuses them and can almost be enticements to sin; but they may be converted to the opposite and bring us favour.' Moreover, we must remember what I said before, that God does not seek sacrifices that are the fruit of an unrighteous activity, as if He were a thieves' 'fence' (*socius furum*). And so He warns believers to keep themselves pure from unrighteousness.

Luke 16.10. *He that is faithful in a very little.* These are proverbial statements from common use and experience, and therefore it is sufficient for them to be true in general. It sometimes happens that a swindler will overlook a small gain and show his wickedness in some big scheme; or many will use the small affair as a sprat to catch a mackerel. As someone says, 'Fraud wins men's confidence in little things so that, when it is worth the candle, the big deal can be brought off.'[1] Yet Christ's statement is not untrue, for, as I said, in proverbs we follow what is common and usual. Therefore Christ tells His disciples that by acting faithfully in small things they will get used to faithfulness in undertaking big things. He also accommodates this idea to the right administration of spiritual graces, disesteemed indeed by the world but certainly far more excellent than the world's fleeting riches. And He teaches that they are not fit for God to commit to them the incomparable treasure of the Gospel and like gifts if they act

[1] Livy: 28, 42.

badly and unfaithfully in unimportant matters, such as the transient riches of the world. And so a tacit threat is implied in these words: We must be afraid lest our abuse of earthly administration deprives us of heavenly gifts. What is true is contrasted with riches in the sense that the substantial and eternal is opposed to the shadowy and transient.

Luke 16.12. *Faithful in that which is another's.* By 'another's' He means what is outside a man. For God does not give us riches for us to be bound to them; but He appoints us as their stewards so that they should not hold us in their chains. For our minds can not live at liberty in heaven unless they treat whatever is on earth as foreign. But He makes spiritual riches, which relate to the future life, our own, because their enjoyment is eternal. He now uses another similitude. We can not hope to use our goods aright and moderately if we deal wickedly or unfaithfully with those of another man. For men misuse their own possessions more carelessly and are less worried about losing them because they are not afraid of being blamed. But they are more careful and anxious about what is entrusted or lent to them and for which they must soon give account. Therefore we understand Christ's meaning to be that they will be bad custodians of spiritual gifts who administer earthly goods badly. Then the statement is made that none can serve God and mammon. This I have explained under Matthew 6, where readers can learn what the word 'mammon' means.

Luke 16.14. *And the Pharisees, who were lovers of money.* Those who think that the Pharisees laughed at Christ for being content with common and simple language and not making a bombastic display have not weighed Luke's words sufficiently. I agree that the teaching of the Gospel seems beneath contempt to the proud and stylish, but Luke expressly says that they laughed at Christ because they were covetous. Because it was a deep-rooted conviction with them that riches were blessed and therefore that there was nothing better than to increase one's possessions by any method and to hold tight to what one has got, they rejected as an absurd paradox whatever Christ said on the opposite side. And indeed, anyone who preaches about despising riches or giving to the poor will seem silly to the covetous. Horace's line is well known: 'The public hissed; but I cried "Well done, me!"' If those condemned by common consent can yet approve of their own actions, how much more shall they ridicule as a fable the philosophy of Christ, which is far removed from common ideas? Yet I do not doubt that the Pharisees were using this as a pretext to laugh off this teaching which attacked their vice. We must remember what moved them. The disease flourishes almost universally that the larger part of mankind think they can reject what does not accord with their de-praved ways. This is why the Word of God is hateful to so many of the wicked and the clowns and the mockers. It summons each man to defend his vices and they think that they can make their jokes a smoke screen to hide their sin.

Luke 16.15. *Ye are they that justify yourselves.* We see that Christ refuses to give way to their scorn, but boldly asserts the authority of His teaching in the face of their ridicule. All ministers of the Gospel must act like this and oppose to the ungodly despisers the fearful judgment of God. And He says that the pretext by which they deceive men will avail them nothing at the judgment seat of God. They did not want it to look as if their jestings were a defence of their avarice. But Christ teaches that the poison bursts from a hidden ulcer—just as today someone might tell the mitred bishops that they are so hostile to the Gospel because it too sharply pierces their inward evil. He says that they are satisfied with being righteous before men and wearing a sanctified appearance, whereas God, who knows the hearts, cannot be kept in the dark about their vices like the world can.

We must note also a distinction between God's judgments and men's. Men applaud outward shows; at God's judgment the sincere heart alone is approved. There is added the remarkable statement that whatever men esteem highly is an abomination to God. Not because God rejects virtues, for He impresses approval of them on men's hearts, but because God abominates whatever men extol from their own understanding. This shows us the place we should give to unauthorized worship invented at the world's will. However pleasing it may be to its framers, Christ declares that before God it is not merely vain and nothing, but even stinking.

*Now there was a certain rich man, and he was clothed in purple and fine linen, faring sumptuously every day: and a certain beggar named Lazarus was laid at his gate, full of sores, and desiring to be fed with the crumbs that fell from the rich man's table; yea, even the dogs came and licked his sores. And it came to pass, that the beggar died, and that he was carried away by the angels into Abraham's bosom: and the rich man also died, and was buried. And in Hades he lifted up his eyes, being in torments, and seeth Abraham afar off, and Lazarus laid in his bosom. And he cried and said, Father Abraham, have mercy on me, and send Lazarus, that he may dip the tip of his finger in water, and cool my tongue; for I am in anguish in this flame. But Abraham said, Son, re-member that thou in thy lifetime receivedst thy good things, and Lazarus in like manner evil things: but now here he is comforted, and thou art in anguish. And beside all this, between us and you there is a great gulf fixed, that they which would pass from hence to you may not be able, and that none may cross over from thence to us. And he said, I pray thee therefore, father, that thou wouldest send him to my father's house; for I have five brethren; that he may testify unto them, lest they also come into this place of torment. But Abraham saith, They have Moses and the prophets; let them hear them. And he said, Nay, father Abraham: but if one go to them from the dead, they will repent. And he said unto him, If they hear not Moses and the prophets, neither will they believe, if one rise from the dead.* (Luke 16.19-31)

Luke inserts other things between verses 15 and 19, but there is no doubt that this parable is a confirmation of the previous discourse. Christ shows what state remains for those who neglect the poor and stuff themselves full with pleasures, who devote themselves to drunkenness and delights and let their neighbours miserably thirst, nay, destroy them with cruel hunger whom they ought to help as they are able. Although to some the parable seems straightforward, yet, because He mentions Lazarus by name, I judge that He is telling a true story. Nevertheless, this is not very important, so long as readers hold the substance of what is taught.

First the rich man is introduced, clothed in purple and fine linen, and indulging himself every day with splendid feasts. The words indicate a very pampered life, full of luxury and display. Not that God dislikes all sartorial elegance and adornment in itself, or that all genteel living is damnable. But it rarely happens that people keep a mean. Those who like to be well-dressed will gradually go further and further in their finery; and those who delight in the pleasures of the table will hardly be able to stop themselves falling into extravagance. But what he is chiefly condemned for is the cruelty that left Lazarus lying at his gate, poor and covered with sores. For Christ interrelated these two things—that the rich man was given up to drunkenness and display, an insatiable whirlpool devouring heaps of food, and yet untouched by Lazarus' poverty and wretchedness but knowingly and willingly letting him waste away of hunger, cold and stinking ulcers. Ezekiel accuses Sodom in the same way that in all its fulness of bread and wine it did not reach out a hand to the poor (16.49). The linen here is very fine stuff, and, as is well-known, it was frequently used by the Orientals for pomp and show. This habit the sacrificing papists imitated with their so-called surplices.

Luke 16.21. *But even the dogs came.* It convicts the rich man of hardness and inhumanity that such a wretched sight did not move him to sympathy. For had there been one drop of humanity in him, he would at least have ordered that some of the kitchen scraps should be

116

given to the poor man. But the height of his ungodliness and worse than animal cruelty was that he did not learn mercy from the dogs. There is no doubt that those dogs were directed by the secret counsel of God to condemn him by their example. Christ brings them here as if to bear witness and reprove the man's accursed hardness. For what greater monstrosity could we conceive than that the dogs should care for a man who was neglected by his neighbour? He would not give even a crumb to this starving man; but the dogs lent him their tongues to heal him. Therefore, as often as strangers, or even animals, take our place to perform a duty that we ought to do, let us know that they are witnesses and judges appointed by God to lay bare our crime.

Luke 16.22. *And it came to pass, that the beggar died.* Here Christ shows how the condition of both is changed at death. Death is common to them both; but for the dead man to be carried by angels into Abraham's bosom is a bliss more desirable than all kingdoms. But to be destined to eternal torments is terrifying, something to be redeemed, if it were possible, by a hundred lives. In the person of Lazarus we are taught very clearly not to think that they are accursed by God who drag their way through life afflicted with troubles and continual sickness. For in him God's graciousness was so hidden, and he was so oppressed by the ugliness of the cross and insults that fleshly understanding could grasp nothing beyond the curse. But if the angels carried him away to the blessed life, we can see how precious was the soul which was concealed within the filth and rottenness of the body. Death was no harm to him; deserted, despised, without any help of man, when he left the prison house of the body heavenly spirits deigned to be beside him, at his command.

Again the rich man is like a bright mirror in which we can see that temporal felicity is not to be sought for if it ends in eternal destruction. Yet we must note that Christ expressly declares that the rich man was buried, whereas He does not say what became of Lazarus—not that his body lay out in the open at the mercy of wild beasts, but it would have been thrown contemptuously and dishonourably into some pit (for from the opposite clause it is easy to infer that they would have spent no more trouble on him dead than when he was alive). The rich man, on the other hand, given a splendid burial corresponding to his riches, still has a sort of remnant of his former pride. For in this matter we see heathen men fighting, as it were, against nature and desiring to have some of their fortune carried over into a splendid and solemn funeral. The ridiculous foolishness of this ambition is testified by their souls in hell.

When He says Lazarus was carried, it is a synecdoche. For in that man's soul is his more excellent part, the name of the whole man is deservedly given to it. It is not for nothing that Christ assigns this office to angels, for we know that they have been given to be ministers to believers to bestow their energies and labours on their salvation.

*Abraham's bosom.* There is no need to relate (and in my opinion it is not expedient) how differently the many interpreters of Scripture have philosophized on 'Abraham's bosom'. It is enough to hold what readers well practised in Scripture will acknowledge to be the genuine sense. Just as Abraham is called the father of believers because the covenant of eternal life was entrusted to his care, first to keep faithfully for his own children and then to hand on to all the nations, and all the heirs of the promise are called his children, so those who receive with him the fruit of the same faith are said to be gathered into his bosom after they die. It is a metaphor taken from children returning, as it were, to the bosom of their father when they meet at home in the evening after their day's work. God's children are strangers and pilgrims in the world, and as during their present course they follow the faith of their father Abraham, so when they die they withdraw to that blessed rest where he awaits them. But it is not necessary to conceive of this as a definite place. All that is indicated is, as I have said, that assembling in which believers will know indeed that since they enjoy the same dwelling in heaven they did not fight in vain under the banner of Abraham's faith.

If it be asked whether today the same state is laid up for believers when they die, or whether Christ did not, in rising from the dead, open His own bosom, in which both Abraham himself and all the godly repose, I reply briefly that just as God's grace shone on us more brightly by the Gospel and as Christ the Sun of righteousness brought us salvation by His coming (a salvation which it was once given to the fathers to see under shadows), so there is no doubt at all that the dead come closer to the fruition of the heavenly life. Yet we must understand that the glory of immortality is deferred until the final day of redemption. So far as the name goes, that quiet haven which opens for believers after the voyage of this present life can be called either Abraham's or Christ's bosom. But because we have gone higher than did the fathers under the law, the distinction becomes clearer if we say that Christ's members are gathered to their Head. And so the metaphor of Abraham's bosom comes to an end, as if the brightness of the risen sun obscured all the stars. Yet we may certainly infer from Christ's way of speaking here that while they were alive the fathers under the Law embraced by faith the inheritance of the heavenly life, which they received when they died.

Luke 16.23. *And in hell he lifted up his eyes.* Although Christ is telling a story, yet He describes spiritual things under figures which

He knew were on the level of our understanding. For souls have not been endowed with fingers and eyes, nor are they tormented with thirst, nor do they hold conversation with one another in the way here described of Abraham and the glutton. The Lord is painting a picture which represents the condition of the future life in a way that we can understand. The sum of it is that believing souls when they leave the body lead a joyful and blessed life outside the world, but that for the reprobate are prepared terrifying torments which can no more be conceived by our minds than can the infinite glory of heaven. For just as by the illumination of God's Spirit we taste through hope only a little part of the glory promised to us (a glory which far transcends all our thoughts), so it is enough to know only obscurely the incomprehensible vengeance of God which awaits the ungodly, to know it sufficiently to be terror-struck. Hence Christ's words give a faint knowledge of these things, one which avails to restrain curiosity: that is, the ungodly are cruelly tortured by a sense of their own misery; they desire relief, but hope is taken from them and they feel a twofold torment; they are the more tormented because they are forced to remember their sins and to compare the blessedness of the faithful with their own unhappy and lost estate. This is why a conversation is described between those who in fact have no intercourse at all. When the rich man calls Abraham 'father' he is expressing another torture he feels, that too late he realises that he is disinherited from the family of Abraham.

Luke 15.25. *Son, remember.* The word 'Son' seems to have been used ironically, so that the sharp reproof might pierce the rich man to the heart, for in his life-time he had falsely boasted of being one of the sons of Abraham. His mind is wounded, so to say, with a burning iron when his hypocrisy and counterfeit trust is held before his eyes. He is said to be tormented in hell because he received his good things in this world. But this must not be taken as meaning that eternal destruction awaits all those who live well and prosperously in the world. In fact, as Augustine shrewdly observed, the pauper Lazarus is carried into the bosom of wealthy Abraham to teach us that the gate of the Kingdom of heaven is shut against no rich man but lies open for all in common who either have used their riches well or have been patient in poverty. All it means is that he who was completely sunk in the pleasures and delights of this present life and so despised God and His Kingdom, is now given the punishment of his sloth.

The pronoun 'thy' is emphatic, as if Abraham said, 'When you had been created for immortal life and the Law of God should have raised you up to practice the heavenly life, you forgot your wonderful heritage and preferred to be like a pig or a dog. You therefore receive a reward fit for your brutish pleasures.' Again, when it is said of Lazarus that he received solace because he had suffered many miseries in the world, it is improper to apply it to all the unhappy. Some of them have profited so little from affliction that their end will be the utmost punishment. What is praised in Lazarus is his bearing of the cross, and this springs always from faith and the sincere fear of God. For a man who obstinately resists earthly ills and persists untamed in his fierceness does not deserve to be praised for patience or to have God repay him with solace for his cross. What it comes to is this: for those who patiently bear the weight of the cross which is laid on them and do not fight against God's yoke and rod, but throughout all their troubles aspire to the hope of a better life, there is laid up in heaven rest when their warfare is ended. But on the other side, for profane despisers of God who gorge on carnal delights and whose minds are so surfeited that there is no room for the exercise of godliness, there is prepared from the moment of death torments which shall banish all empty delights. Moreover, we must remember that the consolation which the children of God enjoy is given on the understanding that when they perceive the crown of glory laid up for them they will wait joyfully and quietly for it. Just as also the sense of future judgment which they see hanging over them torments the ungodly.

Luke 16.26. *There is a great gulf fixed.* These words point to the condition of the future life, as if it had been said that the boundaries dividing the reprobate from the elect can never be crossed. Hence we are warned to return to the way while there is time, lest we should rush headlong into that abyss from which there is no return. It is an imprecise expression to say that the passage is closed, for it is certain that none of the godly have any such wish.

Luke 16.27. *I pray thee, therefore, father.* To fit the story to our use the better, He makes the rich man wish that his brothers still alive might be warned by Lazarus. The Papists argue ineptly about this when they want to prove that the dead have a care for the living—a quite disgusting quibble. By the same argument I will conclude that believing souls are not content with their lot and would be seized by a desire to migrate to hell if they were not separated from it by a fixed gulf. If no-one accepts this nonsense, there is no reason why the Papists should be so pleased with their other invention. But it is not my purpose to dispute on one side or the other; I only want to point out in passing how futile the arguments are that lead them to imagine that the dead pray to God for us.

Now I return to the simple and native sense of the passage. Christ tells us, under the persons of the rich man and Abraham, that, since a sure rule of life has been given to us, we must not expect the dead to rise to teach and exhort us. For while Moses and the prophets were alive they were appointed as teachers to the men of their age in such a way that later generations might also receive fruit from their writings. Since God wishes us to be taught in this way how to live aright, there is no reason why the dead should be sent as witnesses of the rewards or punishments of the future life. Nor will their sloth be excusable who indulge themselves under the pretext that they do not know what happens outside the world. We know that among profane men there is uttered this ungodly saying, or rather this porcine grunting, that those who torture themselves by doubtful fears are foolish, because no-one ever returned from hell to tell the truth. Christ wanted to correct such bewitchments of Satan and so He recalls us to the Law and the Prophets, according to the testimony of Moses, 'After this thou shalt not say, Who will ascend into heaven? or, Who will descend into the abyss? or, Who will cross the sea? The word is near, in thy mouth and heart' (Deut. 30.12-14). Therefore those who deride as fables what the Scripture testifies about future judgment will one day feel how intolerable is the ungodliness that will not believe in the holy oracles of God. Moreover, God arouses His people from this sluggishness, lest they should be misled by hope of going scot-free and so neglect the time of repentance. And this is where Abraham's reply tends, that God gave the doctrine of salvation abundantly to His people through Moses and the Prophets, and therefore nothing remains but for all to assent to it. The greater part are for ever longing for new revelations, for man's spirit is deeply infected with the depraved disease of curiosity. Now nothing displeases God more than for men to transgress greedily their due bounds, and so He forbids them to seek the truth from magicians and soothsayers and to desire false oracles in the manner of the heathen; at the same time, as a sedative for their curiosity, He promises that He will give them prophets to teach the people whatever is useful for salvation (Deut. 18.9-15). If God sent the prophets quite definitely to keep the people under the bridle of the Word, then whosoever is not content with this method of teaching has no real desire to learn but is only titillated by an ungodly mental wantonness. Therefore God complains that He has been done an injury when all, from the living to the dead (Isa. 8.19), do not listen to Him alone. The distinction Abraham makes in the Word of God to the Law and the prophets refers to the age of the Old Testament. But now that the fuller interpretation of the Gospel has come, less tolerable is our ungodliness in despising that doctrine and being carried about hither and thither, in brief, in not letting God's Word rule over us. From this we also gather how much basis there is for the Papist faith in purgatory and such like nonsense, which is based only on phantasmas.

Luke 16.30. *Nay, father Abraham.* This is a *prosopopoeia* (personification), as we have said, in which is uttered rather the thought of the living than the anxiety of the dead. For the teaching of the Law falls flat in the world, the prophets are neglected, no-one troubles to listen to God speaking in His own way. Some lust for angels to come down from heaven, some for the dead to rise from their graves, some for ever new miracles to seal what they hear, some for voices to thunder from heaven. But if it came to pass that God fell in with all these perverted wishes, we should be no further forward, for God has included in His Word whatever it is useful for us to know, and He has witnessed and proved the authority of this Word with genuine seals. Moreover, faith does not depend on miracles or portents. It is the special gift of the Spirit and is born of the Word. Finally, it is the office proper to God Himself to draw us to Him, and it is His will to work effectively through His Word. Therefore there is no hope that those media will avail us which divert us from obedience to the Word. I confess that the flesh is prone to nothing so much as to listen to empty revelations, and we see how ardently those who despise all Scripture rush into Satan's snares. From this come necromancy and like witchcrafts, which the world not only accepts greedily but even grabs with mad desire. But here Christ is only saying that those who are deaf and stubborn against the teaching of the Law cannot be corrected by the dead or brought to a sound frame.

*But who is there of you, having a servant plowing or keeping sheep, that will say unto him, when he is come in from the field, Come straightway and sit down to meat; and will not rather say unto him, Make ready wherewith I may sup, and gird thyself, and serve me, till I have eaten and drunken; and afterward thou shalt eat and drink? Doth he thank the servant because he did the things that were commanded? I think not. Even so ye also, when ye shall have done all the things that are commanded you, say, We are unprofitable servants; we have done that which it was our duty to do.* (Luke 17.7-10)

The point of this parable is that when God claims for Himself as of right all that is ours, and possesses us as His bond-slaves (*nexuque et mancipio*), all the duty that we try to do lays Him under no obligation to us. For since we are His, He can owe us nothing in return. He therefore puts forward the similitude of a slave who, after he has worked hard the whole day, goes on working after he gets home in the evening until his master lets him off. Now Christ is not speaking of the sort of hired servants who minister to us nowadays, but of the slaves of old whose condition was that they received nothing for themselves but were bound to their masters with all their work, care and toil even to blood. Christ here teaches that we are obliged and bound by no less a strait bond of servitude to God. And from this we gather that there is no way by which He can be obliged to us. This is an argument from the lesser to the greater, for if so much power over a man is granted to a mortal man that he can force him to a continual obedience day and night and yet be bound by no contract of mutual compensation, as if he were a debtor, how much more may God lay claim to our powers so long as their strength lasts without owing us anything? Therefore we see that all those who think they can merit something before God and make Him their debtor are condemned of depraved pride. And yet there is no vice more common than such pride. For there is no-one who does not want to call God to a reckoning; and this is why the imagination about merits has reigned in nearly all ages. But we must grasp Christ's statement that we serve God without any pay but are at His command on the understanding that we owe Him all that is in us.

There are two parts to the sentence: our life, even to the end of its course, is completely devoted to God, so that if anyone applied a part of it in doing his duty towards God, he could not strike a bargain to lay off for the rest of the time—just as at the end of ten years military service a good number of men might wish to petition for discharge. From this follows the second part, that, as I have just mentioned, God is not bound to reward us for our duties. Therefore let each one remember that he was created to work and to practise his ministry energetically, and that not only for a time but right until death, so that he shall not only live but also die to the Lord.

But so far as merit goes, a knot must be untied which worries many. Scripture very often promises a reward to works and seems to ascribe something meritorious to them. The solution is easy. The reward is put down only to the promise of God's sheer good will. They are very deceived who join reward and merit together in a mutual relationship, for God is not moved to render a reward by the worthiness of the works but by His free kindness. I confess, of course, that in the covenant of the Law God was bound to men if they performed substantially what was required of them; yet because this obligation was voluntary, it remains an axiom that a man can claim nothing from God as if it were merited. The pride of the flesh is therefore laid low, because even if anyone fulfilled the Law he could not charge it against God as a debt, for he would only be paying what he owed. So the sense in which He says we are unprofitable servants is that God receives nothing

123

extra from us but only gathers the legitimate fruits of His lordship. Therefore we must grasp these two things: that God owes us nothing naturally (nor is any service that we pay Him worth a hair); and that in the covenant of the Law a reward is determined for works, not on account of their worthiness but because God is freely a debtor. And it would be quite intolerable ingratitude for anyone to become proud and haughty on this pretext. For the more open handed and kind God is to us, the more He makes us obliged to Him; and far be it from us to think we have any right to vain confidence. Therefore, whenever we meet with the word 'reward' or it crosses our minds, let us realize that it is the height of the divine goodness towards us that, although He has us completely in His debt, yet He condescends to make an agreement with us. The more hateful is that invention of the Sophists, who dared to invent the doctrine of condign merit (*meritum de condigno*). Even in itself the word merit was heathenish and foreign to the rule of godliness; but it is far worse for men to be drunken with a diabolical pride and think they can merit anything on the basis of equity (*de condigno*).

Luke 17.10. *That which was our duty to do.* That is, we have brought nothing of our own, but only performed our proper duties. Here Christ is speaking of such a perfect keeping of the Law as exists nowhere. For even the most perfect of all are at the furthest pole from what the Law demands. He is not here discussing the question of whether we are saved by works, but whether the observation of the Law deserves any reward from God. And this He denies, since God keeps us as His bondslaves and therefore can claim whatever issues from us as His by right. But even if it were true that a reward was owed to the observation of the Law in respect of merit, yet it would not therefore follow that anyone is justified by the merits of works. For we all fail, not only in that our obedience is defective, but because no part of it accords precisely with God's judgment.

*And he spake a parable unto them to the end that they ought always to pray, and not to faint; saying, There was in a city a judge, which feared not God, and regarded not man: and there was a widow in that city; and she came unto him, saying, Avenge me of mine adversary. And he would not for a while: but afterward he said within himself, Though I fear not God, nor regard man; yet because this widow troubleth me, I will avenge her, lest she wear me out at last by her coming. And the Lord said, Hear what the unrighteous judge saith. And shall not God avenge his elect, which cry to him day and night, and he is longsuffering*

*over them?  I say unto you, that he will avenge them speedily.  How-*
*beit when the Son of Man cometh, shall he find faith on the earth?*
(Luke 18.1-8)

We know how uncommon and difficult a virtue is persistence in
prayer; and in this our unbelief betrays itself, for unless our first
requests are answered, we at once give up hope and also the practice
of prayer.  The only legitimate proof of trust is when anyone who is
disappointed of his desire does not lose heart.  Therefore Christ has
good cause to commend perseverance in prayer to His disciples.  He
uses a parable which is difficult at first sight, but is especially apt for
His purpose in teaching them to wait importunately on God the Father
until at last they wring from Him what it seemed He was not willing
to give.  Not that God is overcome by our prayers and at last unwillingly moved to mercy, but because the actual event does not at
once bear witness to the fact that He is favourable to our wishes.  In
the parable Christ introduces a widow who gets what she wants from
an unfair and cruel judge because she did not stop asking.  The point
of it is that God does not help His people immediately because in a
sense He wants them to tire themselves out with praying.  Moreover,
however wretched and cast down are those who pray to Him, yet so
long as they do not fail in a regular tenor of praying, He will look on
them at last to help them in their necessities.  The comparison is not
completely applicable, for there is a big difference between an ungodly,
cruel man and the God who inclines to mercy.  But Christ wanted to
teach them that believers need not fear that continual praying will not
prevail upon the Father of mercy if they can by their importunity
compel men who are given up to cruelty.  The wicked and hard judge
could not put up with the widow's solicitations and at last he unwillingly gave in.  How then shall the prayers of believers be unfruitful
if only they persist in them?  Therefore if we are weakened by boredom, if when we have done a little we give up, or if our ardour in
prayer languishes because God seems to have deaf ears, let us still be
convinced that success will be assured even if it is not yet seen.  And
in this confidence let us so wrestle against our impatience that a longer
delay does not break our perseverance in prayer.

Luke 18.7. *And shall not God avenge.*  The judge whom Christ por-
trayed as completely beyond hope, who was not only hardened before
God but shamelessly cared nothing what people would think of him,
at last opened his eyes to the widow's miseries.  There is no doubt at
all that believers will experience at least the same success so long as
they do not cease to wait upon God.  But we must observe that, in
accommodating His parable to His teaching, Christ did not make God

like a depraved and human judge, but indicated a very different reason why He puts believers off for a long time and does not at once stretch out His hand to them in action—because He is patient. Therefore if God overlooks our injuries longer than we wish, let us know that it happens of His fatherly purpose, to exercise us in endurance. This temporary and apparent ignoring is not at all an eternal impunity of the wicked. But when He promises that God will avenge them speedily, it should be referred to His providence. We are so headlong and He does not run quickly enough to bring us timely help according to our fleshly mind. But if it were lawful to penetrate into His counsel, we should know (so far as it is good for us) that His help is always prompt and ready and He does not delay one moment but is at hand every second.

Yet it may be asked how Christ can here teach His disciples to seek vengeance when elsewhere He bids them pray for their persecutors. I reply that the fact that Christ was here treating of vengeance in no way discredits that teaching. God declares that He will be the avenger of His believers not so as to loosen the bridle to their carnal affections, but to persuade them that their salvation is dear and precious to Him and that in this way He invites them to trust in His help. If they put away hatred and are pure and free from a depraved desire for revenge and are well-disposed by the moving of the Spirit and then implore God's help, their prayer will be lawful and holy and will be heard by God. But because nothing is more difficult than to put off vicious affections and to conceive pure and sincere prayers, we must pray the Lord to direct and over-rule our hearts by His Spirit, so that we may righteously invoke God's vengeance and He will answer our request.

Luke 18.8. *When the Son of man shall come.* In this sentence Christ tells us that it will not be surprising if afterwards men sink under their evils, for they neglect the true remedy. And He wants to forestall the offence which we are always conceiving at the shameful confusion of everything. There flourish on every hand perfidy, cruelty, plots, frauds, violence, inequitable ways, shamelessness; the poor groan under their oppression, the innocent are harassed arrogantly and insultingly; yet God seems asleep in heaven. And so the flesh imagines a blind rule of fortune. But Christ here tells us that men are justly left without heavenly help if they neither know how, nor wish, to trust in it. For it is not right that those who do nothing but grumble inwardly and give no place to His providence should be helped by the Lord. Christ expressly foretells that from the time of His ascent into heaven until His return men will everywhere be unbelieving; and by these words He means that if the Redeemer does not appear quickly, the blame for His slowness will lie at men's door, since hardly anyone will look for

Him. Would that the result of this prediction were not so obvious among us! But experience shows us that, although a vast accumulation of ills overwhelms the world, there is hardly a weak spark of faith to be seen even in a few. Some take the word 'faith' as 'soundness'; but the former sense seems to fit the context better.

*And he spake also this parable unto certain which trusted in themselves that they were righteous, and set all others at nought: Two men went up into the temple to pray; the one a Pharisee, and the other a publican. The Pharisee stood and prayed thus with himself, God, I thank thee, that I am not as the rest of men, extortioners, unjust, adulterers, or even as this publican. I fast twice on the sabbath. I give tithes of all that I get. But the publican, standing afar off, would not lift up so much as his eyes unto heaven, but smote his breast, saying, God, be merciful to me a sinner. I say unto you, This man went down to his house justified rather than the other: for everyone that exalteth himself shall be humbled; but he that humbleth himself shall be exalted.* (Luke 18.9-14)

Christ now gives us commands about another virtue necessary for praying aright: that believers shall come into God's sight only single-minded and cast down. There is no more deadly disease than pride, yet it is so deep-rooted in all that it can hardly be expelled and torn out by any means at all. It is astonishing that men are so silly as to dare to raise their crests against God and to boast of their merits before Him. For although on a human level we may be bewitched by ambition, yet when we are in God's sight we ought to forget all such confidence. But each thinks himself sufficiently humbled if he has used a sham prayer asking pardon. From this we gather that the Lord's admonition was not unnecessary. Moreover, Christ here rebukes and condemns two faults: a depraved self-trust, and pride in despising our fellow-men. The one springs from the other. For whoever deceives himself with vain confidence cannot but exalt himself above his brothers. And no wonder, for how shall he not despise his equals who vaunts it over God? Whoever is puffed up with self-trust wages war openly on God. Only our self-abnegation makes Him favourable to us, when we are emptied of all trust in our own virtue and righteousness and rest on His mercy alone.

Luke 18.10. *Two men went up.* Christ compares two men who by their praying both presented a front of godly zeal. But in fact they were quite different. For the Pharisee who had put on his outward saintliness came to God and praised his own life and came in his own righteousness to offer the sacrifice of praise. The publican, however, like a wretched outcast, because he knew he was not worthy to come, creeps trembling to make his humble confession. And Christ asserts that God rejected the Pharisee and accepted the prayers of the publican. Now two causes are noted why the Pharisee suffered a repulse: he trusted in his own righteousness, and he esteemed himself and despised others. Yet he is not rebuked because he praised the strength of his free will, but because he trusted that God would be appeased with the merits of his works. For his thanksgiving, made entirely in the first person singular, is not at all a glorying in his own power, as if he had made himself righteous or merited anything by his own industry; rather he ascribes it to the grace of God that he is righteous. But although by thanking God he confesses that all his good works are a sheer benefit from God, yet because he trusts in his works and puts himself before others, he and his prayer are both rejected. From this we infer that men are not truly or completely humbled (even although they reckon that they can do nothing) unless they learn to cease to trust in the merits of their works and place their salvation in God's free goodness, so that all their trust is founded on it.

A remarkable passage! To some it seems sufficient to take from men any glorying in good works inasmuch as they are the gifts of the Holy Spirit. And so they think we are justified freely on the basis that God finds in us no righteousness except what He has given. But Christ goes further than this, and not only ascribes the power of doing right to the grace of the Spirit but also empties us of all trust in works. For the Pharisee was not blamed because he usurped what was proper to God but because he trusted that he had God's favour by merits, inasmuch as he deserved it. Therefore let us realize that although a man may ascribe the praise for good works to God, yet if he imagines that the righteousness of those works is the cause of his salvation, or trusts in it, he is condemned for perverted pride.

And note that this man is accused not of the baseless ambition of those who glory before men when they are all the while aware of their faults, but of hidden hypocrisy. For it is not said that he was singing his own praises but that he prayed silently and inwardly. But even if he had spread his fame abroad at the top of his voice, his inward pride would have been an abomination to God. And his glorying was two-fold. First he releases himself from the common guilt of mankind; and then he advances his own virtues. He denies that he is like the rest, for he is free from the guilt of sin which reigns everywhere in the world. And when he boasts that he fasts twice every sabbath and gives away a tenth of his possessions it is as if he were saying that he did more than the Law demands. In the same way, papist monks proclaim works of supererogation, as if they could easily fulfil God's Law. Although every man is the more obliged to give thanks to their Author for the measure of virtues which God has bestowed upon him and it is a godly exercise for him to count up how much he has received so that he does not bury God's beneficence in ingratitude, yet we must note two things: we must not be puffed up by our trust, as if we had satisfied God; and we must not be insolent and contemptuous towards our brethren. The Pharisee sinned both ways. He falsely claimed righteousness for himself and so left nothing for God's mercy. And he despised all others. But Christ would not have rejected his giving of thanks if it had not been infected with these two vices; but since by winking at his own sins this arrogant hypocrite put forward at God's judgment the fabrication of his sound and perfect righteousness, it was necessary that he and his ungodly, sacrilegious audacity should be beaten down. The one and only hope of the godly, albeit they labour under the infirmity of the flesh, is to flee to the one and only mercy of God as soon as they recognize His goodness and to place their salvation in prayer for forgiveness.

But it may be asked how a man who was blinded by ungodly pride could be endued with such sanctity. For this sort of goodness can only flow from God's Spirit, who most certainly does not reign in hypocrites. I reply, his only trust was in an outward mask, as if the hidden and inward cleanness of the heart did not come in question. Granted that inwardly he was swarming with depraved desires, yet because he was only judged from what was visible, he can firmly plead his innocence. The Lord does not reprove him of vanity in falsely claiming what he did not possess; but we must know that none is free from rapine, injustice, lust, all vices, unless he is ruled by the Spirit of God.

In this place, as often elsewhere, *sabbath* is put for a week. But God never commanded in His Law that His servants were to fast every week; hence this fasting and tithing were voluntary practices and more than the Law prescribed.

Luke 18.13. *But the publican, standing afar off.* Christ is not laying down a general rule here, as if it were necessary to look down at the ground when we pray. He was merely using this as a sign of the humility which He commends to His disciples. Humility is being aware of our sins and preventing God's judgment by condemning them and making a frank confession of guilt so as to be reconciled to God. And this relates also to the shame which always accompanies penitence. For the Lord especially insists on this, that the publican knew only too well that he was wretched and lost and betook him to the mercy of God. For although he was a sinner, he trusted in free pardon and looked to God to be favourable to him. In sum, that he may receive favour he confesses that he is unworthy of it. And indeed, since it is only by the forgiveness of sins that God is reconciled to us, this is where we have to start if we want Him to accept our prayers. Moreover, he who begins by being convicted and guilty and yet asks for forgiveness is renouncing confidence in his works; and what Christ was aiming at was that God will only be entreated by those who flee trembling to His mercy alone.

Luke 18.14. *This man went down justified.* The comparison is imprecise. Christ was not merely giving the publican a higher rank than the Pharisee as if they were both righteous. He means that God accepted him and rejected the Pharisee. This verse teaches clearly what it really is to be justified—to stand before God as if we were righteous. For the publican was not said to be justified because he had suddenly acquired some new quality but because he was received into grace by the cancelling of his guilt and the blotting out of his sins. And from this it follows that righteousness consists in the forgiveness of sins. Because just as the Pharisee's virtues were stinking and polluted with depraved confidence, so that his laudable goodness before men counted for nothing with God, so the publican obtained righteousness by no help of the merits of his works but only by his prayer for pardon. Indeed, his hope was only in the pure mercy of God. But it seems absurd to force all into one rank, when the purity of the saints is very different from that of the publican. I reply that however much a man may advance in the worship of God and in true holiness, yet if he considers how far short he falls, he will be unable to pray in any other way than by beginning with confession of guilt. Some may be more, others less, but all in common are guilty. Wherefore Christ is without doubt laying down a law for all, as if He said that God is appeased only when we cease to trust in our works and pray to be reconciled freely. And even the Papists are forced to confess this to some degree, although they soon adulterate the doctrine with their depraved invention. They concede that all need the remedy of pardon, since none is perfect; but in the first place they make poor souls drunken with a trust in what they call partial righteousness, and then they tack on satisfactions to blot out their guilt. But the one foundation of our faith is that God accepts us, not because we deserve it, but because He does not impute our sins.

*And it came to pass, as he was on the way to Jerusalem, that he was passing through the midst of Samaria and Galilee. And as he entered into a certain village, there met him ten men that were lepers, which stood afar off: and they lifted up their voices, saying, Jesus, Master, have mercy on us. And when he saw them, he said unto them, Go and shew yourselves unto the priests. And it came to pass, as they went, they were cleansed. And one of them, when he saw that he was healed, turned back, with a loud voice glorifying God; and he fell upon his face at his feet, giving him thanks: and he was a Samaritan. And Jesus answering said, Were not the ten cleansed? but where are the nine? There were none found that returned to give glory to God, save this stranger. And he said unto him, Arise, and go thy way: thy faith hath made thee whole. And being asked by the Pharisees, when the kingdom of God cometh, he answered them and said, The kingdom of God cometh not with observation: neither shall they say, Lo, here! or, Lo, there! for behold, the kingdom of God is within you.* (Luke 17.11-21)

In chapter 8 Matthew narrated, as did the other Evangelists, that a leper had been cleansed by Christ. Now Luke relates that a similar miracle of healing was performed on ten lepers. But the aim of this story is different. It shows up the disgusting and incredible ingratitude of the Jewish people, so that we need not be surprised that so many of Christ's benefits should have been suppressed among them, so many mighty works buried. One detail is added which makes their shame even worse. When the Lord had healed nine Jews, none of them returned to thank Him; they just furtively slipped off, as if they had forgotten that they were once diseased. Only the one Samaritan professed what he owed to Christ. Therefore on the one hand Christ's divine power shines forth; on the other there is reproved the ungodliness of the Jews in giving hardly any honour to such a clear miracle.

Luke 17.13. *Jesus, Master.* It would appear that they all had some faith, not only in that they implore Christ's help, but also because they call Him Master. Moreover, we may infer from their prompt obedience, that they were speaking sincerely and not hypocritically, for although they can see the foul sore in their flesh, yet as soon as they are commanded to show themselves to the priests, they obey. Add that they would not have gone to the priests unless they had been moved by faith; for it would have been nonsense for them to offer themselves to the men who had to diagnose leprosy and be attested as clean unless Christ's promise had meant more to them than the present sight of their disease. In their flesh they bear a visible leprosy, but at Christ's word alone they do not hesitate to profess their trust that they are clean. Therefore it cannot be denied that some seed of faith was set in their hearts. And although it is sure that they were not born again by the Spirit of adoption, yet it is not unreasonable that they had some elements of godliness. And this should make us fear lest it happen to us that the sparks of faith shining in us should be extin-

131

guished. For although a living faith which has its roots fixed in the Spirit of regeneration never dies, yet we see elsewhere that many conceive a transient faith which vanishes at once. This particular disease is too common, that our minds are moved to seek God when necessity presses us (and the Lord Himself also invites us by the secret impulse of His Spirit) but after we have received what we ask, an ungrateful forgetfulness swallows up that feeling of godliness. Thus poverty and hunger beget faith and abundance kills it.

Luke 17.14. *Show yourselves unto the priests.* This reply is equivalent to His saying that they were clean. For we know that the discerning of leprosy was committed in the Law to the priests, so that they might distinguish between the clean and the unclean. Thus Christ both leaves them their rights and also makes them witnesses and assayers of His miracle. We have said that these sick men thought piously and reverently of Christ in that they at once conceived a hope of healing merely from His words. But the Papists foolishly build their auricular confession on this. I grant that Christ sent the lepers to the priests; but it was not to vomit up their sins into the priests' ears, but rather that they might offer a sacrifice as the Law laid down. Nor were they sent to cleanse themselves, in the way that confession brings cleansing to the Papists, but to show the priests that they were already clean. They are twice foolish for not reckoning what an evil stain of bad repute they cast on their confession—that they have done well when out of the whole band of those who went to the priests only a tenth returned to Christ and all the rest impiously kept away from Him. They cannot use this as a pretext for their confession without it rebounding on them that none returned from the priests to give glory to God. But setting aside these foolish prescriptions, we should keep to why mention was made of the priests.

*And it came to pass, as they went.* Here the divine power of Christ and His words shines out, and also evidence was given of how pleased God is with the obedience of faith. For this very sudden change came to pass because they had a good hope and did not hesitate to make the journey at Christ's command. If that transient faith, without living roots and only producing the blade, was divinely crowned with such a wonderful result, how much more excellent a reward awaits our faith if it is fixed sincerely and firmly in God? For although the physical healing did not advance the salvation of the nine lepers, and they only received a temporary gift from their fleeting and frail faith, yet under this type we are shown how efficacious true faith will be.

Luke 17.15. *And one of them, etc.* It is not clear whether he returned from the middle of his journey, although Luke's words seem to suggest this. But to me it is more probable that he came to give thanks after he had heard the decision of the priests. For he had to be restored to society by the priests, and it would also not have been right for him to neglect Christ's commandment and to defraud God's temple of a sacrifice. Or perhaps another conjecture might be more acceptable, that as soon as he saw he was clean and before he had received testimony from the priests, he was moved by a godly and holy desire to return to the very author of his healing and begin his sacrifice with thanksgiving.

Christ's words contain an underlying expostulation with the whole nation; for He unfavourably compares with this one foreigner the many Jews who were used to gulping down God's benefits without any feeling of godliness. And this is why Christ won hardly any fame by so many and such wonderful miracles among them. Yet let us know that we are all condemned by this complaint if we do not repay God's benefits with at least the common decency of gratitude.

Luke 17.19. *Thy faith hath saved thee.* Some interpreters restrict the word 'saved' to the physical cleansing. But if this is so, it may be asked, since Christ praises the lively faith of the Samaritan, how the other nine were saved; for they were all alike healed. And so we must say that Christ here estimated God's gift differently from the way heathen men do, in that it was a symbol or pledge of salvation by His fatherly love. The nine lepers were cleansed. But because they were ungodly and forgot God's grace, their ingratitude infected and contaminated their healthiness. And so they do not receive the advantage that they should. Therefore faith alone sanctifies God's gifts to us and makes them pure, and when they are used lawfully they turn out to our salvation. And finally by this word Christ declared how we rightly enjoy the benefits of God. We gather that the eternal salvation of our souls is joined with the temporal gift. The Samaritan was saved by his faith. How? Certainly not in that he was cured of leprosy (for this he had in common with the others), but because he was received into the number of God's children to receive from His hand this token (*tessera*) of His fatherly love.

Luke 17.20. *And being asked by the Pharisees.* Without doubt this question was raised in mockery. For since Christ was continually talking of the nearness of God's Kingdom, although no change occurred in the outward condition of the Jews, wicked and malicious people thought that this would be a handy excuse for harassing Him. Therefore they ask Him sarcastically how long the kingdom is going to take in coming, as if He had been babbling and trifling about God's Kingdom. But if anyone thinks that they asked rather because of the grossness of their opinion than out of mockery, I shall not argue about it.

133

*The Kingdom of God cometh not.* To my mind Christ now turns from these dogs and addresses His reply to the disciples. Often when He was provoked by the wicked He turned it into an opportunity for teaching and thus He divinely eluded their malice and also the truth spoken against their quibbles shone the more brightly. Now Christ here used 'observation' to mean a clearness easily observed; as if He were denying that the Kingdom of God would be transcendent in obvious display. He means that they are quite wrong who look with their physical eyes for the Kingdom of God, since it is in no way physical or earthly but the inward and spiritual renewing of the soul. He tells them that the very nature of the Kingdom puts them in the wrong when they look here and there to observe visible marks of it. It is as if He said: 'The restoration of the Church which God promised is to be sought inwardly; for He quickens His elect to heavenly newness and sets up His kingdom in them.' And here He indirectly rebukes the stupidity of the Pharisees, in that they aspired only after what was earthly and transient. Yet we must also note that Christ was speaking only of the beginnings of God's Kingdom; for we now begin to be reformed to the image of God by His Spirit so that the complete renewal of ourselves and the whole world may follow in its own time.

*And it came to pass, when Jesus had finished these parables, he departed thence. And coming into his own country he taught them in their synagogue, insomuch that they were astonished, and said, Whence hath this man this wisdom, and these mighty works? Is not this the carpenter's son? is not his mother called Mary? and his brethren, James, and Joses, and Simon, and Judas? And his sisters, are they not all with us? Whence then hath this man all these things? And they were offended in him. But Jesus said unto them, A prophet is not without honour, save in his own country, and in his own house. And he did not many mighty works there because of their unbelief.* (Matt. 13.53-58)

*And he went out from thence; and he cometh into his own country; and his disciples follow him. And when the sabbath was come, he began to teach in the synagogue: and many hearing him were astonished, saying, Whence hath this man these things? and, What is the wisdom that is given unto this man, and what mean such mighty works wrought by his hands? Is not this the carpenter, the son of Mary, and brother of James, and Joses, and Judas, and Simon? and are not his sisters here with us? And they were offended in him. And Jesus said unto them, A prophet is not without honour, save in his own country, and among his own kin,*

*and in his own house. And he could there do no mighty work save that
he laid his hands upon a few sick folk, and healed them. And he
marvelled because of their unbelief. And he went round about the
villages teaching.* (Mark 6.1-6)

Matt. 13.53. *When Jesus had finished.* Matthew does not mean that
Christ went into His own country as soon as He had finished preaching;
for it appears from Mark that there was quite an interval between.
But the meaning is that when He had taught for some time in Judaea,
He returned to the Galileans who, however, received Him rather
unkindly. Luke 4 relates a not dissimilar story, but it is not the same.
It is not surprising that Christ's fellow countrymen should at first have
been put off by Him, reckoning that His family was mean and obscure
and His upbringing lowly, nor that this made them grumble at His
teaching, and then afterwards they persisted in their malice and did
not cease to malign Him whenever He wanted to execute His prophetic
office among them. Therefore this second rejection of Christ teaches
us that the citizens of Nazareth were not improved by time but always
made the same contempt an obstacle against hearing Christ.

Matt. 13.54. *Insomuch that they were astonished.* They were stupefied
by the fact that Christ, who had never learned to read or write but had
been employed as a workman from childhood should be such a teacher
and should be animated with such a divine wisdom. They should
have seen God's hand in this miracle, but their ingratitude made
them cover themselves in darkness. Will they or not, they are forced to
surprise; yet they despise Him. What is this but to reject a prophet
divinely taught because he was not brought up in a human school?
In fact they strangle themselves with their own testimony when they
render such a remarkable testimony to Christ's doctrine which yet
found no place among them because it did not have the usual earthly
origin. Why did they not lift up their eyes to heaven to learn that
what transcends human reason comes forth from God? Add that the
mighty works joined to this teaching should have touched them more
strongly, or at least should have aroused their overmuch stupidity to
give glory to God. For indeed, when God acts in unaccustomed ways,
He shows the power of His hand the more clearly. But the Nazarenes
simply made this into a veil with which they maliciously covered their
eyes. We see, then, that men are not simply hindered by ignorance
but deliberately seize hold of offences so that they may not follow
where God calls. But we should argue to the contrary, that when
human means fail, God's power is manifest clearly to us and so should
receive its true praise.

Matt. 13.55. *Is not this the carpenter's son?* We know that it happened by the wonderful purpose of God that Christ lived a private life until He was thirty. It was therefore wrong and unjust of the Nazarenes to conceive this offence. Rather they should have embraced Him reverently, as if He had suddenly come down from heaven. They see God at work in Christ—and deliberately turn their eyes to Joseph and Mary and all His relatives and let their obscure estate be a veil over the manifest light. In the Hebrew manner relatives of any sort are called 'brethren', as we have said elsewhere. It was therefore very ignorant of Helvidius to imagine that Mary had many sons because there are several mentions of Christ's brethren.

Matt. 13.57. *A prophet is not without honour.* I have expounded this sentence more fully in John 4. It could be just a common proverb, that those who are pre-eminent in excellent gifts are nowhere so unappreciated as in their own country. And here man's ingratitude betrays itself when the more He offers Himself to them the more they audaciously reject God in the gifts of His Spirit. But I willingly subscribe to Chrysostom, who thinks that this saying was particularly aimed at the Jews. But Christ properly accommodates to His own Galileans what was usually said of the whole nation, for nowhere was He less respected than in His native land. Therefore He deservedly reproves them for driving Him away when they should have been the first to have embraced the grace He offered. For it is quite senseless that a prophet of God should be despised in the place where he was born when people to whom he is a stranger follow him eagerly.

Matt. 13.58. *And he did not many mighty works.* Mark says more emphatically that He was not able to do any mighty work. But they agree completely in substance: Christ's own fellow townsfolk by their ungodliness prevented Him from performing more mighty works among them. He had already given them some taste; but they deliberately deadened themselves so as not to perceive it. Augustine aptly compares faith to the open mouth of a jar, whereas unbelief is like a lid which covers the jar and prevents the liquid being poured in by God. And this is very true. For when the Lord sees that His power is not received by us, He finally takes it away. And yet we complain that He does not give the help which our unbelief drives far from us! By saying that Christ was not able, Mark magnifies the guilt of those who hindered His goodness. For unbelievers do indeed (as far as lies in them) restrict God's hand by their obstinacy. Not that God is overcome as if He were the weaker, but because they will not allow His power to work. But we must observe how Mark says that nevertheless some sick people were healed. For we learn from this that Christ's goodness fought with their malice and emerged victorious. We experience the same thing with God every day; for although He justly and necessarily restricts His power because it has not an open entrance into us, yet we see that He does not fail to do us good and makes a way where there is none. A wonderful struggle! We try every method of suppressing God's grace and keeping it from us, and yet it breaks through triumphant and does its work in spite of our reluctance.

*At that season Herod the tetrarch heard the report concerning Jesus, and said unto his servants, This is John the Baptist; he is risen from the dead; and therefore do these powers work in him.* (Matt. 14.1-2)

*And king Herod heard thereof, for his name had become known; and he said, John the Baptist is risen from the dead, and therefore do these powers work in him. But others said, It is Elijah. And others said, It is a prophet, or even as one of the prophets. But when Herod heard thereof, he said, It is John, whom I beheaded: he is risen from the dead.* (Mark 6.14-15)

*Now Herod the tetrarch heard of all that was done: and he was much perplexed, because that it was said by some, that John was risen from the dead; and by some, that Elijah had appeared; and by others, that one of the old prophets was risen again. And Herod said, John I beheaded: but who is this, about whom I hear such things? And he sought to see him.* (Luke 9.7-9)

The Evangelists relate this to teach us that Christ's name was famous everywhere, so that the Jews could not plead ignorance. Otherwise this doubt might have stolen over the minds of many: 'Why was it that while Christ lived on earth Judaea was very much at rest, as if He had withdrawn into a corner and had revealed His divine power to no-one?' Therefore the Evangelists bear witness that news about Him was current everywhere and had even penetrated Herod's court.

Matt. 14.2. *And he said unto his servants.* From Luke's words we learn that this was not Herod's own idea but that it was a surmise inspired by popular rumour. I have no doubt that hatred of this tyrant and loathing for the wicked murder was, as often happens, the cause of this rumour. The superstition that the dead return to life in another person was firm in men's minds, as I have said elsewhere. Now they seize on a cognate idea, that when Herod cruelly put this holy man to death he did not achieve his end, for John was suddenly raised from the dead by the wonderful power of God, and would be a fiercer avenger of his enemy's wickedness. But Mark and Luke say that there were various reports. Some thought He was Elijah, others one of the prophets or the equal of the prophets in the excellence of His spirit. We have said elsewhere why He was supposed to be Elijah rather than one of the other prophets. God had promised through Malachi[1] that Elijah would come and collect the scattered Church. But they misinterpreted this prophecy as meaning Elijah himself, whereas it was a simple comparison to this effect. In order that the Messiah may not be obscure when He comes and that the grace of redemption may not elude the people, an Elijah like him of old will come first to restore the ruined state and the overturned worship of God. Therefore he will go before the Messiah in a singular power of the Spirit to make manifest that great day. The Jews, crass interpreters, applied this to Elijah the Tishbite, as if he were to exist anew and perform the prophetic office. Some hazard the guess that either one of the ancient prophets had risen or that he was a great man who did not fall far short of them. It is surprising that when they put forward these different opinions the true one did not occur to any of them, especially since the contemporary situation pointed them to Christ. God had promised them a redeemer to bring help to the wretched and lost. The extreme need into which they were cast demanded above all God's help. The Redeemer is present, first heralded by John and then Himself bearing witness to His office; they are forced to acknowledge something divine in Him, and yet they slip into imaginings and transmute Him into other persons. This is how the world is accustomed by its wicked ingratitude to extinguish the grace which God offers it. As for Herod, as I mentioned a little earlier, it was not his own idea that John was risen; but as bad consciences waver in terror and bend at every breeze, he easily conceived what he feared. And God often alarms the ungodly with blind terrors. They try to harden themselves against outside assaults, but they cannot get any rest from the harsh punishment of their inward tormentor.

*Therefore do these powers work in him.* It is surprising that they should have been led to this conclusion. In all the course of his preaching John performed no sign. Therefore there seems to be no reason for them to imagine that the man whose remarkable miracles they saw was John. But what they are thinking is that he is performing miracles for the first time to prove his resurrection and to witness that he had been a holy prophet of God irreligiously killed by Herod and that now he came forth, so to say sacrosanct, that none might dare to hurt him again. They think that powers 'work' in Him (that is, are effective in Him), so that He may have the greater authority and that it may become plain that the Lord is with Him.

[1] Mal. 4.5-6

*For Herod had laid hold on John, and bound him, and put him in prison for the sake of Herodias, his brother Philip's wife. For John said unto him, It is not lawful for thee to have her. And when he would have put him to death, he feared the multitude, because they counted him as a prophet. But when Herod's birthday came, the daughter of Herodias danced in the midst, and pleased Herod. Whereupon he promised with an oath to give her whatever she should ask. And she, being before instructed by her mother, saith, Give me here the head of John the Baptist in a charger. And the king was grieved; but for the sake of his oaths, and of them which sat at meat with him, he commanded it to be given; and he sent, and beheaded John in prison. And his head was brought in a charger, and given to the damsel: and she brought it to her mother. And his disciples came, and took up the corpse, and buried him; and they went and told Jesus.* (Matt. 14.3-12)

*For Herod himself had sent forth and laid hold upon John, and bound him in prison for the sake of Herodias, his brother Philip's wife: for he had married her. For John said unto Herod, It is not lawful for thee to have thy brother's wife. And Herodias set herself against him, and desired to kill him: and she could not; for Herod feared John, knowing that he was a righteous man and a holy, and kept him safe. And when he heard him, he was much perplexed; and he heard him gladly. And when a convenient day was come, that Herod on his birthday made a supper to his lords, and the high captains, and the chief men of Galilee; and when the daughter of Herodias herself came in and danced, she pleased Herod and them that sat at meat with him; and the king said unto the damsel, Ask of me whatsoever thou wilt, and I will give it thee. And he sware unto her, Whatsoever thou shalt ask of me, I will give it thee, unto the half of my kingdom. And she went out, and said unto her mother, What shall I ask? And she said, The head of John the Baptist. And she came in straightway with haste unto the king, and asked, saying, I will that thou forthwith give me in a charger the head of John the Baptist. And the king was exceeding sorry; but for the sake of his oaths, and of them that sat at meat, he would not reject her. And straightway the king sent forth a soldier of his guard, and commanded to bring his head: and he went and beheaded him in the prison, and brought his head in a charger, and gave it to the damsel: and the damsel gave it to her mother. And when his disciples heard thereof, they came and took up his corpse, and laid it in a tomb.* (Mark 6.17-29)

Luke omits this story now because he has it elsewhere. I also do not want to trouble readers by writing the same thing twice, and so I shall be brief here. The Evangelists relate that John had been taken because he had openly condemned the stealing of Herodias and the incestuous marriage with her. Josephus gives a different reason: that Herod was suspicious of John because he feared an uprising against himself. And it may be that the tyrant made this an excuse for his crime, or that this rumour was spread, for unjust violence and cruelty are open to many accusations. But the Evangelists are relating the event itself—Herod was hostile to this holy man because he had been reproved by him. Moreover Josephus is mistaken in thinking that Herodias was stolen not from his brother Philip but from Herod the king of Chalcis. For in the period at which the Evangelist wrote the crime was not only fresh in memory but had even been committed before everybody's eyes. Josephus elsewhere tells us that Philip was of a mild spirit, and I do not doubt that it made Herod the bolder when he thought that he could injure a quiet, peaceful and modest man with impunity. Another probable conjecture is that Herodias seems to have been married to her uncle Philip rather than to her great uncle, her grandfather's brother, by now old and decrepit. Antipas, the Herod mentioned here, and Philip were not uterine brothers; the one was by Marthaca the third wife of Herod the Great, the other by Cleopatra.

But now to return to the Evangelists. They say that John was thrown into prison because he had rebuked Herod's crime more freely than the tyrant's rage could bear. The atrocity in itself was shocking and infamous. Not only did he keep another man's wife, stolen from her lawful bed, but the man he had injured was his own brother. When John interferes with an open rebuke, Herod has good grounds for fearing that an uprising will break out. His lust would not let him correct his sin; and when he had imprisoned God's prophet he promised himself freedom without interference. It has been due to ignorance of history that many have entered on the unnecessary argument as to 'whether it is lawful for me to marry a woman who has been my brother's wife'. For although natural shame shrinks from such a marriage, yet John condemns the stealing rather than the incest, for Herod had stolen his brother's wife by force or guile. Apart from this, it would have been less lawful for him to marry his niece than his brother's widow. And there is no doubt that such a flagrant crime was everywhere blamed. But whereas others attacked and cursed Herod behind his back, John alone bluntly rebuked him to his face in an effort to bring him to repentance. This teaches us with what inflexible courage God's servants should be armed when they have to do with princes. In nearly every court hypocrisy and servile adulation reign and princes become accustomed to delicacy and will lend their ears to no voice which sharply rebukes their vices. But because God's prophet must not disregard such a shameful crime, John encounters him, even if as a troublesome and unwelcome counsellor, and rather than fail in his duty does not hesitate to incur the tyrant's wrath, especially when he was aware that he had little chance of moving a man infatuated with the harlot's charms.

Matt. 14.5. *And when he would have put him to death*. It seems as if there are some verbal discrepancies between Matthew and Mark. The former says Herod wanted to kill him but was restrained by fear of the people. But Mark accuses only Herodias of this cruelty. The solution is easy. At first Herod was unwilling without compulsion of a stronger necessity to kill the holy man, for he revered him, and indeed religion itself stood in the way of dealing so savagely with a prophet of God. Yet even when he was inspired with madness by that female fury to want the holy man's death, he was held back by a new obstacle, fear of a popular uprising.

Mark's words must be noted. He says that Herodias lay in wait for him. Because Herod was not ready to kill him, she either tried to get round him by cunning tricks or she plotted a secret death for the holy man. I prefer the former view, that she tried to gain her husband's collusion by deceit, but in vain so long as Herod's conscience forbade him to go to extremes with the holy man. Another fear then came over him, that the outrage of his death would provoke an insurrection. But Mark only mentions what hindered Herod from giving way to the harlot's requests. What Herodias wanted, as soon as John had been thrown into prison, was his secret execution. But Herod honoured the holy man and would willingly have followed his counsels.

Moreover, the fear mentioned here was not a dread conceived of someone else, as we fear those who have a certain authority, although we reckon them unworthy the honour. But this fear was a willing respect, in that Herod dared not despise one whom he was convinced was a holy man and a faithful minister of God. And this is important, for although John was well aware that in many respects it was worth his while to have the Tetrarch's favour, yet he was not afraid to alienate him if the price of keeping his favour was a treacherous connivance at a notorious and infamous crime. He could have declared that he was not consulting his own interests and had an eye only to the public good. For it is certain that he asked nothing for himself but only wanted Herod to agree with his godly advice which was related to the legitimate administration of the kingdom. But because he saw that this sort of bargaining was not right, to gain some favours at the price of betraying the truth, he would rather turn a friend into an enemy than by his flattery and silence nourish the evil which he is forced severely to repulse. Therefore by his example John lays down a sure rule for all godly teachers, that they should not connive at the vices of princes even in exchange for the most desirable profit to the common good. In Herod as in a mirror the Spirit of God shows that it often happens that those who do not sincerely revere God are nevertheless ready in some respects to obey His commands so long as He will be a little less strict towards them. But when they are dealt with more strictly, they cast off the yoke and rush into obstinacy and madness. There is therefore no reason why those who accept much sensible advice should be pleased with themselves until they have learned to devote themselves entirely to God.

Matt. 14.6. *But when Herod's birthday came.* The Evangelists now begin to relate the trickery by which Herodias at last achieved John's death which she had long been plotting. She got her chance at the ceremonial banquet that Herod gave on his birthday. For these splendid displays can hardly fail to be accompanied by luxury, pride, unbridled mirth and much other wickedness and evil. Not that it is wrong in itself to give a good party; but such is the propensity of the human mind to wantonness that when the reins are loosed men easily go astray. The old custom of celebrating one's birthday can not be disapproved in itself; for as often as it recurs the day should remind each of us that we must give thanks to the Lord for bringing us into the world and leading us by His blessing through many years; and it should also recall to our mind how we have wasted in evil and uselessness the time divinely allowed us; and lastly, it should make us commend ourselves to God's keeping for the rest of our life. But nothing is so pure but it is corrupted by the vices of the world. A birthday should be holy, but the greater part profane it with disgusting corruptions and hardly any banquet is free from dissolute wantonness—too much drinking, and that opens the gate to impure or shameless talk, and in the end no temperance is observed. This is why the holy Job offered a sacrifice when his sons took it in turns to give feasts; he reckoned that men never moderate themselves so well as not to sin in many ways when companion eggs on companion to mirth. And so it happened that Herod, wishing to treat his guests very magnificently, allowed his wife's daughter to dance. This shows only too well the sort of discipline that prevailed in his court; for although many then allowed themselves freedom in dancing, yet in a marriageable girl dancing was a shameful mark of lasciviousness and harlotry. But Herodias had shaped her daughter Salome to her own morals—no doubt lest she should disgrace her. And what followed? The irreligious murder of a holy prophet. The strong wine so excited Herod that he forgot all gravity and common-sense and promised to give this dancing-girl up to a half of his kingdom. What a shameful way of going on, that a drunken king can not only watch with equanimity this lewd spectacle in his family but can offer such a reward! It teaches us to look out carefully for the devil, lest he should entangle us in like snares.

Mark 6.24. *And she went out and said unto her mother.* It is not surprising that John's death meant so much to Herodias. Some conjecture that she was moved by revenge; but they have no grounds for this. It was rather that a fear of being put away burned and tortured her; for mostly adulterers get ashamed of their lust when they conceive an aversion [for their partner?]. And she hoped that Herod would be bound yet more tightly to her by this crime if the foulness of their adulterous marriage were atoned (*mactatum*) by the blood of the prophet. To rule securely in the future she wanted him wiped out, for she believed he was her one enemy. From this we learn also what a miserable anxiety always torments bad consciences. John was kept in prison. This tyrannical and cruel woman could have kept the prophet shut off from all intercourse with the outside world. But she cannot rest in her worry and fear until he is put out of the way. This also helps to show the power of God's Word, that the voice of the holy man, shut up in prison as he was, can tear the mind of the king's wife like the severest torture.

Mark 6.26. *And the king was exceeding sorry.* As we have said, there was no religion left in his heart; but he foresaw that his crime would be detested and he was afraid of the infamy and condemnation, and this was why he repented of his levity. Yet he did not dare deny the dancing-girl in case he should be accused of inconstancy—as if it were worse to retract a rash and foolish promise than to stand firm in a wicked crime. But because in the usual vanity of kings he does not want to go back on what he has once proclaimed, he orders the prophet to be killed out of hand. Now we gather that Herod was banqueting in the castle of Macherus, where Josephus says that John was imprisoned. It is worth while noting that the Evangelist says that it was on account of his oath and of the guests who were present; from which we infer that if he had sworn a hundred times without any witnesses present he would not have kept his promise. There was no inward religion to restrain Herod; he was driven precipitately by ambition when he did not reckon it honest not to keep his word. It often happens that the ungodly fail in their duty because they do not look to God but are only concerned not to fall under the reproach of men. Moreover, had Herod kept before his eyes only the sanctity of his oath and not a shame of men, he would still have sinned more gravely in foolishly performing what he had promised than if he had broken his oath. First, it was a perverse haste in swearing, to confirm his promise on something doubtful. Then when it became clear that he could not get out of what he had promised and he was compelled to go on with the wicked crime, he had no right to use God's holy name in such a shameful act—for what is more foreign to God than to preside at an ungodly murder? If a personal loss is concerned, let him who swore rashly bear the punishment of his foolishness. But men must beware lest when they have taken God's name in vain they do not double their sacrilege by using their oath as a pretext for committing another crime. From this it follows that monastic vows, when they are tied up with manifest impiety are no more binding on the conscience than are magical exorcisms; for God does not wish His holy name to be used to confirm sin. Yet this verse teaches us to take care not to promise anything thoughtlessly and also not to add obstinacy to levity.

Mark 6.28. *And gave it to the damsel.* This blackens the atrocity still further. After he was dead, the head of this holy man was treated as a matter of jest. But the Lord sometimes subjects His people to the pride of the ungodly until at last He shows how precious their blood is in His sight. Herodias exults that she has gained her desire, and cruelly triumphs over her critic. But later on she would be stripped of her riches and driven out not only from her royal honour but even from her birthplace and all help; in poverty and exile she would drag out a wretched existence. And this was a sweet sight to the angels and to all good men. That the guests are forced to defile their eyes with the sight of this abominable ceremony teaches us that those who frequent royal tables often get mixed up in many crimes. No deed of blood may stain the meal, yet everything is so full of every kind of wickedness that those who go must at least be given up to the tricks of a pimp.

Mark 6.29. *His disciples came.* The woman's savagery went so far as to leave the holy man's corpse unburied. For it is probable that when his disciples performed this duty, it had been thrown out by the tyrant's guards. Although the honour of burial does nothing for the dead, yet the Lord wishes us to observe this ceremony as a symbol of the final resurrection. Therefore this carefulness on the part of John's disciples in coming and committing the body of their master to the grave was pleasing to God. It was also a witness to their godliness, for in this way they professed that the teaching of the dead man still flourished in their hearts. This confession was therefore praiseworthy, especially since it was not without danger; for they could not give honour to the man killed by the executioner without provoking the rage of the tyrant against themselves.

*Now when Jesus heard it, he withdrew from thence in a boat, to a desert place apart: and when the multitudes heard thereof, they followed him on foot from the cities. And Jesus came forth, and saw a great multitude, and he had compassion on them, and healed their sick. And when even was come, the disciples came to him, saying, The place is desert, and the time is already past; send the multitudes away, that they may go into the villages, and buy themselves food. But Jesus said unto them, They have no need to go away; give ye them to eat. And they say unto him, We have here but five loaves, and two fishes. And he said, Bring them hither to me. And he commanded the multitudes to sit down on the grass; and he took the five loaves, and the two fishes, and looking up to heaven, he blessed, and brake and gave the loaves to the disciples, and the disciples to the multitudes. And they did all eat, and were filled: and they took up that which remained over of the broken pieces, twelve baskets full. And they that did eat were about five thousand men, beside women and children. (Matt. 14.13-21)*

*And the apostles gather themselves together unto Jesus; and they told him all things, whatsoever they had done, and whatsoever they had taught. And he saith unto them, Come ye yourselves apart into a desert place, and rest awhile. For there were many coming and going, and they had no leisure so much as to eat. And they went away in the boat to a desert place apart. And the people saw them going, and many knew them, and they ran there together on foot from all the cities, and outwent them and came together unto him. And he came forth and saw a great multitude, and he had compassion on them, because they were as sheep not having a shepherd: and he began to teach them many things. And when the day was now far spent, his disciples came unto him, and said, The place is a desert, and the day is now far spent: send them away, that they may go into the country and villages round about, and buy themselves bread, for they have nothing to eat. He answered and said unto them, Give ye them to eat. And they say unto him, Shall we go and buy two hundred pennyworth of bread, and give them to eat? And he saith unto them, How many loaves have ye? go and see. And when they knew, they say, Five, and two fishes. And he commanded them that they should sit down by companies upon the green grass. And they sat down in ranks, by hundreds, and by fifties. And he took the five loaves and the two fishes, and looking up to heaven, he blessed and brake the loaves; and he gave to the disciples to set before them; and the two fishes divided he among them all. And they did all eat, and were filled. And they took up the broken pieces, twelve basketfuls, and also of the fishes. And they that ate the loaves were five thousand men. (Mark 6.30-44)*

*And the apostles, when they were returned, declared unto him what things they had done. And he took them, and withdrew apart to a desert place of a city called Bethsaida. But the multitudes perceiving it followed him: and he welcomed them, and spake to them of the kingdom of God, and them that had need of healing he healed. And the day began to wear away; and the twelve came, and said unto him, Send the multitude away, that they may go into the villages and country round about, and lodge, and get victuals: for we are here in a desert place. But he said unto them, Give ye them to eat. And they said, We have no more than five loaves and two fishes; except we should go and buy food for all this people. For they were about five thousand men. And he said unto his disciples, Make them sit down in companies, about fifty each. And they did so, and made them all sit down. And he took the five loaves, and the two fishes, and looking up to heaven, he blessed them, and brake; and gave to the disciples to set before the multitude. And they did eat, and were all filled: and there was taken up that which remained over to them of broken pieces, twelve baskets.* (Luke 9.10-17)

Matt. 14.13. *Now when Jesus heard it.* John relates the same story, but does not mention Jesus' purpose in going across to the other side of the lake. Mark and Luke also differ somewhat from Matthew, for they say that the cause of the journey was to give the disciples some rest after they had returned from their mission. But there is no contradiction in this, for it may be that He had intended to assemble the apostles in a desert place where He could train them more easily for greater works, and an unexpected opportunity came at this time with the death of John. For John's death might well frighten their timid minds, in that the great prophet's end was a warning of what threatened them all. Certainly, as was declared earlier, when John was taken Christ removed out of Herod's jurisdiction to escape from his rage for the present. And now we may infer that Christ went away into the desert place to rescue His still fearful disciples from the fire. Moreover, it is not clear how long the apostles spent on their first mission. For, as we have said elsewhere, the time sequence was either neglected or not carefully observed by the Evangelists. To me it seems more probable that they were not sent out only once to publish abroad the Kingdom of Christ, but as occasion served they either repeated it in the same place or after some time went out into different places. And so now I understand that they were assembled together so that they might hereafter be continual comrades of Christ—as if it were said that they did not depart from the Master in such a way as if each perpetually pursued his ordinary office of teaching, but after they had preached for a time they returned afresh to school so as to profit the better.

*They followed him.* Although Christ, who foresaw all things, knew well what would happen, yet He wanted to provide for His disciples on the earthly level, so that the event itself might testify that He cared for them. The great crowd shows how well-known He was everywhere; and therefore the Jews were inexcusable, since their dullness deprived them of the blessing of salvation offered to them. For out of this great crowd who were suddenly inflamed with a desire to follow Christ, only a small number gave themselves to His teaching sincerely and constantly, as appears from John.

Matt. 14.14. *And he had compassion on them.* The other two (and especially Mark) express more clearly what moved Christ to this συμπάθεια—that He saw starving souls carried away by the ardour of desire to leave their homes and go out into the desert. The lack of teaching was a sign of a wretched scattering; and therefore Mark says that Christ had pity on them because they were as sheep without a shepherd. Not that, according to the Spirit of His Godhead, He acknowledges them all as His sheep; but as a man, He made an assessment from a review of the state of things. For it was no small sign of godliness for them to leave their own homes and to flock to the prophet of God, even when He tried to evade them. Then we should note that Christ remembered the person that He sustained. There had been laid on Him the office of teacher; and therefore He should for the time being reckon all the Jews to be of God's flock and Church until they alienated themselves from Him. Moreover, the feeling of compassion prevailed in Christ that, although He and His disciples were tired and worn out with almost continual troubles, yet He did not spare Himself. He sought some relaxation, but not so much for Himself as for His disciples; yet because the demands of His office called Him to a new task, He willingly put aside His own needs and set himself to teach the crowds. But although He has now put off those feelings which befitted Him as a mortal man, yet there is no doubt that He looks down from heaven on the wretched sheep without a shepherd so long as they seek a remedy for their needs.

Mark says that He taught many things, that is, that He preached for a long time so that they might carry away substantial profit. Luke relates that He spoke about the Kingdom of God, and this comes to the same thing. Matthew mentions only the miracles, since they were of greater force in gaining a reputation for Christ. But we may well deduce that He did not fail to teach, since this was the chief thing.

Matt. 14.15. *And when even was come.* The disciples' hope was now gone, for Christ seemed intent on teaching and the crowds were so ready to learn that they had no thought of going home. They therefore tell Christ that He should think of their physical needs and send them away to neighbouring villages. But He had purposely deferred till then the miracle which He had in mind: first so that the disciples might gradually be brought to the pitch of considering it and so profit from it the better; and then that the timing of it should teach them that although He does not forestall their needs or even meet them at once, yet He never renounces His care of them but always has His hand ready to give them help and shows it at the right time.

Matt. 14.16. *Give ye them to eat.* A fuller exposition of this miracle will be found under John 6, and I would refer the reader to that place rather than weary him with a repetition here. Yet I will briefly sketch the sum of it now so that it is not completely passed over. Hitherto Christ had worked in feeding souls; now He extends His office as shepherd to the care of their bodies. And by doing this He confirms His saying that to those who seek God's Kingdom and righteousness the other things will be added. We must not expect that Christ will always give food in this way to the hungry and starving. But it is certain that He will never let His people lack the necessities of life without stretching out His hand from heaven, when He sees that it is expedient, for relieving their needs. But those who want Christ to be their nurse must learn not to long for dainties but to be content with black bread.

Christ commanded the people to sit down in companies. And this He did first of all that the miracle might be the more obvious when they were set out in ranks, and then that they might all be witnesses of this heavenly grace; and thirdly because He saw that the disciples were worried and He wished to test their obedience by telling them to do something that seemed ridiculous. The surprising thing was that, without having any food, Christ should prepare for an apparent feast. What follows points in the same direction. He gave them the loaves so that the wonderful abundance should grow in their very hands and so that they should be ministers of Christ's divine power. As if it were but a small thing for them to be eyewitnesses, Christ wanted them actually to feel His power. By Budé's reckoning 200 *denarii* were worth about 34 French francs (*libras*). Thus they estimate a little bread for each person at one French *terunx*.[1] Their obedience in simply obeying Christ's command and leaving the rest to His will deserves no small praise, for they assessed the price of the large amount of bread necessary to give the people only a small piece each.

Matt. 14.19. *He blessed.* As often elsewhere, 'blessing' here means giving thanks. By His example Christ taught us that food can only be holy and pure to us if we testify our gratitude to God, from whose hand it comes. And so Paul says that whatever food God bestows on us is sanctified by the Word and by prayer (I Tim. 4.5); by which he

[1] See Calvin on John 6.7, where the arithmetic works out rather differently. The Budé reference is to *de Asse*, in *Opera omnia* II, 243-244.

means that brutish men who neither by faith consider God's blessing nor praise it by giving Him thanks infect and defile with the pollution of their unbelief what by nature is pure; they also pollute and corrupt the food which they eat, because to the unbelieving nothing is pure. Christ therefore lays down for His people a manner of eating so that they may not profane themselves and God's benefits with ungodly sacrilege. His lifting up of his eyes to heaven declares His earnest and vehement warmth in prayer. Not that this gesture is always necessary when we pray, but the Son of God did not wish to omit ceremonies which are useful for human weakness. And add to this that to raise up our eyes is an apt stimulus to stir up our slowness, since our minds cling too much to the earth.

Matt. 14.20. *And they took up that which remained over.* The remnants, even after such a host of men had been filled, were twelve times more than had first been handed out. And this not a little heightened the wonder of the miracle. For they all understood that by His power Christ not only created out of nothing enough food for their present use, but that if necessary He could provide also for the needs of the future. And finally, now that the miracle had been performed, Christ wanted clear evidence of it to remain, that those who had been refreshed with food might see it at their leisure.

Now although Christ does not multiply loaves every day, and men do not eat without manual labour or agriculture, yet the fruit of this story still touches us. It is only our dullness and ingratitude that prevent us seeing that it is by God's blessing that corn is increased to supply us with food. That from one year's harvest there is enough both for our food and also for seed for the coming year, does not happen without heavenly increase. And if any of us does not feel this, it is his depravity that prevents him, for the eyes of his mind and of his flesh also are blinded so that he cannot see the manifest work of God. Moreover Christ wished to declare that just as all things were given into His hands by the Father, so the food which we eat comes to us from His grace.

*And straightway Jesus constrained the disciples to enter into the boat, and to go before him to the other side, till he should send the multitudes away. And after he had sent the multitudes away, he went up into the mountain alone to pray: and when even was come, he was there alone. But the boat was now in the midst of the sea, distressed by the waves; for the wind was contrary. And in the fourth watch of the night Jesus came unto them, walking upon the sea. And when the disciples saw him walking on the sea, they were troubled, saying, It is an apparition;*

*and they cried out for fear. But straightway Jesus spake unto them, saying, Be of good cheer; it is I; be not afraid. And Peter answered him and said, Lord, if it be thou, bid me come unto thee upon the waters. And he said, Come. And Peter went down from the boat, and walked upon the waters, to come to Jesus. But when he saw the wind, he was afraid; and beginning to sink, he cried out, saying, Lord, save me. And immediately, Jesus stretched forth his hand, and took hold of him, and saith unto him, O thou of little faith, wherefore didst thou doubt? And when they were gone up into the boat, the wind ceased. And they that were in the boat came and worshipped him, saying, Of a truth thou art the Son of God. (Matt. 14.22-33)*

*And straightway he constrained his disciples to enter into the boat, and to go before him across the lake to Bethsaida, while he himself sendeth the multitude away. And after he had taken leave of them, he departed into the mountain to pray. And when even was come, the boat was in the midst of the sea, and he alone on the land. And seeing them distressed in rowing, for the wind was contrary unto them, about the fourth watch of the night he cometh unto them, walking on the sea; and he would have passed by them: but they, when they saw him walking on the sea, supposed that it was an apparition, and cried out: for they all saw him, and were troubled. But he straightway spake with them, and saith unto them, Be of good cheer: it is I; be not afraid. And he went up unto them in the boat; and the wind ceased: and they were sore amazed in themselves and wondered; for they understood not concerning the loaves, but their heart was hardened. (Mark 6.45-52)*

Matt. 14.22. *Jesus constrained the disciples.* He had to compel them because they would never willingly have left Him and gone across to another place. In this they show how much they give way to Him when they yield to and obey His command even against their own opinion. And it certainly did seem unreasonable, that He should remain alone in the desert when night was coming on. Their readiness was the more praiseworthy in that they put the authority of their heavenly Master before what seemed sensible on the contrary side. We do not obey God properly and substantially unless we simply follow whatever He commands even though it conflicts with our ideas. God always has the best reason for His purpose, but He often hides it from us for a time so that we may learn not to be wise in ourselves but to depend entirely on His will. Thus Christ compels His disciples to cross over, so that He may mould them to the rule of obedience that I spoke of. But there is no doubt that He wanted to make a way for Himself to do the miracle which was to follow.

Matt. 14.23. *He went up into the mountain apart.* The Son of God
certainly knew that a tempest was coming, and it is probable that He
did not neglect to pray for His disciples' safety. But it is surprising
that He did not prevent the danger rather than give Himself to prayer.
But to fulfil both sides of His mediatorial office, He shows Himself to
be truly God and man and gives evidence of both natures so far as was
necessary. Although He held all things in His power, He showed
Himself man by praying, and that not in pretence but with a sincere
affection of human love for us. In this respect His divine majesty was
in a sense quiescent, although at last in its own order it came forth.

Now by going up the mountain He was seeking the possibility of
praying free from all interruption. We know how easily warmth in
prayer can be quenched or at least cooled by the least distractions.
But although Christ did not suffer from this weakness, yet He wished
to warn us by His example to be careful to use all the helps that will
disengage our minds from the snares of the world, so that we may be
carried up to heaven. The most important thing is solitude. Those
who set themselves to pray with God as their only witness will be more
watchful, will pour forth their heart into His bosom, will examine
themselves more carefully, and, knowing that they have to do with
God, will rise above themselves. Yet we must note that He was not
laying down a law, as if we could pray only in solitude; for Paul tells
us to lift up holy hands elsewhere (I Tim. 2.8). And Christ sometimes
prayed when He was with other people; He even taught His disciples
to conceive common prayers when they were met together. But the
freedom to pray in all places does not prevent us praying in secret at
the right time.

Matt. 14.24. *But the boat was now in the midst of the sea.* Readers will
find my exposition of this story under John 6, and therefore I will be
brief here. Christ allowed His disciples to be tossed about by a tempest
and in danger for a time so that they should be the more ready to
accept help when it should come. For the contrary wind got up about
midnight or a little earlier. But Christ appeared only in the fourth
watch, that is, at the latest three hours before dawn. So their faith was
as roughly shaken by terrors as their arms were tired with rowing.
Now although very necessity was urging them to desire their Master's
presence, yet they were so crass that the actual sight of Him frightened
them, as if He were a ghost. This is why Mark says that their hearts
were blinded, and they did not understand about the loaves. For in
that miracle they had been taught enough and to spare that Christ had
the divine power to help His people and that He is careful to provide
for them when necessity demands. Their dullness is now deservedly
condemned, because they do not at once remember the heavenly

power of which an outstanding example had been showed only today and which should still be before their eyes. It is the fault of their slowness that they are amazed, for they had not profited by the earlier miracles as they should have done. In particular their blindness is reproved in that the memory of so recent a display has slipped from them, or rather they have not applied their minds to consider the deity of Christ, although the multiplication of the loaves had been a clear enough mirror of it. Mark expresses two things: that they had not rightly considered Christ's glory shown in the multiplying of the loaves; and the reason he gives is that their hearts were blinded. Now that seems added not only to increase the seriousness of their fault but also that we may be admonished of the defect of our mind and may seek new eyes from the Lord. It was indeed, as I have said just now, too brutish ignorance not to be aware of the almost palpable power of God. Yet because the whole human race suffers from the same disease, Mark deliberately mentions blindness, so that we may know that it is nothing new if men are blind to the clear works of God until they are enlightened from on high. As also Moses said: 'Hitherto the Lord hath not given you an heart to know' (Deut. 29.4). And although 'heart' more often denotes the will or the seat of the affections, yet here, as in the verse from Moses just quoted, it means the mind.

Matt. 14.27. *But straightway Jesus spake.* When He offered Himself in the action Jesus was not recognised as the Liberator: and therefore He invites the disciples to the knowledge of Himself by word of mouth. And the trust which He exhorts them to have He places in His presence, as if He were saying that once they have realized He is present with them they will have solid grounds for good hope. But He corrects the fear which had already filled their minds, so that it shall not hinder and delay their trust. Not that they could be without any fear and overflowing with joy; but it was necessary to calm the fear which ruled them, lest it should overwhelm their trust. And although to the reprobate the voice of the Son of God is deadly and His presence terrible, their effect as described here is very different towards believers. Inward peace and hearty trust win the victory in our hearts, so that we do not yield to carnal fears. But the reason why blind and wild tumults upset us is that we are ungrateful and malicious and do not use God's many benefits as shields; yet if we consider them aright they will be sufficient to sustain us. Although the time was ripe for help when Christ appeared, the tempest did not cease until the disciples had been the more stirred up both to desire and to hope for His grace. And we should observe this in order to know that it is not without cause that the Lord often defers the deliverance which He has in His hand.

Matt. 14.28. *And Peter answered.* The condition he lays down shows that his faith is not yet mature. 'If it is thou', he says, 'bid me come to thee.' But he had heard Christ speaking. Why then was he doubtful and bewildered? In his small and weak faith there breaks out a thoughtless wish. He should have kept to his proper limits and rather sought from Christ an increase of faith so that by its leading and guidance he might at last rise above all seas and mountains. But as it is he wants to fly without the wings of faith, and without Christ's voice having a genuine firmness in his heart, to make the waves solid under his feet. There is no doubt that his desire sprang from a good principle, but because it degenerated into a faulty excess it ceased to be praiseworthy. This is why Peter quickly suffered for his rashness. By this example believers are taught to beware of over-much rashness. Whithersoever the Lord calls we must energetically run; but anyone who goes too far will experience at last the unhappy outcome of transgressing his limits.

We might ask why Christ grants Peter's wish. By doing so He seems to approve it. But the solution is easy. God often looks after us better by denying what we ask. But sometimes He gives way to us so as to convince us of our foolishness by experience. Thus by yielding to them more than is expedient He daily trains His believers in sobriety and moderation for the future. Add that this was profitable for Peter and the rest and is profitable for us today. Christ's power shines forth more brightly in Peter when He makes him His comrade than if He had walked on the water alone. Yet Peter knew, and the others saw plainly, that because he did not abide in a firm faith and rest on the Lord's Word the secret power of God which had made the water solid failed. But Christ deals kindly with him, for He did not want him to sink completely. Both these things concern us also. Just as Peter began to sink as soon as he was overtaken by fear, so our frail and transient fleshly ideas sometimes cause us to sink in the course of our activities. Yet the Lord pardons our weakness and stretches out His hand lest the waters should swallow us up. We must also observe that when Peter saw that his temerity had turned out badly, he committed himself to Christ's mercy. Wherefore we also, even when we are suffering a punishment we deserve, must flee to Him to have mercy on us and give us the help we do not deserve.

Matt. 14.31. *O man of little faith.* Christ mercifully saves Peter, yet without condoning his fault. This is the meaning of the reproof which condemns the weakness of his faith. Yet we might ask whether any fear argues a lack of faith, since Christ's words seem to suggest that there is no place for doubt where faith reigns. I reply that the doubting rebuked by Christ is that which is directly contrary to faith. It could happen that a man might doubt without sin; say when he does not yet think of a word of the Lord that will give him certainty. But with Peter it was quite different. He had been armed with Christ's command and already knew His power, but he fell away from that twofold firmness into a vain and perverse fear.

Matt. 14.33. *They that were in the boat.* I consider that this is spoken not only of the disciples but also of the sailors and other passengers. Those who had not yet professed Him as Master suddenly gave Him the title of Messiah. For although the sublime mystery was not commonly known how God would be manifest in flesh, yet because they had learnt from the prophets that their future Redeemer would be called the Son of God, those who honour Christ with this title declare that they believe He is the Christ.

*And when they had crossed over, they came to the land of Gennesaret. And when the men of that place knew him, they sent into all that region round about, and brought unto him all that were sick; and they besought him that they might only touch the border of his garment: and as many as touched were made whole.* (Matt. 14.34-36)

*And when they had crossed over, they came to the land of Gennesaret, and moored to the shore. And when they were come out of the boat, straightway the people knew him, and ran round about that whole region, and began to carry about on their beds those that were sick, where they heard he was. And wheresoever he entered, into villages, or into cities, or into the country, they laid the sick in the market places, and besought him that they might touch if it were but the border of his garment: and as many as touched him were made whole.* (Mark 6.53-56)

Matt. 14.34. *They came to the land of Gennesaret.* The Evangelists mean that region which takes its name from the lake; although it is not clear whether perhaps the name of the country did not give its name to the lake. But it is not very important. What we have especially to note as we follow the Evangelists is that Christ's glory was not testified by just one or two miracles but that that part of Judaea was filled with innumerable testimonies, the news of which could well spread to Jerusalem and the other towns in every direction. From this we gather how shameful and ungodly was the ingratitude of the nation, which shut its eyes maliciously to the present brightness of the divine glory, or even tried, so far as it could, to extinguish it altogether. But now it is for us in this multitude of miracles to understand why Christ came—as a physician to heal all the diseases of all who came to Him. We must remember what Matthew had earlier drawn out of

Isaiah, that by healing the body He had foreshadowed something greater, the restoration of health to our souls and that it was His office to take away spiritual disease. And although He does not walk the earth today, yet it is certain that in heaven He is mighty to exercise the same graces of which a visible example was then shown. But because we are all afflicted with every kind of disease until He heals us, not only should each one of us come to Him, but also we should take care to bring others who need the same remedy.

Matt. 14.36. *That they might touch the border of his garment.* It would seem that there was some superstition mixed up in this, in that they tied the grace of Christ to their touching His clothes. At the least they cheated Him of some part of His honour in not expecting a miracle at His mere word. But He would not quench the smoking flax, and so accommodated Himself to their childishness. But this offers no handle to those who would please themselves and seek God's grace in a piece of wood, or nails, or clothes: for Scripture expressly declares that whatever we conceive of Christ now is unlawful unless it is consistent with His spiritual and heavenly glory. Their weakness was tolerated at the time, because, although they did not know that Christ was God, they desired to come closer to Him. Now that He fills heaven and earth with the scent of His grace we must apprehend, not by hands or eyes, but by faith, the salvation He offers us from heaven.

*Then there come to Jesus from Jerusalem Pharisees and scribes, saying, Why do thy disciples transgress the tradition of the elders? for they wash not their hands when they eat bread. And he answered and said unto them, Why do ye also transgress the commandment of God because of your tradition? For God said, Honour thy father and thy mother: and, He that speaketh evil of father or mother, let him die the death. But ye say, Whosoever shall say to his father or his mother, That wherewith thou mightest have been profited is given by me; he shall not honour his father and his mother. And ye have made void the word of God because of your tradition. Ye hypocrites, well did Isaiah prophesy of you, saying, This people honoureth me with their lips; but their heart is far from me. But in vain do they worship me, teaching as their doctrines the precepts of men.* (Matt. 15.1-9)

*And there are gathered together unto him the Pharisees, and certain of the scribes, which had come from Jerusalem, and had seen that some of his disciples ate their bread with defiled, that is unwashen, hands. For the Pharisees, and all the Jews, except they wash their hands diligently, eat not, holding the tradition of the elders: and when they come from the*

155

*market place, except they wash themselves, they eat not: and many*
*other things there be, which they have received to hold, washing of cups,*
*and pots, and brasen vessels, and tables. And the Pharisees and the*
*scribes ask him, Why walk not thy disciples according to the tradition of*
*the elders, but eat their bread with defiled hands? And he said unto them,*
*Well did Isaiah prophesy of you hypocrites, as it is written, This people*
*honoureth me with their lips, but their heart is far from me. But in vain*
*do they worship me, teaching as their doctrines the precepts of men. Ye*
*leave the commandment of God, and hold fast the tradition of men, the*
*washing of pots and cups: and many other such like things ye do. And*
*he saith unto them, Full well do ye reject the commandment of God,*
*that ye may keep your tradition. For Moses said, Honour thy father*
*and thy mother; and, He that speaketh evil of father or mother, let him*
*die the death: but ye say, If a man shall say to his father or his mother,*
*That wherewith thou mightest have been profited by me is Corban, that*
*is to say, Given; ye no longer suffer him to do aught for his father or his*
*mother; making void the word of God by your tradition, which ye have*
*delivered: and many such like things ye do.* (Mark 7.1-13)

Matt. 15.1. *There come to Jesus.* This is a noteworthy passage, in
that it corrects a vice no less dangerous than common. We see how
bold men are in systems and ways of worshipping God. They are
always inventing new forms of worship, and cleverness in this respect
is taken as a sign of superior wisdom in general. I am not now speaking
of the heathen, but of those in the household of the Church to whom
God has particularly given the honour of holding the rule of godliness
which He has dictated with His own mouth. God has laid down how He
wishes us to worship Him, and He has comprehended perfect holiness
in His Law. But a great number search out many additions from all
kinds of sources, as if it were a light and trivial thing to obey God and
observe what He commands. Those in authority bring forward their
own inventions, as if they possessed something more perfect than the
Word of the Lord. Then crept in tyranny. For when once men have
given themselves the freedom to command, they demand a strict
observance of their laws and will not bear the least letter of the law to
be left out either by contempt or by oversight. The world is impatient
of legitimate rule and especially stubborn against bearing the yoke of
God. Yet it will quickly and willingly ensnare itself in empty traditions; nay, many seem to desire such slavery. And so the worship of
God is vitiated, for its principle and head is obedience. The authority
of men is preferred to His rule. The masses are forced harshly and
tyrannically to devote themselves completely to trifles. But this
passage teaches us: first, that no invented worship pleases God at all,

since He wishes to be heard alone, so as to form and train us by His will in true godliness; secondly, that those who are not satisfied with God's Law alone but weary themselves in keeping human traditions are wasting their time; and thirdly, that it is an injury to God when men's inventions are elevated so high that they almost overthrow the majesty of the Law, or at least cool off respect for it.

*From Jerusalem scribes.* It is not said why these scribes came to Jesus, but it seems likely to me that they had been impressed by what they had heard and came with a desire to learn, since He seemed a suitable teacher. Yet it may be that they were sent as spies. However it was, they brought their pride with them and the least offence quickly annoyed them and made them snap and bite at Christ. This shows us how difficult it is to turn to sound doctrine those who are full of ambition and a lust for power. In particular, those who are devoted and long used to ceremonies will admit nothing new, but will obstinately condemn anything unusual. In brief, one cannot imagine a sort of people more domineering or hypercritical than these. Both the Evangelists mention that they were scribes and Pharisees, but Matthew puts the scribes first, Mark puts them second. But they mean the same thing, that the scribes came from other parties but the Pharisees were the leaders; they had the most honour and the government at that time was in their hands. And it is not surprising that they were more quickly scandalized at His neglect of the laws which they had composed. For, as we have said elsewhere, although they claimed to be the interpreters of the Law (and this is why they were given the name 'Pharisees'[1]) they corrupted the purity of God's Word with their inventions. Thus it was their press that published the traditions then in force among the Jews; and this made them show the more energetic and fierce zeal for them.

Matt. 15.2. *Why do thy disciples transgress?* Since it is dealing with human traditions, this question has nothing to do with political laws, the use and aim of which differs from precepts on how God is to be worshipped. But because human traditions vary, a distinction is to be observed. The impiety of some is quite plain, when they set up perverse forms of worship which are diametrically opposed to God's Word. But others vitiate its purity by mixing the worship of God with profane ineptitudes. Other forms, with more apparent excuse, are not infected with any notable vice but are condemned because they are thought to be necessary for worshipping God. And so men fall away from true obedience to the one God and their consciences are caught in a snare. It is certainly this last sort which is treated here, for the washing of hands which the Pharisees emphasized could not in

[1] See vol. I, p. 183.

157

itself be branded as a depraved superstition—Christ would not have suffered the water pots to stand there at the wedding unless this ceremony had been permissible. Their fault was in thinking that God could not be worshipped aright without the washing. The ceremony of washing when first introduced was not without plausible cause. We know how strictly the Law of God demanded outward cleanness, not that the Lord wanted His servants to be entirely taken up with it but that they might keep themselves the more carefully from all spiritual defilement. And the Law keeps to a certain mean in ablutions. Then along came these teachers who thought that they would not be considered clever enough if they did not add something to the Word of God; and this was how the washings grew up, although the Law made no mention of them. The lawgivers did not claim to be offering anything new but only to be adding certain cautionary rules which would be of assistance in keeping God's Law. But the corruption followed hard on this, for the ceremonies introduced by men began to be thought a part of the divine worship. And then a necessity was imposed on things free and voluntary. For God (as has already been said) wished always to be worshipped according to what was laid down in His Word, and therefore any addition to His Law is intolerable. Although He permits His believers to have external ceremonies, yet He will not allow them to be mixed with His Word as if religion were placed in them.

*For they wash not their hands.* Mark explains more fully the cause of this offence; but the whole point of it was that there were many customs in use among the scribes which they observed of their own will. These were secondary laws invented by scrupulous men, as if the simple command of God were not sufficient. God commanded that anything which had contracted any pollution was to be washed. This covered cups and jugs, clothes, and other household things, so that no-one should touch anything polluted or unclean. But to invent new ablutions was an empty vanity. Certainly there seemed some excuse for it, as Paul says that men's inventions have a show of wisdom (Col. 2.23). But if they had rested in God's Law alone, their modesty would have won more approval than their scrupulous care did. They wanted to ensure that no-one unclean should eat food thoughtlessly; but for the Lord it was enough that they should wash away the stains that they knew. Moreover this sort of carefulness has neither end nor mean; they could scarcely move a finger without incurring some new uncleanness. But the corruption was far worse because it was bound on consciences as a religion that a man who did not sometimes wash his body in water was guilty of pollution. Perhaps they allowed common men to omit this ceremony. But they reckoned Christ and

His disciples as far above the masses. And this is why it seemed wrong that the disciples of a master who professed something better than the present state should not observe rites which had been handed down from the elders and whose observance was holy among the scribes.

Now they are much at fault who compare with the Jewish washings that sprinkling of purifying water which Papists call holy water. By this continual repetition the Papists are blotting out, as far as they can, the once for all baptism. And this paltry sprinkling is extended to exorcisms. Yet even if it were lawful in itself and void of all such corruptions, the necessity for it which they urge would always have to be condemned.

Matt. 15.3. *Why do ye also transgress?* Christ gives a double reply. The first is personal, as they say; the other contains a definition of the matter and its cause. The order is inverted in Mark, who first represents Christ as speaking on the subject as a whole, and then adding His rebuke against the hypocrites. We shall follow Matthew's order. When the Lord in His turn was asking the scribes why they violated God's Law by their traditions, He was not yet completely freeing the disciples from the charge levelled against them, but was only saying how unfair and perverse was the hypercritical attitude of the scribes. They think it is wicked not to keep human commandments precisely. But how much more wicked they are to give all their care to keeping them while they neglect God's Law! That they put men before God in this way made it clear that they were offended rather from ambition than from righteous zeal. Moreover, we may easily infer from the context in what sense He says that they transgress God's commandments. They did not openly or professedly abolish the Law of God so as to make anything lawful which it had forbidden. Their transgression was indirect, in that they allowed the duties divinely enjoined to be omitted. The example which Christ brings forward is clear and homely: The Law of God says that children shall honour their parents. Now the sacred offerings brought gain to the priests, and therefore they demanded them so strictly that they made it a graver sin to omit the free will offering than to defraud parents of the honour due to them. Hence what in the Law of God was voluntary was in the eyes of the scribes more important than one of the chiefest of God's commandments. Therefore whenever we are so intent on keeping man-made laws that we pay less heed to keeping the Law of God, we are judged to have transgressed it. A little later He will say that God's commandment is rendered vain for the sake of the traditions of men, because the scribes so held the people captive to their views that no place was left for hearing the Word of God. And again, the fact that they thought that those who obeyed the traditions to the letter had done their duty wonderfully was a licence for sin. For whenever holiness is placed elsewhere than in keeping of the Law of God, people will believe they can break it unpunished.

Now let everyone just consider whether this wickedness does not flourish more today in the Papacy than of old among the Jews. The Pope, along with all the dirty rabble of his clergy, does not deny that God must be obeyed. But when it comes to the point, they detest an ordinary meal of meat as a capital crime, whereas theft or adultery is only a venial fault for them. And in this they overturn God's Law for the sake of their traditions; for it is completely insufferable that men's views should take anything from the observance which is due to God alone. Moreover, the honour which God commands to be given to parents covers all the duties of godliness. The latter clause that Christ adds, that he who curses his father or mother deserves to die, is intended to teach us that the commandment on honouring parents cannot be common or light, since its violation is punished so severely. But it magnifies the guilt of the scribes not a little that such a harsh denunciation does not frighten them from giving liberty to despisers of parents.

Matt. 15.5. *But ye say, etc.* Mark gives this incomplete sentence more fully when he adds, 'Ye no longer suffer him to do aught.' And the sense is that the scribes are wrong to absolve those who will not do their duty to their parents, if they only make up for this failure with a voluntary sacrifice, which could be omitted without offending God. For we should not understand Christ's words as meaning that the scribes prohibited men from any righteous duty, but they were so keen to get their loot that in the meanwhile children neglected their parents.

Matt. 15.7. *Well did Isaiah prophesy of you.* The Lord now goes further. He declares what was the cause of this, and divides it into two parts. The first is that by making it stand in external ceremonies only they thought nothing of true holiness, which consists of a genuine integrity of heart. The second is that they perversely worship God at their own will. And although He seems merely to be rebuking them personally when He censures their pretended and feigned goodness, yet in fact He embraces the sum of the doctrine; for the full definition of it was that the worship of God is spiritual and is not placed in sprinkling with water or in other ceremonies. Then there is no other rational service of God than that which is formed to the rule of His Word. Now although Isaiah was not prophesying for the future but was aiming at his contemporaries, yet Christ says that the prophecy fits the Pharisees and the scribes because they are like the hypocrites of old with whom the prophet was doing battle. Christ does not quote this verbatim, but the prophet expressly mentions these two vices by which the Jews provoked God's wrath against themselves—that their godliness was feigned, a mere lip-service and outward profession, and that they fall away to false worship. First, then, it is ungodly hypocrisy when men honour God only with outward show; yet in itself it is not wrong to draw near to God with mouth and lips so long as the heart comes first. The sum therefore is that the worship of God is spiritual, and only that is pleasing to Him when there is inward sincerity of heart, so that they are hypocrites who set holiness in external display.

Matt. 15.9. *But in vain do they worship me.* The actual words of the prophet are: 'Their fear was taught by the commandment of men' (Isa. 29.13). But Christ renders the sense faithfully and aptly, that God is worshipped in vain when men's wills are susbstituted for teaching. Moreover, it is perfectly clear that these words condemn all ἐθελοθρησκείας, as Paul calls it (Col. 2.23). For, as we have said, because God wishes to be worshipped according to His will alone, He will not at all permit new forms of worship to be invented. Therefore, as soon as men allow themselves to wander outside God's Law, all their efforts and care in worshipping Him will only bring them the greater judgment, since religion is profaned by such figments.

There is an apposition in the words *teaching doctrines, the precepts of men.* For Christ says that they err who obtrude men's commandments in the place of doctrine, or who seek from them a rule for worshipping God. Therefore let this remain firm, that, because obedience is more to God than saciifice, all false worship is empty in His sight, nay, accursed and detestable, according to the prophet (I Sam. 15.22-23).

*And he called to him the multitude, and said unto them, Hear, and understand: Not that which entereth into the mouth defileth the man; but that which proceedeth out of the mouth, this defileth the man. Then came the disciples, and said unto him, Knowest thou that the Pharisees were offended when they heard this saying? But he answered and said, Every plant which my heavenly Father planted not, shall be rooted up. Let them alone: they are blind leaders of the blind. And if the blind guide the blind, both shall fall into a pit. And Peter answered and said unto him, Declare unto us the parable. And he said, Are ye also even yet without understanding? Perceive ye not yet, that whatsoever goeth into the mouth passeth into the belly, and is cast out into the draught? But the things which proceed out of the mouth come forth out of the heart: and they defile the man. For out of the heart come forth evil thoughts, murders, adulteries, fornications, thefts, false witness, railings:*

*these are the things which defile the man: but to eat with unwashen hands defileth not the man.* (Matt. 15.10-20)

*And he called to him the whole multitude again, and said unto them, Hear me all of you, and understand: there is nothing from without the man, that going into him can defile him: but the things which proceed out of the man are those that defile the man. If any man have ears to hear, let him hear. And when he was entered into the house from the multitude, his disciples asked him of the parable. And he saith unto them, Are ye so without understanding also? Perceive ye not yet, that whatsoever from without goeth into the man, it cannot defile him; because it goeth not into his heart, but into his belly, and goeth out into the draught purging all meats? And he said, That which proceedeth out of the man, that defileth the man. For from within, out of the heart of men, evil thoughts proceed, adulteries, fornications, murders, thefts, covetings, wickednesses, deceit, lasciviousness, an evil eye, railing, pride, foolishness: all these evil things proceed from within, and defile the man.* (Mark 7.14-23)

*And he spake a parable unto them, Can the blind guide the blind? shall they not both fall into a pit?* (Luke 6.39)

Matt. 15.10. *And he called to him the multitude.* To the teachable people now turning to Him Christ explains more fully what He had mentioned at first, that, as Paul puts it, the Kingdom of God does not consist in food and drink (Rom. 14.17). For since outward things are by nature pure, their use is also free and pure, and uncleanness is not contracted from the good creatures of God. It is therefore the general statement that uncleanness does not enter a man from outside, but its well-spring lies hidden within him. It is a synecdoche when He says that all the evil that a man does comes out of his mouth. For He is alluding to the present case, as if He were saying that we do not take in uncleanness along with our food and drink but the various kinds of uncleanness flow out of us.

Matt. 15.12. *Knowest thou that the Pharisees.* Because the scribes were proud and unteachable, Christ did not waste much time in appeasing them—only enough to repel their hypocrisy and pride. Their original taking of offence was only doubled when they saw that it was not out of lack of interest but quite deliberately that Christ despised their washings as trifles. And since Christ did not hesitate to inflame the more these malignant and virulent spirits by His attack, let us learn from His example not to be greatly worried about whether our deeds and words are pleasing to all. But the disciples (as is usual with the inexperienced and ignorant) imagine that because the result is unfavourable Christ's reply was unfortunate and out of place. For their reproof suggests that Christ ought to correct the severity of what He said and smooth over the offence they had taken. It is very common for the weak to judge hardly of the doctrine which is seen to be taken amiss. Certainly it would be fine if everyone approved of it quietly and without offence; but because Satan blinds the minds of many and inflames their hearts to madness and holds many souls whelmed in a brutish dullness, it cannot happen that the true teaching of salvation will please everyone; and in particular it is no wonder if those who nurse the inward poison of malice and obstinacy should be exasperated. We must take care (so far as it is right) that our manner of teaching shall not give rise to offence; but it would be complete madness to want to tone ourselves down to a greater prudence than our heavenly Master has taught us. We see that wicked and perverse men took offence at His preaching; but we also see that He held in contempt the sort of scandal which sprang from malice.

Matt. 15.13. *Every plant, etc.* Christ wanted to put right the harm which had been done to their weak minds by the lack of success of the preaching. And the remedy which He applies is that the good have no cause to be upset or to think less highly of the doctrine itself if it brings death to many. Some expound this passage amiss, that every invention of man and all that does not proceed from the mouth of God ought to be rooted out and destroyed. But Christ was looking rather to men; and the meaning is that it is not surprising if the teaching of salvation is deadly to the reprobate, for they are carried headlong into the destruction to which they are appointed. Understand those who are planted by God as those who are by His free adoption grafted into the tree of life—in the way that Isaiah calls the Church renewed by Christ's grace a branch planted by the Lord (Isa. 60.21). Moreover, because salvation is of God's election alone, it is necessary that the reprobate shall in some way or other perish. Not that those destroyed by God are innocent and blameless, but because from their innate malice they turn whatever is offered to them into a means of destruction. This is why, as Paul says, the Gospel is an odour of death unto death for those who willingly perish. For although it is set before all for their salvation, it has this result only in the elect. It is for the faithful and good teacher so to adapt what he puts forward that all may profit from it. But whenever things turn out differently let us be consoled by Christ's reply. The parable expresses beautifully the fact that the cause of destruction does not lie in the doctrine but that when reprobates, without any root in God, are confronted with the doctrine, they vomit out their hidden poison and hasten the death to which they were appointed. Add that Christ particularly has in mind hypocrites, who

163

for a time seem just like branches of good trees. For the Epicureans, noteworthy for their gross and wicked contempt of God, can not really be likened to trees. It must be those in whom gleams some sort of empty piety. Such were the scribes who stood out like cedars of Lebanon in the Church of God. And this makes their failure seem the more inconsonant. Moreover, although Christ might have said that those who unworthily reject salvation deserve to perish, He goes further and says that no-one will stand firm continually unless his salvation is fixed in God's election. In these words He expressly says that the primary origin of our salvation flows from the grace by which God chose us to be His children before we were made.

Matt. 15.14. *Let them alone*. He says that they are not worth troubling about; and therefore that there is no need for them to be an offence to us. This is the basis for the common distinction in the avoidance of offences, that we should take care not to give offence to the weak but that if anyone takes offence out of obstinacy and malignity there is no help for it. For Christ, who is the rock of offence, would have to be buried if we wanted to satisfy the stubbornness of everybody. Therefore it is important to make a distinction between the weak who take offence out of ignorance and soon return to their senses and the proud and hypercritical who voluntarily seize on offences. Let the wicked obstinately fasten on offences, but let us go on quietly in the midst of offences. For he who does not spare his weak brethren grinds them underfoot instead of holding out a helping hand. It would be inconsistent, if we desire to keep to the right path, to pay heed to those who are going to take offence any way. When it happens that they separate and defect from Christ under some slight pretext, we must leave them be, or they will drag us down with them.

*If the blind guide the blind*. Christ means that those who follow their own will wherever it leads will wretchedly perish; for they stumble on the good road because they are voluntarily blind. Now, how can anyone let himself be guided by them without falling into the same ditch? But Christ, who is the Sun of righteousness enlightening us, not only shows us the way by the torch of His Gospel but expects us to tread it, and He rightly calls His disciples back from their indolence so that they shall not, by following the blind, wander in darkness. From this also we infer that all those who under cover of simplicity or modesty give themselves up to being deceived and ensnared by errors are without excuse.

In quoting this sentence Luke mentions no details but only says in general that Christ used this parable. He is often silent about the purpose for which Christ preached the discourses he mentions. It may be that Christ said the same thing quite often. But, since no better place could be found, I have not hesitated to insert it here, because Luke does not refer it to any particular time.

Matt. 15.15. *And Peter answered and said.* Christ deservedly reproves the disciples for showing so much ignorance, and He blames them that so far they had lacked understanding, even though He had not failed in teaching them. Matthew ascribes the reply to Peter by name, but in the same sense Mark relates that they all made the request. And this appears from Christ's reply where He rebukes the ignorance, not of Peter alone, but of them all alike.

The sum of it is that men are not polluted by foods but have within themselves the defilements of vices and these come into the open in their actions. If anyone objects that intemperate eating is a defilement, the answer is easy. Christ is only dealing with the natural and legitimate use of those things which the Lord has offered us. In itself eating and drinking is a thing free and indifferent. If it is corrupted, this arises from man himself and so should be accounted internal and not external.

Matt. 15.19. *For out of the heart come forth.* From this we infer, as I have said, that Christ had earlier used the word 'mouth' for the sake of the present passage; for now He does not mention the mouth but only says that whatever is sinful and stains by its uncleanness flows from a man's heart. Mark differs from Matthew in that he enumerates many vices, like lusts or immoderate desires (some have translated this as 'avarice', but I prefer to take it generally), and also guile and intemperance and their results. This is an imprecise way of speaking and it is enough to grasp Christ's meaning, that all vices proceed from the evil and corrupt affections of the heart. It is also imprecise to say that an evil eye comes out of the heart, although in reality there is nothing absurd or ambiguous in saying that an impure heart contaminates the eyes, so that they are the ministers or instruments of evil desires. But Christ is not restricting the evil which is in a man to open sins, but says that the witness and fruit rests in the sins themselves, so that He may the more clearly teach that man's heart is the seat of all evils. For 'pollute' the Greek has 'make common', just as a little before Mark said 'common hands' for 'impure hands'. It is a Hebraism; for the Lord had set aside the Jews on the condition that they should be separated from all defilements of the Gentiles, and therefore whatever was alien to this holiness was called 'common' as if it were unholy.

*And Jesus went out thence, and withdrew into the parts of Tyre and Sidon. And behold, a Canaanitish woman came out from those borders, and cried, saying, Have mercy on me, O Lord, thou son of David; my daughter is grievously vexed with a devil. But he answered her not a word. And his disciples came and besought him, saying, Send her away; for she crieth after us. But he answered, and said, I was not sent but unto the lost sheep of the house of Israel. But she came and worshipped him, saying, Lord, help me. And he answered and said, It is not meet to take the children's bread and cast it to the dogs. But she said, Yea, Lord, for even the dogs eat of the crumbs which fall from their master's table. Then Jesus answered and said unto her, O woman, great is thy faith; be it done unto thee even as thou wilt. And her daughter was healed from that hour.* (Matt. 15.21-28)

*And from thence he arose, and went away into the borders of Tyre and Sidon. And he entered into a house, and would have no man know it: and he could not be hid. But straightway a woman, whose little daughter had an unclean spirit, having heard of him, came and fell down at his feet, (now the woman was a Greek, a Syrophoenician by race) and she besought him that he would cast forth the devil out of her daughter. And Jesus said unto her, Let the children first be filled: for it is not meet to take the children's bread and cast it to the dogs. But she answered and saith unto him, Yea, Lord: for even the dogs under the table eat of the children's crumbs. And he said unto her, For this saying go thy way; the devil is gone out of thy daughter. And she went away unto her house, and found the devil gone out and the child laid upon the bed.* (Mark 7.24-30)

In this miracle we are taught in what way Christ's grace began to flow to the Gentiles. Although the fulness of time was not yet come when Christ declared Himself to the whole world, He wished to give a certain prelude of the common mercy which at last, after His resurrection, was revealed indiscriminately to Jews and Gentiles. A remarkable image of faith is depicted in the Canaanite woman, to teach us by comparison that the Jews, whose ungodliness was so stupid, were justly deprived of the promised redemption. Matthew calls the woman a Canaanite, but Mark says she was Greek, a Syrophoenician by race. There is no inconsistency here, for we know that it was a common way of speaking among the Jews to call all foreigners Greeks. This is the reason for the frequent antithesis between Greeks and Jews in Paul. Moreover, she came from the parts of Tyre and Sidon, and it is not surprising that she was called Syrophoenician, for the name of the country was Syria and it was a part of Phoenicia. The Jews called all the natives of that country by the opprobrious term Canaanites. And we can well believe that most of them were descended from the people of Canaan who were driven out of their country and found refuge in this neighbourhood. They both agree that a woman who came of a heathen nation, not taught in the doctrine of the Law, came of her own accord to Christ to supplicate His help.

We must also notice the detail that Mark mentions, that Christ did not come there with flags flying, but to remain hidden in that quiet corner for a time as a private person. But Mark is speaking in an ordinary human sort of way; for although by His divine Spirit Christ foresaw what would happen, yet so far as He was the minister and envoy of His Father He kept Himself humanly within the limits of the vocation laid upon Him. And this is why it is said that He could not do what as a man He wished to do. Yet, as I said, this fact is very damning of the Jews, because when Christ put before them the promised redemption with a clear voice and the reinforcement of miracles, they were blind and deaf, though all the while they claimed to be the heirs of the Lord's covenant. His own possession, a priestly Kingdom. But this woman, who had nothing in common with the children of Abraham and who apparently had no part or lot in the covenant, runs to Him of her own accord invited by no word, no sign.

Matt. 15.22. *Have mercy on me, O Lord.* Although this woman was outside the Lord's flock, she had received a certain taste of godliness, for without some knowledge of the promises she could not have called Christ the Son of David. Although the Jews had revolted, or at least swerved away, from the pure and sound teaching of the Law, yet there was a vigorous and widespread awareness of the promised redemption. And because the restoration of the Church was based on David's kingdom, it was quite common to call the Messiah the Son of David, and indeed this confession was universal. But when true faith fell into disuse among them, it happened by the wonderful and incredible goodness of God that the odour of the promises spread into Gentile lands. Therefore, although this woman had not received direct teaching from any master, yet she did not rashly invent for herself a faith about Christ, but conceived one from the Law and the prophets. Therefore that dog Servetus was absurd as well as ungodly in misusing this example to strip faith of the promises. According to this sense I do not deny that there may sometimes be a certain implicit faith, that is, one that does not consist in an express and distinct knowledge of sound doctrine. But we must hold that faith is always born of God's Word and takes its beginning from true elements, so that it may always be joined to a certain light of knowledge.

Matt. 15.23. *But he answered her not a word.* The Evangelists praise the woman's faith in different ways. At this point it is her unconquered constancy. For Christ's silence was a sort of repulse and it would not have been surprising for her to have been cast down by this temptation.

But her persistence was testified by her persevering in prayer. Yet this seems to be contrary to the nature of faith and prayer as Paul describes it in Rom. 10.14—that no-one can pray aright unless the Word of God has led the way. Who can say, then, that this woman was endowed with faith, who, when Christ was silent, breathes out her trust from her own feelings? But since there are two ways in which Christ speaks and is silent, we must note that although He then suppressed His words, He spoke inwardly to the woman's mind and so this secret instinct stood in place of the external preaching. Add that, since her prayer was born of the hearing of faith, although Christ did not reply at once, yet there was always sounding in her ears the teaching which she had once learnt, that Christ came as the Redeemer. Thus the Lord often addresses His believers and at the same time is silent; for they trust in the testimonies of Scripture and when they hear Him speaking they do not doubt that He will be favourable to them although He does not at once answer their desires and prayers and only seems to be pretending to hear them. Therefore we see that Christ's motive in being silent was not to quench the woman's faith but rather to sharpen her zeal and kindle her fervour. Now, if a tiny seed of doctrine could bear such rich fruit in the Canaanite woman, it certainly does not behove us to faint if He ever keeps us in suspense and does not immediately vouchsafe a kind reply.

*Send her away.* The disciples ask nothing on her behalf. Simply because her importunity is a nuisance to them, they desire that she be sent away, no matter how. For the rest, it was a childish invention for the Papists to use this passage in their attempt to make departed saints into patrons for us. For even if we grant (which cannot be drawn out of the passage) that the woman was seeking from the disciples some support or assistance, yet between the dead and the living the case is different. Add that the disciples heard her in a disdainful frame of mind, so that, even if they had had any idea of helping her with their patronage, they would have obtained nothing.

Matt. 15.24. *I was not sent.* He tells the disciples that the reason why He was not listening to the Canaanite woman was that He wished to devote Himself entirely to the Jews, to whom alone He had been appointed the minister of divine grace. He therefore argues from the calling and command of the Father that He was to give no help to foreigners. Not that the power of Christ was to be enclosed forever within such narrow limits, but it was a question of the time; because He made a beginning with the Jews He devoted Himself peculiarly to them at that time. For, as was said in chapter 10, not until after the resurrection was the wall broken down and Christ could preach peace to the Gentiles outside the Kingdom of God. Elsewhere He commanded the Apostles to sow the seed of the Gospel first in Judaea alone. (Matt. 10.5). Hence in this verse He says truly that He was sent only to the Jews, until the Gentiles also should follow in their turn.

By *the sheep of the house of Israel* He means not only the election but all who were descended from the holy patriarchs, for the Lord embraced them all in His covenant and the Redeemer was promised to all alike, just as He showed and offered Himself to all without exception. It is also noteworthy that He declared that He was given for the lost sheep, and elsewhere He bore witness that He had come to save that which was lost. Now since today His grace is common to us and to the Jews, let us grasp what our condition is until He appears to us as the Saviour.

Matt. 15.25. *She came and worshipped him.* The woman looks as if she is wrestling with a sort of obstinacy in Christ and trying to wring something out of Him unwillingly. But there is no doubt that what inspired her was the faith she had conceived in the goodness of the Messiah. When Christ directly denies that this is His office, the repulse does not frighten her or turn her from her purpose. And this is because, as I said, her original feeling of faith was deeply fixed in her and she rejected everything contrary to her hope. And this is the true proof of faith, when we do not permit the general principle of our salvation, which is founded in the Word of God, to be shaken from us in any way.

Matt. 15.26. *It is not meet.* In this reply Christ seems to be cutting away all hope even more harshly than before. For He not only says that He owes the Jews all the grace He has received from the Father and must dispense it to them if they are not to be defrauded of their special right, but also with a certain insult compares the woman to a dog, meaning that she does not deserve to become partaker in His grace. Now, to bring out the meaning clearly, we should understand that what is called 'the children's bread' is not God's gifts in general but only those which He gave particularly to Abraham and his race. For from the beginning of the world God's goodness was shed abroad— nay, filled heaven and earth—in such a way that all mortals felt Him to be the Father. But because He honoured the children of Abraham above the rest of the human race, He calls the children's bread whatever relates strictly to the adoption by which the Jews alone were chosen as children. The Gentiles enjoyed in common with the Jews the light of the sun, the breath of life, the fruits of the earth; but the blessing which was to be hoped for in Christ resided only in the house of Abraham. Therefore to lay open to all and sundry what God has deposited in the possession of one nation as a unique privilege, would simply be an abolishing of God's covenant, for in this way the Gentiles would be

169

made equal to the Jews who were, as was right, more excellent. Therefore Christ uses the word 'cast', meaning that it is out of place to take this from the Church of God and make it common to the heathen.

But this should be restricted to the time when men called on God only in Judaea. For from the time when the Gentiles were admitted into fellowship of the same salvation (which happened when Christ shone everywhere through the Gospel), the distinction was removed and those who were formerly the dogs are now reckoned among the children. The pride of the flesh must needs be humbled to the ground when we hear that by origin we are dogs. Certainly there was in the beginning a greater excellence in the human nature in which the image of God shone and this shameful name did not belong to all nations nor to kings themselves, whom God adorned with His own title; but the perfidy and defection of Adam brought it to pass that the Lord deservedly cast on to the dung-heap along with the dogs those who by the fault of the first parent became degenerate. This is specially true when there is a comparison between the Jews, exempt from the common lot, and the Gentiles, who were exiles from God's Kingdom.

Christ's intention is more clearly expressed in Mark, where it says, *let the children first be filled.* For He is warning the Canaanite that she is acting out of turn when she raids the table in the middle of supper, so to say. Now although He was chiefly concerned with making a trial of the woman's faith, yet at the same time He was teaching that a horrible vengeance would remain for the Jews who deliberately rejected the incomparable blessing offered to them although He denied it to others who eagerly and fervently desired it.

Matt. 15.27. *Yea, Lord.* The woman's reply shows that she was not carried away by a blind or obtuse passion to attack Christ's word frontally. Since God had put the Jews before the rest, she also relinquished the honour of adoption to them and declares that she has nothing against Christ satisfying them according to the divinely appointed order. All she asks is that a crumb, falling maybe by chance, may reach the puppies. And indeed, God never so enclosed His grace among the Jews that He did not sprinkle the Gentiles with at least a little taste of it. For expressing the dispensation of God's grace which then flourished, nothing more apt or shrewd could be said.

Matt. 15.28. *Great is thy faith.* First He praises the woman's faith; then He declares that He will yield to her prayers for the sake of her faith. The greatness of her faith showed itself chiefly in that, with only a moderate glimmer of teaching to lead her, she not only recognized the genuine office of Christ and ascribed heavenly power to Him, but kept steadily on through such hard obstacles. She allowed herself to be emptied so long as she could hold fast to what she was convinced of—that she would get Christ's help. In short, she so seasoned her confidence with humility that she did not lay rash claim to anything and yet did not shut herself off from the fountain of Christ's grace by the sense of her own unworthiness. But the ingratitude of the people who claimed to be holy unto God is condemned by this praise of a heathen woman. I have already mentioned how the woman is said rightly to believe when she was not only destitute of any promise of Christ but was even repulsed by His antagonistic words. Although He apparently rejects her prayers harshly, yet she is convinced of the salvation divinely promised in the Messiah and does not cease to hope. And she thinks the door is closed on her, not to drive her away altogether, but rather to make her try in faith to get through the cracks in the wood.

The last clause contains the useful lesson that faith will obtain anything from the Lord, for He values it so highly that He is always ready to grant our prayers so far as it is proper.

*And Jesus departed thence, and came nigh unto the sea of Galilee; and he went up into the mountain, and sat there. And there came unto him great multitudes, having with them the lame, blind, dumb, maimed, and many others, and they cast them down at Jesus' feet; and he healed them: insomuch that the multitude wondered, when they saw the dumb speaking, the maimed whole, and the lame walking, and the blind seeing; and they glorified the God of Israel. And Jesus called unto him his disciples, and said, I have compassion on the multitude, because they continue with me now three days and they have nothing to eat: and I would not send them away fasting, lest they faint in the way. And his disciples say unto him, Whence should we have so many loaves in a desert place, as to fill so great a multitude? And Jesus saith unto them, How many loaves have ye? And they say, Seven, and a few small fishes. And he commanded the multitude to sit down on the ground. And he took the seven loaves and the fishes, and gave thanks and brake, and gave to the disciples, and the disciples gave to the multitudes. And they did all eat, and were filled: and they took up that which remained over of the broken pieces, seven baskets full. And they that did eat were four thousand men, besides women and children. And he sent away the multitudes, and entered into the boat, and came into the borders of Magadan. (Matt. 15.29-39)*

*And again he went out from the borders of Tyre and Sidon and came unto the sea of Galilee, through the midst of the borders of Decapolis. And they bring unto him one that was deaf, and had an impediment in his speech; and they beseech him to lay his hands upon him. And he took him aside from the multitude privately, and put his fingers into his* ears, and he spat, and touched his tongue; and looking up to heaven, he sighed, and saith unto him, Ephphatha, that is, Be opened. And his ears were opened, and the bond of his tongue was loosed, and he spake plain. And he charged them that they should tell no man: but the more he charged them, so much the more a great deal they published it. And they were beyond measure astonished, saying, He hath done all things well: he maketh even the deaf to hear, and the dumb to speak.

In those days, when there was again a great multitude, and they had nothing to eat, Jesus called unto him his disciples, and said unto them, I have compassion on the multitude, because they continue with me now three days, and have nothing to eat; and if I send them away fasting to their home, they will faint in the way; and some of them are come from far. And his disciples answered him, Whence shall one be able to fill these men with bread here in a desert place? And he asked them, How many loaves have ye? And they say, Seven. And he commandeth the multitude to sit down on the ground: and he took the seven loaves, and having given thanks, he brake, and gave to his disciples, to set before them; and they set them before the multitude. And they had a few small fishes: and having blessed them, he commanded to set these also before them. And they did eat, and were filled: and they took up of the broken pieces that remained over, seven baskets. And they that did eat were about four thousand: and he sent them away. And straightway he entered into the boat with his disciples, and came into the parts of Dalmanutha. (Mark 7.31-37 and 8.1-10)

Matt. 15.29. *And Jesus departed thence.* Matthew and Mark without doubt narrate the same return journey of Christ from the region of Sidon, but in some things they disagree. It is unimportant that the one says that He came into the coasts of Magdala but the other into the parts of Dalmanutha, for these were neighbouring cities on the Lake of Gennesareth over against Mount Tabor, and it is not surprising if the name of both was ascribed to the region between them. Decapolis was so called from the ten cities and, as it bordered on Phoenicia and maritime Galilee, Christ would have passed through it when He returned from Phoenicia to Judaean Galilee. A more serious discrepancy seems to be that He healed many afflicted with various diseases, whereas Mark mentions only one deaf man. Yet this knot is easily untied. Mark chose for commemoration a miracle that was performed on the journey and the news of which, when it spread, caused such general excitement among the natives of that land that they brought to Christ many to be healed. And we know that the Evangelists are not scrupulous to relate everything that Christ did, but were so sparing in speaking of His miracles that they only refer to a few as examples.

Moreover, Mark thought it sufficient to put forward merely one in which Christ's power shone, as it did in those others of the same sort which followed soon after.

Mark 7.32. *And they bring unto him one that was deaf.* Why they prayed Him to lay His hands on him is gathered from earlier passages. For the imposition of hands was a solemn symbol of consecration, by which also the gifts of the Holy Spirit were conferred. There is no doubt that Christ frequently made use of this rite, so that these men were asking nothing but what they knew He had used for a long time. But Christ employs other symbols too; for He anointed the dumb man's tongue in His spittle and put His finger in his ears. The mere laying on of hands would have been efficacious enough in itself—nay, if He had not moved a finger, His will alone would have prevailed. But it is plain that He used outward signs freely so as to help men by them. So that now, by sprinkling his tongue with His spittle, He wanted to indicate that the faculty of speech flows from Himself alone, and by putting His finger in the man's ears He taught that it was His proper office to perforate, as it were, deaf ears. There is no need to flee to allegories, and we see that those who have played that game the most subtly have offered nothing substantial but rather made the explaining of Scripture a mockery. Therefore let this one thing suffice sober readers, that through prayer we receive speech and hearing from Christ inasmuch as He inspires His power into our tongues and penetrates into our ears by His fingers. The reason why He takes the deaf man aside from the crowd is partly that He wanted the ignorant and those who were not yet satisfactory witnesses to behold the glory of His Godhead from afar, and partly that He might pour out the fervour of His praying more freely. For His looking up into heaven and sighing was a sign of His powerful emotion—and it shows us His singular love towards men when He so much sympathized with their miseries. Nor is there any doubt that by transferring His spittle from His own mouth into the man's mouth and by inserting His fingers into his ears He wanted to testify and express the same affection of kindness. Yet He demonstrates that He has the supreme rule in correcting human faults and healing them when He simply commands the tongue and the ears to be opened. For Mark did not use this Chaldean word thoughtlessly but as a witness to Christ's divine power. Among other trifles with which foolish men have adulterated baptism there is this piece of play-acting too.[1] This example warns us that there is no half-way house in licence when men wanton at their will in the mysteries of God.

[1] Calvin means the so-called *Effeta* in the Roman rite, when the ears and lips of the catechumen were anointed with spittle.

Mark 7.36. *And he charged them, that they should tell no man.* There are many expositors who twist these commands round to mean the opposite, as if Christ had deliberately stirred them up to publish abroad the news of the miracle; but to me it seems more simply (as I have mentioned before) that He only wanted this to be deferred to a more opportune and ripe time. Therefore I do not doubt that their enthusiasm was untimely when they, who were commanded to be silent, hastened to speak. But it is not surprising that people who were not accustomed to Christ's teaching should be carried away by an immoderate zeal at the wrong time. Yet Christ turns their imprudence to His glory, for the miracle was made known and all that region was made inexcusable for despising the author of the heavenly gifts.

Mark 7.37. *He hath done all things well.* After Matthew has collected together several miracles he finally adds the clause that the crowds were amazed and gave glory to the God of Israel, because by showing His power in these unusual ways He renewed the memory of His covenant. But there is perhaps an antithesis hidden in Mark's words; for because the rumour about Christ was varied, 'crowd' signifies that it was the ungodly and malicious who maligned His actions when in fact everything that they slandered deserved the highest praise. And even our natural sense teaches us that nothing is more unfair than for blessings to be made matters of accusation and hatred.

Matt. 15.32. *I have compassion on the multitude.* Here is related a miracle not very different from the other which we expounded earlier. The only difference is that instead of Christ feeding five thousand men with five loaves and two fishes, He now feeds four thousand with seven loaves and some fishes. And instead of twelve baskets being filled with the fragments, there is less left over from a larger supply. This teaches us that God's power is not tied to means or helps and that it does not matter to Him whether there be much or little, as Jonathan said of His small forces and the huge multitude of the enemy (I Sam. 14.6). But just as God's blessing is enough to feed a great crowd whether with one loaf or twenty, so without His power a hundred loaves are not sufficient to feed a hundred men. For when the staff of bread is broken, although the full weight of flour may come from the mill, of bread from the oven, yet it will profit nothing but to cram the belly. Do not understand the three days' fasting of which Christ speaks as their having gone without food for three days; but a desert does not offer much in the way of resources, and of necessity they lacked ordinary food. Add that in those hot lands they did not get so hungry as we do in our thick and cold climate. So it is not surprising if they can go without food longer.

Matt. 15.33. *Whence should we have, etc.* The disciples betray a too

174

Kingdom of God should be completely restored. When there was nothing more to level against His teaching they ask Him to give a sign from heaven. But it is certain that they would have yielded no more to a hundred signs than to the testimonies of Scripture. Add that the power of Christ had already set many miracles before their eyes, almost at the touch of their hands. They neglect the signs by which Christ revealed Himself familiarly to them. How much less, then, will they profit from a distant and obscure sign? So today the Papists, as if the teaching of the Gospel had never been sealed, ask that it should be proved to them by new miracles.

And we must observe that although the Sadducees were engaged in a bitter struggle with the Pharisees, so that not only was there bad feeling but quarrels were continually breaking out between them, yet nevertheless they league together against Christ. The ungodly may disagree, but their mutual discord never prevents them from conspiring against God and as if by a pact reaching out their hands to oppress the truth. By the word 'tempting' the Evangelists signify that it was not in sincerity or with a desire to learn but by deceit that they were seeking what they thought He was going to deny them, or at least, what they imagined was not in Christ's power. For because they were convinced that there was nothing but meanness and lowliness in Him, they had only the one aim of uncovering His weakness and overthrowing all the esteem He had won among the people. Thus unbelievers are said to tempt God when they grumble that they have not been given whatever they desire and accuse God of weakness.

Matt. 16.2. *When it begins to be evening.* In these words Christ tells them that His power was sufficiently declared for them to know the time of their visitation—unless they evaded the open light by deliberately closing their eyes. And He uses a beautiful and very apt metaphor; for although the state of the weather is changeable, so that now a storm will suddenly get up and now it is unexpectedly fair, yet men foretell from natural signs that tomorrow will be bright or cloudy. Christ therefore asks why they do not recognize the Kingdom of God when it is manifest by no less clear signs. For this showed quite clearly that they were too devoted to earthly and transitory interests and despised what concerned the heavenly and spiritual life. They were blind, not so much from error, as from deliberate malice. Also He calls them 'hypocrites' because they pretend to be seeking what they did not want to see when it was shown them. Now the same rebuke is relevant to almost the whole world. Because men bend their wits and apply their senses to the use of the present, there is hardly anyone who in this respect is not sufficiently strong and capable or at least does not know pretty well how to achieve what will be profitable to him.

Is not the reason why the signs by which God invites us to Himself are meaningless, that each of us quenches the light offered by giving himself to a willing dullness? But Christ's calling and the present revelation of eternal salvation was visible to the scribes from the Law and the prophets as well as from His teaching and the miracles joined to it. There are very many today who chatter away that on difficult problems they rightly suspend judgment because they must wait for a sure definition of it. They even think that it is wisdom to avoid deliberately any inquisition into the truth. As if it were not wicked slothfulness, when they take so much trouble about fleshly and earthly things, to neglect the eternal salvation of their souls and all the while find themselves empty excuses for their gross and supine ignorance. But it is quite absurd when some unlearned men deduce from this passage that it is unlawful to study the skies or forecast the temperature and storms. Christ is rather arguing from the right order of nature that those who are quite clever in the affairs of this present life, but cover over the heavenly light knowingly and willingly by their dullness, justly perish from their ingratitude.

Mark adds that Christ *sighed deeply in his spirit.* By these words he means that He took it sadly and bitterly when He saw those ungrateful men obstinately resisting God. And certainly all who desire the glory of God and have a concern for men's salvation should be so minded that nothing hurts them more than to see unbelievers deliberately blocking their own way to faith and applying their whole mind to obscuring the brightness of God's Word and works with their own mists. I consider that the word 'spirit' is emphatic, to tell us that this sigh came from the very depths of His heart; and so no sophist can say that Christ was pretending a sorrow that He did not feel. His holy soul, governed by the spirit of zeal, could not fail to be deeply saddened by such ungodly wilfulness.

Luke 12.57. *And why even of yourselves.* Here Christ uncovers the spring of their evil and as it were touches the ulcer with His scalpel—that they do not descend into their consciences nor inwardly consider before God what it is. This is why hypocrites are so bold in their quibbling and throw their boasts boldly forth. They do not collect their thoughts or place themselves before God's judgment seat so that they may know the truth and it may have the victory.

Luke tells us that this was said to the crowds, and this does not disagree with what Matthew and Mark relate, for it is probable that Christ was in general addressing the scribes' followers and disciples and such like despisers of God whom He saw were far too numerous. Thus His complaint or rebuke was aimed at the whole gang.

Matt. 16.4. *An evil and adulterous generation.* This passage was expounded in chapter 12. The sum of it is that the Jews will accept no signs but eventually get a depraved urge to test God. He does not call them an adulterous generation simply because they seek a sign (for God sometimes allows this for His people), but because they set out to provoke God; and He threatens them that He will be like the prophet Jonah risen from the dead. This is in Matthew; Mark does not mention Jonah. But the meaning is the same, that it would not even be a sign to them if Christ rose from the dead and uttered everywhere the resounding voice of His Gospel.

*And the disciples came to the other side and forgot to take bread. And Jesus said unto them, Take heed and beware of the leaven of the Pharisees and Sadducees. And they reasoned among themselves, saying, We took no bread. And Jesus perceiving it said to them, O ye of little faith, why reason ye among yourselves, because ye took no bread? Do ye not yet perceive neither remember the five loaves of the five thousand, and how many baskets ye took up? Neither the seven loaves of the four thousand, and how many baskets ye took up? How is it that ye do not perceive that I spake not to you concerning bread? But beware of the leaven of the Pharisees and Sadducees. Then understood they how that he bade them not beware of the leaven of bread, but of the teaching of the Pharisees and Sadducees.* (Matt. 16.5-12)

*And they forgot to take bread; and they had not in the boat with them more than one loaf. And he charged them, saying, Take heed, beware of the leaven of the Pharisees and the leaven of Herod. And they reasoned one with another, saying, We have no bread. And Jesus perceiving it saith unto them, Why reason ye, because ye have no bread? do ye not yet perceive, neither understand? have ye your heart hardened? Having eyes, see ye not? and having ears, hear ye not? and do ye not remember? When I brake the five loaves among five thousand, how many baskets full of broken pieces took ye up? They say unto him, Twelve. And when the seven among the four thousand, how many baskets of broken pieces took ye up? And they said unto him, Seven. And he said unto them, Do ye not yet understand?* (Mark 8.14-21)

*In the meantime, when the many thousands of the multitude were gathered together, insomuch that they trode one upon another, he began to say unto his disciples first of all, Beware of the leaven of the Pharisees which is hypocrisy.* (Luke 12.1)

Matt. 16.5. *And the disciples came.* Here Christ exhorts His disciples, on the basis of what had happened earlier, to beware of all the corruptions that infect sincere godliness. A little before, the Pharisees had come, a real example of poisonous wilfulness. The Sadducees were their companions. In quite another camp stood Herod, the worst of the lot and an enemy and corrupter of true doctrine. In the midst of all these perils it was necessary to warn the disciples to take care. For since the human spirit inclines of itself to vanity and errors, there is nothing easier than to fall away from the true and genuine purity of the Word of God when we are set about with perverted inventions of corrupt doctrine and similar pests. And if they once got a hold on us, it could never happen that true religion would reign alone in us. But we must consider Christ's words, so that the whole thing may become clearer.

Matt. 16.6. *The leaven of the Pharisees.* Matthew joins with the Pharisees and the Sadducees, but Mark puts Herod instead. Luke mentions only the Pharisees (although it is not clear whether he is relating the same discourse of Christ), and defines leaven as hypocrisy, but he only touches on this sentence as if there were no ambiguity in it at all. Although the metaphor of leaven, which is here referred to false doctrine, might elsewhere have been transferred to hypocrisy of life and morals, or the same thing might have been said twice; yet there will be nothing absurd in our saying that whereas the other two narrate the course of the story more fully, Luke speaks a little differently and just mentions it without reference to its place or order. And yet there is no discrepancy in this. If we may follow this conjecture, then hypocrisy means something different from a counterfeit and forged show of wisdom, namely, the very fount and substance of empty display which seems something great before men but is nothing in God's eyes. For Jeremiah (5.3) bears witness that the eyes of the Lord look upon the truth, and He instructs believers by His word into sound godliness so that they may cleave to righteousness with a perfect and sincere heart. Just as also it is said in Deuteronomy 10.12: 'And now, O Israel, what doth the Lord require of thee but to cleave to Him with all your heart and all your soul?' But in opposition, neglecting spiritual worship, they bring in the traditions of men in their transitory disguises, as if God could be snared in such traps. For although external ceremonies may be impressive, before God they are childish trifles, save in so far as by their help we are trained in true godliness.

Now let us understand why Luke classes hypocrisy as invented doctrine and by this name embraces the leavens of men which only swell them up and in the sight of God contain nothing solid, and indeed which only pervert men's minds from the true study of godliness to empty and worthless ceremonies. But it will be best to keep to Matthew's exposition, which is clearer. Since the disciples at last understood the Lord's rebuke as a command to beware of false doctrine, it is certain that Christ's intention was to fore-arm them against the present corruptions which beset them on all sides.  And He spoke expressly of the Pharisees and Sadducees because these two parties reigned tyrannically at that time in the Church and kept the teaching of the Law and the prophets under by their corrupt doctrines, so that hardly anything healthy or whole remained.  Yet it may be asked why Mark numbers Herod among the false teachers when he never professed any such office.  I reply that since he was a half-Jew, degenerate and faithless, he could try by all sorts of tricks to seduce the people to his side.  For it is the manner of all apostates to compound some admixture in order to invent a new religion and abolish the old.  And therefore, because he was cunningly working to overturn the principles of true and ancient godliness in favour of a religion which would best fit in with his tyranny, or rather because he was trying to introduce a new form of Judaism, it is not without cause that the Lord bids them beware of his leaven.  The scribes sowed their errors from the temple of God, and Herod's court was Satan's other publishing house for manufacturing different errors.

Just as today in the Papacy we see that anti-Christ not only vomits his deceits in temples and the caves of the sophists and the monks but also that his kingdom is buttressed by the help of the theological schools, and no trick is left untried.  And even as at that time Christ forestalled the present evils and stirred up the minds of His people to beware of what was especially harmful, we today are warned by this example to consider wisely what sort of corruptions may harm us.  You will sooner mix fire with water than reconcile the Papist inventions with the Gospel.  And so whoever desires sincerely to give himself as a disciple to Christ must study to keep his soul pure from that leaven.  If he has already been tainted by it, he must strive to purify himself until nothing of these dregs or filthiness sticks to him.  Now on the other hand, because there are troublemakers who have tried in various ways to corrupt sound doctrine, believers must watch out carefully and beware of such tricks and so celebrate a perpetual passover in the leaven of truth.  But because there now flourishes everywhere an atheistical (*Lucianica*) ungodliness, a most pernicious leaven, a more than deadly poison, they must apply all their senses to this caution, which is necessary above all others.

Matt. 16.8. *Why reason ye within yourselves?*  The disciples again show how little they had profited both from the Master's teaching and from His wonderful works.  When He spoke of bewaring of leaven, they took it as if Christ merely wanted to take them away from outward business.  Because it was usual among the Jews not to eat with the heathen, the disciples think that the Pharisees are being reduced to that order and number. This ignorance was not unendurable; but because they had already forgotten the recent blessings, they did not think that the remedy was in Christ's hands to stop them having to pollute themselves by eating and drinking, and so He rebuked them more sharply, as they deserved. And surely their ingratitude was too gross. Only recently they had seen enough bread created out of nothing to fill many thousands of people, and this had been done twice. Yet now they are so worried about food, as if the same power were not still in the Master. From these words we gather that all are convicted of unbelief who have experienced God's power once or twice but mistrust for the future. For just as faith cherishes the memory of God's gifts in our hearts, so, unless faith has fallen asleep, forgetfulness of them will never steal over us.

Matt. 16.12. *Then understood they, etc.* It is quite clear that Christ was setting the word 'leaven' in opposition to the simple and pure Word of God. Earlier Christ had used the word in a good sense saying that the Gospel was like leaven; but generally Scripture indicates by this word a foreign element which infects the native purity of something. In this passage, without doubt, there are two interrelated antitheses—the simple truth of God and the figment which men invent out of their own ideas. No sophist should try to slip out of this by denying that this should be understood of any doctrine, for there is no other doctrine which deserves to be called true and unleavened than that which comes from God. From this it follows that it is anything mixed in from outside that is called leaven; just as Paul tells us that faith is adulterated as soon as we are led away from the simplicity of Christ (II Cor. 11.3).

And now we must see whose teaching the Lord bids them beware of. At that time the ordinary power in the Church was in the hands of the scribes and priests, and the Pharisees were in the chief position. Since Christ warns His disciples off their teaching in particular it follows that all those are to be rejected who mix inventions with the Word of God or impart something alien, however honourable a rank or title they may boast. Therefore the subjection of those who willingly submit to the fictions and laws of the Pope is accursed and false.

*And they come unto Bethsaida. And they bring to him a blind man, and beseech him to touch him. And he took hold of the blind man by the hand, and brought him out of the village; and when he had spit on his*

181

*eyes, and laid his hands upon him, he asked him, Seest thou aught?*
*And he looked up, and said, I see men; for I behold them as trees walking.*
*Then again he laid his hands upon his eyes; and he commanded him to*
*look, and he was restored, and saw all things clearly. And he sent him*
*away to his home, saying, Do not even enter into the village, nor speak*
*to anyone in the village.* (Mark 8.22-26)

This miracle, omitted by the others, seems to have been related by Mark especially on account of the circumstance that Christ restored the blind man's sight little by little and not suddenly, as He usually did. And this was probably done to set up in the man a proof of His freedom of activity, that He was not tied to any rigid form, but exercised His power in this way or in that. Therefore He did not enlighten the eyes of the blind man to perform their duty immediately but instilled an obscure and confused sight in them; then, by another imposition of His hands He gave them perfect sight. Thus the grace of Christ which on others was poured out all at once, flowed upon this man drop by drop.

Mark 8.24. *I see men.* He had asked the blind man for the sake of the disciples, so that they might learn that something had been given to him already, but yet only a slight beginning of healing had taken place. He replies that he sees men, since he could make out some people walking who were upright, like trees. And by these words he confesses that his sight is still not so clear that he can tell men from trees, but yet that he has been given some faculty of sight, because from their movement he conjectures that what he saw standing upright were men—it is in this sense, too, that he says they are like trees. Wherefore we see that it was only by conjecture that he said he saw men.

Mark 8.26. *And he sent him away to his home.* Christ did not let him go back to Bethsaida where many had witnessed the miracle. Some imagine that this was because Christ wished to punish the inhabitants of the place by depriving them of the enjoyment of His grace. Whatever the cause, it is certain that He did not perform the miracle so that it might be forever buried, but wanted to hide it among many others until the sins of the world should be expiated by His death and He should ascend to the glory of His Father.

*Now when Jesus came into the parts of Caesarea Philippi, he asked his*
*disciples, saying, Who do men say that the Son of man is? And they*
*said, Some say John the Baptist; some, Elijah: and others, Jeremiah, or*
*one of the prophets. He saith unto them, But who say ye that I am?*

*And Simon Peter answered and said, Thou art the Christ, the Son of the living God. And Jesus answered, and said unto him, Blessed art thou, Simon Bar-Jonah: for flesh and blood hath not revealed it unto thee, but my Father which is in heaven. And I also say unto tnee, that thou art Peter, and upon this rock I will build my church; and the gates of hell shall not prevail against it. And I will give unto thee the keys of the kingdom of heaven: and whatsoever thou shalt bind on earth shall be bound in heaven: and whatsoever thou shalt loose on earth shall be loosed in heaven.* (Matt. 16.13-19)

*And Jesus went forth, and his disciples, into the villages of Caesarea which is called Philippi: and in the way he asked his disciples, saying unto them, Who say men that I am? And they answered him, John the Baptist: and others, Elijah; but others, One of the prophets. And he said to them, But who say ye that I am? Peter answereth and saith unto him, Thou art the Christ.* (Mark 8.27-29)

*And it came to pass, as he was praying alone, the disciples were with him: and he asked them, saying, Who do the multitudes say that I am? And they answering said, John the Baptist; but others say, Elijah; and others, that one of the old prophets is risen again. And he said unto them, But who say ye that I am? And Peter answering said, The Christ of God.* (Luke 9.18-20)

**Matt. 16.13.** *Into the parts of Caesarea Philippi.* Mark tells us that this conversation took place on a journey. But Luke says it was when He was praying and He had only His disciples with Him. Matthew does not indicate the occasion so precisely. Yet it is certain that they are all referring to the same story, and it may be that Christ questioned the disciples on the journey after He had prayed at some resting place.

There were two Caesareas, an old and more famous one which at first was the tower of Strato, and this one, situated at the foot of Mount Lebanon not far from Jordan; and so the distinguishing epithet was added. Some think that it was built on the same place where once was the town of Dan, yet because it had been recently built by the tetrarch Philip, it was called Philippi.

*Who do men say.* It could seem that the meaning is: What is the general rumour about the Redeemer who became the Son of Man? But the question is different: What do men think about Jesus the Son of Mary? According to His custom He takes the name 'Son of Man'; as if He were saying, 'Now that I live on earth, clothed in flesh and one man among all the others, what is the judgment on me?' And it was Christ's purpose to establish His disciples solidly in a sure faith, so that they should not waver between many opinions, as we see at once.

Matt. 16.14. *Some say John.* This does not refer to the professed enemies of Christ or to heathenish despisers but to the more healthy and sound part of the people and as it were the choice flower of the Church. For the disciples mention only those who speak well of Christ; and yet, although the truth was set before them, none of them reached towards that mark, but they all melted away into their dreams. From this we can see how weak is the human spirit, which not only can conceive of itself nothing right and true but even fabricates errors out of true principles. Add that Christ is the unique sign of concord and peace by whom God gathers the whole world to Himself and yet the greater part seizes from this an occasion of greater discord. Certainly among the Jews unity of faith existed only in Christ, and yet those who at first seemed to have some agreement among themselves now break up into various opinions. We can see how error often begets error. The idea that was settled in peoples' minds that souls migrate into different bodies made them the more prone to this false imagination. But although the Jews were divided in this way by Christ's coming, yet such a variety of opinions should not hinder the godly from desiring the pure knowledge of Him. For if anyone used this as an excuse to give himself up to sloth and neglected to seek Christ, even by our judgment there would be no excuse for him. Much less would he escape God's judgment if he shrank from Christ because of the sects or made the false opinions of men a reason for contempt and not deigning to give himself to Christ.

Matt. 16.15. *But who say ye that I am?* Here Christ distinguishes His disciples from the rest of the crowd. And this makes it all the more absurd, however much others may reject it, that we should be distracted from the unity of faith. For whoever give themselves simply to Christ and do not try to mix anything from their own head with the Gospel, shall never lack sure light. But we have to be careful and vigilant in keeping firmly to Christ while the whole world slips away into its inventions. As Satan could not take from the Jews the conviction they held from the Law and the prophets about the coming of the Christ, he transfigured Him in all sorts of ways and, so to say, cut Him into pieces. Then he put forward many fictitious Christs, that the true Redeemer might be lost. Afterwards with the same tricks he did not cease either to tear Christ asunder or to give Him a different appearance. Therefore, among the confused and discordant voices of the world we must always let sound in our ears this voice of Christ which separates us from wandering and erratic men, so that we may not go with the multitude and our faith may not be tossed about among the contrary waves of opinions.

Matt. 16.16. *Thou art the Christ.* A brief confession, but one which contains the whole sum of our salvation. In the praise of Christ is comprehended His eternal Kingdom and Priesthood, that He reconciles God to us and wins perfect righteousness, expiating our sins by His sacrifice, that He keeps His own, whom He has received into His trust and care, and adorns and enriches us with every kind of blessing. Mark has only 'Thou art the Christ', where Luke has 'the Christ of God', but the meaning is the same. In times past the kings, divinely anointed with oil, were called the christs of God. And Luke used this expression earlier in saying that a reply was given to Simeon from heaven that he should not die until he had seen the Lord's Christ. For the divine redemption was clear which God revealed by the hand of His Son. Therefore it was right that He who was to be the Redeemer should come forth from heaven marked with the anointing of God. In Matthew the term is clearer—'the Son of the living God'. For although it may be that Peter did not yet grasp distinctly how Christ was begotten of God, yet he believed Him to be so excellent as to originate from God, not like the rest of men, but as living and true Godhead clothed in flesh. By ascribing the epithet 'living' to God, he is indicating a distinction between Him and dead idols which are nothing.

Matt. 16.17. *Blessed art thou, Simon.* Since this is life eternal, to know the one God and Jesus Christ whom He has sent, Christ has every reason to pronounce blessed the man who sincerely made this confession. But He did not speak this privately to Peter, but wanted to show where the unique felicity of the whole world was set. And to aspire after Him the more heartily we must first understand that by nature men are all wretched and accursed until they find the remedy in Christ. And also it must be added that whoever has attained Christ lacks absolutely nothing of perfect blessedness, since we may not desire anything more than the eternal glory of God, to the possession of which Christ leads us.

*Flesh and blood.* In the person of one man, Christ admonishes all men that they must seek faith from His Father and give Him the praise for His grace. For here flesh and blood are set over against the special illumination of God. From this we infer that human minds lack the ability to perceive the mysteries of heavenly wisdom hidden in Christ; more, all human senses fail in this respect until God opens our eyes to see His glory in Christ. And so let no-one, trusting in his own insight, break out in pride, but let us humbly allow ourselves to be taught inwardly by the Father of lights, that His Spirit alone may enlighten our darkness. And now let those who have been given faith learn to be aware of their own blindness and to refer to God what they have received.

Matt. 16.18. *And I say unto thee.* By these words, which give Peter so great a reward, Christ declares how pleased He is at his confession. For although He had already given His disciple Simon the name of Peter and freely appointed him an apostle, yet He ascribes these free gifts to faith as if they were a kind of reward—and this is not uncommon in Scripture. Moreover, He gives Peter a two-fold honour, the first in regard to his own salvation, the second to his apostolic office.

When He says *Thou art Peter,* He is confirming that He did not bestow this name on him in vain, but that he holds his firm position as a living stone in the temple of God. This extends to all believers, each of whom is a temple of God, and compact together by faith make up one temple (Eph. 2.20). But it also marks out Peter's pre-eminence, as each in his own order receives more or less according to the measure of the gift of Christ.

*Upon this rock.* From this it appears how the name Peter belongs both to Peter and to other believers; that is, founded on the faith of Christ they are fitted by a holy concord into the spiritual building, so that God may dwell in their midst. For since Christ here declares that this is the common foundation for the whole Church, He wishes to join with Peter all the believers who are going to exist in the world. It is as if He said, 'You are now just a tiny number of men, and therefore your confession has little worth at present; but the time will soon come when it will stand out splendidly and will spread far wider.' And this availed not a little to encourage the disciples to constancy; because, although their faith was obscure and lowly, yet they were chosen by the Lord as first fruits so that at last from this insignificant beginning there should arise the new Church which would stand triumphant against all the designs of hell. For although the pronoun 'it' can refer either to faith or the Church, the latter sense fits better, because the Church shall stand victorious against all the power of Satan; that is, the truth of God on which her faith rests shall ever remain unshaken. This corresponds to John's saying: 'This is the victory that overcomes the world, even your faith' (I John 5.4).

In particular this promise is worthy of note, that those who are united in Christ and acknowledge Him to be Christ and Mediator, shall remain safe from all harm even unto the end. For what is said of the body of the Church refers to each individual member, so far as they are one in Christ. But this also warns us that so long as the Church is a pilgrim on this earth she will know no rest but will be exposed to many assaults. For the reason why He denies that Satan will gain the upper hand is because He will always oppose him. Therefore, we are stayed on this word of Christ and exult safely against Satan and already by faith triumph over all his forces; but we must also learn that the

186

trumpet has, so to say, sounded, to prepare us for the battle. The word 'gates' without doubt denotes a kind of power and fortification.

Matt. 16.19. *And I will give unto thee the keys.* Here Christ begins to speak about Peter's public office, that is, his apostolate. He adorns its dignity with a twofold encomium. For Christ says that ministers of the Gospel are like gate-keepers of the Kingdom of heaven, because they bear its keys. And secondly He adds that they are endowed with a power of binding and loosing which is effective in heaven. The metaphor of 'keys' fits in well with the office of teaching, as Christ says in Luke 11.52 that the scribes and Pharisees, as interpreters of the Law, likewise have the key of the Kingdom of heaven. For we know that the gate of life is only opened to us by the Word of God. From this it follows that the key is put into the hand of the minister of the Word. Those who think that 'keys' was put in the plural because the apostles were appointed not only to open but also to shut have some likelihood on their side. Yet if anyone takes it less subtly, let him hold his own view. It may be asked why the Lord promises that He will give to Peter what it seems He gave him when He first created him an apostle. But this problem was solved in chapter 10, when I said that the twelve were at first only temporary heralds, so that when they returned to Christ they had fulfilled their commission. But when Christ had risen from the dead, they began to be appointed as ordinary doctors of the Church. In this respect the honour is bestowed upon him for the future.

*Whatsoever thou shalt bind.* This second metaphor or similitude strictly denotes the forgiveness of sins. For Christ, by setting us free by His Gospel from the guilt of eternal death, looses the snares of the curse by which we were held bound. Therefore He declares that the doctrine is appointed for loosing our chains, so that, loosed by the voice and testimony of men on earth we may in actual fact be loosed also in heaven. But because very many ungodly not only reject the liberation offered to them but also by their obstinacy bring upon themselves more grievous judgment, the power and mandate of 'binding' is also given to ministers of the Gospel. Yet we must note that this is accidental and as it were unnatural to the Gospel. As Paul teaches when talking of vengeance which he says is held ready against all unbelievers and rebels; he at once adds, 'When your obedience is fulfilled' (II Cor. 10.6). Unless the reprobate turn life into death by their own fault, the Gospel is the power of God to all for salvation. Yet because when it is heard the ungodliness of many breaks out openly and provokes God's wrath the more, it must of necessity be an odour of death to them.

The sum of it is that Christ wants to teach His own about the salvation promised them in the Gospel so that they may await it no less confidently than if He Himself descended from heaven as a witness. But, again, He also wished to strike terror into the despisers lest they should think they could mock ministers of the Word with impunity. And both these are very necessary; for because the incomprehensible treasure of life is set before us in earthen vessels, unless the authority of eternal doctrine is confirmed in this way, their faith would fail at almost every moment. Again, the ungodly behave so boldly because they think that they have to do only with men. Therefore Christ pronounces that it is by the preaching of the Gospel that there is revealed on earth what God's future and heavenly judgment will be, and that we must not look elsewhere for certainty of life or death. It is a great honour that we are God's interpreters to bear witness to the world of His salvation. The highest majesty of the Gospel is that it is called the ambassadorship of the mutual reconciliation between God and men. And finally, it is a wonderful consolation to godly souls that they know that the news of salvation brought to them by some little mortal man is ratified before God. Let the ungodly ridicule the doctrine which is preached at God's command if they like. They will feel at the last that it was really and truly God who was threatening them by the mouth of men. Finally, armed with this confidence, godly teachers may boldly be sureties to themselves and others of the quickening grace of God, and yet no less courageously threaten the obstinate despisers of their teaching.

So far I have expounded clearly the native sense of the words, so that no more would need to be said. But the Roman antichrist, wishing to bring in some excuse for his tyranny, has dared to pervert this whole passage not less wickedly than unbelievingly. And although the mere light of the true interpretation which I have contributed seems sufficient to wipe away his darkness, yet lest godly readers should be hindered, I will briefly refute his disgusting falsehoods. First, he pretends that Peter is called the foundation of the Church. But who cannot see that what he transfers to the person of a man was said about Peter's faith in Christ? I grant that in Greek Peter (*Petros*) and stone (*petra*) mean the same thing, save that the first word is Attic, the second from the common tongue. But this variation is not put down thoughtlessly in Matthew, but is rather a deliberate kind of change to express something different. And I have no doubt that Christ in His own language signified such a distinction. Hence Augustine wisely said that *petra* [stone] does not come from Peter, but Peter from *petra*, just as we are all Christians from Christ. But to be brief, Paul's saying should be held as sure and certain among us, that the Church can be founded only on Christ (I Cor. 3.11); and therefore the Pope's invention of another foundation can be nothing but sacrilegious blasphemy. And indeed no words can express how much we should detest the Papist tyranny from this one name alone. For its sake the foundation of the Church has been taken away, so that the opened pit of hell swallows up unhappy souls. Add that (as I mentioned at first) this clause does not yet relate to Peter's public office. It was simply that he was given just one of the chief places among the sacred stones of the temple. The praises which follow do, however, relate to the apostolic office. Whence it follows that nothing is said to Peter that does not belong also to the rest of his colleagues. For if the apostolic dignity is common to them all, that which is annexed to it must also be in common. But Christ addresses Peter only by name. Just as one had confessed in the name of all that Christ was the Son of God, so His word in response was directed to one, but belonged to them all equally. But we must not slight the reason which Cyprian and others inferred, that He commends unity to the Church. They argue in reply that he to whom this was specially given was preferred before all others. But this is just as if they were insisting that he was more of an apostle than his colleagues; for the power of binding and loosing could no more be taken from the teaching office and the apostolate than heat or light from the sun. But even if we grant that Peter was pre-eminent among the apostles because he had been given more than the rest, yet the Papists' inference is stupid that the primacy was given to him so that he might be the universal head of the whole church. For dignity is a different matter from gathering the whole world under his arms. And certainly Christ laid no more weight on him than he could bear. He was commanded to be a gate-keeper of the Kingdom of Heaven, he was commanded to dispense God's grace by binding and loosing, and to execute His judgment on earth—that is, as far as the faculty of a mortal man extends. Therefore, whatever was given to him must be restricted to the measure of the grace given for the edification of the Church. Thus that vast empire which the Papists arrogate to him collapses.

But even if there were no controversy or quarrel about Peter, the Pope's tyranny would still gain nothing from this. For the principle which the Papists hold and which no-one in his senses will concede to them, is that what was given to Peter was then transmitted to his successors as by hereditary right. For he was not permitted to give anything to his successors. The Papists therefore make him free of another man's property. Finally, if the continual succession were in fact valid, the Pope would wring nothing from it until he had proved that he was Peter's lawful successor. And how will he prove that? Because Peter died at Rome; as if Rome by the murder of an apostle had won herself the primacy! But they also claim that he was bishop there. How futile this is I have sufficiently taught in my *Institutio*[1]; and I would prefer the complete course of this argument to be sought there rather than to repeat it here to the trouble and boredom of the reader. Yet this brief statement may be added; even if the successor of Peter had been Bishop of Rome by right, yet when by his teaching he usurped so much honour to himself, he lost whatever Christ conferred on Peter's successors. That the Pope's court is at Rome is well enough known; but there they show no mark of the Church. They no less abhor the true office of pastor than they strive greedily for their domination. Certainly Christ omitted no praise in extolling the heirs of Peter; but He was not so lavish as to transfer His own honour to apostates.

*Then charged he the disciples that they should tell no man that he was Jesus the Christ. From that time began Jesus to show unto his disciples, how that he must go unto Jerusalem, and suffer many things of the elders and chief priests and scribes, and be killed, and the third day be raised up. And Peter took him, and began to rebuke him, saying, Be it far from thee, Lord: this shall never be unto thee. But he turned, and said unto Peter, Get thee behind me, Satan: thou art a stumbling-block unto me: for thou mindest not the things of God, but the things of men. Then said Jesus unto his disciples, If any man would come after me, let him deny himself, and take up his cross, and follow me. For whosoever would save his life shall lose it: and whosoever shall lose his life for my sake shall find it. For what shall a man be profited, if he shall gain the whole world, and forfeit his own soul? or what shall a man give in exchange for his soul? For the Son of man shall come in the glory of his Father with his angels; and then shall he render unto every man according to his deeds. Verily I say unto you, There be some that stand here, which shall in no wise taste of death, till they see the Son of man coming in his kingdom.* (Matt. 16.20-28)

*And he charged them that they should tell no man of him. And he began to teach them, that the Son of man must suffer many things, and be rejected by the elders, and the chief priests, and the scribes, and be killed, and after three days rise again. And he spake the saying openly. And Peter took him, and began to rebuke him. But he turning about, and seeing his disciples, rebuked Peter, and saith, Get thee behind me, Satan: for thou mindest not the things of God, but the things of men. And he*

[1] Strictly, the reference is to 1550 *Inst.* cap. VIII. §§ 98-102. In 1559 the reference is IV.vi.11-15.

*called unto him the multitude with his disciples, and said unto them, If*
*any man would come after me, let him deny himself, and take up his cross,*
*and follow me. For whosoever would save his life shall lose it; and who-*
*soever shall lose his life for my sake and the gospel's shall save it. For*
*what doth it profit a man, to gain the whole world, and forfeit his own*
*soul? Or what shall a man give in exchange for his soul? For whoso-*
*ever shall be ashamed of me and my words in this adulterous and sinful*
*generation, the Son of man also shall be ashamed of him, when he cometh*
*in the glory of his Father, with the holy angels. And he saith unto them,*
*Verily I say unto you, There be some here among them that stand by,*
*which shall in no wise taste of death, till they see the kingdom of God*
*come with power.* (Mark 8.30-38; 9.1)

*But he charged them, and commanded them to tell this to no man; saying,*
*The Son of man must suffer many things, and be rejected of the elders*
*and chief priests and scribes, and be killed, and the third day be raised up.*
*And he said unto all, If any man would come after me, let him deny*
*himself, and take up his cross daily, and follow me. For whosoever would*
*save his life shall lose it; but whosoever shall lose his life for my sake,*
*the same shall save it. For what is a man profited, if he gain the whole*
*world, and lose or forfeit his own self? For whosoever shall be ashamed*
*of me and of my words, of him shall the Son of man be ashamed, when*
*he cometh in his own glory, and the glory of the Father, and of the holy*
*angels. But I tell you of a truth, There be some of them that stand here,*
*which shall in no wise taste of death, till they see the kingdom of God.*
(Luke 9.21-27)

Christ had given a sample of His future glory, and now He tells His
disciples that He must suffer, so that they also may prepare themselves
for bearing their cross. The time of the struggle was at hand and He
knew that they were quite unequal to it unless they were armed with
a new fortitude. But what was specially necessary was for Christ to
show them that His Kingdom would be ushered in, not in great pomp,
not with great riches, not with the joyful applause of the world, but
by a shameful death. Nothing was more difficult for them than to
overcome such an offence, especially if we reckon the deep-seated
persuasion they had of the Master; for they imagined that He would
be the author of earthly happiness. They hang therefore on an empty
hope, greedily longing for the moment of time when Christ should
suddenly reveal the glory of His Kingdom. Of the ignominy of the
cross they had so little thought that they believed it would be completely out of keeping for anything disgraceful to happen to him. It
also was a serious matter to be reproved by the elders and scribes, who
held the primacy in the Church. And from this it is easy to grasp how

necessary was this admonition. But because the mere mention of the cross could not fail to upset their weak minds terribly, He at once heals the wound and says that on the third day He would rise from the dead. And certainly, since in His cross there appears only the weakness of the flesh, until our faith comes to His resurrection, in which shone the power of the Spirit, it will find nothing on which to stand or maintain itself. Hence this method must be prudently kept by ministers of the Word who desire to teach successfully, that they shall always join the glory of His resurrection with the ignominy of His death. But it is surprising that Christ did not want the apostles to bear witness to Him, when He had already laid this office upon them. For why had they been sent, save as heralds of the redemption which depended on Christ's coming? The solution is not difficult if we keep in mind what I then explained, that they were appointed not as teachers who should bear a sure and full testimony to Christ, but only to prepare disciples for the Master, that is, make those teachable and attentive who were very slothful. And moreover, it was a temporary mandate, brought to an end by the preaching of Christ Himself. The time of His death was now near, but they were not yet ready to testify to their faith—in fact, the weakness of their faith would have made their confession a mockery. Therefore the Lord commands their silence until others know that He is the conqueror of death and He endues them with a new constancy.

Matt. 16.22. *And Peter began to rebuke him.* It was a sign of immoderate warmth that Peter rebuked the Master, though it seems that he was also moved by reverence to take Him aside by Himself, because he did not dare rebuke Him in front of witnesses. Yet it was going too far altogether to tell Him to spare Himself, as if He were lacking in sense. But thoughtless enthusiasm moves men and even drives them, so that they do not hesitate to subject God Himself to their will. Peter judges it absurd that God's Son, the future Redeemer of the people, should be crucified by the elders, and that He, the Author of life, should be put to death. He therefore tries to drag Christ back from exposing Himself to death. It seems quite plausible; but we must defer more to Christ's judgment than to Peter's zeal, however excusable his reasons may be. And here we are taught how much what are thought to be good intentions avail before God. So innate is pride in men that they complain that they are done an injury unless what they consider right is also pleasing to God. And thus we see how obstinately the Papists boast of their devotions; but while they applaud themselves so boldly, God not only rejects what they are convinced deserves the highest praise but also severely condemns it as ungodly madness. Certainly, if the sense and judgment of the flesh counted, Peter's intention would be godly or at least probable. But Christ could not have rejected it more harshly or more insultingly. What, I ask you, is the significance of His sharp reply? He who everywhere maintains such mildness that He would not break a bruised reed, how is it that He now thunders so fiercely against His chosen disciple? The reason is certainly clear. In the person of one man He wanted everyone to restrain themselves and not give way to their enthusiasm. For although it is difficult to restrain the lusts of the flesh, which are like wild animals, yet there is no more ravening beast than the wisdom of the flesh. Christ attacks it so fiercely that He so to say beats it down with a hammer of iron, so that we may learn to be wise from the Word of God alone.

Matt. 16.23. *Get thee behind me, Satan.* Some philosophize ineptly on the word 'behind', as if Peter were commanded to follow and not to lead the way. But in Luke 4 it is related that the Lord repulsed the devil with just the same words. And the word ὕπαγε means 'go away', and from it is derived the Latin word *Apage* (Begone!) Christ dismisses His disciple because in his perverse zeal he played the part of Satan. For He does not simply call him His opponent, but gives him the name of the devil as a sign of His utter hatred.

We must note well the reason that is at once added: *thou art a stumbling-block unto me, for thou thinkest according to men and not according to God.* Peter was an offence to Christ when he set himself against His vocation. From this it also appears how mad men are in their perverse zeal. For when Peter tried to interrupt the Master's course, it was no thanks to him that he did not deprive himself and the whole of mankind of eternal salvation. Therefore we are taught in one word how much we should flee from all that leads us away from obedience to God. And first Christ opens up the well of all evil, when He says that Peter is wise according to men. Therefore, lest the heavenly Judge should deliver us and our endeavours to the devil let us learn not to be devoted to our own sense but obediently to embrace what the Lord approves. Now let the Papists go and laud their notions to the skies! They will realize at last, when they come to the heavenly judgment seat, how much the boasting is worth which Christ pronounces Satanic. But for ourselves, unless we want deliberately to shut the door of salvation by deadly obstacles, let us desire to learn our wisdom only from the mouth of God.

Matt. 16.24. *Then said Jesus unto his disciples.* Because Christ sees that Peter has a horror of the cross and knew that all the others had the same feeling, He speaks in general of bearing the cross. He not only constrains the twelve but places the same law upon all the godly. We have almost the same statement in Matthew 10.28, although there the

apostles were warned about the persecution which they would encounter as soon as they began to fulfil their duty. But here He gives
ordinary instruction to beginners and so to say initiates in the first
elements all those who wish to enrol under the Gospel.

But He expressly says *if any man would come after me*, to refute Peter's
imagining. For by making Himself an example of self-denial and
patience for each man He showed that He had to suffer what Peter
considered to be foreign to His Person. And then He invites each
member of His body to imitate Him. The words should be resolved
like this: 'If any one wishes to be mine, when he has denied himself and
taken up his cross, let him follow me', or, 'let him conform to my
example'—meaning that none can be considered Christ's disciple who
is not a true imitator of Him and prepared to run the same course.
Moreover, He lays down a short rule of imitation to teach us in what
particularly He wishes us to be like Him. And this consists in two
aspects: denial of ourselves and the voluntary bearing of the cross.
The denial is far reaching: that, renouncing our own intelligence and
bidding farewell to all the affections of the flesh, we are prepared to
be reduced to nothing so that God may live and reign in us. We know
how men are by nature involved in a blind love of themselves, how they
are given to themselves, what a price they set on themselves. But if
we want to join Christ's school, we must begin at that foolishness to
which Paul exhorts us (I Cor. 3.18): and then we must go on to tame
and subdue all our affections. The reason why He preached about
bearing the cross was that, although man's life is subject to all the
common troubles, yet God exercises His own in a special way to
conform them to the image of His Son, and so it is not surprising that
He gave this law to them. And although God burdens with the cross
both bad and good, yet only they are said to bear the cross who freely
take it on their shoulders. For although a fierce and unruly horse will
carry a rider, yet he will not endure him. The patience of believers
therefore consists in willingly bearing the cross laid on them.

In Luke is added the particle 'daily'; which is very weighty, for
Christ means that there will be no end to our military service until we
leave this world. Therefore let it be the constant practice of the godly
to get ready for new endurance when they have passed through many
troubles.

Matt. 16.25. *For whosoever would save his soul.* A most apt consolation, that those truly gain life who freely suffer death for Christ. For
Mark expressly says that this is the cause of the death of believers in this
respect; and it is also implied in Matthew's words. For it often happens
that ambition or desperation drives heathen men to a contempt for
life, and they go courageously to their death, but without profit. The

194

contrary threatening has also great power to shake off the sloth of the flesh, when He warns those who are greedy of the present life that their only profit will be that they will lose it. There is an antithesis between the temporal and the eternal life, as we are taught in chapter 10, where readers may find the rest.

Matt. 16.26. *For what shall a man be profited.* The word 'soul' should be taken strictly, for Christ is telling them that man's soul was not created merely to enjoy the world for a few days but that its immortality stands firm only in heaven. It is as if He said: 'How great is this sloth and how brutish the stupor, that the world should hold men bound and fill their minds, so that they do not consider why they were born and that their immortal soul was given to them that they should live for ever in heaven after their earthly course is run.' Everyone confesses that the soul is more than all riches and delights of the world; yet the sense of the flesh blinds them and they cast their souls knowingly and willingly into destruction. Therefore, lest the world should bewitch us with its charms, let us remember the excellency of our souls. If we consider this earnestly, it will easily shake off the empty imaginings of earthly happiness.

Matt. 16.27. *For the Son of man shall come.* In order that the former teaching might penetrate their minds the better, Christ sets the future judgment before their eyes. For if this transitory life is to become paltry to us, we must be deeply touched by a sense of the heavenly life. But to look up to heaven, our slow and sluggish minds need help. Hence Christ summons believers to His judgment seat, so that at each moment they may reflect that they live for no other reason than to aspire to the blessed redemption which He will reveal at His own day. And the point of this admonition is that we may know that those for whom the confession of the faith is more precious than their own lives do not fight in vain. It is as if Christ said: 'Place your lives boldly in my hand and keeping. At the last I will be present as your avenger to restore you whole again, although for a time it will look as if you are perishing.'

He speaks of 'the glory of the Father and the angels' lest the disciples should assess His Kingdom by its present appearance; for hitherto He had lain mean and lowly under the habit and appearance of a slave. He therefore promises that He will be very different when He shall come as Judge of the world. Readers will find the additional material in Mark and Luke expounded under Matthew 10. Also I have treated of the reward of works elsewhere, and no more is necessary here. The sum is this: whenever a reward is promised to good works, it is not contrasting their merit with the free righteousness of faith nor showing the cause of salvation but only encouraging believers to try to act aright since they are certain that their labour is not vain. Therefore these two things agree excellently, that we are justified freely because God accepts us irrespective of our merits, and yet according to His good pleasure He repays our works with a reward which is not owing to them.

Matt. 16.28. *Verily I say unto you.* Since the disciples might still be doubtful as to when that day would be, the Lord rouses them to a closer trust, that an example of His future glory would soon be given. We know the truth of the common proverb that for desire even speed seems slow; but this is particularly true of us when our salvation is delayed until the coming of Christ. Therefore, that the Lord may bear up His disciples in the meanwhile, He strengthens them by setting before them an interim period, as if He said, 'If the time of waiting for the day of my coming seems too long, I will anticipate it very soon. For before you die that Kingdom of God on which I bid you to rely will be visible to your eyes.' This is the genuine sense of the words; for what some invent here about John is ridiculous.

Understand 'the coming of the kingdom of God' as the manifestation of the heavenly glory which Christ inaugurated at His resurrection and showed more fully by sending the Holy Spirit and by performing wonderful miracles. For in those beginnings He gave His people a taste of the newness of the heavenly life, when by true and sure experiences they knew that He sat at the right hand of the Father.

*And after six days, Jesus taketh with him Peter, and James, and John his brother, and bringeth them up into a high mountain apart: and he was transfigured before them: and his face did shine as the sun, and his garments became white as the light. And behold, there appeared unto them Moses and Elijah talking with him. And Peter answered and said unto Jesus, Lord, it is good for us to be here: if thou wilt, let us make three tabernacles; one for thee, and one for Moses, and one for Elijah. While he was yet speaking, behold, a bright cloud overshadowed them, and behold a voice out of the cloud, saying, This is my beloved Son, in whom I am well pleased; hear ye him. And when the disciples heard it, they fell on their face, and were sore afraid. And Jesus came and touched them and said, Arise, and be not afraid. And lifting up their eyes, they saw no one, save Jesus only.* (Matt. 17.1-8)

*And after six days Jesus taketh with him Peter, and James, and John, and bringeth them up into a high mountain apart by themselves: and he was transfigured before them: and his garments became glistening, exceeding white; so as no fuller on earth can whiten them. And there appeared unto them Elijah with Moses: and they were talking with*

*Jesus. And Peter answereth and saith to Jesus, Rabbi, it is good for us to be here: and let us make three tabernacles; one for thee, and one for Moses, and one for Elijah. For he wist not what to speak; for they became sore afraid. And there came a cloud overshadowing them: and there came a voice out of the cloud, saying, This is my beloved Son; hear ye him. And suddenly looking round about, they saw no one any more, save Jesus only with themselves.* (Mark 9.2-8)

*And it came to pass about eight days after these sayings, he took with him Peter and John and James, and went up into the mountain to pray. And as he was praying, the fashion of his countenance was altered, and his raiment became white and dazzling. And behold, there talked with him two men, which were Moses and Elijah; who appeared in glory, and spake of his decease which he was about to accomplish at Jerusalem. Now Peter and they that were with him were heavy with sleep: but when they were fully awake, they saw his glory, and the two men that stood with him. And it came to pass, as they were parting from him, Peter said unto Jesus, Master, it is good for us to be here: and let us make three tabernacles; one for thee, and one for Moses, and one for Elijah: not knowing what he said. And while he said these things, there came a cloud, and overshadowed them: and they feared as they entered into the cloud. And a voice came out of the cloud, saying, This is my beloved Son, my chosen: hear ye him. And when the voice came, Jesus was found alone.* (Luke 9.28-36)

We must first see Christ's purpose in putting on His heavenly glory for a little while and in admitting only three out of His disciples as witnesses of the event. The view of some that He did this to fore-arm them against the testing which was imminent in His death seems improbable to me. For why should He deprive the others of this same remedy? More, why should He expressly forbid them to say what they had seen before His resurrection, save because the fruit of the vision would come after His death? I have no doubt that Christ wanted to testify that He was not dragged unwillingly to death but went to it of His own free will, to offer the sacrifice of obedience to His Father. The disciples did not think of this until after Christ had risen. Nor was it even necessary for them in that moment of time to conceive the divine power of Christ which they recognized victorious in the cross. But at another time they were taught both for themselves and for us not to be offended by Christ's weakness, as if He would suffer of necessity and by superior force. For it is always clear that it would have been no more difficult for Christ to give His body immunity from death than to adorn it with heavenly glory. And so we learn that He was subject to death because He wished to be, that He was crucified because He offered Himself. For that same flesh which was sacrificed on the cross and lay in the tomb could have been immune from death and sepulchre, since it had already been partaker of the heavenly glory. We are taught that although Christ took the form of a servant and existed in the world and His majesty was hidden under the weakness of the flesh, nothing had been taken away from Him, for He emptied Himself of His own free will. But now the resurrection lifted the veil which had covered His power for a time. Moreover, it was sufficient for the Lord to choose three witnesses, since this was the number laid down in the Law for establishing anything (Deut. 17.6). The discrepancy in the time should not worry us at all. Matthew and Mark enumerate the passing of six full days; but when Luke says it happened almost eight days after he was including both the day on which Christ was speaking and also that on which He was transformed. We see, therefore, that the same meaning is contained in the different words.

Matt. 17.2. *And he was transfigured.* Luke says this happened as He was praying, and from the time and place we may well infer that He had prayed for what He obtained—that there might be, in the glory of a new form, a visible image of His deity. Not that He needed either to seek by prayer from outside for something that He did not possess or that the Father's will was doubtful, but because in the whole course of His humiliation He referred to the Father whatever He Himself did as God, and by His example He wanted to stimulate us to pray.

This transformation did not absolutely reveal Christ to the sight of His disciples as He now is in heaven but gave them such a taste of His infinite glory as they were able to receive. Then His face shone like the sun; now it far transcends the sun's glory. A strange brightness glowed in His robe; now apart from clothes His divine majesty shines in all His body. Thus once God appeared to the holy fathers, not as He was in Himself but so far as they could bear the rays of His infinite splendour. For John declares that believers will not see Him as He is until they are made like to Him (I John 3.2).

There is no reason for anyone to dispute subtly about the whiteness of His robe or the shining of His face, for this was not a substantial revelation of Christ's heavenly glory, but He gave them in symbols, consonant with the capacity of their flesh, a partial taste of what they could not yet receive fully.

Matt. 17.3. *There appeared unto them Moses and Elijah.* It might be asked whether it was really Moses and Elijah who were present or whether only their spectres were set before the disciples, just as often the prophets saw visions of absent things. Although there is much to be said on both sides, as they say, yet it seems more likely to me that they really were brought to that place. For it is not absurd, if God has bodies and souls in His hand that at His will He restores the dead to life for a time, when it is expedient. But Moses and Elijah were not raised for themselves but to be present at Christ's side. If anyone again asks how the apostles knew they were Moses and Elijah whom they had never seen, the reply is easy. When God brought them forth He provided also signs and marks by which they should be recognized. It was by an extraordinary mode of revelation that it came to pass that they knew for certain that here were Moses and Elijah. As to why these two appeared rather than others from the band of the holy fathers, it should be sufficient for us to realise that the Law and the prophets had no other goal than Christ. For it concerned our faith greatly that Christ did not come without a witness but as one commended by God. And there is truth in another reason often given, that Elijah was chiefly chosen to represent all the prophets. Although he left no writings, yet after Moses he was the chief, restoring the vitiated worship of God; he was the incomparable champion of the Law and true godliness, almost extinct in his day. That they appear with Christ and speak with Him is a sign of agreement. What their talk was about, only Luke says—that they spoke of the end which awaited Christ at Jerusalem. This should not be restricted to them as private individuals but rather to the embassy once laid upon them. For the Lord wished, although they were long dead and the course of their vocation was done, to seal again by their voice what they had taught in life, so that we might know that set before us in the sacrifice of Christ we have a salvation in common with the holy fathers. Now, when the old prophets foretold the death of Christ, He, the eternal wisdom of God, was seated on the secret throne of His glory. From this it follows that when He was clothed in flesh He was only subject to death so far as He submitted Himself freely.

Matt. 17.4. *Lord, it is good.* Luke relates that Peter said this when Moses and Elijah were going away. From this we gather that he was afraid that their departure would bring that sweet and blessed sight to an end. But it is not surprising that Peter was so ravished by this sweetness that he despised everything else and was satisfied with the enjoyment of that alone—just as it says in the Psalm: 'In thy presence is fulness of joy.'[1] Yet his request was out of place in that he did not take into account the purpose of the vision. He was also foolish enough to put the servants on the same level as their Lord. Thirdly, he was in error in wanting to build transitory tabernacles for men who had been received into heavenly and angelic glory. I say that the

[1] Ps. 16.11.

purpose of the vision was unknown to him. For, although he had heard Moses and Elijah say that the time of Christ's death was nigh, yet in his stupor he dreamed that this appearance, in fact temporary, would be eternal. Why did he narrow down Christ's Kingdom to a little space of twenty or thirty feet? Where was the redemption of the whole Church? Where the fellowship of eternal salvation? It was also very perverse to think that Elijah and Moses were colleagues of the Son of God, as if it were not necessary for all to be forced into their proper place so that He alone might be pre-eminent. If Peter was content with his lot, why did he think they needed earthly helps, they at whose sight he knew himself to be so happy? The two Evangelists therefore rightly make the annotation *He knew not what he said.* Mark adds the reason: *for they became sore afraid.* For God did not then wish the apostles to go any further than seeing momentarily the deiyt of His Son as in a living mirror. Later, in course of time, He corrected their faulty judgment by showing them the fruit of it. Mark therefore means that Peter was ravished into an ecstasy and spoke like a man astonished.

Matt. 17.5. *Behold, a bright cloud.* The cloud was set before their eyes to teach them that they were not yet fit to contemplate the brilliance of the heavenly glory. For when the Lord gave signs of His presence He at the same time added certain coverings which restrained the boldness of the human mind. Thus now He hides the sight of the heavenly glory from their eyes in order to train them in humility. This admonition belongs to us too, lest we should want to break into secrets which transcend our thoughts. No, each of us should contain himself soberly within the measure of his faith. Finally, this cloud ought to be like a bridle to us to hold back our frisky curiosity. Then the disciples were told that they must return to their previous military service, in case they should promise themselves victory before the time.

*And behold, a voice out of the cloud.* It is noteworthy that God's voice sounded out of the cloud; His body or His face was not seen. Therefore we may remember the saying of Moses: 'God did not put on a visible form, lest we should be deceived and think that He is like a man' (Deut. 4.12, 15). True it is that in times past He appeared in divers forms to the holy fathers, in which they might know God. Yet He always abstained from symbols which offered a possibility of fabricating idols. And indeed, since human minds are more than prone to gross phantasies, it would be useless to add oil to the flames. This was an especially bright manifestation of God's glory. From the interposing veil He invites us to Himself by His voice. How absurd it is, then, to want Him to be present before our eyes in a block of wood or stone! Therefore we learn that it is not by the eyes of the flesh that we penetrate to the light inaccessible in which God dwells, but by faith alone. The voice was uttered from the cloud so that the disciples might know that it came from God and receive it with the reverence due to it.

*This is my beloved Son.* I readily accept the view of those who think this contains a tacit antithesis of Moses and Elijah with Christ. It was as if Christ commanded His disciples to be content with the only Son. For the word 'Son' is emphatic and raises Him above the servants. Moreover Christ is here adorned with two titles no less honourable in themselves than useful for our faith. The one is 'beloved Son'; the other is 'Teacher'. When the Father calls Him the Beloved, in whom He is well-pleased, He declares that He is the Mediator in whom He reconciles the world to Himself. When He commands them to hear Him, He sets Him in authority as the highest and unique Doctor of His Church. For since it was His purpose to distinguish Him from all the rest, so that we truly and properly infer from these words that He was by nature the unique Son, we may similarly infer that He alone is loved by the Father, and alone appointed Teacher, so that the whole authority may be in His hands. If anyone objects that God loves also angels and men, the explanation is simple. The fatherly love of God which is shed forth on angels and men comes from that well-spring. For the Son was not so loved by the Father that He had only hatred for other creatures but in order that He might share with them what belonged to Himself. The case was different between us and the angels: they were never alienated from God or needed a Reconciler; but we were enemies on account of our sin until Christ propitiated Him to us. Yet let this remain firm: God was propitious to both inasmuch as He embraced us in Christ and because the angels could have no established union with God without the Head. Now since it was the Father who spoke here and who designated Himself other than the Son, it follows that their persons are distinct, although the essence is one and the majesty the same.

*Hear ye him.* I have just said that this voice was recalling the Church to its unique Teacher Christ, that it might hang on His lips alone. For although Christ came to affirm the faith of the Law and the Prophets, yet He occupied the highest position to such a degree that He absorbed in the brightness of His Gospel those sparks which glimmered in the Old Testament. For He is the Sun of righteousness at whose advent the bright day shines. And this is why the Apostle says in Hebrews,[1] 'God, who at sundry times and in divers manners spake in time past through the prophets, hath in these last days spoken by his Son.' Fin-

---

[1] Hebrews 1.1

ally, Christ is heard today no less in the Law and the prophets than in His Gospel, so that the authority of the Master rests in His power, just as He claims it for Himself alone in Matthew 23.10. Nor does He preserve His prerogative unless all human tongues keep silence. Wherefore, to detain us under His teaching, He must cast down and kill whatever men invent. He does, it is true, send out teachers today. But they are men who sincerely and in good faith put forward what they have learnt from Him, not those who contaminate the Gospel with their additions. In sum, none is a faithful teacher of the Gospel save he who is himself the disciple of Christ and who brings others to Him to be taught.

Matt. 17.6. *And when the disciples heard this.* God wanted to strike the disciples with such terror that the memory of the vision might be imprinted more firmly on their hearts. And we see how weak our nature is, which is so afraid to hear God's voice. For the ungodly either mock at it or neglect it brazenly; and this is because God does not compel them effectively. As soon as we feel God's majesty it must of necessity cast us down. But it is Christ's office to raise up the prostrate; for He descends to us so that believers, led by Him, might boldly appear in the sight of God and that His Majesty, which otherwise would consume all flesh, might no longer be terrifying to them. Add that He does not only comfort them by word but also confirms it by touching them.

Where at the last they are said to see Christ only, the point is that the glory of the Law and the prophets was temporary, so that Christ alone might remain glorious. For the right use of the works of Moses is not to cleave to him but take care to be led by his hand to Christ, whose minister he is together with all the others. Moreover, this place may be accommodated to the condemnation of the superstitions of those who so mix Christ in with not only the prophets and the apostles, but also with hosts of saintlings that He becomes just one among many. But God's graces are given to saints for a very different purpose from snatching a share in the honour which belongs to Christ. And we can see the fount of the error in the disciples themselves. For although they were frightened by the majesty of God, their minds wandered off, seeking for men. But when Christ sweetly raised them up, they saw Him alone. For if there flourishes in us the consolation with which Christ cures our fears, all the foolish affections which drag us hither and thither vanish away.

*And as they were coming down from the mountain, Jesus commanded them, saying, Tell the vision to no man, until the Son of man be risen from the dead. And his disciples asked him, saying, Why then say the scribes, that Elijah must first come? And Jesus answered and said, Elijah indeed cometh first, and shall restore all things: but I say unto you, that Elijah is come already, and they knew him not, but did unto him whatsoever they listed. Even so shall the Son of man also suffer of them. Then understood the disciples that he spake unto them of John the Baptist. (Matt. 17.9-13)*

*And as they were coming down the mountain, he charged them that they should tell no man what things they had seen, save when the Son of man should have risen again from the dead. And they kept the saying, questioning among themselves what the rising again from the dead should mean. And they asked him, saying, Why say the scribes that Elijah must first come. And he answered and said unto them, Elijah indeed cometh when he shall first restore all things; and how it is written of the Son of man, that he should suffer many things and be set at naught. But I say unto you, that Elijah is come, and they have also done unto him whatsoever they listed, even as it is written of him. (Mark 9.9-13)*

*And they held their peace, and told no man in those days any of the things which they had seen. (Luke 9.36)*

Matt. 17.9. *And as they were coming down.* We have said why the time was not yet ripe for the vision to be published. And certainly no-one would have believed the apostles unless Christ had given them the plainer token of His glory in the resurrection. But after He had exercised His divine power openly, that temporary sight of His glory also began to have its place, so that it might be established that, although He was emptied for a time, yet He kept entire His deity, even if it was hidden under the veil of His flesh. He therefore has good reason to command the disciples to be silent until He had risen from the dead.

Matt. 17.10. *And his disciples asked him.* As soon as Christ mentioned His resurrection, the disciples imagined that His Kingdom was beginning. For this is how they interpreted the saying that the world would know Him to be the Messiah. They got a different image of the resurrection from what Christ intended, as we see in Mark, who says: 'They questioned among themselves what the rising from the dead should be.' It may be that the madness already prevailed which is held as a certain oracle among the rabbis, that the advent of the Messiah would be twofold—in the beginning contemptible, but this soon succeeded by His royal dignity. This error has a certain plausibility about it, since it is based on a sound principle. Scripture also puts forward two advents of the Messiah. It promises that He will be the Redeemer who will expiate the sins of the world by His sacrifice. To this relate the prophesies: 'Rejoice, O daughter of Zion; behold, thy king cometh, poor, and sitting upon an ass, etc.,' (Zech. 9.9). Again: 'We see him and he has no beauty: he has no form and is like a leper, so that we esteemed him not' (Isa. 53.2-3). Then it sets Him forth as the Conqueror of death, who subjects all things to Himself. But we see that the rabbis deprave the genuine teaching of Scripture with their inventions. But since in the days of Christ everything was very corrupt, it is possible that the people were also imbued with this notion. We have shown two or three times how grossly they erred about the person of Elijah. Perhaps they were also trying maliciously and cunningly to use Elijah as an instrument to detract from Christ. Elijah had been promised as the fore-runner of the Messiah, to prepare the way for Him; and it was easy for them to accuse Him of coming without Elijah. Today the devil bewitches the Papists with almost the same trick—that they should not expect the day of judgment until Elijah and Enoch have appeared. We may well conjecture that the scribes seized on this deliberately to discredit Christ as lacking the legitimate sign of the Messiah.

Matt. 17.11. *Elijah indeed cometh.* We have said elsewhere how this error arose among the Jews. In restoring the broken state of the Church John the Baptist would be like Elijah, and Malachi also gave this name to him. But it was wantonly seized on by the scribes as if Elijah the Tishbite himself would return to the world. Christ declares that Malachi foretold nothing in vain, but that his prophecy had been twisted awry. It is as if He said: 'It was a true promise about the coming of Elijah and it has been fulfilled. But Elijah has already been rejected by the scribes, and they oppose to me his empty name.' The restoration which is attributed to the Baptist was not complete; but he handed what he had done straight to Christ to perfect it. But because the scribes undeservedly rejected John, Christ warns His disciples that they need not be hindered by these errors, and also that they must not be surprised if they reject the Master with the same freedom with which they had earlier rejected His servant. And lest anyone should be disturbed by this unexpected thing, the Lord says that they were both foretold in the Scriptures—that the Redeemer of the world would be rejected and suffer at the hands of false and ungodly teachers just as Elijah His herald did.

*And when he was come to the multitude, there came to him a man, kneeling to him, and saying, Lord, have mercy on my son: for he is lunatic, and suffereth grievously: for oft-times he falleth into the fire, and oft-times into the water. And I brought him to thy disciples, and they could not cure him. And Jesus answered and said, O faithless and perverse nation, how long shall I be with you? how long shall I bear with you? bring him hither to me. And Jesus rebuked it; and the devil went out from him: and the boy was cured from that hour.* (Matt. 17.14-18)

*And when he came to the disciples, he saw a great multitude about them, and scribes questioning with them. And straightway all the multitude, when they saw him, were greatly amazed, and running to him saluted him. And he asked the scribes, What question ye among yourselves? And one of the multitude answered him, Master, I brought unto thee my son, which hath a dumb spirit; and wheresoever it taketh him, it dasheth him down: and he foameth, and grindeth his teeth, and pineth away: and I spake to thy disciples that they should cast it out; and they were not able. And he answereth them and saith, O faithless nation, how long shall I be with you? how long shall I bear with you? bring him unto me. And they brought him unto him: and when he saw him, straightway the spirit tare him grievously; and he fell on the ground, and wallowed foaming. And he asked his father, How long time is it since this hath come unto him? And he said, From a child. And oft-times it hath cast him both into the fire and into the waters, to destroy him: but if thou canst do anything, help us and have compassion on us. And Jesus said unto him, If thou canst! All things are possible to him that believeth. Straightway the father of the child cried out, and said, I believe, O Lord; help thou mine unbelief. And when Jesus saw that a multitude came running together, he rebuked the unclean spirit, saying unto him, Thou dumb and deaf spirit, I command thee, come out of him, and enter no more into him. And having cried out, and torn him much, he came out: and the child became as one dead; inasmuch that many said, He is dead. But Jesus took him by the hand, and raised him up; and he arose.* (Mark 9.14-27)

*And it came to pass, on the next day, when they were come down from the mountain, a great multitude met him. And behold, a man from the multitude cried saying, Master, I beseech thee to look upon my son; for he is mine only child: and behold, a spirit taketh him, and he suddenly crieth out; and it teareth him that he foameth, and it hardly departeth from him, bruising him sorely. And I besought thy disciples to cast it out; and they could not. And Jesus answered and said, O faithless and perverse nation, how long shall I be with you, and bear with you? bring hither thy son. And as he was yet a coming, the devil dashed him down, and tare him grievously. But Jesus rebuked the unclean spirit, and healed the boy, and gave him back to his father. And they were all astonished at the majesty of God.* (Luke 9.37-43)

We will follow Mark's wording, since it is fuller and explains each part expressly. In the first place, he shows the cause of this unwonted sharpness in Christ, when He cried that the Jews were not worth putting up with any longer because of their twisted malice. We know how kindly He used to receive others, even if they were only worrying Him to get something out of Him. This father asks for his only son; he urges his extreme need; restrainedly and humbly he begs for Christ's mercy. Why then did He, in a way so out of character, suddenly flare up and say that He could not put up with it? Some interpreters have been led astray because they could not find the cause for such harshness in Matthew and Luke, and have regarded the rebuke as aimed either at the disciples or at the father of the afflicted lad. But if we weigh well the whole complex of this story as it is in Mark, it will be easy to decide that Christ is angry at the malice of the scribes rather than trying to harass the ignorant and weak. When the lunatic boy was brought there during Christ's absence, the scribes saw a good opportunity to persecute Christ, and they seized on it greedily. They press the disciples to show if they have any power by healing the boy. The disciples probably tried and were unsuccessful; and so the scribes exult as the winners and not only jeer at them but also snap their fingers at Christ, as if it was His power that had failed in their persons. But this more than wicked ungodliness was allied to a like ingratitude; they maliciously suppress the many miracles which taught them what great power Christ had. For they deliberately try to extinguish the light set before their eyes. And so Christ has good cause to exclaim that He could not bear it any longer, and that they were an unbelieving and perverse nation. For they ought, from so many previous proofs, to have got at least as far as not snatching at opportunities of disparaging Him.

Mark 9.14. *He saw a great multitude.* There is no doubt that the disciples were held up to public scorn, as the enemies of the truth are accustomed to seek an audience for their triumphs even when they are empty. Therefore the scribes by their commotion exposed the disciples to the mockery of the crowd. And yet it would seem that some were not ill affected, for as soon as Jesus appeared they saluted Him; more, His presence repressed the scribes' insolence, for when He asked what they were disputing about, they were dumb.

Matt. 17.17. *Master, I brought unto thee my son.* Matthew says it was one sort of disease, Mark another; for Matthew says the man was

206

'lunatic'. But they are in agreement that he was dumb and driven to frenzies at certain times. They are called lunatics who during the waning of the moon, suffer from epilepsy or are tormented with dizziness. I do not accept what Chrysostom imagines, that this name was devised as a trick of Satan to defame the good creation. For sure experience teaches us that those illnesses increase or decrease according to the course of the moon. Yet this does not mean that Satan does not mix his attacks with natural means. And so I consider that this man was not deaf and dumb naturally, but that his tongue and ears were possessed by Satan. Then, when the weakness of his brain and nerves made him liable to epilepsy, the sickness was made worse by the same Satan. Hence it came to pass that he put himself in danger everywhere; he was torn asunder and fell down senseless and as if dead. From this we learn how many ways Satan has to harm us unless he is held off by God's hand. All the weaknesses of the flesh and soul, which we feel to be innumerable, supply him with darts to wound us. Therefore we are more than stupid if our wretched state does not move us to pray. But the incomparable goodness of God shows itself in the way that, although we are exposed to so many different evils, yet He guards us by His help—especially if we consider how fiercely our enemy burns to destroy us. But there ought to come to our minds this comfort, that Christ came to bridle his raging, and that we remain safe among so many perils because the heavenly medicine is greater than our ills. The circumstance of the time also relates to this. The father replies that his son has been afflicted unhappily like this since childhood. If Satan was allowed so much licence during his tender years, what should not we fear who by our vices continually expose ourselves to deadly blows, who even supply our enemy with weapons and over whom he could rule as of right unless by the wonderful goodness of God his lust was restrained and cast down?

Matt. 17.17. *O faithless nation.* Christ seems to speak to the lunatic's father but there is no doubt He was aiming at the scribes; not rebuking the ignorant and weak, but those who are bound by their own malice and obstinacy to resist God. Christ therefore says that they do not deserve to be endured any longer and threatens to cut himself off from them at once. There can be nothing worse than for Him to desert us. And it is no light reproach that they so arrogantly reject the grace of His visitation. We must also note that men must be dealt with differently, each according to his character. For He invites the teachable with the greatest kindness, He upholds the weak, He stirs up the slow as they need it, but He does not spare the winding, devious serpents whom He sees can be healed by no remedy.

Mark 9.20. *When he saw him.* That the devil should savage the man more cruelly still when he is brought to Christ is not surprising. For the nearer the light of Christ's grace comes and the more effectively it works, the more impotently does Satan rage. Christ's presence therefore arouses him like the call of a trumpet, and he profoundly disturbs whoever he can and fights with what power he has. Lest our faith be upset, we ought to consider in good time how our enemy here attacks more violently than usual when Christ's grace appears on the scene. We must understand something else, too. The true beginning of our healing is when we are afflicted so profoundly that we are next door to death. Add that from the furious onslaught of Satan the Lord lights a torch to illuminate His grace. For men would have been aghast at that horrible sight, and so it served to show up the better the power of Christ which quickly followed.

Mark 9.21. *From a child.* From this we gather that this was not a punishment inflicted on the man for his sins but was a secret judgment of God. It is of course true that as soon as babies come from the womb they are not innocent in God's sight and free from guilt. But God's scourgings sometimes have hidden causes, and this is to prove our obedience. For we only render just honour to God if reverently and humbly we adore His righteousness, which is hidden from us. If anyone wishes to learn more about this, let him look in John 9 under the verse 'Neither this man sinned, nor his parents'.

Mark. 9.22. *If thou canst do anything, help us.* We see how little honour he gave to Christ. He thought He was some prophet whose capability was finite and so comes to Him doubtfully. But the first foundation of faith is to embrace the infinite power of God. Also, the first entry into prayers is to rise above all obstacles so that we are firmly convinced that our praying will not be in vain. But because this man thinks of Christ only as a man, his false opinion is corrected. His faith has to be formed, so that he may become capable and fit to receive the grace he asked for. Christ did not openly reprove him in His reply but gave the man back the words he had spoken amiss and so showed him his fault and told him to seek the remedy. For this objection *If thou canst believe* was as good as saying: 'You ask me to help you so far as I am able. But you will find an inexhaustible spring of power in me if only you will bring a large enough measure of faith.' From this we gather the useful lesson, which applies to us all alike, that it is not the Lord's fault if a great abundance of blessings does not flow from Him to us, but it must be imputed to the narrowness of our faith, that it only comes drop by drop—sometimes, indeed, we do not feel even a drop, because unbelief blocks up our hearts. Some want to be very subtle here and make Christ mean that a man can believe of himself. But this is in vain, for His only purpose was to throw the blame for their poverty back on men when they weaken God's power by their own unbelief.

Mark 9.23. *All things are possible to him that believeth.* There is no doubt that Christ taught that the Father had given Him the fullness of all good things and that no sort of help at all could be hoped for from Himself save as it came from the Father's hand. It was as if He said, 'Only believe, and you will obtain.' And how faith obtains anything we shall see shortly.

Mark 9.24. *Lord, I believe.* He declares that he believes, and yet confesses his unbelief. Although these two things seem inconsistent, there is no-one who does not experience the same thing in himself. Nowhere is there a perfect faith, and therefore it follows that we are partly unbelievers. Yet in His kindness God pardons us and reckons us as believers on account of our small portion of faith. Meanwhile it is for us to shake off carefully the remnants of unbelief that remain within us, and fight against them and ask the Lord to correct them; and so often as we toil in this struggle we must flee to Him for succour. If we consider aright what is given to each man, it will be very clear that those who excel in faith are rarest, those with a middling faith are few, and the most are endowed with only a small measure.

*Then came the disciples to Jesus apart, and said, Why could not we cast it out? And Jesus saith unto them, Because of your unbelief: for verily I say unto you, If ye have faith as a grain of mustard seed, ye shall say unto this mountain, Remove hence to yonder place; and it shall remove; and nothing shall be impossible unto you. Howbeit this kind goeth not out by prayer and fasting. (Matt. 17.19-21)*

*And when he was come into the house, his disciples asked him privately, Why could not we cast it out? And he said unto them, This kind can come out by nothing, save by prayer and fasting. (Mark 9.28-29)*

*And the apostles said unto the Lord, Increase our faith. And the Lord said, If ye have faith as a grain of mustard seed, ye would say unto this sycamine tree, Be thou rooted up, and be thou planted in the sea; and it would have obeyed you. (Luke 17.5-6)*

Matt. 17.19. *Then came the disciples to Jesus.* The disciples were surprised that the power with which they had once been furnished had been taken away: but they had deprived themselves of it by their own fault. Christ ascribes this lack to their unbelief and repeats something which He had said earlier and explains it more fully—that to faith nothing is impossible. It is true that it is an hyperbole when He declares that faith will remove trees and mountains. But it all comes to this, that God will never fail us so long as we open the gate to His grace. He does not mean that God will give us whatever comes heedlessly into our minds or mouths. In fact, since there is nothing more contradictory to faith than the foolish and unconsidered wishes of our flesh, it follows that where faith reigns there is no asking for anything indiscriminately, but only for what the Lord promises. Therefore we must observe the moderation of not desiring more than is promised to us and of giving our prayers to what this rule prescribes. If anyone objects that the disciples did not know whether the Lord would be pleased to heal the epileptic, the reply is easy—this happened from their own fault. For Christ is now really dealing with special faith, which had its secret instincts as the matter in hand required. And this is the faith which Paul refers to in I Cor. 12.4ff. How then did it happen that the apostles were without the power of the Spirit which earlier they had possessed, so as to work miracles? Was it not because they suffocated it with their sloth? But what Christ says of particular faith in this context extends to the common faith of the whole Church.

Matt. 17.21. *This kind goeth not out.* With these words Christ was rebuking the sluggishness of some, to teach them that there was need for an extraordinary faith. Otherwise they might have objected that they were not completely without faith. The meaning therefore is that, when we have to fight earnestly against Satan, any sort of faith is not enough. Strenuous efforts are required. As the remedy for a languid faith He prescribes prayer, to which He adds fasting as an assistance. 'You', He says, 'are soft exorcists. You engage in a sort of unreal and make-believe battle. But you are up against a real antagonist who will only be overcome by the most strenuous efforts. Therefore your faith must be stirred up by prayers. And because you are slow and cold in praying you need also to have the assistance of fasting.' This shows clearly how ridiculous is the Papist reliance on fasting as an antidote for driving out devils, when the Lord's only intention in it is to sharpen zeal in prayer. But since He affirms that that kind of demon can only be cast out by prayers and fasting, the meaning is that where Satan fixes deep roots and has ruled by a long possession, or where he attacks with unbridled fury, victory is hard and difficult and we must fight with all our strength.

*And while they abode in Galilee, Jesus said unto them, The Son of man shall be delivered up into the hands of men; and they shall kill him, and the third day he shall be raised up. And they were exceeding sorry.*

*In that hour came the disciples unto Jesus, saying, Who then is greatest in the kingdom of heaven? And he called to him a little child, and set him in the midst of them, and said, Verily, I say unto you, Except ye be converted, and become as little children, ye shall in no wise enter into the kingdom of heaven. Whosoever therefore shall humble himself as this little child, the same is the greatest in the kingdom of heaven. And whoso shall receive one such little child in my name receiveth me.* (Matt. 17.22-23; 18.1-5)

*And they went forth from thence, and passed through Galilee; and he would not that any man should know it. For he taught his disciples, and said unto them, The Son of man is delivered up into the hands of men, and they shall kill him; and when he is killed, on the third day he shall rise again. But they understood not the saying, and were afraid to ask him. And they came to Capernaum: and when he was come in the house he asked them, What were ye reasoning in the way? But they held their peace: for they had disputed one with another in the way, who was the greatest. And he sat down, and he called the twelve; and he saith unto them, If any man would be first, he shall be last of all, and minister of all. And he took a little child and set him in the midst of them: and taking him in his arms, he said unto them, Whosoever shall receive one of such little children in my name, receiveth me: and whosoever receiveth me, receiveth not me, but him that sent me.* (Mark 9.30-37)

*But while all were marvelling at all the things which he did, he said unto his disciples, Let these words sink into your ears: for the Son of man shall be delivered up into the hands of men. But they understood not this saying, and it was concealed from them, that they should not perceive it: and they were afraid to ask him about this saying. And there arose a reasoning among them, which of them should be greater. But when Jesus saw the reasoning of their heart, he took a little child, and set him by his side, and said unto them, Whosoever shall receive this little child in my name receiveth me: and whosoever receiveth me receiveth him that sent me: for he that is lesser among you all, the same is great.* (Luke 9.43-48)

Matt. 17.22. *And while they abode in Galilee.* The nearer the time of His death drew, the more often Christ warned His disciples, lest that particular sorrow should undermine their faith. This talk took place soon after He had performed the miracle. Mark says that He had left that place to go for a quiet rest in Galilee; for He had decided to go to Jerusalem at the solemn day of sacrifice, because He was to be sacrificed at the next Passover. Although they had several times been warned about this, they are now as upset as if they had never heard anything of it before. The presumptive idea holds sway and darkens their minds in the midst of clearest light. The apostles imagined that the state of Christ's Kingdom would be pleasant and joyful; they thought that, as soon as it was made known, it would be received with great acclaim by all. It never crossed their minds that the priests and scribes and other leaders of the Church would oppose it. With this error firmly entrenched they keep out whatever is said to the contrary—Mark says that they did not know what the Lord meant. But were they not ignorant, when He had spoken so openly and clearly, because this empty illusion held a veil across their minds? That they did not dare ask any further was partly due to their reverence, but also I do not doubt that they were bound fast in their sorrow and could not speak because they were overcome by the absurdity which they had made up for themselves. This shamefastness was not entirely laudable, for it fed their perplexed doubting and their faulty sadness.

Meanwhile it was an implicit seed of godliness rather than any clear knowledge of the truth which kept them bound to Christ and did not let them run away from His school. There was indeed a certain beginning of faith and true understanding implanted in their hearts, so that their zeal in following Christ was far from the implicit faith of the Papists. But because they had not yet got so far as to learn the nature of the Kingdom of God and of the renewal promised in Christ, I say that what was active in them was more a desire for godliness than a distinct knowledge. From this we can gather what deserves praise or blame in them. Moreover, although their stupidity was not excusable, we need not be surprised that the clear and express declaration of the Master's cross and ignominy should be an enigma to them. And this, not only because it was alien to the glory of the Son of God to be rejected and condemned, but because there was nothing less consonant than that the grace promised particularly to the Jews should be rejected by the Gentiles. But because the overwhelming horror of the cross which suddenly seized them shut the door on the comfort derived from the hope of the resurrection, we learn that whenever there is mention of the death of Christ, it includes the whole three days, and His death and sepulchre should lead to blissful triumph and the new life.

Matt. 18.1. *In that hour.* It appears from the other two that the disciples did not come to Christ of their own accord, but were dragged into the light out of their shadows when they were arguing secretly on the way. But there is nothing wrong in Matthew's hurrying on to Christ's reply and not relating the whole context of the story but omitting the beginning and only summarizing why Christ corrected the foolish itch for primacy among the disciples. But when He asks about their surreptitious conversation and the disciples have to confess what they would rather have suppressed, we are taught that we should beware of all ambition, even when it is masked. We must also note the circumstances and the occasion. The prediction of His death made them sad and worried. Yet as if they had heard sheerly delightful things, as if they had drunk the nectar of the poets, they start quarrelling at once about who shall be first. How could it be that their anxiety should vanish in a moment, save because men's minds are so addicted to ambition that they forget the war is still on in the delusion of their false imagining and rush forward to triumph? If the remembrance of His recent words slipped so quickly from the apostles, what will happen to us if for a long time we cease to live under the cross (*meditationi crucis*) and give ourselves over to dullness and sloth or idle speculations? But it may be asked what caused the disciples' quarrel? I reply that, since the flesh willingly shakes off all unhappiness, they overlooked what would sadden them and just seized on what was said about the resurrection, and thus the argument broke out because they thought all was well. And because they fled from the first part of the teaching, which is distasteful to the flesh, God let them be deceived about the resurrection, so that they day-dreamed of what would never happen—that by preaching alone Christ would win His Kingdom, and that He would soon arise to blissful riches. In this argument the fault was twofold. The aposltes were perverse in laying down the responsibility of military service to which they had been called and demanding in advance, rest and a good pension, like retired soldiers. Secondly, when they should have been striving with one mind to help one another and to desire success for their brethren no less than for themselves, some try in their malicious ambition to beat others. Therefore, if our course is to be approved by the Lord, let us learn to bear patiently the weight of the cross laid on us until the time is fulfilled when we shall receive the crown. And also, as Paul exhorts us, let us prefer one another in honour (Rom. 12.10). Nowadays what is akin to the first fault is the vain curiosity of those who too soon give up the lawful course of their vocation and vault over the sky. In His Gospel the Lord invites us to His Kingdom and by so doing shows us the way there. Light-headed men think nothing of faith, patience, prayer to God and other exercises and dispute what goes on in heaven. But this is just like a man who is going on a journey and asks where he will be able to stay the night, but does not put one foot forward. When the Lord bids us to walk on earth, anyone who inquisitively argues about how the dead live in heaven are in fact delaying their own arrival in heaven.

Matt. 18.2. *And he called to him a little child.* The sum of it is that those who seek greatness, to be above their brethren, will be so far from getting it that they will not even possess a tiny corner. And he argues from the contrary that only humility raises us up. Because a visible example affects people more, He puts forward a child, as a type of humility. When He bids His people to be like a child, He is not extending it to all indiscriminately. We know that there are many faults in children. This is why Paul wants us to be children, not in understanding but in malice, and elsewhere he tells us to strive after manhood (I Cor. 14.20, Eph. 4.13). But because children are not yet aware what rivalry is, Christ wishes by their example to drive from the minds of His disciples what heathen men and children of the world are always worrying about—the sweetness of honours. He does not want them to be excited by ambition. If anyone objects that pride is inborn in infants from the womb so that they want to get the first care and attention, the reply is easy. We should not try to make the likenesses exact or precise so that they agree in every respect. It is because there is still so much simplicity reigning in infancy that they are ignorant of degrees of honour and provocations to pride, that Christ deservedly and rightly puts them forward as examples. And this is the point of the conversion He mentions. The disciples were too inured to the common habits of men, and therefore, to make for this goal they had to be turned back from their course. Each one wanted the first or the second place, but Christ regarded as worthy of even the lowest bench only the man who forgot his superiority and humbled himself. And on the other hand He declares that they are greatest who abase themselves, lest we should think we lose anything when we willingly surrender all greatness. And from this we may gather a brief definition of humility: He is truly humble who neither claims anything for himself over against God nor proudly despises his brethren, affecting superiority, but regards it sufficient to be reckoned as one of the members of Christ and desires nothing but that the Head alone have the pre-eminence.

Matt. 18.5. *And whoso shall receive.* Christ now metaphorically calls children those who set aside their loftiness and settle themselves to modesty and subjection. It is added as a consolation, so that submission should not seem vexatious or hard to us. By it Christ not only re-receives us into His protection but also commends us to men. And in this way believers are taught how they should prize one another by their mutual subjection. For is not the mutual friendship of the children of this world based on a general acceptance of the greed of the others? And so whoever is the more greedy of glory, he usurps the power more boldly, so as to be lifted up to the heights; but the humble are mocked or lie despised. Christ, however, commanded that the more a man humbled himself, the more he should be honoured. And the clause that Luke adds comes to the same thing. For He does not command us to think more highly of the deservedly contemptible but of those who empty themselves of all pride and are reduced to nothing.

*But whoso shall offend one of these little ones which believe in me, it is profitable for him that a great millstone should be hanged about his neck, and that he should be sunk in the depth of the sea. Woe unto the world because of offences! for it must be that the offences come; but woe to that man through whom the offence cometh! And if thy hand or thy foot causeth thee to stumble, cut it off, and cast it from thee: it is good for thee to enter into life maimed or halt, rather than having two hands or feet to be cast into the eternal fire. And if thine eye causeth thee to stumble, pluck it out, and cast it from thee: it is good for thee to enter into life with one eye, rather than having two eyes to be cast into the hell of fire. See that ye despise not one of these little ones; for I say unto you, that in heaven their angels do always behold the face of my Father which is in heaven. (Matt. 18.6-10)*

*And whosoever shall cause one of these little ones that believe in me to stumble, it were better for him if a great millstone were hanged about his neck, and he were cast into the sea. And if thy hand cause thee to stumble, cut it off: it is good for thee to enter into life maimed, rather than having thy two hands to go into hell, into the unquenchable fire: where their worm dieth not, and the fire is not quenched. And if thy foot cause thee to stumble, cut it off: it is good for thee to enter into life halt, rather than having thy two feet to be cast into hell, into the fire that never shall be quenched: where their worm dieth not, and the fire is not quenched. And if thy eye cause thee to stumble, cast it out: it is good for thee to enter into the kingdom of God with one eye, rather than having two eyes to be cast into hell-fire; where their worm dieth not, and the fire is not quenched. (Mark 9.42-48)*

*And he said unto his disciples, It is impossible but that offences should come: but woe unto him, through whom they come! It were well for him if a millstone were hanged about his neck, and he were thrown into the sea, rather than that he should cause one of these little ones to stumble. (Luke 17.1-2)*

Matt. 18.6. *But whoso shall offend.* This seems to have been added as a comfort to the godly lest they should think their lot wretched when the world despises them. For it is a great obstacle to submitting themselves to a voluntary humility when they think it makes them contemptible. Yet it is hard when the proud not only despise them but almost trample them under foot. Therefore Christ heartens His disciples with the consolation that if the world exults over their insignificance, God certainly does not neglect them.

Yet there seems to be another point in this, in that there had arisen a quarrel about being first. From this it is easy to infer that the apostles were infected with a depraved desire (*potestate*) to be superior. Now anyone who is too pleased with himself is bound to despise his brethren or want to prefer himself to everyone else. To heal this disease Christ pronounces a horrifying punishment on a man who in his pride casts down poor men already humbled of their own accord. The word 'offence' embraces more than a prohibition to despise. Yet the reason why anyone should carelessly offend the weak must be because he does not honour him as he should.

Now there are various species of offence, but we must understand what the genus itself is. If anyone by our fault either stumbles or is led astray from the right way, or is hindered, we are said to offend him. Therefore whoever wants to avoid this punishment which Christ severely threatens must stretch out his hand to the little ones who are abject in the sight of the world and help them lovingly on their way. Christ commends them to us as opportunities for our willing humility, just as Paul prescribes a rule to the children of God, to accommodate themselves to the lowly (Rom. 15.1).

Christ speaks of a form of punishment which was then particularly terrifying and used for the most atrocious crimes. From this we can see how dear and precious God regards those who are mean and despised before the world.

Matt. 18.7. *Woe unto the world.* This verse can be explained in two ways. Actively, that Christ curses the authors of offences. In this sense, by the word 'world' will be understood all unbelievers. Or passively, that Christ bewails the evils which He sees ready to burst upon the world because of offences; as if He said that there was no more dangerous plague, bringing more disasters in its train, than for many to be troubled or to fall away through offences. And this sense is the more consonant; for I do not doubt that if the Lord had meant the other He would have spoken at greater length to make His disciples more attentive and cautious. Lest Satan should overcome us while we are asleep, the Lord exclaims that there is nothing to be more afraid of than offences. Satan has innumerable at hand and does not cease to put fresh ones before almost every step we take—and we easily succumb because we are too weak or lazy. And so it happens that few make much progress in the faith of Christ, and of the few who start the race, hardly one in ten keep on to the goal without failing.

Since Christ's purpose was to wake us up, woe to our irresponsibility if we do not set ourselves strenuously to overcome them.

*For it must needs be that offences come.* To quicken the disciples' care and heedfulness the more, the Lord tells them that it cannot be but that they will journey through all sorts of offences; as if He said that this evil is inevitable. Thus it is a confirmation of the former statement which Christ uses as a basis to teach them how much trouble comes from offences, for the Church will never, can never, be free from this evil. But He does not declare the reason for the necessity, as Paul does when he talks of heresies and says that they arise so that they which are approved may be made manifest (I Cor. 11.19). But we must understand that God wishes men to be exposed to offences, to exercise their faith and to separate out the hypocrites like the sweepings and the chaff from the pure corn. But if anyone argues and complains that it is all wrong for the Lord to give the reins to Satan so that he can work the destruction of wretched men, then it is for us to think reverently of the secret counsels of God, and one of them is that it is necessary that the world be disturbed by offences.

*But woe to that man.* After He has exhorted His disciples to beware of the offences, He again attacks their originators. And to make His threatening the more forcible He adds that we must spare neither right eye nor right hand if they are causing us to stumble. I interpret that this was put in to amplify what had been said. To paraphrase: 'You must resist offences so carefully and steadfastly that you should rather pluck out your eye and cut off your hand than encourage offences. For if anyone hesitates to do such an injury to his members, he will cast himself into eternal destruction by his indulgence.' What a horrifying vengeance awaits those who destroy their brethren by offences! (Since these two verses were explained under chapter 5, it is sufficient now to mention why Christ repeats the same statement here.)

Matt. 18.10. *See that ye despise not.* Pride is the mother of insult, and contempt begets the insolence of giving offence. To apply an opportune remedy for healing this disease, Christ therefore prohibits any despising of the little ones. And indeed, as we mentioned above, whoever is rightly solicitous for his brethren will never easily break out into giving them cause for offence.

The end of Christ's talk points in the same direction as the beginning, that among us there should be a striving after submission and humility, for God embraces the little ones in His special love. But it would be completely perverse if those whom God so prizes should be despised or set at naught by mortal men. He proves this love by saying that the angels, the ministers of their salvation, enjoy familiarly the sight of God. Yet, in my judgment, He did not simply intend to teach what honour God accords them by assigning angels to be their guardians, but He was also threatening their despisers. It was as if He said, 'They are not despised with impunity, for they have angels very close at hand who will exact vengeance.' And so we must beware lest we should disprize their salvation when angels are given the task of looking after it.

Some take this verse as if God ascribed a particular angel to each individual; but this is weak. For Christ's words do not say that one angel is devoted to this or that person all the time; and indeed it conflicts with the whole teaching of Scripture, which bears witness that the angels camp around the godly (Ps. 34.7)[1] and that many, and not just one, are appointed as guardians of each believer. Let us then be done with the invention about the good and evil genius and be content to hold that to the angels is committed the care of the whole Church and that they succour individual members so far as their necessity and situation demands.

If anyone asks whether, although by nature they excel us, the condition of the angels is inferior to ours, because they are appointed to be our ministers, I reply that it does not prevent them offering their service to God in the free favour which He bestows on us. They are called ours because they spend their labours on us.

*For the Son of man is come to save that which was lost. How think ye? if any man have a hundred sheep, and one of them be gone astray, doth he not leave the ninety and nine, and go unto the mountains, and seek that which goeth astray? And if so be that he find it, verily, I say unto you, he rejoiceth over it more than over the ninety and nine which have not gone astray. Even so it is not the will of your Father which is in heaven, that one of these little ones should perish.* (Matt. 18.11-14)

*Now all the publicans and sinners were drawing near unto him for to hear him. And both the Pharisees and the scribes murmured, saying, This man receiveth sinners, and eateth with them. And he spake unto them this parable, saying, What man of you, having a hundred sheep, and having lost one of them, doth not leave the ninety and nine in the wilderness, and go after that which was lost, until he find it? And when he hath found it, he layeth it on his shoulders, rejoicing. And when he cometh home, he calleth together his friends and his neighbours, saying unto them, Rejoice with me, for I have found my sheep which was lost.*

[1] Calvin interprets the 'angel' of Ps. 34.7 in the plural. See his comments on this verse.

*I say unto you, that even so there shall be joy in heaven over one sinner that repenteth, more than over ninety and nine righteous persons, which need no repentance. Or what woman having ten drachmas, if she lose one drachma, doth not light a lamp, and sweep the house, and seek diligently until she find it? And when she hath found it, she calleth together her friends and neighbours, saying, Rejoice with me, for I have found the drachma which I lost. Even so, I say unto you, there shall be joy in the presence of the angels of God over one sinner that repenteth.* (Luke 15.1-10)

Matt. 18.11. *For the Son of man is come.* By His own example Christ now exhorts us to honour our weak and lowly brethren; for He descended from heaven to be the Redeemer, to save not only them, but even the dead, those who were lost. And it is unworthy to reject in our pride those for whom the Son of God did so much. Our pride would be inexcusable even were the weak labouring under faults which could make them worthy of contempt; for they are not to be assessed according to their own virtues but according to the grace of Christ. And whoever does not conform to the pattern of that grace is altogether too critical and proud.

Matt. 18.12. *How think ye?* Luke makes the occasion for this parable come earlier, when the scribes and Pharisees blamed the Lord for mixing daily with sinners. In that case Christ wanted to show that a good teacher must no less labour to recover the lost than to keep what he already has in his hand. In Matthew, however, the parable goes further; that we must not only lovingly cherish Christ's disciples but also bear with their faults and when they go wrong try to bring them back to the right way. For although it happens that they sometimes go astray, yet, because they are the sheep over whom God made His Son the shepherd, we ought to gather them out of their wandering and certainly not be so inhuman as to drive them away or banish them. For the whole point of Christ's words is that we are to take care not to lose what God wishes to save. Luke's account has a rather different object: because the whole human race belongs to God, those who are estranged are to be gathered in, and it is as much cause for rejoicing when the lost reform as when someone finds something precious which he had given up for lost.

Luke 15.10. *There is joy in the presence of the angels.* If the angels on their side rejoice to see the lost restored to the flock, we who have like and equal cause should be their companions in rejoicing. But how is it that the angels are said to rejoice over the repentance of one ungodly man more than over the perseverance of many righteous men? For nothing delights the angels more than a continuous and steady course of righteousness. I reply, although it is more consonant with the wishes of the angels (as also it is more desirable) that men should always stand fast in pure integrity, yet because the mercy of God shines more brightly in the liberating of a sinner who was already devoted to destruction and like a rotten member cut off from the body, He ascribes to the angels, as if they were human beings, greater joy at an unexpected blessing.

The word 'repentance' should be applied specially to the conversion of those who had been completely turned away from God and, so to say, rise from death to life. For in another sense repentance should be a continual and life-long exercise, and no-one is exempt from this necessity, for his very sins urge him to progress in it daily. But it is one thing to strive for the goal amid offences or failures or deviations when you have already started on the race, and another to turn round from the wrong direction altogether, or to begin the right course from the starting point. They do not lack such repentance who have already begun to form their lives to the rule of the divine law, and begin a holy and godly life, although they groan under the weaknesses of their flesh and need to labour at correcting them.

*And he said, A certain man had two sons: and the younger of them said to his Father, Father, give me the portion of thy substance that falleth to me. And he divided unto them his living. And not many days after the younger son gathered all together, and took his journey into a far country; and there he wasted his substance with riotous living. And when he had spent all, there arose a mighty famine in that country; and he began to be in want. And he went and joined himself to one of the citizens of that country; and he sent him to his farm to feed swine. And he would fain have filled his belly with the husks that the swine did eat: and no man gave unto him. But when he came to himself he said, How many hired servants of my father have bread enough and to spare, and I perish with hunger! I will arise and go to my father, and will say unto him, Father, I have sinned against heaven, and in thy sight; I am now not worthy to be called thy son: make me as one of thy hired servants. And he arose, and came to his father. But while he was yet afar off, his father saw him, and was moved with compassion, and ran, and fell on his neck, and kissed him. And the son said unto him, Father, I have sinned against heaven, and in thy sight, I am not henceforth worthy to be called thy son. But the father said to his servants, Bring forth the best robe, and put it on him; and put a ring on his hand, and shoes on his feet: and bring the fatted calf, and kill it, and let us eat, and make*

*merry: for this my son was dead, and is alive again; he was lost, and is*
*found. And they began to be merry.* (Luke 15.11-24)

This parable is simply a confirmation of the one before. The first part shows how ready and willing God is to pardon our sins, and the second, which we shall deal with in its proper place, shows how maliciously and perversely they act who disparage His mercy. Under the person of a prodigal young man who was brought to extreme poverty through his lechery and wastefulness and then returned as a suppliant to his father whom he had injured and rebelled against, Christ describes all sinners who become disgusted at their own madness and return to the grace of God. He compares God to a human father who not only pardons his son's misdemeanours, but runs to meet him. For God is not content with forgiving those who beg for it but prevents them with His fatherly loving-kindness. Now let us consider the details.

Luke 15.12. *And the younger of them said.* He first points to a sign of ungodly lack of wisdom in the young man, that when he wanted to leave his father he did not think he could be happy without casting off his father's control and doing what he pleased without fear. There was also the ingratitude of not only depriving the old man he was deserting of his due services, but also breaking up and diminishing the family fortune. And lastly he wasted all his goods in wild extravagance and a dissolute and evil life. Sinning so much, he deserved to find his father unforgiving. But there is no doubt that under this image there is depicted the infinite goodness, the incomparable kindness of God, so that not the most atrocious crime need deter us from hoping for pardon. It will not be an unapt analogy (*anagoge*) to compare this foolish and impudent young man to anyone who is blessed by God with an abundance of possessions yet is moved by a blind and mad desire to be separated from Him and be completely free, as if the most desirable of all states were not to live under the fatherly care and governance of God. But I am afraid that this allusion may be too subtle, and therefore I will be content with the literal sense—not that I do not think that under such a figure there is reproved the madness of those who imagine that they will live happily if they have something of their own and are rich apart from their heavenly Father, but because I now keep within the proper limits of an interpreter.

Christ here relates something that often happens to young men when their own disposition gets control. With their lack of prudence and their hot intemperance they are not at all fit to rule themselves. And so when they are not constrained by fear or shame they cannot fail to throw themselves into whatever their lust urges and hasten shamelessly into disgraceful poverty. Then He describes the punishment which by God's just judgment usually awaits prodigal spendthrifts. When they have wickedly wasted their goods they have to go hungry, and because they did not know how to use carefully an abundance of the best bread they are reduced to acorns and husks. They become companions of pigs and feel unworthy to eat human food. For it is swinish gluttony to waste what was given to sustain life. Some explain this subtly, that it is just punishment for ungodly pride to be famished and have recourse to the husks when they reject the good bread in the family of their heavenly Father. This is true and valuable and there is no theological reason (*religio*) why we should not use this similitude; but yet we must always remember how allegories differ from the genuine sense.

Luke 15.16. *And he fain would have filled.* He means that in his hunger he forgot all about the old delicacies and was avidly gorging himself on husks, a food he possessed in plenty when he was giving it to the swine. There is a famous saying of Cyrus when he had been hungry for a long time during a flight. After refreshing himself a little with common black bread he said that he had never tasted good bread before. So the young man in the parable is forced by necessity to develop an appetite for husks.

The reason is added: *no man gave unto him.* For the conjunction should be made causal, in my judgment. It is not spoken of the husks, which were there ready to hand; but I take it as meaning that no one had pity on his poverty. For no-one will acknowledge prodigals who dissipate their goods recklessly. In fact, because they are accustomed to waste everything, nothing seems to be given to them.

Luke 15.17. *But when he came to himself.* Here is described to us the way in which God invites men to repentance. If they are sensible of their own accord and show themselves teachable, He attracts them sweetly. But because they do not lower themselves to be obedient unless they are tamed by the rod, He punishes them harshly. Affluence made this young man wild and untamed; for him hunger was the best teacher. We are taught by his example not to think that God is cruel to us if He sometimes presses us with serious troubles, for this is how He educates the obstinate and the pleasure-lovers in obedience. Finally, whatever miseries we suffer are a valuable invitation to repentance. But since we are slow, we scarcely ever return to a sound mind unless we are forced by extreme evils. For until difficulties press on us from every side and desperation has us in its grip, the flesh will always exult or at least shrink back. From this we gather that it is not surprising if the Lord lays on us violent and repeated blows to break our obstinacy and drives tough wedges into tough knots, as the proverb says. We must also note that hope of a better fortune if he returns to

222

his father gives the young man a desire to repent. For no burden of punishment will soften our depravity or make us displeased with our sins until it seems profitable. Therefore just as this young man is aroused by his trust in his father's pity to seek a reconciliation, so the recognition of the divine mercy must be the beginning of our repentance and stir us up to a good hope.

Luke 15.20. *While he was yet afar off.* This is the central point of the parable. If men, by nature vindictive and tenacious of their rights, are moved by fatherly love mercifully to forgive their children and in pity to seek out the lost, God will act no more harshly to us, He whose infinite goodness surpasses the love of any father. And surely nothing is here related of an earthly father which God does not promise to be true of Himself. 'Before they call', He says, 'I will hear' (Isa. 65.24). And there are David's well-known words: 'I said, I will confess my unrighteousness to the Lord against myself, and thou forgavest the iniquity of my sin' (Ps. 32.5). Therefore, just as this father is not only open to the prayers of his son but even goes out to meet him as he comes and before he has said a word embraces him, neglected and dirty as he is, so God does not wait for a long prayer but as soon as the sinner sets out to confess his fault, meets him willingly. There is a disgusting quibble which some squeeze out of this, that God's grace is not shown to sinners before they themselves turn to Him in repentance. They say that there is set before us here a father who is ready to forgive, but only after his son returns to him. Therefore God has no respect to, nor is gracious to, any save those who take the initiative in seeking it. It is true that for a sinner to beg for forgiveness demands a sorrow of conscience and displeasure at himself. But it is wrong to infer from this that repentance, which is the gift of God, is contributed by men as the movement of their own heart. And in this respect it is ignorant to compare a mortal man with God. An earthly father can not renew the perverse heart of his son by a secret movement of the Spirit in the way that God makes hearts of flesh out of stone. And finally, this is not discussing whether he is converted and returns to Him of himself; under the figure of a man it simply praises God's fatherly kindness and readiness to pardon.

Luke 15.21. *Father, I have sinned against heaven.* Here another part of repentance is indicated; the sense of sin is conjoined with sorrow and shame. For he who does not grieve that he has sinned and does not have his fault before his eyes will try anything before he thinks of returning to a good course. Therefore it is necessary that displeasure goes before repentance. And this expression is very weighty, when the young man is said to come to himself, inasmuch as he was wandering in the errors of his desires and thus carried away to forgetfulness of himself. And indeed, so aberrant are the impulses of the flesh, that whoever gives himself to them will vanish away and be gone out of himself. This is why transgressors are commanded to return to their heart (Isa. 46.8). There follows the confession—not the sort the Pope invented, but by which the son appeased his offended father. For this humbling is completely necessary for taking away the offence. The expression *I have sinned against heaven and before thee* is equivalent to saying that he had injured God in the person of his earthly father. And certainly nature teaches us that whoever is insolent against his father also rises up impiously against God, who subjects children to their parents.

Luke 15.22. *Bring forth the best robe.* Although (as has often been said) it is foolish to apply all the details in parables, yet it will not twist the literal meaning if we say that our heavenly Father not only so pardons our sins that He buries the memory of them, but He also restores the gifts of which we were stripped. Just as on the other hand He takes them from us to punish our ingratitude and forces us to shame at the reproach and immodesty of our nakedness.

*Now his elder son was in the field: and as he came and drew nigh to the house, he heard music and dancing. And he called to him one of his servants, and inquired what these things might be. And he said unto him, Thy brother is come; and thy father hath killed the fatted calf, because he hath received him safe and sound. But he was angry, and would not go in. Therefore his father came out, and entreated him. But he answered and said to his father, Lo, these many years do I serve thee, and I never transgressed a commandment of thine: and yet thou never gavest me a kid, that I might make merry with my friends. But when this thy son came, which hath devoured thy living with harlots, thou killedst for him the fatted calf. And he said unto him, Son, thou art ever with me, and all that is mine is thine. But it was meet to make merry and be glad: for this thy brother was dead, and is alive again; and was lost, and is found.* (Luke 15.25-32)

This final part of the parable charges with inhumanity those who want maliciously to restrict God's grace, as if they grudged poor sinners their salvation. For we know that the pride of the scribes is here accused. They considered that the reward owing to their merits was not paid if Christ admitted publicans and the masses to the hope of the eternal inheritance. The sum of it therefore is: if we want to be reckoned the children of God, we must in a brotherly way forgive our brethren their faults which He pardons in a fatherly way. Those who think that by 'first-born son' is meant a type of the Jewish people, although there is some reason in it, do not seem to me to be attending sufficiently to the context as a whole. For what gave rise to this parable was the grumbling of the scribes, who could not bear Christ's humanity towards the wretched and men of doubtful lives. He therefore compares the scribes, swollen with their arrogance, to thrifty and canny men who by their honest and careful life have always taken good care of the household. They are even obedient sons who throughout their lives have patiently borne their father's government. But although they did not at all deserve this praise, Christ speaks according to their view of themselves and imputes feigned holiness to them as a virtue by way of concession. It is as if He said: 'Although I grant you what you falsely claim, that you have always been obedient sons of God, yet you must not reject your brethren so proudly and cruelly, when they repent of their wasted lives.'

Luke 15.28. *And his father came out.* With these words He is telling the hypocrites that their pride is unbearable, when they have to be begged by their Father not to grudge mercy to their brothers. Now, granted God does not beg us, yet He exhorts us by His own example to bear with the faults of our brethren. To take away all excuse from such wicked rigorism. He not only represents the hypocrites speaking, and can refute their false boasting, but also asserts that even if anyone had fulfilled absolutely all the offices of piety to his father, yet he would have no just cause for complaint that pardon was given to his brother. It is certain that sincere worshippers of God are always clean and free from this malignant attitude, but Christ's purpose is to show that they are unfair (even though they may be as holy as the angels) who object to their brethren being received into grace.

Luke 15.31. *Son, thou art ever with me.* There are two points in this reply. The first is that the elder son has no cause for anger at seeing his brother received kindly and without condemnation. The other is that he has no interest in his brother's welfare when he is grieved at the happiness of his homecoming.

*All that is mine is thine,* he says: that is, 'Although you have never actually taken anything out of my house, you have not lost it, because everything remains as it is for you. Then why are you offended at our joy, when you ought to be joining in it? For it was right that we should rejoice that your brother whom we thought lost is now safe home again.' We must note these two reasons. We lose nothing if God kindly receives into His favour those who were alienated from Him by their sins. And it is hard-hearted not to rejoice when we see our brethren revived from death.

225

*And if thy brother sin against thee, go, shew him his fault between thee
and him alone: if he hear thee, thou hast gained thy brother. But if he
hear thee not, take with thee one or two more, that at the mouth of two
witnesses or three every word may be established. And if he refuse to
hear them, tell it unto the church: and if he will not hear the church also,
let him be unto thee as the Gentile and the publican. Verily, I say unto
you, What things soever ye shall bind on earth shall be bound in heaven,
and whatsoever ye shall loose on earth shall be loosed in heaven. Again
I say unto you, that if two of you shall agree on earth as touching anything that they shall ask, it shall be done for them of my Father which
is in heaven. For where two or three are gathered together in my name,
there am I in the midst of them.* (Matt. 18.15-20)

*Take heed to yourselves: if thy brother sin, rebuke him; and if he repent
forgive him.* (Luke 17.3)

Matt. 18.15. *And if thy brother sin against thee.* He had preached to
them about bearing the weaknesses of brethren, and so now He shows
more clearly how they are to be borne, for what purpose, and to what
extent. If He had not done this it would be easy to object that we can
only beware of giving offence if each connives at the faults of others
and so makes the bad worse by indulgence. Christ therefore lays
down a middle way which does not offend the weak over-much and
yet will heal their diseases. For severity compounded as a medicine is
useful and praiseworthy. In sum, Christ bids His disciples to forgive
one another in such a way as nevertheless to try to correct their faults.
And this is something to be considered prudently, for there is nothing
more difficult than to spare men and yet to be open in reproving them.
Nearly all lean to the one side or the other; they either deceive one
another with deadly flatteries or they attack too fiercely the person
they should be healing. But Christ commends to His disciples a
mutual love, and this is far from adulation. Only He tells them to
season their admonitions with a moderation so that they do not dis-
courage the weak by being too strict and harsh.

He expressly sets out three degrees in brotherly correction. The
first is to warn the offender privately. The second is, if he shows any
sign of obstinacy, to repeat the warning before witnesses. And the
third is, if this has done no good, to deliver him over to the public
judgment of the Church. But, as I have said, the aim of all this is not
to destroy love under pretext of a fervent zeal. Since the greater part
of men are moved by ambition, and this makes them ready to drag
the failings of their brethren into public gaze, Christ forestalls this fault
in good time and commands us to cover over the shame of our
brethren so far as we can. For those who take pleasure in the shame

and disgrace of their brethren are surely motivated by hatred and malevolence; if love were living in them they would simply think of the brother's feeling of shame.

But it may be asked whether this rule should be applied indiscriminately to any sort of sin. For there are many who allow no public censure until the sin has been admonished privately. For Christ's words contain a manifest limitation. He does not say that whoever without exception has sinned is to be warned and rebuked privately and without a witness; but He wants us to try this way when we have been offended privately, not indeed as our own affair, but because we should be smitten with sorrow whenever God is offended. Christ was not here speaking of bearing injuries, but teaching in general that kindness should be so cultivated among us that we do not destroy the weak, who ought to be saved, by treating them too harshly. Therefore the phrase 'against thee' does not indicate an injury done to a person, but is a distinction between hidden and open sins. For if anyone sins against the whole Church, Paul says he is to be publicly reproved, and that even elders are not to be spared. For he makes an express command on this to Timothy, that by rebuking them openly before all he may set them up as an example to others (I Tim. 5.20). And certainly it would be absurd for anyone who committed an open, notorious and flagrant sin to be warned a thousand times. Wherefore we must keep to the distinction which Christ expressly made, so that no-one shall accuse his brother rashly and needlessly by publishing his hidden sins.

*If he hear thee.* Christ confirms His teaching by its value and fruit. For it is no small thing to win for God a soul enslaved to Satan. But it is not often that the fallen repent; and why is this, save because, when they are treated as hated enemies, they become thick-skinned and obstinate? There is nothing better than gentleness; it reconciles to God those who were cut off from Him. But anyone who gives way to an immoderate and foolish indulgence goes out of his way to make shipwreck of his brother's salvation, which is in his hand. In Luke, Christ expressly commands us to be satisfied with a private reproof if a brother is brought to repentance. From this also we gather how necessary is a mutual freedom for reproof among believers. For since each of us sins very often every day it would be more than cruel to abandon by our silence and insincerity the salvation of those whom we should rescue from destruction by a friendly reproof. For although it does not always succeed, yet he is very guilty who neglects to use the remedy prescribed by the Lord for looking after his brother's salvation. It is also noteworthy that the Lord transfers His own honour to us to make us more energetic in doing our duty. It belongs to Him alone, and to no other, to convert a man; yet all undeservedly He gives us this credit of having gained a lost brother.

Matt. 18.16. *If he hear thee not.* The second degree is to take witnesses and again warn him if towards one man he is acting obstinately or at least is less than tractable. Some object that it is no good calling witnesses if one is dealing with a man who is hard and rebellious, since their presence will not turn him to a recognition of his guilt but rather make him deny it more relentlessly. But this difficulty is easily resolved if you distinguish between the different sorts of denying and evasiveness. The person who denies the fact straight out and asserts that he is accused falsely and slanderously should be left alone, for it is no good pressing him in front of witnesses. But there are many who impudently make light of their wrong and sinful action, or shamelessly excuse it, until they encounter a higher authority. For them this method is useful. Moreover it is clear that Christ's discourse should be understood from the word 'argue'.[1] To argue is to convince by demonstration. But how shall I argue with one who fiercely denies the whole thing? If he brazenly denies that he has committed the sin, he is shutting the door on any second admonition. Now we can see why Christ wanted witnesses to be present: so that the warning should be more weighty and solemn. Moses' words have a rather different meaning, but they are not inconsistent with this. Moses prohibits any pronouncement on a matter unknown, and defines the legitimate method of proof as being the testimony of two or three witnesses. Christ alludes to this law and says that the case will be clear when two or three witnesses arise to condemn a man's contumacy, at least to make the Church fully aware of it. For he who refuses to hear the two or three will not be able to complain and ask why he is dragged into the public gaze.

*Tell it to the church.* It may be asked what is meant by the word 'Church'. For Paul commands that the man of Corinth who committed incest should be excommunicated not just by a chosen number but by the whole assembly of the godly. And therefore it might seem likely that judgment is here placed with the whole people. But since there was not as yet any Church grouped around Christ, no such society founded, the Lord was Himself speaking in a common and accepted manner, and there is no doubt that He alludes to the order of the old Church, just as He accommodates His word in other places to the customary usage. When He commands us to leave at the altar the gift we wish to offer until we are reconciled to our offended brother (Matt. 5.23), there is no doubt that He is wanting to teach

---

[1] i.e. in verse 15: ὑπαγε ἐλεγξον αὐτὸν. Calvin takes ἐλέγχειν as equivalent to *arguere* here.

228

from the contemporary legal form of the worship of God that we cannot pray aright nor offer anything to God while there is discord between us and our brethren. So in this case, too, He was looking to the accepted form of discipline among the Jews, for it would have been absurd to place the judgment with the Church which did not yet exist.

Moreover, since among the Jews the power of excommunication rested with the elders, representing the whole Church Christ appositely says that those who sinned were only to be brought before the Church publicly if they arrogantly despised or jestingly evaded the private admonitions. We know that from the time they returned from the Babylonian exile the Jews committed the censure of morals and doctrine to an elected council, which they called the Sanhedrin, in Greek *synedrion*. This was a lawful government and approved by God, and it served as a bridle to keep the wanton and intractable in the way of duty. If anyone objects that in Christ's day it had all become corrupt and perverted, a tyranny which certainly could not be regarded as a judgment of the Church, the answer is easy. Although it was then an adulterated and perverse system, what Christ was deservedly praising was the tradition handed down by the fathers. But a little later He set up the Church and then He removed the corruption and restored the pure usage of excommunication. Yet there is no doubt that the system of discipline which flourished under the rule of Christ took the place of the older one. And indeed, since even heathen nations kept a shadowy rite of excommunication, it appears that there was from the beginning divinely imprinted on men's minds that if there were any who were impure and polluted they should be separated from the holy assemblies. It would therefore have been wrong and shameful for God's people to be quite without discipline, of which there remained some vestiges among the Gentiles. And what was preserved under the Law Christ transmits to us, since it is a system common to us and to the fathers of old. It was not Christ's purpose to send His disciples away to the synagogue, which willingly fostered disgusting uncleanness in its bosom and so excommunicated the true and genuine worshippers of God. But He tells us that in His Church the same order is to be kept that was instituted of old under the holy Law.

What is then added about 'Gentiles and publicans' confirms the interpretation I have given. Because the Gentiles and publicans were at that time hated like poison by the Jews, He compares to them impure and incurable men who will submit to no admonitions. Certainly He did not mean to give a command about the Gentiles, of whom the Church was then composed, that they should flee from themselves; nor today is there any reason why believers should abhor publicans.

But Christ, in order to be understood more easily by the simple, borrowed a form of speaking from the contemporary custom of His nation. And the meaning is that we should have nothing to do with despisers of the Church until they repent.

Matt. 18.18. *What things soever ye shall bind.* He now repeats the words He had used in chapter 16, but with a different meaning. There He wanted to assert the authority of teaching; but here He is establishing discipline, which is an appendix to teaching. There Christ said that the preaching of the Gospel would not be in vain but would prove either a quickening or a killing odour; here He affirms that, although the ungodly might deride the judgment of the Church, it would not be in vain. The distinction to be held is that He is talking simply about the Word preached, but here about public censures and discipline. Moreover, readers should seek the meaning of the metaphor of binding and loosing in that place. The sum of it is that whoever admits his fault humbly acknowledges and prays forgiveness for his sin, and begs the Church to pardon him, is absolved not only by men but by God Himself. And on the other hand, anyone who makes a mockery of the rebukes and threatenings of the Church, will, if he is condemned by her, have this human judgment confirmed in heaven. If anyone objects that this makes God into a sort of lower official who just subscribes to the decision of mortal men, the solution is easy. Christ is not asserting an authority of His Church which will jeopardize the right of Himself and His Father, but one which confirms the majesty of His Word. For just as in chapter 16 He wanted to establish not some undefined teaching but that which proceeded out of His mouth, so in this place He is not saying that any sort of judgment would be constant and ratified but that in which He Himself presides as judge; and that not only by the Spirit, but also by the Word. From this it follows that men's judgment is not primary when they do nothing but declare from His mouth and only try faithfully to carry through what He has appointed. For although Christ is the unique Judge of the earth, yet in the interim He wishes to have ministers as heralds of His Word. Then He wants the Church to put forward His own judgment. Thus He derogates nothing from Himself by appointing a ministry of men, for it is He alone who absolves and binds.

But there is a problem here. The Church tolerates many hypocrites and also absolves many who only pretend to be penitent. Are such people absolved in heaven too? I reply that this word is addressed to those who are truly and sincerely reconciled to the Church. He wanted to give comfort to troubled consciences and release them from fear, and so He declares that whoever has sinned is freed from guilt before God if he is reconciled to the Church. For this is appointed as a sort of pledge of heavenly favour and does not relate to hypocrites, who pervert the pure use of reconciliation. But for the godly it gives no little confidence also to be pardoned by the Church at the same time as they hear that their sins are blotted out before God and His angels. In the other clause Christ's meaning is not at all ambiguous. The stubborn and proud are prone to despise the Church's judgment on the grounds that they do not wish to be submissive to men (and this is why ungodly rascals will often boldly appeal to the judgment of heaven). But Christ wants to break down obstinacy by fear and declares that the judgment which they now despise will be ratified in heaven. And he encourages His people to a righteous severity so that they may not give way to the wicked obstinacy of those who reject or throw off discipline.

From this also we may see how foolishly the Papists twist this present passage to hide all sorts of tyranny. It is certain that the right of excommunication is given to the Church, and every sane man acknowledges this. Shall then some fellow or other, not even called by the Church but created by a horned and masked beast, utter his empty groans of excommunication at his will? But it is certain that the lawful government of the Church was given to the elders (*presbyteris*) and this means not only the ministers of the Word but also those from the laity (*ex plebe*) who were joined to them as censors of morals. Not satisfied with this shamelessness, however, they have even up till now tried to prove from this passage that all the burdens which they impose are to be borne. I will be silent on the way these worst enemies of the Church usurp and snatch for themselves the power permitted to the Church, and will merely say that, since Christ is here concerned only with the correction of sins, those who ensnare souls in their laws abuse His testimony foolishly and wickedly.

Their defence of auricular confession from this verse is of the same character. For the fact that Christ wanted a man who had been brought for his fault before public judgment to be reconciled to the Church does not mean that He laid an obligation on individuals to unload their sins into the ear of a priest. But their nonsense is so weak that it is not necessary to spend much time in refuting it.

Matt. 18.19. *Again I say unto you.* He confirms His previous statement. God will not only give the Spirit of counsel and wisdom to those who ask, but will also bring to pass that whatever they do from His Word shall not lack its power and effect. By joining agreement to prayer He warns them how soberly and reverently believers should behave in all the exercises of religion. The sinner is to be warned, and then, if he does not submit to correction, excommunicated. Here we must not only consult God's holy mouth so that nothing may be

231

established save from His Word, but we must also make a start with prayers. From this what I said earlier appears more clearly, that men are not given the freedom to do what they like, but God is declared to be the protector of the government of the Church, that it may decree and ratify the judgments of which He is the author. When believers meet together, they are taught to join their wishes and to have common prayer, not only to testify the unity of their faith but that God may hearken to their general agreement. Therefore, as God often promises elsewhere that He will be favourable to the prayers of individuals, so Christ here honours public prayers with a special promise and so invites us more earnestly to apply ourselves to them.

Matt. 18.20. *Where two or three are gathered together.* This promise is far broader than the former one. The Lord declares that whenever two or three are assembled in His name, He will be present to direct their counsel and to prosper everything they have embarked upon. There is therefore no reason for those who give themselves to be ruled by Him to doubt that they will experience good fruit from His presence. It is an inestimable blessing to have Christ as the President in all affairs, to bless deliberations and outcomes; and on the other hand there is nothing worse than being deprived of His grace. Therefore this promise should stir us up not a little to grow into a godly and holy unity. For whoever either neglects the sacred assemblies or separates himself from his brethren and is slothful in cultivating unity demonstrates by this fact that he cares nothing for Christ's presence. But the first thing to realize is that those who desire Christ's presence will meet in His name. And we must also grasp the definition of this term, for we see how the ungodly will falsely, impudently and wickedly use His holy name to sanction their conspiracies. Therefore unless we want to prostitute Christ to their mockeries and to overturn what He promises, let us know in particular the meaning of this expression, so that those who meet together may lay aside all the hindrances which prevent them coming to Christ and aspire after Him and devote themselves to His Word in obedience and permit His Spirit to govern them. When this simplicity rules we need not fear but that Christ will show that the assembly has not met together under His auspices in vain.

In this is betrayed the gross ignorance of the Papists. They cry out that councils cannot err and that we must accept all their decrees because whenever two or three are met together in Christ's name He is in their midst. But the first thing to ask is whether they really are met in the name of Christ when their faith, doctrine and piety are doubtful. When the Papists leave this out or wrap it up, who cannot see that they are cunningly confusing the difference between holy and profane assemblies and transferring the power of doing anything from the Church to the sworn enemies of Christ? Let us know, therefore, that only the faithful worshippers of God, who seek Christ sincerely, are heartened to confidence, so that they are not afraid He is absent from them. But we may leave out the false and abortive councils which have woven a web from their own imaginings, and allow Christ alone, with the doctrine of His Gospel, to have the pre-eminence among us.

*Then came Peter, and said to him, Lord, how oft shall my brother sin against me, and I forgive him? until seven times? Jesus saith unto him, I say not unto thee, Until seven times: but, Until seventy times seven. Therefore is the kingdom of heaven likened unto a certain king, which would make a reckoning with his servants. And when he had begun to reckon, one was brought unto him, which owed him ten thousand talents. But forasmuch as he had not wherewith to pay, his lord commanded him to be sold, and his wife, and children, and all that he had, and payment to be made. The servant therefore fell down and worshipped him, saying, Lord, have patience with me, and I will pay thee all. And the lord of that servant, being moved with compassion, released him, and forgave him the debt. But that servant went out, and found one of his fellow-servants, which owed him a hundred pence: and he laid hold on him, and took him by the throat, saying, Pay what thou owest. So his fellow-servant fell down and besought him, saying, Have patience with me, and I will pay thee. And he would not: but went out and cast him into prison, till he should pay that which was due. So when his fellow-servants saw what was done, they were exceeding sorry, and came and told unto their lord all that was done. Then the lord called him unto him, and saith to him, Thou wicked servant, I forgave thee all that debt, because thou besoughtest me: shouldest not thou also have had mercy on thy fellow-servant, even as I had mercy on thee? And his lord was wroth, and delivered him to the tormentors, till he should pay all that was due. So shall my heavenly Father do unto you, if ye forgive not every one his brother from your hearts their trespasses.* (Matt. 18.21-35)

*And if he sin against thee seven times in a day, and seven times turn again to thee saying, I repent; thou shalt forgive him.* (Luke 17.4)

Matt. 18.21. *Lord, how often, etc.?* This objection comes up out of Peter's ordinary fleshly thought and understanding. It is innate in everyone to want to be forgiven; and if they are not forgiven immediately they complain that they are treated severely and unkindly. But those who ask to be treated mercifully themselves, are far from

233

showing themselves easy towards others. When, therefore, the Lord had exhorted His disciples to be gentle, the doubt came into Peter's mind, 'Will it not happen that, if we are ready to pardon, our gentleness will engender further sinning?' Therefore he asks whether it is right to forgive sinners frequently (for the number seven is to be taken as meaning a great number, and the adverb 'seven times' is equivalent to saying, 'How frequently, Lord, do you want us to be reconciled to sinners? For it is absurd and useless for them to find us reconcilable repeatedly.') But Christ is far from being swayed by this objection. He expressly declares that no limit should be set to forgiving. It is not that He intends to lay down some definite number, but rather to enjoin us never to give up. Luke differs somewhat from Matthew, in that he simply relates Christ's command to be ready to forgive seven times. But the meaning is the same, that we must be ready to forgive not just once or twice but as often as a sinner comes to himself. The only difference is that in Matthew the Lord, to chide Peter because he is too limited, exaggerates the number, and this is sufficient of itself to show the sum of what is meant. For Peter was not asking whether he should forgive seven times because this was as far as he wished to go, but to suggest a great absurdity and draw Christ away from His opinion, as I have already said. He who is ready to forgive seven times will be reconcilable to the seventieth offence.

But Luke's words provoke another question: Christ does not command us to forgive save when the sinner is turned to us and declares his penitence. This seems to be giving permission to His people to deny pardon and mercy to the wicked. I reply that sins are forgiven in two ways. If anyone does me an injury and I set aside any feeling of revenge and do not cease to love him and even repay him with benefits instead of injuries; although I may think badly of him, as he deserves, yet I may be said to forgive him. For when the Lord bids us wish our enemies well, He does not demand that we shall approve in them what He Himself condemns, but only wishes our minds to be purged of hatred. In this sort of forgiveness it is not a question of someone who has sinned coming spontaneously to be reconciled to us or of an obligation upon us to love those who set out to exasperate us and reject our friendliness, and heap up old offences against us. The second sort of forgiving is when we receive a brother into our favour in such a way as to think well of him and be convinced that the memory of his fault is wiped out before God. And this is what I said at first. Christ is not talking here only about the injuries done to us but about any sort of sin at all. For He wants those who have fallen to be raised by our mercy. And this doctrine is very necessary, because by nature we are nearly all too critical; and Satan impels us to a most harsh rigour under the guise of strictness. Because of this, sadness and desperation swallow up unhappy men who are denied forgiveness.

But this also may be asked: Ought we straightway to believe anyone when he professes to be repentant? If we do this we shall of necessity err willingly and knowingly. For where will discretion be if someone mocks us with impunity to the hundredth fault? I reply: first that this is said of daily faults, and in this the best man needs pardon. When we have such a slippery road to tread and so much weakness of the flesh, what will happen if all hope of pardon is cut off at the second or third fall? Secondly, we must add that Christ is not depriving believers of discretion, to be foolishly credulous at the merest word, but only wishes them to be fair and humane and to reach out a hand to the penitent when they show signs of being sincerely displeased with themselves. Penitence is a holy thing, and therefore needs to be examined carefully. But whenever a sinner gives a probable sign of conversion, Christ wants him to be admitted to reconciliation and not to be broken and lose heart by being repulsed. Thirdly, we must note, when anyone makes himself suspect of levity and unsteadiness, we can still forgive him when he asks for pardon in such a way that we keep an eye on his behaviour in the future, lest he should make a mockery of our toleration and kindness, which come from the Spirit of Christ. For the purpose of the Lord Himself is to be kept to: our mercy must help those who have fallen to rise. And certainly we must imitate the goodness of the heavenly Father, who goes a long way to meet sinners and invite them to salvation. Add that since repentance is a wonderful gift of the Spirit and the creation of a new man, we do God an injury if we despise it.

Matt. 18.23. *Therefore is the kingdom of heaven likened.* Because it is difficult to orientate ourselves towards mercy, especially if we have to bear with many faults in our brethren, and a weariness steals over us, the Lord confirms His teaching with an apt parable. The sum of it is that those who are unbending in forgiving the faults of brethren, certainly have not their own interests at heart, and are setting up a standard too hard or heavy for themselves, for they will find God to be equally strict and inexorable towards them. The similitude stands chiefly in three parts. The lord is set over against the slave, the huge sum against the small or middling, and the extraordinary mercy against the extreme cruelty. If we mark these three things, it will be easy to gather Christ's meaning. For what are we, if we compare ourselves with God? And what is the sum each of us owes to Him? Finally, how light are the offences that our brethren have committed against us, if weighed against our own obligation to God! How undeserving, then, of God's mercy is the pigmy man who is himself laden with an

235

immense mass and yet is implacable to others in like case and will not forgive their least sin! As for the words, 'Kingdom of heaven' here means the spiritual state of the Church. It is as if Christ said: 'Between God and men, considered in their soul and spiritual life, things stand on the same footing as financial and worldly affairs between a civil and earthly lord and his slave.'

Matt. 18.25. *His lord commanded him to be sold.* It would be silly and too subtle to investigate the details here. For God does not always show strictness at first, when we are compelled to pray and ask forgiveness: in fact He forestalls us by His free goodness. But He is only saying what would happen to us if God used complete justice towards us. Then, if He decided to demand from us what is owing, how much we should need to flee to prayer, the unique refuge for sinners. Note also the big difference between the sums of money. If one talent is more than a hundred denarii, what are a hundred denarii in proportion to ten thousand talents!

Matt. 18.31. *So when his fellow-servants saw.* There is no mystery lurking in these words. They contain nothing but what nature tells us and what we learn daily; and we must know that the men among whom we live will be witnesses against us in God's sight. Cruelty cannot fail to be displeasing and hateful to them, especially when each one is afraid that what seems to be done to another will rebound on his own head. As to the next statement, there is no point in asking how God punishes the sins He has once forgiven. The meaning is simple. Granted He offers mercy to all, yet strict creditors, who will grant no relief, are unworthy to enjoy His forgiveness. But the Papists are ridiculous when they infer the flame of purgatory out of the adverb 'till', for it is certain that what Christ indicates here is eternal death and not a temporal punishment by which God's judgment is satisfied.

*And when they were come to Capernaum, they that received the didrachma came to Peter, and said, Doth not your master pay the didrachma? He saith, Yea. And when he came into the house, Jesus spake first to him, saying, What thinkest thou, Simon? the kings of the earth, from whom do they receive toll or tribute? from their sons, or from strangers? Peter said to him, From strangers. Jesus said unto him, Therefore the sons are free. But, lest we cause them to stumble, go thou to the sea, and cast a hook, and take up the fish that cometh up first; and when thou hast opened his mouth, thou shalt find a stater: that take, and give unto them for me and thee.* (Matt. 17.24-27)

236

Matt. 18.24. *And when they were come.* The first thing to observe is the scope of this story. Christ freely declared that He was subject by paying the tribute money; just as He put on the form of a servant. Yet He shows by His words and miracles that it was not by coercion or necessity but by a free and voluntary submission that He so emptied Himself that the world regarded Him merely as one of the crowd. This was not a toll that had to be paid on a journey, but an annual capital tax levied on the Jews. Thus they paid to tyrants what they were once accustomed to give to God alone. We know that this tax was laid on them by the Law so that by paying a half stater a year they would confess that God, who had redeemed them, was their sovereign king. The Asiatic monarchs appropriated the tax and then the Romans followed their example. In this way the Jews were, so to say, alienated from God's rule and paid the sacred tax enjoined in the Law to heathen tyrants. Now it might well seem absurd that Christ should not be immune from the tribute when He appeared as the Redeemer of the people. To obviate this offence, He taught first by word of mouth that He bound Himself to this of His own free will, and then He proved by a miracle that He who was the Lord of the sea and the fishes could exempt Himself from earthly rule.

*Doth not your master pay?* Some think that Christ was being censured by the tax-collectors as putting Himself outside the common law. Therefore, that sort of man being impudent and insulting, I interpret this as said abusively. And this teaches us that there was nowhere at all where Christ was left in peace, for the custom was for people to pay the tax in their own town. These men, therefore, ask whether He is to be free from laws because He travels about here and there without a fixed abode. And Peter's reply was a mild excuse to soothe them. 'He will pay', he says. From this we gather that it was Christ's habit to pay, since Peter promises it as something not at all doubtful. I suspect that the reason why they addressed Peter rather than the other disciples was because Christ lived with him; for if they had all lodged together, the payment would have fallen on them all.

The Papists are ridiculous in making Peter share Christ's dignity for such a weak reason. They say that He chose him as His deputy (*vicarium*) and gave him equal honour with Himself when He made him His equal in paying the tribute. But by this reckoning they make all swineherds vicars of Christ, in that they paid as much as He did. If Peter's primacy depends on the paying of tribute, why do they claim exemption from taxes? But those who deprave Scripture at their will are bound to play the fool in this disgusting way.

Matt. 18.25. *What thinkest thou, Simon?* Christ gave visible evidence of His divinity by showing that nothing was hidden from Him. But

237

what was the object of His saying? Did He want to exempt Himself and His disciples from subjection to the laws? Some do expound this as meaning that in relation to the state system Christians are free by right but subject themselves freely because this is the only way that society can be maintained. But to me the meaning seems more simple. There was a danger that the disciples might think that Christ had come in vain, since by paying the tax He ruled out any hope of liberation. And therefore He simply affirms that He freely paid it of His own right and power. From this they gathered that His kingdom was not decreased in any way. But why did He not openly claim what was His own? Because His majesty was unknown to the tax-collectors. For although His Kingdom is spiritual, He, the only Son of God, must be regarded as the Heir of the whole world, to subject all things to Himself and put them in their proper place in His sight. The meaning therefore is that kings and governments are not appointed by God over the human race so that He who is the Son should be placed in the same order of service with others but that He should freely be the servant alongside others until the glory of His Kingdom is revealed. The Pope succeeds in perverting this testimony very foolishly to exempt His clergy from the law—as if shaven pates made them the sons of God and immune from tributes and taxes. All Christ intended was to claim for Himself the title of being the King's Son, so as at least to have a residence where He enjoyed immunity from the common law. The Anabaptists, too, stupidly twist these words so as to weaken the political order; for it is quite certain that Christ says nothing at all about a special common law for believers, but only uses the comparison of kings's sons who, with their staff, are free in this respect.

Matt. 18.27. *Cast a hook.* Although I agree that Christ's purse was not always full, yet I consider that He was not forced by poverty to tell Peter to do this, but to prove by a miracle that His Kingdom was broader than that of earthly kings, for even the fishes paid Him their tribute money. And we only once read that this happened; one example was sufficient in the whole of His life. A stater was equivalent to a shekel—i.e. four drachmas or two didrachmas.

*And it came to pass when Jesus had finished these words, he departed from Galilee, and came into the borders of Judaea beyond Jordan; and great multitudes followed him; and he healed them there.* (Matt. 19.1-2)

*John answered him, saying, Master, we saw one casting out devils in thy name, and he did not follow us: and we forbade him, because he followed us not. But Jesus said, Forbid him not: for there is no man*

238

*which shall do a mighty work in my name, and be able quickly·to speak evil of me. For he that is not against us is for us.*

*And he arose from thence, and cometh into the borders of Judaea through the region which is beyond Jordan: and multitudes come together unto him again; and, as he was wont, he taught them again.* (Mark 9.38-40; 10.1)

*And John answered and said, Master, we saw one casting out devils in thy name; and we forbade him, because he followeth not with us. And Jesus said unto him, Forbid him not: for he that is not against us is for us. And it came to pass, when the days were well-nigh come that he should be received up, he steadfastly set his face to go to Jerusalem, and sent messengers before his face: and they went, and entered into a village of the Samaritans, to make ready for him. And they did not receive him, because his face was as though he were going to Jerusalem. And when his disciples James and John saw this, they said, Lord, wilt thou that we bid fire to come down from heaven, and consume them as Elijah did? But he turned, and rebuked them saying, Ye know not what spirit ye are of. For the Son of man came not to destroy men's lives, but to save them. And they went to another village.* (Luke 9.49-56)

Mark 9.38. *Master, we saw one.* From this it is clear that Christ's name was at this time so renowned that even some who were not among His close disciples used it, or maybe misused it. On this last point I dare not be definite. It may be that the man mentioned had embraced Christ's doctrine and devoted himself to performing miracles out of a good intention; but because Christ gave this ability only to the chosen heralds of His Gospel, I judge that he undertook, or snatched up, the office presumptuously. But although he acted out of turn in daring to imitate the disciples without any mandate, his audacity was not fruitless, for it pleased the Lord to make His name illustrious by this means also—just as He sometimes works through those whose ministry He does not approve as legitimate. This does not rule out the possibility that some one who is imbued with a special faith may follow a blind impulse, and throw himself into performing miracles.

I now come to John and his comrades. They say that they have forbidden a man to work miracles. Why did they not first ask whether it was lawful or not? For now they are doubtful and uncertain and seek the Master's decision. From this it follows that they took the right to forbid on themselves thoughtlessly. Therefore, whoever undertakes more than he knows God's Word allows him is condemned of recklessness. Moreover, we may suspect Christ's disciples of being ambitious, since they are striving to assert the privilege of their own

239

honour. For why is it that they suddenly forbid an unknown man to do miracles except because they want to claim the right for themselves alone? They allege as their reason that he did not follow Christ; as if they said, 'He is not your close friend like us, so why should he equal us in honour?'

Mark 9.39. *Forbid him not.* Christ did not want him to be forbidden. This was not because He was the author of what he had done, or approved of it, or even because He wished the disciples to approve of it, but because when God is glorified in any event, we should accept it and rejoice at it. Thus Paul, although he did not like the greed of those who used the Gospel for self-advertisement, rejoices that by their doing this Christ's glory is proclaimed. And we must note the reason that is given: it is impossible that a man who did great works in Christ's name should curse Him; and this should be reckoned as gain. For it follows from this, that unless the disciples had been more addicted to their own glory than careful and desirous of promoting the Master's glory, they would not have taken it badly when they saw His glory being extolled and increased. When, however, Christ declares that those who are not open enemies should be regarded as friends, He was not telling us to open the gate to thoughtless men and to be silent while they throw things into confusion as they wish and upset the whole order of the Church (for such licence we must restrain, so far as our calling demands). But he says that they are doing wrong who try hard to stop the Kingdom of God being promoted by any sort of means at all. He does not recognize as His own or regard as belonging to His flock those who are midway between being enemies and friends; but He means that, inasmuch as they do not harm, they profit and help. There is a proverb which tells us not to go to war until we are provoked.

Luke 9.51. *When the days were come.* Luke alone relates this story, which yet is valuable in many respects. He describes in the first place Christ's courage and constancy in despising death; secondly, the way that religious disagreements engender deadly hatred; thirdly, how man's nature is carried away by a headlong fervour to impatience; then how easy it is to fall into an imitation of the saints; and finally he recalls us to follow Christ's example of meekness.

He calls Christ's death a receiving up, not only because He was then taken away, but because He left the lowly prison of His body and ascended on high.

*He steadfastly set his face.* By this word Luke declares that when Christ saw death before His eyes, He overcame His fear and advanced to meet it. Yet at the same time a struggle is indicated, so that He vanquished fear and courageously offered Himself to death. For if He

240

had encountered no dread, no difficulty, no struggle, no anxiety, what would be the point of His setting His face steadfastly? But He was not deadened, not endowed with drunken recklessness; He had to be moved by the cruel and bitter death, the dreadful and horrifying torture, which He knew hung over Him from the strict judgment of God. But that was so far from obscuring or lessening His glory that it was a wonderful proof of His infinite love for us. He cast off all care for Himself, devoted Himself to our salvation, and walked through the midst of terrors towards the death which He well knew was near at hand.

Luke 9.52. *And sent messengers.* It is probable that He took with Him a great crowd of friends. The messengers were not sent to prepare a fine feast or to choose some splendid palace but only to say that a great host of strangers was on the way. But they were shut out and repulsed, and so wait for the Master. From this we learn, as I noted in the second place, that when men disagree on the teachings of religion, they soon break out into a mutual hatred. For it was a sign of very bitter hatred to refuse food to the hungry, to deny lodging to the weary. But the Jewish religion is in such ill odour and so irritates the Samaritans that they think its adherents deserve no kindness. Perhaps, too, they were annoyed at the insult they were very conscious of, that the Jews hated their temple as something profane and regarded them as degenerate and corrupt worshippers of God. But since the superstition once admitted stuck firmly, they fought with a depraved jealousy to defend it to the end. At length the quarrel grew so hot that it destroyed both nations in one fire; for Josephus bears witness that it was the torch that lit the Jewish war. Although it would have been easy for Christ to have avoided this ill-will, He preferred to profess Himself a Jew rather than buy a lodging with an implied denial.

Luke 9.54. *And when his disciples.* Perhaps it was the country itself that made them want to thunder against the ungodly. For it was there that Elijah had cast down the king's soldiers with fire from heaven when they were sent to take him (II Kings 1.10). It therefore came to their minds that the Samaritans were appointed to a like destruction for rejecting the Son of God so undeservedly. And here we see how a foolish imitation of the saints may drive us on. James and John bring forward the example of Elijah; but they do not consider how far they differ from Elijah. They do not examine carefully their intemperate zeal; they do not think of God's calling. The Samaritans covered their idolatry with a similar specious mask, as we read in John 4.20. But they are both wrong, for they have no discrimination and aped rather than imitated the holy fathers. Although it is not clear whether they imagine they themselves have the power to do this, or whether they are asking Christ to give it them, to me it seems more probable that they are elated with foolish confidence and do not doubt they have the strength to exercise vengeance if Christ lets them. Luke 9.55. *Ye know not what manner of spirit.* With this reply Christ not only restrains the wild impulse of these two disciples but lays down a rule for us all that we should not let our zeal have its own way. For whoever undertakes anything should be conscious of having God's Spirit as its author and leader and of being moved by His right and pure instinct. Many are driven on by their enthusiasm. But if they lack the Spirit of prudence it is all so much froth. It also often happens that wild and fleshly feelings are mixed up with the enthusiasm and those who seem the keenest zealots for God's glory are blinded by their own fleshly mind. Therefore, unless the Spirit of God rules over our zeal it will be no excuse to claim that we undertook nothing but out of holy zeal. But the Spirit Himself will rule us by His counsel and wisdom so that we shall attempt nothing beyond our duty outside our calling, nothing imprudently or inopportunely. He will cleanse our minds from all filth of the flesh and imbue them with a righ-attitude, lest we should desire anything apart from what God come mands. Christ also reproves the disciples for being so far from tht spirit of Elijah and yet wrongly usurping what he had done. For Elijah executed God's judgment as it was commanded him by the Spirit. But they were not acting under God's order but just rushing in at the impulse of the flesh to punish the Samaritans. Therefore the examples of the saints are no defence to us unless the same Spirit who directed them dwells in us.

*And there came unto him Pharisees, tempting him, and saying to him, Is it lawful for a man to put away his wife for any cause? And he answered and said to them, Have ye not read, that he which made them from the beginning, made them male and female? And he said, For this cause shall a man leave his father and mother, and shall cleave to his wife; and the twain shall become one flesh? So that they are no more twain, but one flesh. What therefore God hath joined together, let not man put asunder. They say unto him, Why then did Moses command to give a bill of divorcement, and to put her away? He saith unto them, Moses for your hardness of heart suffereth you to put away your wives: but from the beginning it hath not been so. And I say unto you, Whoso-ever shall put away his wife, except for fornication, and shall marry another, committeth adultery.* (Matt. 19.3-9)

*And there came unto him Pharisees, and asked him, Is it lawful for a man to put away his wife? tempting him. And he answered and said unto them, What did Moses command you? And they said, Moses suffered to write a bill of divorcement, and to put her away. But Jesus said unto them, For your hardness of heart he wrote you this commandment. But from the beginning of the creation, male and female made he them. For this cause shall a man leave his father and mother, and shall cleave to his wife; and the twain shall become one flesh: so that they are no more twain, but one flesh. What therefore God hath joined together, let not man put asunder. And in the house his disciples asked him again of this matter. And he said unto them, Whosoever shall put his wife away, and marry another, committeth adultery against her: and if the woman shall put away her husband, and marry another, she committeth adultery.* (Mark 10.2-12)

The Pharisees are setting traps for Christ and are attacking Him cunningly so as to overthrow Him. Yet their malice turns out usefully for us, just as the Lord knew how to convert wonderfully to the use of His disciples all the schemes of the ungodly to destroy true doctrine. For there was solved by this occasion the question as to the permissiveness of divorce, and a sure law was delivered on the sacred and indissoluble bond of marriage (*sacro et insolubili coniugii nexu*). But they seize it as a basis for disagreement, so that He would have to give an answer that would annoy them whichever side He took. They ask whether it is right for a man to divorce his wife for any cause at all. If Christ denies it, they cry in their ungodly way, He will be abrogating the Law. If He affirms it, they will say that He is no prophet of God but simply a pimp, out to indulge men's lusts. This is what they conceive in their minds, but the Son of God, who knew how to take the wise in their own cunning, disappointed them. He stood out strictly against unlawful divorces, and yet at the same time showed that He put forward nothing that was not consonant with the Law. For He comprehends the whole matter under two heads: that the order of creation should be as a law, so that a man should be faithful to his wife all his life; that divorce was permitted, not because it was lawful, but because God was dealing with a stubborn and intractable people.

Matt. 19.4. *Have ye not read?* Christ does not reply directly to what they ask, yet He does fully satisfy the implied question. It is just as if today someone were to be asked about the Mass and expounded faithfully the mystery of the holy Supper and they drew the conclusion that any who dared to add to or detract from the pure institution of the Lord would be sacrilegious and falsifying. By saying this he would obviously overturn the fictitious sacrifice of the Mass. Now Christ takes as an axiom this: From the beginning God joined the husband

243

to the woman and the two became a complete man. Therefore he who divorces his wife tears from himself half of himself. And it is quite against nature for a man to tear his body asunder. He adds another argument, from the minor to the major.

The bond (*vinculum*) of marriage is holier than that which binds children to parents.

But piety binds children to parents in an indissoluble bond (*nexu*). Much less, therefore, can a husband renounce his wife.

Hence it follows that if a man divorces his wife the divine bond (*divinum vinculum*) is broken.

But here the sense of the words is that God, the Creator of the human race, made male and female so that each should be content with a single wife and not desire others. For He emphasizes the dual number, just as the prophet Malachi,[1] inveighing against polygamy, uses the same argument, that God, whose Spirit was so abundant that it was in His power to create more, in fact made one man, that is, as it is here described by Christ. Therefore from the order of creation is proved the indivisible society (*individua societas*) of one man with one woman. If any object that in this way it will not be lawful when the first wife is dead to take another, the reply is easy; not only does death loose the bond, but a second wife is put by God in the place of the first, as if she were one and the same.

Matt. 19.5. *For this cause shall a man leave.* It is not clear whether Moses makes Adam or God speak these words. But whichever you choose will not affect the present place much, for it was sufficient to quote an oracle of God even if spoken through Adam's mouth. Now He does not simply command the man who takes a wife to leave his father; for God would be inconsistent if He abolished for the sake of marriage the piety He demands from children to their parents. But when a comparison between the two duties is made, the wife is preferred to the father and mother. But if a man should repudiate his father and shake off the yoke to which he is bound, no one would be friendly with such a monster. Therefore far less is permission given to dissolving a marriage.

*And the twain shall become one flesh.* This statement condemns both polygamy and also permissiveness in divorcing wives. For if the mutual conjunction between the two was consecrated by the Lord, the intermingling of three or four is a falsifying. But Christ (as I said a little before) applies this to His purpose in a different sense, that anyone who divorces his wife tears himself asunder because the force of holy marriage is that the husband and wife join together to make one man. It was not Christ's intention to introduce Plato's impure and obscene

[1] Mal. 2.14-16.

speculation, but to speak reverently of the order divinely appointed. The husband and wife live together in such a way as to cherish either the other no less than as half of himself. And the husband should rule as the head of his wife, not as a tyrant; and on her side the wife should submit herself in modest obedience.

Matt. 19.6. *What therefore God hath joined together.* In this sentence Christ bridles men's lust, so that they may not break the sacred knot by divorcing their wives. But just as He says that it does not lie in men's will to dissolve marriage, so also He lays down a law for all others that they are not to confirm illegal divorces on their own authority. For the magistrate who gives a man permission to divorce his wife is abusing his power. Strictly speaking, Christ's intention was that everyone who had given his troth should religiously keep it, and that those who were tempted to divorce by lust or by a depraved mind should have this thought: Who are you to want to make a break from this divine bond? But this doctrine can be extended further. The Papists, imagining a Church separated from Christ its Head, are left with a truncated and mutilated body. In the holy Supper, when Christ joined the bread and the wine, they have dared to deprive the whole people of the use of the cup. Against these diabolical corruptions we may well oppose the words, 'What God hath joined, let not man separate.'

Matt. 19.7. *Why then did Moses.* They had thought up this artifice in case Christ should (and this was the more probable) demand a legitimate cause for divorce. For it seems that whatever God permits in His Law is lawful, since His will alone establishes the distinction between good and bad. But Christ refutes this false ill-will with an apt reply: Moses conceded this because of their obstinacy, not because he approved of it as lawful.

He confirms this statement with the excellent argument: *but from the beginning it hath not been so.* He takes it for granted that when God instituted marriage from the beginning, He fixed a perpetual law which would last until the end. If the institution of marriage is to be regarded as an inviolable law, it follows that, whatever leads astray from it, does not lie in its very nature but comes from man's vice. Yet it may be asked whether it was right for Moses to permit what in itself was bad and vicious. I reply: The fact that he did not strictly forbid it is imprecisely called a permission. He did not give a law about divorce and approve of it by his consent, but when men's wickedness could be restrained by no other means, he applied the most tolerable remedy, so that a man might at least bear witness to his wife's chastity. For the Law was only given for the sake of women, so that they should not incur any disgrace by being unjustly rejected. From this we gather that it was rather a punishment inflicted on men than an indulgence or permission to kindle their desire. Add that the spiritual government differs greatly from the social and external order. The Lord comprehends what it is meet and right to do in ten words. Since it can happen that many things are never tried before a human court which yet worry and convict the conscience, it is not surprising if the laws of a country wink at them. Let us take a familiar example. The law gives us a greater liberty to go to law than the rule of love allows. Why so? Because individuals cannot get their right unless a door is opened for them to demand it. Yet the inward law of God declares that what love dictates must be followed. This is no reason, however, why magistrates should make their laziness an excuse, if they deliberately refrain from correcting vices or omit what their duty demands. But private men must see to it that they do not double their guilt by covering their vices under the law. For the Lord is here indirectly accusing the Jews in that, not satisfied with having their obstinacy tolerated, they also want to make God the author of their iniquity. If the rule of holy and godly living is not always nor everywhere to be sought in the laws of a state, far less are they in custom.

Matt. 19.9. *And I say unto you.* Mark relates that this was said privately to the disciples when they had gone home. But Matthew leaves out these circumstances and joins the sentence to the discourse. The Evangelists often omit some intervening event and regard it as sufficient to gather the heads of the matter. There is therefore no disagreement, save that the one explains it more precisely than the other. And the sum of it is that although the Law does not punish divorces (although they are dissonant with God's first institution) yet he who rejects his wife and takes another is adulterous. For it lies not in a man's will to dissolve the bond of marriage, which the Lord wishes to remain settled; and thus she who occupies the bed of a lawful wife is a concubine.

But an exception is added. A woman who commits adultery sets her husband free, for she cuts herself off from him as a rotten member. Those who think out other reasons for divorce, and want to be wiser than the heavenly Master, are rightly to be rejected. They want leprosy to be a just cause for divorce because not only the husband but also the children may be infected. But for my part, while advising a godly man not to come in contact with his wife if she is a leper, I do not permit him to divorce her. If anyone objects that those who cannot live a celibate life need a remedy so that they may not burn, I say that the remedy is not to be sought outside God's Word. I also add that they will never lack the gift of continency if they give themselves to be ruled by the Lord and follow what He commands. Say that someone starts to take an aversion to his wife and cannot bear to lie with her. Is this evil going to be cured by polygamy? Or the wife of another man may be smitten by paralysis or have a stroke or suffer some other incurable disease. Is her husband going to cast her out because he cannot live continently? But we know that those who walk in His ways never lack the help of the Spirit. Paul says, 'To avoid fornication, let each man have his own wife' (I Cor. 7.2). Even if everything does not turn out as he hoped, yet the man who has done this has fulfilled his part in the matter; and if anything is lacking, it will be made good by God's help. To go beyond is simply to tempt God. But Paul also points to another cause: When unbelievers reject their spouse because they hate their godliness, the godly brother or sister is not subject to the bondage (I Cor. 7.12, 15). This is not contrary to Christ's meaning. For Paul is not dealing with just causes for divorce, but only whether a woman continues to be bound to an unbelieving husband after he has wickedly rejected her because he hates her God and she can only be reconciled to him at the price of denying God. Therefore it is not surprising that Paul prefers separation from a mortal man to alienation from God. But the exception which Christ mentions seems unnecessary. For if the adulteress was punished by death, what is the point of talking about divorce? But because it was the husband's duty to bring the adultery of his wife to judgment so as to purge his house of disgrace, however the event might turn out, Christ releases from his bond the husband who convicts his wife of unchastity. And it may be that this crime went largely unpunished among the corrupt and decadent people. Similarly today it is the perverted indulgence of magistrates that makes it necessary for men to divorce their impure wives, inasmuch as there is no punishment for adultery. But we must note that each party has a common and mutual right, just as their obligation of loyalty is mutual and equal. A man may hold the primacy in other things, but in bed he and his wife are equal, for he is not the lord of his body. Therefore if he commits adultery he has defected from marriage and the wife is given freedom.

*He that marrieth her.* Many expositors have interpreted this clause very badly. They think generally and confusedly that it commands celibacy always after a divorce, so that if a husband puts away his adulterous wife, they must both of necessity be celibate thereafter. As if the freedom to divorce consisted merely in sleeping apart from the wife; as if also Christ did not obviously permit in this case what the Jews were accustomed to claim for themselves indiscriminately at their pleasure. Hence, this was a gross error. When Christ accuses of adultery the man who marries a divorced woman, it is certain that He is restricting it to unlawful and frivolous divorces. Paul commands

247

those who were put away to remain unmarried or to be reconciled to their husbands because marriage is not abolished by quarrels and disagreements (I Cor. 7.10-11). And this can be inferred also from Mark when he expressly speaks of a wife leaving her husband. Not that wives had the right to give their husbands a bill of divorce, except so far as the Jews had lapsed into the customs of foreigners; but Mark wanted to note that the Lord censured contemporary corrupt practice of the remarriage of both partners after voluntary divorce. This is why he does not mention adultery.

*The disciples say unto him, If the case of the man is so with his wife, it is not expedient to marry. But he said unto them, Not all men can receive this saying, but they to whom it is given. For there are eunuchs, which were born so from their mother's womb: and there are eunuchs, which were made eunuchs by men: and there are eunuchs, which made themselves eunuchs for the Kingdom of heaven's sake. He that is able to receive it, let him receive it. (Matt. 19.10-12)*

As if it would be a hard lot for men to be so bound to their wives that, so long as they are chaste, they are forced to put up with everything else and not leave them, the disciples are upset by Christ's reply and argue that it is better to be without a wife altogether than fall into such a snare. But why do they not think on their side how hard was the bondage of their wives? Simply because they are thinking only of themselves and their own convenience and are so motivated by the mind of the flesh that they forget others and want only themselves to be considered. Their ungodly ingratitude betrays itself that they reject this wonderful gift of God out of fear of one inconvenience or out of boredom. According to them it would be better to flee marriage altogether than to tie oneself to a perpetual bond of fellowship. But if God instituted marriage for the common welfare of the human race, it is not to be rejected because it carries with it some things which are less agreeable. Therefore we learn that, if there is anything in God's benefits that does not please us, we are not to be so discriminative and critical that we do not use them reverently. This depravity we must especially beware of in holy marriage, for, because there are many troubles bound up in it, Satan is always trying to make it seem hateful and disgraceful, so that he can put men off it. And Jerome gave proof of a too obvious spirit of malice and perversity in not only maligning that sacred and divine order of life but heaping up all the bad examples he could out of profane authors to destroy its beauty and honour. But

248

we should call to mind that all the troubles in marriage are accidental, in that they come from man's vice. And we should also remember that when our nature had become corrupt, marriage began to be a medicine, and it is not surprising if there is some bitter taste mixed with the sweetness. But we must see how the Lord refutes this foolishness. By saying that all are not capable of what He has said, He means that the choice is not in our hands, as if we had the power to make up our own minds. If anyone imagines that it is to his advantage to be without a wife and so without further consideration decides to be celibate, he is very much in error. For God, who declared that it was good that the woman should be the help meet for the man, will exact punishment for contempt of His ordinance. Men arrogate too much to themselves when they try to exempt themselves from their heavenly calling. That it is not open to all to choose which state they please, Christ proves from the fact that continency is a special gift. For when He says that only those are capable of it to whom it is given, He plainly means that it is not given to all. This convicts the arrogance of those who do not hesitate to claim for themselves what Christ so clearly refuses them.

Matt. 19.12. *For there are eunuchs.* Christ speaks of three sorts of eunuchs. Eunuchs by nature or who have been castrated are debarred from marriage because they are not men. Others He calls eunuchs who have made themselves eunuchs, so as to give themselves the more freely to God. He says that these are free from the necessity to marry. From this it follows that all others who shrink from marriage are fighting against God with the impious audacity of Titans. It is very weak for the Papists to emphasize this phrase 'make themselves eunuchs', as if men can impose a rule of continency at their will. For Christ has already said that God gives it to whom He pleases. And a little later He asserts again that anyone who is not endowed with this special gift is acting presumptuously if he chooses celibacy. Hence the 'self-castration' does not rest in men's free-will. The sense simply is that, although some are by nature capable of marriage, yet if God grants them immunity from it they are not tempting Him if they abstain.

*For the kingdom of heaven's sake.* Many explain this absurdly as meaning 'To deserve eternal life', as if celibacy contained some meritorious service—just as the Papists imagine it is an angelic state. But all Christ intended was that the unmarried should set the aim before them of being more ready for the exercises of religion if they are freed from all cares. It is foolish to imagine that celibacy is a virtue, for this is no more pleasing to God in itself than fasting is, nor does it deserve to be reckoned among the duties required of us. It ought in fact to be seen in quite a different connection. Christ meant to say expressly that, although a man might be pure from fornication, his celibacy would not be approved by God if he merely aimed at his own ease and pleasure. The only thing that can excuse him is an aspiration after a free and unfettered practice of the heavenly life. In sum, Christ teaches us that it is not enough for a celibate to live chastely: but he may deliberately abstain from marriage in order to free himself for better duties.

*He that is able to receive it.* In this verse Christ warns them that marriage is not to be shunned unless we want to throw ourselves headlong into destruction through our blind recklessness. He had to lay a hand on His disciples when He saw them rushing on without any judgment. But the warning is useful to everyone, for in deciding what kind of life to lead, few reckon what has been given to them, but charge forward without choosing wherever their thoughtless zeal bears them. I wish this had been heard in the past; but men's ears were blocked by I know not what bewitchments of Satan, so that in opposition to nature and against God's·will, those whom God had called to marriage took on themselves the snare of perpetual celibacy. Afterwards wretched souls were caught in the snare of a deadly vow and out of that ditch there was no emerging.

*Then were there brought unto him little children, that he should lay his hands on them, and pray: and the disciples rebuked them. But Jesus said to them, Suffer the little children, and forbid them not, to come unto me: for of such is the kingdom of heaven. And he laid his hands on them, and departed thence.* (Matt. 19.13-15)

*And they brought unto him little children, that he should touch them: and the disciples rebuked them that brought them. But when Jesus saw it, he was moved with indignation, and said unto them, Suffer the little children to come unto me: forbid them not: for of such is the kingdom of heaven. Verily I say unto you, Whosoever shall not receive the kingdom of God as a little child, he shall not enter therein. And he took them in his arms, and blessed them, laying his hands upon them.* (Mark 10.13-16)

*And they brought unto him also their babes, that he should touch them: but when the disciples saw it, they rebuked them. But Jesus called them unto him, saying, Suffer the little children to come unto me, and forbid them not: for of such is the kingdom of God. Verily I say unto you, Whosoever shall not receive the kingdom of God as a little child, he shall not enter therein.* (Luke 18.15-17)

This story is very useful. It teaches us that Christ does not receive only those who voluntarily come to Him of a holy desire and moved by faith, but also those who may not yet be old enough to realize how much they need His grace. These small children still have no understanding that they should seek His blessing. Yet when they are brought He receives them kindly and lovingly and consecrates them to His Father in a solemn ceremony of blessing. We must notice the purpose of those who brought the children. It would have been meaningless for them to have offered their children had there not been a conviction in their minds that into His possession was given the power of the Spirit which He would pour out on the people of God. There is therefore no doubt that they ask for the children a participation in that grace. This is why Luke adds the adverb 'also'. It is as if he said that, when they had learned how He helped grown-ups in various ways, they hoped also for their children that if He laid His hands on them they would not go away without receiving some of the gifts of the Spirit. Now the laying on of hands (as we have said elsewhere) was an ancient and renowned symbol of blessing among the Jews. It is therefore not surprising if they desire Christ to pray for their children by using that solemn ceremony. Moreover, since the greater bless the lesser (Heb. 7.7) they ascribe to Him the right and honour of the supreme prophet.

Matt. 19.13. *And the disciples rebuked them.* If a crown had been placed on Jesus' head, they would have accepted the fact willingly and with rejoicing; for they did not yet grasp what His real office was. But they think it is beneath His dignity to receive children. There is some excuse for their mistake. For what had the supreme Prophet, the Son of God, to do with children? But this teaches us that they judge perversely who assess Christ according to the mind of the flesh, for they will continually despoil Him of His real qualities and give Him others, which seem honours but do not at all belong to Him. This is how the immense mass of superstitions arose which brought a fictitious Christ into the world. We learn therefore not to think of Him otherwise than He Himself taught nor to give Him another role (*personam*) than that which the Father laid on him. We can see what has happened in the Papacy. They think they are paying Christ great honour if they prostrate themselves before a bit of bread. Before God this is a stinking abomination. Again, because they thought it was not honourable enough for Him to undertake the office of Advocate for us, they have created numberless patrons. But in so doing they have taken from Him the honour of Mediator.

Matt. 19.14. *Suffer the little children.* He bears witness that He wishes to receive children, and in the end He both embraces them in His arms

251

and blesses them by laying His hands upon them. From this we gather that His grace reaches to this age of life also. And no wonder, for when the whole race of Adam was shut up under the penalty of death, it was inevitable that all should perish, from the least to the greatest, save those whom one Redeemer should rescue. It would be too cruel to exclude that age from the grace of redemption. Therefore it is not thoughtlessly that we oppose this shield against the Anabaptists. They deny baptism to infants because they are not capable of understanding the significance of its mystery. We on the contrary argue that since baptism is the pledge and figure of the free forgiveness of sins and of divine adoption, it should certainly not be denied to infants, whom God adopts and washes with the blood of His Son. The objection that it also figures repentance and newness of life is easily resolved. They are renewed by God's Spirit according to the measure of their age until by degrees and in its own time this power hidden within them increases and shines forth openly. But they contend that we are reconciled to God and become heirs of the adoption only by faith. We confess that this is true of adults; but that it applies also to infants this passage proves to be false. The laying on of hands was certainly no frivolous or empty symbol, nor did Christ pour forth His prayers into the empty air. But He could not solemnly present them to God without giving them purity. And what was His prayer for them but that they might be received among the children of God? From this it follows that they were regenerate by the Spirit in the hope of salvation. And finally, that He embraced them was a testimony that Christ reckoned them in His flock. And if they were partakers of the spiritual gifts which baptism figures, it is absurd that they should be deprived of the outward sign. It is an irreligious audacity to drive from Christ's fold those whom He nursed in His bosom, and to shut the door on them as strangers when He did not wish to forbid them.

*Of such is the kingdom of heaven.* By this word He comprehends both little children and also those who are like them. It is foolish for the Anabaptists to exclude children; they ought to make a beginning with them. But He uses this present occasion to exhort His disciples to empty themselves of malice and pride and to put on the nature of a child. This is why Mark and Luke add that no-one can enter into the Kingdom of heaven save he who becomes like a child. But we must remember Paul's admonition that we must be babes, not in understanding, but in malice (I Cor. 14.20).

*And behold, one came to him and said, Good Master, what good thing shall I do, that I may have eternal life? And he said unto him, Why callest thou me good? There is none good save one, even God: but if thou wouldest enter into life, keep the commandments. He saith unto him, Which? And Jesus said, Thou shalt not kill, Thou shalt not commit adultery, Thou shalt not steal, Thou shalt not bear false witness, Honour thy father and thy mother: and, Thou shalt love thy neighbour as thyself. The young man saith unto him, All these things have I observed from my youth up: what lack I yet? Jesus said unto him, If thou wouldest be perfect, go, sell what thou hast, and give to the poor, and thou shalt have treasure in heaven: and come, follow me. But when the young man heard the saying, he went away sorrowful: for he was one that had great possessions.* (Matt. 19.16-22)

*And as he was going forth into the way, there ran one to him, and kneeled to him, and asked him, Good Master, what shall I do that I may inherit eternal life? And Jesus said unto him, Why callest thou me good? none is good save one, even God. Thou knowest the commandments, Do not commit adultery, Do not kill, Do not steal, Do not bear false witness, Do not defraud, Honour thy father and mother. And he answered and saith unto him, Master, all these things have I observed from my youth. And Jesus looking upon him loved him, and said unto him, One thing thou lackest: go, sell whatsoever thou hast, and give to the poor, and thou shalt have treasure in heaven: and come, take up the cross and follow me. But his countenance fell at the saying, and he went away sorrowful: for he was one that had great possessions.* (Mark 10.17-22)

*And a certain ruler asked him, saying, Good Master, what shall I do to inherit eternal life? And Jesus said unto him, Why callest thou me good? none is good save one, even God. Thou knowest the commandments, Do not commit adultery, Do not kill, Do not steal, Do not bear false witness, Honour thy father and thy mother. And he said, All these things have I observed from my youth up. And when Jesus heard it, he said unto him, One thing thou lackest yet: sell all that thou hast, and distribute unto the poor, and thou shalt have treasure in heaven: and come, follow me. But when he heard these things, he became exceeding sorrowful; for he was very rich.* (Luke 18.18-23)

Matt. 19.16. *And behold, one came.* Luke says he was a ruler, that is, a man in the front rank of authority, not just one of the people. Although riches alone may win a man honour, yet this man seems also to have been regarded as sensible and good. And having weighed all the circumstances, I do not doubt that, although he was called 'young', yet he was the sort of man who cultivated an old-fashioned integrity in frugality and chastity. He does not come out of guile, like

253

the scribes, but with a desire to learn. And so both his words and his kneeling down bear witness that he revered Christ as a faithful teacher. But a blind confidence in his own works prevents him from learning from Christ, although in other respects he wanted to show himself teachable. Thus today we see some who are not ill-affected, yet, because they are taken up with I know not what shadowy holiness, they barely taste the teaching of the Gospel. But to judge the significance of the reply better, the form of the question must be noted. He does not ask simply how and by what road he can attain to life, but what good thing he must do in order to acquire it. He therefore dreams of merits as a payment for which he can be owed eternal life. Hence Christ directs him to the keeping of the Law which is certainly the way of life, as I shall soon explain more fully.

Matt. 19.17. *Why callest thou me good?* I do not take this correction in the subtle sense that many interpreters do, as if Christ were hinting at His deity. They think the words equivalent to saying, 'If you recognize in me nothing higher than human nature, you are in error to transfer to me the title of "good", which belongs to God alone.' I agree, of course, that properly speaking men are not worthy of this honourable title, nor for that matter, are the angels, for they have no drop of goodness of their own but hold it as a loan from God. And moreover, goodness has only begun in them, it is not perfected. But Christ's only aim was to assert the authority of His teaching, as if He should say, 'You are in error to call me a good Master unless you acknowledge that I have come from God.' He is therefore not affirming the essence of His deity, but leading the young man to trust the authority of His teaching. He was indeed already imbued with a certain attitude of obedience, but Christ wanted him to rise higher and hear God speaking. It is a habit in men to make angels out of devils and so to call quite indiscriminately good teachers men in whom they are aware of nothing divine; and this is a profanation of God's gifts. It is not surprising therefore if Christ, to establish the authority of His teaching, calls the young man back to God.

*Keep the commandments.* Some of the fathers interpreted this verse badly, and the Papists have followed them. They make Christ teach that the keeping of the Law can merit us eternal life. But Christ is not concerned with men's capabilities. He is replying to the question put to Him: 'What is the righteousness of works?' namely, what the Law lays down. And certainly we must hold that in His Law God embraced the way of holy and righteous living, in which righteousness is contained. For Moses' saying was no empty form of words: 'If a man does these things, he shall live in them' (Lev. 18.5). And again, 'I call heaven and earth to witness that today I show you life' (Deut.

254

30.19). Therefore we must not deny that the keeping of the Law is righteousness, by which the perfect observer of the Law would gain life for himself. But because we all lack the glory of God, there is found in the Law only a curse. Nothing remains for us but to flee to the free gift of righteousness. And so Paul lays down a twofold righteousness, of the Law and of faith. The former he places in works, the second in the sheer grace of Christ. From this we gather that Christ's reply was 'legal', in that it was first necessary to teach this young man who was enquiring about the righteousness of works that none can be accepted as righteous before God save he who satisfies the Law (a thing impossible), so that he might be convicted of his own weakness and make use of the help of faith. I therefore agree that, because God promises the reward of eternal life to those who keep His Law, this would be the right way were it not for the weakness of our flesh. But Scripture teaches that because of our sin we do not receive it as a merit, but it is necessary that it be given to us. If anyone objects that righteousness is in vain set before us in the Law since no one can ever possess it like this, I reply that as the elementary means by which we are led to pray for righteousness (*ad precariam iustitiam*) it is not superfluous. When therefore Paul says that the doers of the Law shall be justified, he is excluding all from the righteousness of the Law. This passage also destroys all the figments which the Papists fabricate for acquiring righteousness. For they are not only deceived in wanting God to be under an obligation to good works and pay salvation back as a debt. But when it comes to doing good works, they forget the teaching of the Law and are particularly concerned with the inventions they call devotions. Not that they openly repudiate God's Law, but they far prefer human traditions. But what does Christ say? That the only service which God approves is what He Himself commands; that obedience is better than all sacrifices. Therefore whoever intends to frame his life to obedience to Christ, must give his whole study to keeping the commandments of the Law, whereas the Papists busy themselves with their foolish traditions.

Matt. 19.18. *Thou shalt not kill.* It is surprising that, since Christ wished us to be devoted to the whole Law, He referred only to the second table; but He did this because the state of the mind is seen better from the duties of love. Duty towards God comes first; but because hypocrites often seem to be keeping the first table, the second table proves better for making examination. Let us know, therefore, that Christ chose out the commandments which contain a testimony of true righteousness; but by synecdoche He indicates the whole under a part. There is no significance in His placing the commandment about honouring parents last, for He was not precise about the order. Yet it is worth noting that He assigned it to the second table; so we should not be deceived by Josephus' error of thinking that it belonged to the first table. His final words 'thou shalt love thy neighbour' contain nothing different from the earlier commandments but are a general explanation of them.

Matt. 19.20. *The young man saith unto him.* The Law must have been a dead letter to him that he should dream that he was so righteous. For unless he had been self-satisfied by his hypocrisy, the best admonition to teach him humility would have been to see his stains and impurities in the mirror of the Law. But he soberly and securely boasts his false confidence that he had done his duty well from childhood. Paul confesses that the same thing happened to him. He was convinced he was alive so long as the power of the Law was hidden from him. But after he had felt what power the Law had, a deadly wound was inflicted on him. Hence Christ's response was directed to the man's character. Yet Christ was not demanding of him something beyond the commands of the Law, but because he was unmoved by the simple assertion, He used other words to uncover the hidden disease of avarice.

I acknowledge that the Law never commands us to sell all we have; but since the purpose of the Law is to lead men to deny themselves, and since also it expressly condemns covetousness, we see that Christ's only purpose was to correct the young man's wrong attitude. For if he had really had any self-knowledge, he would, at the mention of the Law, have confessed that he was subject to God's judgment. Now, because the bare words of the Law are insufficient to convict him of his guilt, the inward meaning is expressed in different words. For if Christ were now requiring something beyond the commands of the Law, He would be inconsistent. He had just said that perfect righteousness was contained in the commandments of the Law. How then will it be consistent to accuse the Law of lacking something? Moreover, Moses' testimony which I quoted earlier would be false. Therefore Christ means that the young man lacked something, not apart from the observance of the Law, but within the observance of the Law. For although the Law nowhere compels us to sell everything, yet because it annihilates all our vicious covetousness, because it trains us to bear the cross, because it intends us to be prepared for hunger and poverty, the young man is very far from keeping it fully so long as he is devoted to his wealth and burns with covetousness.

And He says *one thing thou lackest* because there was no need to preach to him about adultery and murder; but He points out his own particular disease, as if He were touching an ulcer with His finger. But we must note that He tells him not only to sell but also to give to the poor. For to renounce riches is not in itself virtuous, but rather an empty ambition. Crates the Theban is praised by secular historians for casting his money and anything precious he had into the sea, since he did not think he would be safe unless he lost all his riches. As if it would not have been better to give to others what he thought he did not need! Love is the bond of perfection; and those who defraud others along with themselves of the use of money deserve no praise. And so Christ is commanding him not simply to sell but to be liberal in helping the poor.

By saying 'Follow me' Christ presses more strongly the mortification of the flesh. For He not only commanded him to give, but to submit his shoulder to carrying his cross, as Mark expressly says. And he had to be pricked by this goad, for at home he was used to living quietly and comfortably and he never conceived the slightest idea of what it was to crucify the old man and to tame his fleshly desires. But the monks are too ridiculous in claiming a state of perfection for themselves on the basis of this verse. First, it is easy to grasp that not all are indiscriminately commanded to sell everything. A farmer who has to live by his labour and support his children would be wrong in selling his farm, except under force of circumstances. Therefore to hold what God places in our hand is a greater virtue than to waste everything, so long as we care for ourselves and our family thriftily and moderately and give some part to the poor. But what is that wonderful selling that the monks boast of? A lot of them have plunged into monasteries as if they were pig-sties, because they did not find enough swill at home. They are all taking good care to batten idly on the bread that others provide. A very honourable exchange! They are commanded to give to the poor what they rightly possess; but they prefer to snatch what belongs to others!

Mark 10.21. *And Jesus looking upon him loved him.* It is too childish altogether that the Papists deduce from this that morally good works (which do not come from the moving of the Spirit but precede regeneration) merit *de congruo*. For if merit is inferred from the love of God, then frogs and fleas must be said to merit, since God loves all His creatures without exception. It is therefore important to distinguish degrees of love. So far as relates to the present place, it is enough to hold in sum that God embraces in His fatherly love only His children, whom He regenerates by the Spirit of adoption, and that, because of this love, they are accepted at His judgment seat. According to this sense, to be loved by God and to be justified before Him are synonymous. But sometimes God is said to love those whom He neither approves nor justifies. The preservation of the human race is dear to Him (the preservation which consists in righteousness, justice, modera-

257

tion, prudence, loyalty, temperance), and therefore He is said to love the social virtues; not that they merit salvation or grace, but because they aim at something which He approves. In this sense, according to different relations, He both loved and hated Aristides and Fabricius. For inasmuch as He had ennobled them with outward righteousness, and that to the common good, He loved His work in them. Yet because their hearts were unclean, their outward appearance of righteousness did nothing to obtain righteousness for them. For we know that hearts are cleansed by faith alone and the Holy Spirit of uprightness is given only to Christ's members. Thus the question which might be put is answered, that Christ loves the proud and hypocritical man, although there is nothing more hateful to God than these two vices. For there is no absurdity in God loving the good seed which He has sown in some natures, while rejecting the persons and their works on account of their corruption.

Matt. 19.22. *He went away sorrowful.* His going away shows how far the young man was from the perfection to which Christ called him. Why was it that he left Christ's school, but because it was hard for him to give up his riches? But unless we are ready to bear poverty, it is plain that covetousness is still reigning in us. And this is what I said at first. That Christ bids him sell everything is not an addition to the Law, but a testing of his latent vice; so when it is reproved he is dragged out into the light of day. And this example teaches us that if we are to keep on steadily in Christ's school we must renounce the flesh. This young man left Christ, even though he had come modestly and with a desire to learn, because it was too hard for him to bid farewell to his dear fault. The same thing will happen to us unless the sweetness of Christ's grace makes all fleshly delights tasteless to us. Whether this temptation was only temporary and the young man later repented, we do not know. Yet the probable conjecture is that his avarice pulled him back and kept him back.

*And Jesus said unto his disciples, Verily I say unto you, It is hard for a rich man to enter the kingdom of heaven. And again, I say unto you, It is easier for a camel to go through a needle's eye than for a rich man to enter into the kingdom of God. And when the disciples heard it, they were astonished exceedingly, saying, Who then can be saved? And Jesus looking upon them said to them, With men this is impossible; but with God all things are possible.* (Matt. 19.23-26)

*And Jesus looked round about, and saith unto his disciples, How hardly shall they that have riches enter into the kingdom of God! And the disciples were amazed at his words. But Jesus answered again, and saith unto them, Children, how hard is it for them that trust in riches to enter into the kingdom of God! It is easier for a camel to go through a needle's eye, than for a rich man to enter into the kingdom of God. And they were astonished exceedingly, saying unto him, Then who can be saved? Jesus looking upon them saith, With men it is impossible, but not with God: for all things are possible with God. (Mark 10.23-27)*

*And when Jesus saw that he was very sorrowful, he said, How hardly shall they that have riches enter into the kingdom of God! for it is easier for a camel to go through a needle's eye, than for a rich man to enter into the kingdom of God. And they that heard it said, Then who can be saved? But he said, The things which are impossible with men are possible with God. (Luke 18.24-27)*

Matt. 19.23. *It is hard for a rich man.* Christ is warning them, not only how serious and deadly a plague is avarice, but also what a hindrance riches are. Mark softens the harshness of His saying by restricting it to those who put their trust in riches. But I consider that by these words the first statement is confirmed rather than corrected, as if He said that it should not seem surprising to them that He made entry into the Kingdom of heaven so difficult for the rich, since it is an ill common to nearly all to trust in their wealth. This teaching is very useful for everyone: for the rich, that they are warned to beware of their danger; for the poor, that they may be content with their lot and not greedily seek what would do them more harm than good. It is, of course, true that by their nature riches do not prevent us following God. But (and this is the depravity of the human spirit) it must almost certainly happen that those who are well supplied will drown themselves in their riches. So Satan holds the very affluent bound as in chains, lest they should aspire after heaven. Nay, they bury and constrict themselves and enslave themselves completely to this world. The simile of the camel which is then added, emphasizes the difficulty; for He means that the rich are too swollen with pride and confidence to let themselves be reduced to the narrow straits in which God contains them. I judge that the word 'camel' means rather a ship's rope than the animal.

Matt. 19.25. *And when the disciples heard it.* The disciples were amazed, for it should make us not a little anxious that the one way into the Kingdom of God is blocked for the rich. For wherever we turn our eyes, a thousand obstacles stand in our path. But we may notice that although they were struck with astonishment, they did not run away from Christ's teaching. The man we were talking of just now was quite different. The austerity of the commandment so de-

259

terred him that he separated himself from Christ. But these men although they are afraid and wanting to know who can be saved, do not swerve from Him but desire to conquer their despair. When God threatens and proclaims something sad and fearful it is good for us to tremble, so long as we are not discouraged but rather aroused. Matt. 19.26. *With men this is impossible.* Christ completely frees their minds from all anxiety. It is useful for them to know how hard is the ascent to heaven; first, so that they may bend all their energies to this effort, and then that they may distrust themselves and pray for strength from heaven. We see how lazy and secure we are. What would happen if believers thought they could walk sweetly and happily along a smooth and pleasing plain? This, then, is the reason why, although He sees the disciples are frightened, Christ does not pretend the danger is less but rather emphasizes it. At first He had said it was only difficult; now He declares it is impossible. This shows how perverse those teachers are who are so afraid to speak harshly that they gratify the laziness of the flesh. We ought rather to follow Christ's rule. He so tempered His Word that He taught men who were humbled in themselves to rest on God's grace alone, and at the same time stirred them up to pray. Thus He helped men's weakness wisely, not attributing anything to them, but rousing their minds to the hope of God's grace. Christ's reply also refutes the common axiom, which the Papists took from Jerome: 'Whoever shall say that it is impossible to keep the Law, let him be anathema.' For Christ clearly proclaims that it is not possible for men to keep to the way of salvation save in so far as God's grace succours them.

*Then answered Peter and said unto him, Lo, we have left all, and followed thee; what then shall we have? And Jesus said unto them, Verily, I say unto you, that ye which have followed me in the regeneration, when the Son of man shall sit on the throne of his majesty, ye also shall sit upon twelve thrones, judging the twelve tribes of Israel. And everyone that hath left houses, or brethren, or sisters, or father, or mother, or wife, or children, or lands, for my name's sake, shall receive a hundredfold, and shall inherit eternal life. But many shall be last that are first; and first that are last. (Matt. 19.27-30)*

*Peter began to say unto him, Lo, we have left all, and have followed thee. Jesus answered and said, Verily I say unto you, There is no man that hath left house, or brethren, or sisters, or father, or mother, or wife, or children, or lands, for my sake and the gospel's, but he shall receive a hundredfold now in this time, houses, and brethren, and sisters, and mothers, and children, and lands, with persecutions; and in the world to come eternal life. But many that are first shall be last; and the last first.* (Mark 10.28-31)

*And Peter said, Lo, we have left all, and followed thee. And he said unto them, Verily, I say unto you, There is no man that hath left house, or parents, or brethren, or wife, or children, for the kingdom of God's sake, who shall not receive manifold more in this time, and in the world to come eternal life.*

*But ye are they which have continued with me in my temptations; and I appoint unto you a kingdom, even as my Father appointed unto me, that ye may eat and drink at my table in my kingdom; and ye shall sit on thrones judging the twelve tribes of Israel.* (Luke 18.28-30; 22.28-30)

Peter tacitly compares himself and the other disciples to the rich man whom the world had separated from Christ. And because they were leading a poor and unsettled life, with some disgrace and troubles, and there seemed no hope of things improving, he rightly asks whether they have given up everything and given themselves to Christ in vain. For it was all wrong that they should be despoiled by the Lord and not better recompensed. But what were the 'all things'? They were unimportant and poor men, and they hardly had even homes to leave. The boast could therefore seem ridiculous. And certainly experience shows how highly men usually price their duty towards God. Today those in the Papacy who can hardly be called beggars arrogantly grumble that they have suffered great loss for the cause of the Gospel. Yet the disciples can be excused, for, although they may not have had splendid fortunes, yet they were just as happy at home doing their manual work as the richest man alive. And we know that simple men, used to a quiet and modest life, take it harder to be separated from wife and children than do those who are ruled by ambition or whom the breeze of prosperity blows hither and thither. Certainly, unless some reward had been set aside for the disciples they would have been foolish to change their way of life. Nevertheless, although they are excusable in this respect, yet they sin in demanding to see the victory before the battle is over. If we are overtaken by such weariness at the delay and are tempted to be impatient, let us learn first to reckon up the comforts with which the Lord softens the harshness of the cross in this world and bestir ourselves to hope for the heavenly life. For Christ's reply is contained in these two parts.

Matt. 19.28. *Verily I say unto you.* Lest the disciples should think they have laboured in vain and be sorry that they have started on this course, Christ tells them that the glory of His Kingdom, hitherto hidden, was going to be revealed. It is as if He said, 'There is no reason why your low fortunes should dismay you. I, who am humbled almost beneath the lowest, shall at last ascend the throne of majesty. Hold out for a little while until the time of the revelation of my glory shall come.' What is He promising them? That they shall share in the same glory. For by ascribing thrones to them, on which they shall judge the twelve tribes of Israel, He compares them to ambassadors, or to high judges and presidents, who occupy the foremost seats in the regal court. We know the twelve apostles were chosen to testify that God wished to gather together at Christ's coming the dispersed remnants of His people. This was the highest dignity, but it was yet hidden. Therefore Christ keeps their hopes in suspense until the final revelation of His Kingdom, so that they may then perceive the fruit of their calling. And although Christ's Kingdom is partially manifested in the preaching of the Gospel, there is no doubt that Christ was here speaking of the last day.

*In the regeneration.* Some connect this phrase with what follows and make regeneration simply the newness which follows our restoration, when what is mortal is swallowed up by life, and our vile body is transfigured into the heavenly glory of Christ. But I would rather relate 'regeneration' to Christ's first coming, for it was then that the world began to be renewed and the Church emerged from death's darkness into the light of life. And this way of speaking comes everywhere in the prophets and fits the details of this passage very well. For the oft promised renovation of the Church gave hope of a wonderful happiness when the Messiah should appear. To control that mistake Christ therefore distinguished between the beginning and the completion of His Kingdom.

Luke 22.28. *But ye are they which have continued.* Although Luke seems to refer to a different discourse of Christ, spoken at a different time, I do not doubt that it belongs to the same occasion. He is narrating not a single sermon of Christ's but unconnected sayings, without regard to the order of time, as we have to say again soon. But he uses more words than Matthew. Christ pronounces that, because the disciples had been His companions in temptations and had stood firm, they would share in His glory.

It may be asked what He means when He calls them *His* temptations. I consider that He is referring to the struggles in which God exercised Him and the disciples in common. And 'temptations' is used quite rightly, because according to the understanding of human nature His faith and patience were tested.

Luke 22.29. *And I appoint unto you a kingdom.* He here makes them, not only leaders (*praesides*), but kings, for He communicates to them the Kingdom He has received from the Father. And the word 'appoint' is emphatic. In their enthusiasm they must not be in too great a hurry to occupy the Kingdom, for He alone is the rightful Arbiter in appointing it, and by His example He exhorts them to be patient. For although the Father had determined Him as King, He was not yet raised to His glory, nay, He emptied Himself and it was through the disgrace of the cross that He obtained His regal honour.

'To eat and to drink at his table' is a metaphor meaning that they would be His companions sharing in His glory.

Matt. 19.29. *And everyone that hath left.* After He has raised their minds to the hope of the future life, He sustains them with present consolations and strengthens them to bear the cross. For although God allows His people to be sorely afflicted, yet He never deserts them, but counterbalances their distresses with His helps. Here He is not addressing the apostles only but is using it as an occasion to speak to all believers. The sum of it is: He who voluntarily loses all this for Christ's sake will have greater joys in this life than if he had kept them, and above all a reward is laid up for him in heaven. Yet His promise of a hundredfold recompense does not seem to square with experience. For usually those who for the testimony of Christ are deprived of parents or children and other relatives, or of their marriage partners, or have lost all their money, do not recover but struggle out their life in lonely and deserted exile and in poverty. I reply that if anyone rightly assesses God's present grace by which He alleviates the miseries of His children he will confess that it is to be preferred to all the riches of the world. Unbelievers may flourish, but because they do not know what the morrow may bring they cannot help being worried and fearful, and they can only enjoy their good fortune by, so to say, stupefying themselves. Yet God gladdens His people, so that the bit of good which they enjoy is far more to them, far sweeter, than if apart from Christ they possessed immense riches. I interpret that this is the sense in which Mark adds the words 'with persecutions', as if Christ were saying: 'Although there will always be persecutions for the godly in this world, and the cross will as it were stick to their backs, yet so sweet is the flavouring of the grace of God which gladdens them that their state is more desirable than the delights of kings.'

Matt. 19.30. *But many shall be last.* This sentence was added to take away the laziness of the flesh. Although they had hardly started the race, the apostles were already clamouring for the prize. And we are nearly all like this at heart. Within a month of enlisting we are roughly demanding a gratuity, as if we had come to the end of our service. But Christ is exhorting those who have begun well to keep going energetically. At the same time He tells them, that to have

263

begun the race fast will do no good if they break down in the middle. So also Paul says that not all who run receive the prize (I Cor. 9.24). And elsewhere he exhorts believers by his own example to forget what lies behind and to press on to the remaining part of the race (Phil. 3.13). Therefore, so often as we think of the heavenly crown, it should prick us with ever new incitements so that we should be less slack in future.

*For the kingdom of heaven is like unto a man that is an householder, which went out early in the morning to hire labourers into his vineyard. And when he had agreed with the labourers for a denarius a day, he sent them into his vineyard. And he went out about the third hour, and saw others standing in the marketplace idle; and to them he said, Go ye also into the vineyard, and whatever is right I will give you. And they went their way. Again he went out about the sixth and ninth hour, and did likewise. And about the eleventh hour he went out, and found others standing idle; and he saith unto them, Why stand ye here all the day idle? They say unto him, Because no man hath hired us. He saith unto them, Go ye also into the vineyard and whatever is right you will receive. And when even was come, the lord of the vineyard saith unto his steward, Call the labourers, and pay them their hire, beginning from the last unto the first. And when they came that were hired about the eleventh hour, they received every man a denarius. And when the first came, they supposed that they would receive more; and they likewise received every man a denarius. And when they received it, they murmured against the householder, saying, These last have spent but one hour in work, and thou hast made them equal to us, which have borne the burden of the day and the scorching heat. But he answered and said, to one of them, Friend, I do thee no wrong: didst not thou agree with me for a denarius? Take that which is thine, and go thy way; it is my will to give unto this last, even as unto thee. Is it not lawful for me to do what I will with mine own? or is thine eye evil, because I am good? So the last shall be first, and the first last; for many are called, but few chosen.* (Matt 20.1-16)

Since this parable is just the confirmation of the last sentence, 'The first shall be last' (Matt. 19.30), we must now see how it is to be applied. Some interpreters say that the point of it is that because the inheritance of heaven is not obtained by the merits of works, but is given freely, the glory of all will be equal. But Christ is not arguing either on the equality of the heavenly glory or on the future state of the godly, but is only declaring that those who come first in time have no cause for boasting or crowing over others, because the Lord can, whenever He wishes, call those whom He seemed at the time to overlook, and to make them equal with the first or even put them before them. To want to examine the details of this parable precisely would be empty curiosity. We should look for nothing more than Christ intended to tell us. But we have already said that His one aim was continually to incite His people to keep going. We know that slackness is nearly always the fruit of over-confidence. And this is why many sit down in the middle of the race as if they had got to the end. Paul bids us forget what lies behind us and think of what still remains so that we may spur ourselves on to running energetically. But it will do no harm to glance through the words so as to throw light on the teaching.

Matt. 20.1. *For the kingdom of heaven.* The meaning is that the divine calling follows the same method as a man hiring labourers in the morning at a certain price to cultivate his vineyard and then later bringing in others without an agreement but giving them the same wage. He speaks of the Kingdom of heaven to compare the spiritual life with the earthly, the reward of eternal life with the wages men earn by their labours. Some understand this passage subtly, as if Christ were distinguishing Jews from Gentiles. They say that at the first hour the Jews were called for an agreed wage, in that the Lord promised them eternal life on condition that they fulfilled the Law, whereas in the calling of the Gentiles there was no agreement, at any rate of works, but salvation was offered to them freely in Christ. But cleverness like this is out of place. The only distinction the Lord made was in time, in that those who went last to the vineyard, in the evening, received the same reward as the first. For although God of old promised to the Jews a reward for keeping the Law, yet we know that this failed in effect, in that no-one ever received salvation by his merits. Why then (say some) did Christ expressly mention an agreement when He spoke of the first but was silent in regard to the others? Simply to teach that, without injury to any, the last were given as much honour as if they had been called at the beginning. For properly speaking, He owes nothing to anyone and has a perfect right to demand from us whom He holds as His own, whatever duties lie in us. But because He freely offers us a reward, He is said to hire our work, which in fact we owe Him. This is why He honours with the name of reward the crown which He freely gives us. Moreover, to show that we have no cause to remonstrate with God if He makes those our comrades who followed after us after a long time, He made the parable different from the usual custom of men, who agree on a wage before they send the labourers to their work. But if anyone infers from this that men were created for activity and that each has his divinely appointed station, so that he shall not sink into laziness, he will not be twisting Christ's words. We may also gather that our whole life is useless and we are justly condemned of laziness until we frame oui life to the command and calling of God. From this it follows that they labour in vain who thoughtlessly take up this or that kind of life and do not wait for God's calling. Finally we may also infer from Christ's words that only they are pleasing to God who work for the advantage of their brethren.

A *denarius* (which was worth a little more than four French *caroli*) was probably the ordinary wage for a day's work. The third, sixth and ninth hours are singled out because the ancients divided the day into twelve hours, from sun-rise to sun-set, with three-hourly subdivisions; just as the night was divided into four watches. Hence the eleventh hour means the end of the day.

Matt. 20.8. *And when even was come.* There is nothing mysterious in the householder telling his steward to start at the last, as if God will first crown those who come last in time. For this invention certainly does not agree with Paul's teaching. He says that those who are left at Christ's coming will not go before those who at first fell asleep in Christ but will follow them. But Christ uses a different order in this passage, because only so could He express, as He adds at the end, that the first-comers grumbled because they were given no more. Moreover, He did not wish to say that this grumbling would occur at the last day, but only to deny that they had any cause for grumbling. The *prosopopeia* (personification) which He employs sheds no little light on this teaching, that God's liberality in honouring the unworthy with rewards beyond their deserts does not expose Him to any human complaints. Therefore some have quite missed the point when they have imagined that the Jews were being rebuked by these words for harbouring malice and hatred against the Gentiles. For it would be absurd to make them receive an equal reward with the childen of God. But this malice of arguing with God does not belong to believers. The simple sense of it is that God is free to give a reward He does not owe to those whom He calls at a late hour, for He is defrauding no-one of their just reward.

Matt. 20.16. *So the last shall be first.* He is not comparing the Jews with the Gentiles, as elsewhere, nor the reprobate who fall away from faith with the elect who persevere. And so the sentence which many insert, 'many be called, but few chosen', is quite out of place. Christ's meaning simply was that anyone who is called before others should run the more swiftly. He is also exhorting everyone to be modest and not put themselves before others but willingly let them share the common prize. It would have seemed that the apostles, as the firstfruits of the whole Church, might claim a certain supremacy; and Christ does not deny that they will sit as judges to rule the twelve tribes of Israel. But lest they should be seized by ambition or any vain confidence, they are at once warned that others who would be called long after them would be their companions in the same glory; for God is obliged to nobody, but whomsoever He will He freely calls, and He pays those whom He has called the reward which seems good to Him.

*And as Jesus was going up to Jerusalem, he took the twelve disciples apart on the way, and said unto them, Behold, we go up to Jerusalem; and the Son of man shall be delivered unto the chief priests and scribes; and they shall condemn him to death, and shall deliver him unto the Gentiles to mock, and to scourge, and to crucify: and the third day he shall be raised up.* (Matt. 20.17-19)

*And they were in the way, going up to Jerusalem; and Jesus was going before them: and they were amazed; and they that followed were afraid. And he took again the twelve, and began to tell them the things that were to happen unto him, saying, Behold, we go up to Jerusalem; and the Son of man shall be delivered unto the chief priests and scribes; and they shall condemn him to death, and shall deliver him unto the Gentiles; and they shall mock him, and shall scourge him, and shall spit upon him, and shall kill him; and on the third day he shall rise again.* (Mark 10.32-34)

*And Jesus took unto him the twelve, and said unto them, Behold, we go up to Jerusalem, and all the things that are written by the prophets concerning the Son of man shall be accomplished. For he shall be delivered up unto the Gentiles, and shall be mocked, and shamefully entreated, and spit upon: and they shall scourge and kill him: and the third day he shall rise again. And they understood none of these things; and this saying was hid from them, and they perceived not the things that were said.* (Luke 18.31-34)

Although the apostles had been already warned what death awaited the Lord, yet they had not taken in sufficiently what He had said so often; and now He repeats it all afresh. He sees the day of His death approaching; He is ready for action, to offer Himself as a sacrifice. But He also sees that the disciples are not only timid but stricken with blind fear. He exhorts them to stand fast, lest they should sink under the temptation. And He encourages them in two ways. By telling them in advance what was going to happen, He not only arms them so that they shall not give way when they are overtaken suddenly by an unexpected evil, but He also sets over against His cross the proof of His deity so that they may not be broken-hearted at His brief humiliation but be convinced that He is the Son of God and therefore victor over death. The second way in which He strengthens them is from the nearness of His resurrection.

But we must look at the words more closely. Mark says something about which the other two are silent: that before the Lord privately told the disciples that He was going straight into the sacrifice of death, both they and His other followers had been sad and frightened. But it is not plain why they had been overtaken by this fear, unless they had already learnt that they had determined enemies in Jerusalem. They would therefore have preferred Christ to wait quietly in retirement and out of range rather than deliberately to encounter such dangerous enemies. Now, although this fear was wrong in many respects, yet their following of Christ was a sign of no common allegiance and piety. It would, of course, have been far better if they had hurried swiftly and without regrets to wherever the Son of God wanted to lead them; but their reverence deserves praise, for they would rather do violence to themselves than desert Him.

Matt. 20.17. *He took the twelve.* It might seem strange that, when all alike need comforting (for fear had stolen upon all), He tells the secret only to the twelve. But I consider that He did not publish His death lest the rumour of it should spread abroad before the time. Moreover, He was not looking for any present fruit from His warning, and so held it sufficient to deposit it with the few who should afterwards be witnesses to it. For just as seed sown on the ground does not at once germinate, so we know that Christ said many things to His disciples which did not bear fruit immediately. If all indiscriminately had been admitted to this declaration, they might have been overcome with fear and run away and spread the rumour everywhere. And so Christ's death would have been brought into disrepute from His seeming to encounter it recklessly. Thus He speaks secretly to the apostles, and does not choose them because they are fit to profit from His words, but (as I have just said) so that they might be witnesses in the future. In this respect Luke speaks more fully, for he relates, not only that Christ foretold what was imminent, but at the same time that He adds the teaching that what was written through the prophets would be fulfilled in the Son of man. For the best way to overcome the temptation was to recognize in the very disgrace of the cross the marks by which the prophets pointed to the promised author of salvation. Now there is no doubt that the Lord is also showing from the prophets what fruit should be looked for from His death. For the prophets teach not only that Christ suffered, but also add the cause, to reconcile the world to God.

Matt. 20.18. *Behold, we go up to Jerusalem.* From this we perceive that Christ was trained by a divine courage to conquer the terrors of death, for wittingly and willingly He hastens to submit to it. For why, without coercion, does He take the path to a horrible slaughter save because the unconquerable power of the Spirit subdued His fear and raised Him above all human feelings? By describing the circumstances more closely He shows the more shining evidence of His deity. For in His humanity He could not guess that after He had been condemned by the scribes and priests He would be delivered to the Gentiles, that He would be spat upon and insulted, flogged, and at last taken away to execution on the cross. And we must note that although the weakness of His disciples was certainly not hidden from the Lord, He did not conceal from them the very worst of the scandal. For, as we have said elsewhere, at that time nothing could shock the believers so seriously as to see the whole sacred order of the Church against Christ. Yet He does not spare their weakness by deceiving them, but openly declares the truth and so shows how the temptation is to be overcome —by looking firmly to the resurrection. But because it was necessary that His death should come first, He places their triumph in hope.

Luke 18.34. *And they understood none of these things.* How dull they were not to understand what Christ said to them so clearly and intimately! It was not something sublime or recondite, and in fact they themselves had arrived at a suspicion of it. But here we must also remember what I have said elsewhere, that they were held in their gross ignorance because they imagined they were making good and successful progress and so thought it completely nonsensical that Christ should be disgracefully crucified. From this we gather how a deceiving imagination makes men insane. And therefore we must the more beware lest we get wound up in these inventions and become blind in day-light.

*Then came to him the mother of the sons of Zebedee with her sons, worshipping him, and asking a certain thing of him. And he said unto her What wouldst thou? She saith unto him, Command that these my two sons may sit, one on thy right hand, and one on thy left hand, in thy kingdom. But Jesus answered and said, Ye know not what ye ask. Are ye able to drink the cup that I am about to drink? and to be baptized with the baptism that I am baptized with? They say unto him, We are able. He saith unto them, My cup indeed ye shall drink and be baptized with the baptism that I am baptized with: but to sit on my right hand, and on my left hand, is not mine to give, but it is for them for whom it hath been prepared by my Father.* (Matt. 20.20-23)

*And there came near unto him James and John, the sons of Zebedee, saying unto him, Master, we would that thou shouldest do for us whatsoever we shall ask of thee. And he said unto them, What would ye that I should do for you? And they said unto him, Grant unto us that we may sit, one on thy right hand, and one on thy left hand, in thy glory. But Jesus said unto them, Ye know not what ye ask. Are ye able to drink the cup that I drink? or to be baptized with the baptism that I am baptized with? And they said unto him, We are able. And Jesus said unto them, The cup that I drink ye shall drink; and with the baptism that I am baptized withal shall ye be baptized: but to sit on my right hand or on my left hand is not mine to give: but it is for them for whom it hath been prepared.* (Mark 10.35-40)

This story is a clear mirror of human vanity. It teaches that ambition or some other fault of the flesh is often entwined in a right and godly zeal, so that Christ's followers have a different aim from what they should. And they are wandering from their goal who are not content with Him alone but seek this or that outside Him and His promises. It is not enough for a mind to be sincerely directed to Christ in the beginning, but it must keep on always in the same path of purity; for often depraved thoughts and feelings come over us in the middle of our race and turn us off course. Thus it is probable that the two sons of Zebedee had at the outset dedicated themselves to Christ, but when they see that He is exceptionally friendly with them and hear Him say that the Kingdom is at hand, at once their minds are carried away with a wicked greed and they are irked at the thought of remaining in their submission. If this happens to two of the foremost disciples, how carefully we ought to walk if we do not want to swerve from the straight line! And especially when some plausible occasion offers, we must beware lest a greed for honours infect our attitude of godliness.

There is some verbal discrepancy between Matthew and Mark, but in the heart of the matter they are in agreement. Matthew says that Zebedee's wife came and asked for her sons that they might have the highest seats in Christ's Kingdom. Mark represents them as asking for themselves. But it is probable that when their shame prevented them from asking, they cunningly brought in their mother who could ask more boldly. That the wish came from themselves may be gathered from the fact that Christ replies to them and not to their mother. Moreover, the fact that their mother kneels down and shows that she has something she wishes to ask before she brings out what she is thinking, and that they themselves in Mark stipulate that they shall get whatever they ask, all this timid hinting bears witness that they were conscious that they were doing wrong.

Matt. 20.21. *In thy kingdom.* It was praiseworthy in the sons of Zebedee that they were looking for some Kingdom of Christ when no shadow of it had yet appeared. They saw that He was lowly in the ignoble habit of a slave; they saw Him despised by the world and subjected to many reproaches. Yet they are convinced that He will soon be a magnificent king—just because He said so. This was certainly a wonderful example of faith. But we can see how easily the pure seed, as soon as it is sown in our hearts, degenerates into corruptions. For they imagined some shadowy kingdom, and soon fell into a greed for the chief places. Since therefore this perverted greed flowed from the general principle of faith, in itself certainly praiseworthy, we should ask the Lord not only to open the eyes of our mind but also to continue to direct them and keep them fixed on the right aim. We should ask Him not only to inspire us with faith, but to keep our faith pure and unadulterated.

Matt. 20.22. *Ye know not what ye ask.* Their foolishness receives a twofold condemnation. First, because in their ambition they desire more than they should; and secondly, because they conceive an aery phantasm in place of Christ's heavenly Kingdom. In regard to the first, whoever is not content with God's free adoption but desires to rise above it, wanders outside his bounds and takes on himself more than he should, and so is displeasing to God. For it is quite perverse to measure the spiritual Kingdom of Christ by our fleshly understanding. And indeed the more that a man's spirit delights in idle speculations, the more he should beware of them—just as we see that books of the sophists are stuffed full of such empty fragments.

*Are ye able to drink the cup?* To correct their ambition and recall them from their perverted desire, He sets before them the cross and all the sufferings which the children of God must undergo. It is as if He said, 'Have you got so much spare time in your present military service that you can organize already the triumphal march?' If they had been earnestly given up to the practices of their calling they would have had no room for this wicked imagination. Therefore in this sentence Christ tells those who snatch untimely at the prize that they must occupy themselves in practising the offices of godliness. And certainly ambition is best curbed by this rein, because our state is such while we are pilgrims in this world that we should rid ourselves of vain delights. A thousand perils throng us. The enemy attacks us now with various ambushes, and now with open force. Is not that man worse than a fool who among so many deaths safely amuses himself

271

by painting the triumph? The Lord does indeed tell His people to be sure of victory, and to sing the triumphal song in the midst of death, for otherwise they would not be heartened to fighting energetically. But it is one thing, in the divinely-inspired hope of reward, to prepare for the battle and to direct all our efforts keenly to this. And it is quite another to forget that a battle is raging, to avoid the enemy and set aside the dangers, and anticipate the triumph which should be waited for in its own time. Add that this unseasonable haste usually leads men away from their calling. For just as it is the laziest soldiers who are greediest for the loot, so in the Kingdom of Christ none desire the primacy more than those who avoid all the trouble and work. And so Christ justly keeps at their post those who are puffed up with vain glory. The sum of it is that there is a crown prepared for none but him who has genuinely fought; and especially that none shall share in Christ's life and kingdom save he who has first suffered and died with Him.

In the word 'baptism' there is an apt metaphor. For we know that in baptism believers are initiated into self-denial, into crucifying the old man, and into bearing the cross.

In the word 'cup' it is doubtful whether the Lord is alluding to the mystery of the Holy Supper; but because this was not yet being observed, I prefer to take it more simply for the measure of affliction that the Lord appoints for each. For because it is for Him to lay on each man his burden, according to His will (just as a householder distributes and divides portions among his dependents), so He is said to give the cup to drink. Within these words there lies no common consolation for softening the harshness of the cross, when Christ joins us in this. For what could be more desirable than to have everything in common with the Son of God? Thus it comes to pass that the things which at first seem death-dealing, yield us salvation and life. But how can he be reckoned among Christ's disciples who wants to be quite free from the cross, who refuses to undergo His baptism? For this is simply to withdraw secretly from the first lessons. Now, whenever there is mention of baptism, let us remember that we are baptized under this condition and for this end—to fix the cross to our shoulders. It is a sign of carnal confidence in John and James that they boast so firmly that they are ready to drink this cup; for when we are out of range nothing seems impossible to us. It was not long before the disgraceful event betrayed their rashness. Yet it was a good thing in them that they were ready for both outcomes, and offered themselves to bear the cross.

Matt. 20.23. *My cup indeed.* As disciples, it was necessary for them to be conformed to their Master. Christ warns them of what is going

272

to happen, so that they may compose themselves to patience—and this is addressed under the person of these two men to all His followers. For although many believers die quietly, without violence, without bloodshed, yet it is common to all (as Paul says in Rom. 8.29) to be conformed to the image of Christ. And so throughout their lives they are sheep appointed for the slaughter.

*Is not mine to give.* By this reply Christ is not belittling Himself, but only saying that the Father did not lay on Him the task of assigning a special and distinct place to each in the Kingdom of heaven. He came to collect all His people into eternal life, but it should suffice us that there awaits us the inheritance won by His blood. It is not ours to inquire in what degree some surpass others; nor does God wish Christ to reveal this to us. It is delayed until the final revelation. Now we can grasp Christ's purpose. He is not disputing here about His power, but only wishes us to consider why He was sent by the Father and what belongs to His calling. And therefore He distinguishes the office of teaching laid on Him from the secret counsel of God. This is a useful admonition, that we may learn to be soberly wise and not try to burst through into the hidden mysteries of God, and especially not to be over inquisitive in investigating the state of the future life. For it does not yet appear what we shall be, until God makes us like Himself (I John 3.2). But we should note that there is not an equality among God's children after they have been received into heavenly glory; rather to each is promised that degree of honour to which he is destined in the eternal counsel of God.

*And when the ten heard it, they were moved with indignation concerning the two brethren. But Jesus called them unto him, and said, Ye know that the rulers of the Gentiles lord it over them, and their great ones exercise authority over them. Not so shall it be among you: but whosoever would become great among you shall be your minister; and whosoever would be first among you shall be your servant: even as the Son of man came not to be ministered unto, but to minister, and to give his life a ransom for many.* (Matt. 20.24-28)

*And when the ten heard it, they began to be moved with indignation concerning James and John. And Jesus called them to him, and saith unto them, Ye know that they which are accounted to rule over the Gentiles lord it over them; and their great ones exercise authority over them. But it is not so among you: but whosoever would become great among you, shall be your minister: and whosoever would be first among you, shall be servant of all. For even the Son of man came not to be ministered unto, but to minister, and to give his life a ransom for many.* (Mark 10.41-45)

*And there arose also a contention among them, which of them is accounted to be greatest. And he said unto them, The kings of the Gentiles have lordship over them; and they that have authority over them are called Benefactors. But ye shall not be so: but he that is the greater among you, let him become as the younger; and he that is chief, as he that doth serve. For whether is greater, he that sitteth at meat, or he that serveth? is not he that sitteth at meat? but I am in the midst of you as he that serveth.* (Luke 22.24-27)

Matt. 20.24. *And when the ten heard it.* Luke seems to refer this quarrel to a different occasion. But anyone who carefully considers his chapter 22 will see clearly that he is stringing together sayings from various times without regard for their sequence. Hence the argument about who should be first, which Luke mentions, arose because the sons of Zebedee desired the foremost seats in Christ's Kingdom. And yet the indignation which moved the ten was not at all righteous. For although the foolish ambition of those two was very blameworthy so that they left Christ in shame, how did their foolish desire for what they did not receive hurt the other ten? For although they were justly jealous, they should have been reconciled by their repulse. But the Lord wanted to use this as an opportunity of uncovering the latent disease in them. For no-one will willingly give way to others; but each cherishes within himself a secret hope of being first. Thus it happens that they are jealous and quarrel, while all the time a perverse desire reigns in them all. Now if this vice was inborn in simple and obscure men and broke out at the least occasion or almost at no occasion at all, how careful we should be when there is fuel to feed the hidden fire. And so we see how ambition burns in men of great power and station, and sends out its flames far and wide unless the Spirit of modesty from heaven quenches man's inherent and natural pride.

Matt. 20.25. *Ye know, that the rulers of the Gentiles.* It is first said that Christ called them to Him to reprove them. From this we gather that when they grew ashamed of their greed, they did not grumble openly, but as it were growled and grumbled under their breath, and secretly each one put himself first. Now He does not say in general what a deadly plague ambition is, but simply warns them that it is utterly stupid to fight about nothing. For He shows that the primacy which was the cause of their quarrel is nothing in His Kingdom. They are deceived who apply this saying indiscriminately to all believers, for

274

Christ was only telling the apostles in this particular situation how ridiculous they were to dispute about degrees of power or honour in their order, because the office of teaching to which they had been appointed had nothing in common with worldly empire. I agree, of course, that this lesson applies both to private men and also to kings and magistrates; for none deserves to be reckoned among Christ's flock save him who has so advanced under the schoolmaster humility that he claims nothing for himself but submits himself to cherishing brotherly love. This is certainly true; but Christ's purpose was, as I have said, to distinguish the spiritual government of His Church from earthly empires, so that the apostles should not assume courtly graces. When a nobleman is loved by the king, he wins preferments and riches. But Christ appoints as pastors of His Church not those who lord it but those who serve. This refutes the error of the Anabaptists who will have no kings and magistrates in the Church of God, because Christ will not let His disciples be like them. But the comparison is made, not between Christians and heathen, but between offices. For it might happen that a man who is lord of a country or town is forced by urgent necessity to take up the office of teaching also. But Christ was doing no more than treating of what relates to the apostolic office and what is alien to it.

Yet it may be asked why Christ, who instituted distinct orders in the Church, here repudiates all degrees of order. For this seems to cast down, or at least level them, so that none is higher than the rest. But the order of nature teaches us something very different. And when Paul describes the government of the Church, he enumerates the various ministries in such a way as to make the dignity of the apostolate superior to the office of pastors; and he enjoins (without doubt by God's command) Timothy and Titus to be preferred in authority to others. I reply, if we carefully examine the details, even kings do not rightly and truly rule unless they serve; but the apostolic office differs from earthly principalities in that their being servants does not prevent kings and magistrates from bearing sway and indeed, rising above their subjects in magnificent splendour and pomp. Thus David, Hezekiah, and others like them, although they were voluntarily the servants of all, were yet adorned with the sceptre, the crown, the orb and the other insignia of royalty. But the government of the Church permits nothing of this sort. Christ gives to pastors nothing more than that they shall be servants and completely abstain from domination. It also must be observed that His words relate rather to the thing itself than to the attitude. Christ separates the apostles from the order of kings, not because kings are allowed to be haughty, but because the royal state differs from the apostolic office. It behoves both to be humble; but the apostles must always consider what form of ruling His Church the Lord instituted.

As for the words: where Matthew has 'their kings exercise authority over them', in Luke it runs, 'they are called Benefactors'. This means the same thing, as if He said that kings are very wealthy and possess great riches so that they can be bountiful and liberal. For although kings rejoice more in their power and prefer it to be founded rather on fear than on the agreement of the people, yet they are greedy to be praised for their bounty. And from this comes a name that they have in Hebrew. They are called נְדִיבִים because they bestow gifts; for taxes and tributes are paid to them simply so that they may have sufficient for the necessary expenses of their pomp.

Matt. 20.26. *Not so shall it be among you.* There is no doubt that Christ is reproving the foolish imagination which He sees deceiving the apostles. He says, 'You are foolishly and wickedly imagining a kingdom which I hate. If you desire to do me faithful service, you must think very differently from this: each of you must strive to serve the others.' He is speaking imprecisely when He tells him who wishes to be great to become a minister. For ambition will not suffer a man even to devote himself to his brethren, far less subject himself. I confess that those who aspire for honours servilely flatter, but nothing is further from their minds than to serve. But Christ's meaning is perfectly plain. He declares that the love for oneself which carries everyone away should be transferred to another. It is as if He said, 'Your unique greatness, excellence and dignity is to submit yourselves to your brethren. Let your primacy consist in being the servants of all'.

Matt. 20.28. *Even as the Son of man.* Christ confirms His teaching by Himself as the exemplar; He freely assumed the role of servant and emptied Himself, as also Paul teaches (Phil. 2.7). Moreover, to show more clearly how far He had descended from the height, He recalls them to His death, as if He said, 'Because I have chosen you as being next to me in honour, you are tempted by a perverse ambition to become rulers. But you should frame your life by my example, and I did not come to be arrogant or to claim some sort of kingship. Rather I have put on a mean and lowly flesh and taken on me the ignominy of the cross.' If anyone objects that Christ was exalted by the Father so that every knee should bow to Him, the solution is easy: what He is saying now refers to the time of His humiliation. This is why in Luke it is added that He lived among them as if He were a servant. Not that He was inferior to them either in appearance, or in title, or in fact (for He wished always to be acknowledged as Master and Lord). But He was a servant in that He undertook to bear their infirmities. We must also remember that this is a comparison of the

276

major and the minor, as in John 13.14: 'If I, your master and Lord, have washed your feet, much more should you prefer others before yourselves.'

*And to give his life a ransom.* As we have said, Christ spoke of His death to draw the disciples away from their perverse idea of an earthly kingdom. Yet He aptly and well expresses the power and fruit of His death when He declares that His life was the price of our redemption. From this it follows that our reconciliation with God is free, for the only price paid for it is Christ's death. And so this one word overthrows all that the Papists babble about their disgusting satisfactions. Moreover, since Christ won us as His own by His death, the submission of which He speaks is so far from derogating from His infinite glory that in fact it makes it more glorious. 'Many' is used, not for a definite number, but for a large number, in that He sets Himself over against all others. And this is its meaning also in Rom. 5.15, where Paul is not talking of a part of mankind but of the whole human race.

*And as they went out from Jericho, a great multitude followed him. And behold, two blind men sitting by the way side, when they heard that Jesus was passing by, cried out, saying, Lord, have mercy on us, thou son of David. And the multitude rebuked them, that they should hold their peace: but they cried out the more, saying, Have mercy on us, O Lord, thou son of David. And Jesus stood still, and called them, and said, What will ye that I should do unto you? They say unto him, Lord, that our eyes may be opened. And Jesus, being moved with compassion, touched their eyes: and straightway they received their sight, and followed him.* (Matt. 20.29-34)

*And they came to Jericho: and as he went out from the city of Jericho, with his disciples and a great multitude, the son of Timaeus, Bartimaeus, a blind beggar, was sitting by the wayside. And when he heard that it was Jesus of Nazareth, he began to cry out, and say, Jesus thou son of David, have mercy on me. And many rebuked him, that he should hold his peace; but he cried out the more a great deal, Thou son of David, have mercy on me. And Jesus stood still, and commanded him to be called. And they call the blind man, saying unto him, Be of good cheer: rise, he calleth thee. And he, casting away his garment, sprang up, and came to Jesus. And Jesus answered him, and said, What wilt thou that I should do unto thee? And the blind man said unto him, Rabboni, that I may receive my sight. And Jesus said unto him, Go thy way; thy faith hath made thee whole. And straightway he received his sight, and followed Jesus in the way.* (Mark 10.46-52)

*And it came to pass, as he drew nigh unto Jericho, a certain blind man sat by the way side begging: and hearing a multitude going by, he inquired what this meant. And they told him, that Jesus of Nazareth passeth by. And he cried, saying, Jesus, thou son of David, have mercy on me. And they that went before rebuked him, that he should hold his peace: but he cried out the more a great deal, Thou Son of David, have mercy on me. And Jesus stood, and commanded him to be brought to him: and when he was come near, he asked him saying, What wilt thou that I should do unto thee? And he said, Lord, that I may receive my sight. Then Jesus said unto him, Receive thy sight: thy faith hath made thee whole. And immediately he received his sight, and followed him, glorifying God: and all the people, when they saw it, gave praise unto God.* (Luke 18.35-43)

Matt. 20.29. *And as they went out.* Osiander thinks he is very clever to make one blind man into four. In fact, there is nothing sillier than his idea. Because he sees that the Evangelists disagree in a few words, he imagines that sight was restored to one blind man at the entry into the city, and then to a second, and two others were enlightened when Christ went away again. But all the details hang together so well that no sane man can believe that these are different stories. To deal with only one point. We are asked to believe that, when Christ's companions had tried to silence the first blind man and saw that beyond all his hope he was healed, they tried to do the same thing with the three others. There is no need to take up the details which show clearly that they are all narrating one and the self-same story.

But the discrepancy troubles some that Matthew and Mark say that the miracle was performed either on one blind man or on two, when Christ had already left the city; but Luke says it was done before He entered the city. And whereas Mark and Luke speak of only one, Matthew says that there were two together. But we know that it happens everywhere in the Evangelists that one of them will pass over what is said by the others, and again what is omitted by them, the one will explain more clearly. So we should not find this strange and unexpected in the present passage. I conjecture that when Christ was approaching the city, the blind man cried out; and when he could not make himself heard because of the noise, he took his seat at the road going out of the city, and it was there that he was called by Christ. And so Luke starts out from what was true but does not tell the whole story, passing over Christ's stay in the city. But the other two mention only the time about the miracle. And it is a probable conjecture that

278

as Christ wanted to prove men's faith and often put them off for a little, so He tested this blind man in the same way. The solution of the second problem is quite simple. We see elsewhere that Mark and Luke related that one demoniac was healed, while Matthew spoke of two, just as in this passage. Yet they do not disagree. The likely conjecture is that when at first one blind man implored Christ's grace, another was moved by his example and therefore on this occasion sight was restored to the two. But Mark and Luke spoke only of one, either because it was the better known or because Christ's power was shown no less remarkably in the one than in the two. Certainly Mark seems to have chosen him because he was well known, for he mentions both his name and that of his father—this could not have been from the nobility of his family or from his wealth, since he was a beggar, one of the masses. From this it would appear that, since his sad case was widely known, the miracle on his person was the more celebrated. This seems to me the reason why Mark and Luke mention him alone and are silent about the other, who was a sort of second string. But Matthew, as an eye-witness, did not want to pass over this man too, even though he was more obscure.

Matt. 20.30. *Lord, have mercy on us.* I have just said that at first only one man was calling out. But a similar need quickly drove the other to add his voice too. It was no common honour that they paid to Christ when they asked Him to help them in their misery. For they had to be convinced that the help or remedy they needed lay in His hand. But their faith is to be seen even more in the fact that they confess Him to be the Messiah—for we know that the Messiah was known by this title among the Jews. They therefore flee to Christ, not only as to some prophet or other, but as to the unique Author of salvation, promised by God. Their crying out was an indication of their vehement emotion. For when they knew that many who had no regard for Christ's honour disliked what they said, the fervour of their desire overcame their fear and made them lift up their voices boldly.

Matt. 20.31. *And the multitude rebuked them.* It is incredible that Christ's disciples, those who followed Him out of loyalty and reverence, should want to drive the unhappy away from Christ's grace and block, so far as they could, the way to His power. But it usually happens that the greater part of those who profess allegiance to Christ would rather hinder or delay our coming to Him than invite us to Him. If Satan tried to put an obstacle in the path of those two blind beggars through godly and sincere men who were drawn by a certain piety to follow Christ, how much more will he do it through hypocrites and traitors unless we take good heed? There is need of con-

279

stancy to transcend all hindrances, and the more barriers that Satan erects, the more must we be kindled to prayer, just as we see the blind men redoubling their cries.

Matt. 20.32. *What will ye that I should do?* He asks kindly and friendly what they would like, for He had decided to grant their requests. Without doubt they had prayed by the special moving of the Spirit, since, just as the Lord does not intend to save all from their physical ills, so He does not permit this merely to be asked. There is laid down for us a rule as to what, and how, and how far we ought to ask. It is wrong to swerve from this unless (as rarely happens) the Lord suggests some special request by the secret moving of His Spirit. But Christ questions them, not so much for their sakes as for the whole people. For we know that the world swallows God's benefits without thought unless it is prompted and stirred up. Christ therefore arouses the crowd by His voice to look at the miracle, as a little after by a visible sign when He opens their eyes by His touch. When Matthew says that Jesus was sorry for them, it is not the participle of the verb which He had used about the blind men.[1] They implore Christ's mercy, that He would help their misery. And now the Evangelists express, not only that Christ was moved to heal them by His free goodness, but that He sympathised with all their ill. It is a metaphor taken from the inward parts in which reside the humanity and mutual compassion which stir us to help our neighbours.

Mark 10.52. *Thy faith.* By the word 'faith' is meant not only his trust that he would recover his sight, but a deeper conviction, in that this blind man acknowledged Jesus to be the divinely promised Messiah. We must not imagine that this was some confused idea, for we have already seen that this confession was taken from the Law and the prophets. For the blind man did not thoughtlessly give Christ the name of 'the Son of David', but embraced Him as the one whom the divine oracles had taught him would come. And Christ ascribes it to faith that the blind received sight because, although God's power and grace penetrate sometimes to unbelievers as well, yet none can enjoy His blessings aright save he who receives them by faith—in fact, for unbelievers the use of God's gifts is not only not salutary but downright harmful. Therefore the salvation of which Christ speaks is not restricted to the outward healing but includes also the healing and salvation of the soul. It is as if Christ said that it was by faith that the blind man obtained God's answer to his prayer. If God gave the blind man His grace because of his faith, it follows that he was justified by faith.

[1] The blind men said: 'Ἐλέησον ἡμᾶς—Miserere nostri. Of Jesus it is said: σπλαγχνισθείς—misertus.

Matt. 20.34. *They followed him.* It was a sign of gratitude that the blind men joined the company of Christ. And although it is not clear how long they stayed with him, yet it was a mark of their gratitude that they were ready to be a spectacle of Christ's grace to many on this journey. Luke adds that the people gave glory to God, which helps to prove the certainty of the miracle.

*And he entered and was passing through Jericho. And behold, there was a man by name Zacchaeus; and he was a chief publican, and he was rich. And he sought to see Jesus who he was; and could not for the crowd, because he was little of stature. And he ran on before, and climbed up into a sycamore tree to see him: for he was to pass that way. And when he came to the place Jesus looked up, and saw him, and said unto him, Zacchaeus, make haste, and come down; for today I must abide at thy house. And he made haste, and came down, and received him joyfully. And when they saw it, they all murmured, saying, He is gone in to lodge with a man that is a sinner. And Zacchaeus stood, and said unto the Lord, Behold, Lord, the half of my goods I give to the poor; and if I have wrongfully exacted aught of any man, I restore it fourfold. And Jesus said unto him, Today is salvation come to this house, forasmuch as he also is a son of Abraham. For the Son of man came to seek and to save that which was lost.* (Luke 19.1-10)

From this it is clear that Luke was not particular in keeping to the time sequence. Having related the miracle, he now tells us what happened in the city of Jericho. And he says that when Christ was walking through the streets in the sight of everybody, Zacchaeus was the one man most eager to see Him. For it was a sign of his vehement desire that he climbed the tree, when rich men are usually proud and want to appear serious. It may well be that others had the same desire, but Luke deservedly celebrates this man before all the rest, and that both because of his station in life and of his wonderful and sudden conversion. But although faith was not yet formed in Zacchaeus, this was a certain preparation for it. He was moved by God to desire so much to see Christ—to the purpose, I mean, which was at once realized. For no doubt empty curiosity moved some to come to see Christ, even from a distance. But from what happened it is clear that there was a seed of godliness in Zacchaeus' mind. The Lord often, before He reveals Himself to them, inspires in men a blind feeling which brings them to Him although He is still hidden and unknown. And though they have not yet any fixed purpose, He does not disappoint them but in time reveals Himself to them.

281

Luke 19.5. *Zacchaeus, make haste, and come down.* A memorable example of grace! The Lord forestalls Zacchaeus, does not wait for an invitation, but asks straight out to be his guest. We know how much the very name of publican was then disliked, even detested—something that Luke expresses a little later. It was therefore a remarkable kindness that the Son of God should take the initiative and come to him whom men commonly shunned. Yet it is not surprising that He honours him like this, for He had already drawn him to Himself by the secret movings of the Spirit. And it was a more wonderful gift to dwell in his heart than to enter his house. And by this saying He declared that men never seek Him in vain if they sincerely desire to know Him. For Zacchaeus received far more than he had looked for. And the fact that Zacchaeus obeyed so readily and came down out of the tree to receive Christ shows the more clearly the power and directing of the Holy Spirit. For although he was not yet imbued with pure faith, his readiness and obedience were the beginning of faith.

Luke 19.7. *And when they saw it.* The townsfolk, and maybe some of Christ's companions, grumble when He turns uninvited to a man of an evil and disgraceful occupation. Thus the world, when it neglects the grace of God set before it, complains and criticizes if this is offered to others instead. But we see how unfair this grumbling was. They think it wrong that Christ should give so much honour to a wicked man. For 'sinner' here, as in many other places, is not to be taken in the ordinary sense, but means a man of disgraceful and infamous life. Granted that Zacchaeus was like this; but first we must ask for what purpose Christ invited Himself to his house. For while they are grumbling in public, inwardly God is illuminating wonderfully the glory of His name and so rebuts their wicked slander. For Zacchaeus' conversion was a wonderful work of God; yet there was no good reason why Zacchaeus should be stigmatized with infamy. He was a collector of taxes. There is nothing wicked in itself in collecting taxes; but among the Jews this system was considered so disgraceful and hateful that they could imagine nothing more disgraceful than having to pay tribute. But whatever sort of a man Zacchaeus was, Christ's kindness was laudable, not blameworthy, in not withholding His help from this poor man but bringing him from destruction to salvation. And so their wicked taking offence did not frighten Him from proceeding to fulfil the Father's command. And all His ministers should be endued with the same greatness of mind, so that the salvation of one soul should be more to them than the grumblings of all the ignorant people, and they should not cease to do their duty even when all their actions and words seem to lay them open to slanders.

Luke 19.8. *And Zacchaeus stood.* It is from this outcome that they should have judged Christ's action; but men are so hasty and perverse that they leave no place for God. Zacchaeus' conversion is described from its fruits and outward signs; since it is probable that he had grown rich to the hurt of many, he is ready to repay fourfold any whom he had defrauded. Moreover, he would devote a half of his possessions to the poor. Now it might be that a man bestowed all his goods on the poor and yet his liberality could be nothing in God's sight. But although there is here no mention of inward repentance, yet Luke means that the godly resolve which he commends in Zacchaeus came from a living root. In the same way Paul, in speaking of repentance, exhorts us to these duties so that men may understand that we are changed for the better—'Let him that stole, now not steal; but rather let him labour with his hands, so that he may help the poor and needy' (Eph. 4.28). Therefore, it all begins in the heart, but at the same time our repentance is attested by our works. And let us note that Zacchaeus was not at all offering God a share in his plunder, as many rich people give God a part of their thievings so as to be able to steal with greater freedom in the future and go scot-free for the injuries of the past. But Zacchaeus sacrifices a half of his goods to God in such a way as to make recompense for the losses he had caused. From this we gather that the riches he possessed were not gained illicitly. Thus Zacchaeus was not only ready to make satisfaction if he had defrauded anyone but also shared his lawful patrimony with the poor; and in this he shows that he had been converted from a wolf into not merely a sheep but even a shepherd. And as he puts right the sins he has already committed, so he renounces his evil tricks in the future; for God demands of His people that they abstain from all evil. Now Zacchaeus' example does not at all put the same necessity on others to give away a half of their goods. We must only hold the rule which the Lord prescribes, that we consecrate ourselves and all we have to holy and lawful purposes.

Luke 19.9. *Today is salvation.* Christ bears testimony to Zacchaeus that he has said nothing false. Yet He does not ascribe the cause of his salvation to Zacchaeus' good works, but because his conversion was the sure pledge of his divine adoption, He rightly gathers that his house should inherit salvation, and this is the significance of the words. For because Zacchaeus was one of Abraham's children He argues that his house is saved. But for anyone to be reckoned among the sons of Abraham he must imitate his faith. Scripture strictly attributes to faith the praise that it distinguishes the genuine sons of Abraham from strangers. Let us know, then, that what is chiefly praised in Zacchaeus is that on account of which it came about that his own good works

283

were also pleasing to God. Yet there is no doubt that Christ's teaching preceded Zacchaeus' conversion. Therefore the origin of his salvation was that he heard Christ teaching on the free mercy of God, on the reconciliation of men with Himself, on the redemption of the Church and that he embraces this teaching by faith. Since the Greek word οἶκος is masculine, this verse has been explained in two ways. The Vulgate refers it to Zacchaeus; and this interpretation I prefer. Erasmus would rather translate it that the house itself was the daughter of Abraham. I would not deny this, but I consider it is explained better of Zacchaeus. For because the Lord, when He adopts the father of a family, promises to be the God of the whole family, the salvation extends from the head to the whole body. And the copula καὶ is emphatic. For Christ means that Zacchaeus was no less the son of Abraham than the other Jews who so arrogantly cursed him. And lest his earlier life should seem to have shut the gate of salvation on him, He argues from His own office that there is nothing in this charge to offend anyone, since He was sent by the Father to save those who were lost.

*For it is as if a man, going into another country, called his own servants, and delivered unto them his goods. And unto one he gave five talents, to another two, to another one; to each according to his several ability and he went on his journey straightway. He that received the five talents went and traded with them, and made other five talents. In like manner he also that received the two gained other two. But he that received the one went away and digged in the earth, and hid his lord's money. Now after a long time the lord of those servants cometh, and maketh a reckoning with them. And he that received the five talents came and brought other five talents, saying, Lord, thou deliveredst unto me five talents: lo, I have gained other five talents through them. His lord said unto him, Well done, good and faithful servant: thou hast been faithful over a few things, I will set thee over many things: enter thou into the joy of thy lord. And he also that received the two talents came and said, Lord, thou deliveredst unto me two talents: lo, I have gained other two talents through them. His lord said unto him, Well done, good and faithful servant: thou hast been faithful over a few things, I will set thee over many things: enter thou into the joy of thy lord. And he also that had received the one talent came and said, Lord, I knew thee that thou art a hard man, reaping where thou didst not sow, and gathering where thou didst not scatter and I was afraid, and went and hid the talent in the earth: lo, thou hast thine own. But his lord answered and said unto him,*

*Thou wicked and slothful servant, thou knowest that I reap where I sowed not, and gather where I did not scatter; thou oughtest therefore to have put my money to the bankers, and at my coming I should have received back mine own with interest. Take ye away therefore the talent from him, and give it unto him that hath the ten talents. For unto every one that hath shall be given, and he shall have abundance: but from him that hath not, even that which he hath shall be taken away. And cast ye out the unprofitable servant into the outer darkness: there shall be the weeping and gnashing of teeth.* (Matt. 25.14-30)

*And as they heard these things, he added and spake a parable, because he was nigh unto Jerusalem, and because they supposed that the kingdom of God was immediately to appear. He said therefore, A certain nobleman went into a far country, to receive for himself a kingdom, and to return. And he called ten servants of his and gave them ten pounds, and said unto them, Trade ye herewith until I come. But his citizens hated him, and sent an ambassage after him, saying, We will not let this man reign over us. And it came to pass, when he was come back again, having received the kingdom, that he commanded these servants, unto whom he had given the money, to be called to him, that he might know what they had gained by trading. And the first came before him, saying, Lord, thy pound hath made ten pounds more. And he said unto him, Well done, thou good servant: because thou wast found faithful in a very little, have thou authority over ten cities. And the second came, saying, Thy pound, Lord, hath made five pounds. And he said unto him also, Be thou also over five cities. And another came, saying, Lord, behold, here is thy pound, which I have kept laid up in a napkin: for I feared thee, because thou art an austere man: thou takest up that thou layedst not down, and reapest that thou didst not sow. He saith unto him, Out of thine own mouth will I judge thee, thou wicked servant. Thou knowest that I am an austere man, taking up that I laid not down, and reaping that I did not sow; then wherefore gavest thou not my money into the bank, and I at my coming should have required it with interest? And he said unto them that stood by, Take away from him the pound, and give it to him that hath the ten pounds. And they said unto him, Lord, he hath ten pounds. For I say unto you, that unto every one that hath shall be given; but from him that hath not, even that which he hath shall be taken away from him. Howbeit these mine enemies, which would not that I should reign over them, bring hither, and slay them before me. And when he had thus spoken, he went on before, going up to Jerusalem.* (Luke 19.11-28)

Luke 19.11. *And as they heard these things.* It was like some deformity that as soon as the disciples were warned of the approaching death of Christ their thoughts flew away to His Kingdom. And it was a twofold error to imagine blessed peace without the cross and, too, to reckon the Kingdom of God by their fleshly sense. It shows how weak and clouded was their faith, for although they had had a taste of the hope of the resurrection, yet it was too small a taste to hold anything sure and steady about Christ. They believe He is the Redeemer who was promised of old; and from this they conceive hope of the restoration of the Church. But their knowledge soon degenerated into an imagination which either perverted or obscured the power of His Kingdom. It was quite absurd that so many warnings should be forgotten without any profit to them. When Christ had recently declared quite definitely that a hard and ignominious death was at hand for Him, it was a brutish stupor in them not merely to remain secure but to hurry, as it were, to a joyful victory.

Luke 19.12. *A certain nobleman.* Matthew put this parable among others without regard for the time sequence. But because it seems his purpose from chapter 22 onwards to collect together Christ's final sayings, there is no reason why readers should worry much as to which was spoken on the first or the second or the third day in that short time. But it is important to observe how Matthew and Luke differ. The one deals with only one aspect, the other with two. That which is common to them is that Christ is like a nobleman who to win a kingdom undertook a distant expedition and entrusted his money to his servants to administer, and so on. What is peculiar to Luke is that the prince's subjects took advantage of his absence to stage a revolution and throw off his yoke. In both parts Christ's meaning was that the disciples were very deceived in thinking that His Kingdom was already established and that He was going to Jerusalem to set up a prosperous state. He takes from them the hope of a present Kingdom and exhorts them to hope and patience. For He teaches them that they must undergo troubles for a long time before they enjoy that glory which they do not greatly desire.

*Into a far country.* Since the disciples thought that Christ was even now entering into possession of His Kingdom, He first corrects the error that His Kingdom had to be won by a long journey. Those who seize on sophistries argue too subtly about the significance of 'a far country'. To me Christ merely seems to mean His long absence from the time of His death to His second coming. For although He sits at the right hand of the Father and has the rule in heaven and on earth, and from His ascension into heaven has been given all power, so that before Him every knee should bow, yet because He has not been revealed, He is not improperly said to be absent from His people, until He shall come again, adorned with a new kingship. Yet it is true that

286

He now reigns when He regenerates His people into the heavenly life, and fashions them anew to the image of God and makes them fellows with the angels, when He governs the Church by His Word, guards it by His grace and upholds it by His power, and supplies whatever is necessary for its salvation, when He restrains the fury of Satan and all the ungodly and overthrows all their schemes. But because the mode in which He reigns is hidden by His flesh, its manifestation is properly delayed until the last day. Therefore when the apostles foolishly grasped at the shadow of a kingdom, the Lord declared that He must seek His Kingdom afar, so that they may learn to bear delay.

Luke 19.13. *And he called ten servants.* There is no more particular significance in the number of the servants than there is in the sums of money. By mentioning differing amounts, Matthew contains a richer teaching, that Christ does not make all these men bear an equal burden of business, but to one was committed a small sum, to another a greater. Both Evangelists agree that Christ would in a way be living apart from His people until the final day of resurrection, yet that it would be quite wrong for them to sit idle and useless in the meanwhile; for to each is entrusted a certain office in which he may engage. Therefore he should be zealous in his business, and energetically administer the affairs of the Lord. Luke says simply that a *mina* was given to each, because whether it be more or less that the Lord commits to us, each alike must render account for himself. As I have said, Matthew is fuller and plainer in that he makes distinct degrees. For we know that the Lord does not give to all indiscriminately the same measure of gifts but distributes them variously, as seems good to Him, so that some men excel others (Eph. 4.7). Moreover, we learn that all the gifts the Lord bestows on us are like money deposited with us, for us to make some gain out of it (I Cor. 12.7). For there is nothing worse than keeping God's graces buried and not making use of them, since their force consists in their fruit.

Matt. 25.15. *To each according to his several ability.* Christ is not here distinguishing nature from spiritual gifts; for there is neither power nor skill which should not be referred to God. Thus whoever is willing to share with God will leave nothing for himself. What, then, does it mean when the head of the family is said to commit to each more or less according to his ability? Simply that God, as He disposes every man and gives him natural gifts, so also He lays this or that responsibility upon him, engages him in activities, advances him to various functions, supplies him with excellent ability for activity and also gives him the opportunities. The Papists are ridiculous to deduce from this that God's gifts are conferred according to the measure of a man's deserving. For although the Vulgate uses the word 'virtue'

287

(*virtutis*), it does not mean that the virtue is divinely given according as men have behaved well and obtained praise for their virtue, but only so far as the head of the family judged them fit. However, we know that none is found fit by God until he is made so: and there is no ambiguity in the Greek word which Christ used.

Matt. 25.20. *And he that received the five talents.* Those who use to advantage what God deposits with them are said to trade. For the life of the godly is aptly compared to business, since they should deal among themselves to maintain fellowship; and the industry with which each man prosecutes the task laid on him, and his very vocation, the ability to act aright, and the rest of the gifts, are reckoned as merchandise, since their purpose and use is the mutual communication among men. And the fruit of which Christ speaks is the common profit which lightens up the glory of God. For although God is neither enriched nor increased by our works, the man who greatly profits his brethren and applies to the use of their salvation the gifts he has received from God is said to give fruit or gain to God Himself. For the heavenly Father esteems so highly the salvation of men that whatever contributes to it He wishes to be reckoned to His account. And in order that we shall not grow weary in well doing, Christ declares that their labour will not be in vain who practice their vocation faithfully. In Luke he who had gained five *minae* is said to become ruler over five cities. By these words He declares that the glory of His Kingdom at His final advent will be very different from how it appears now. For now we are laboriously looking after the business of one who is as it were absent; but then He will have a full and manifold supply of honours in His hand to adorn us with magnificently. In Matthew the form of speaking is simpler: 'Enter thou into the joy of thy Lord.' By this He means that faithful servants, whose activities He approves, will be His fellows in the blessed wealth of all good things.

But it may be asked what He means when He adds, 'Take away the *mina* from him and give it to him who has ten.' For this overthrows all economic sense. I reply: We must remember, as I said earlier, that it is wrong to insist precisely on the individual details. The native sense is: Although lazy and useless servants are now furnished with gifts of the Spirit, at last they will be stripped of all and their poverty and shameful need will bring glory to the good. And Christ says that lazy men bury the talent or *mina* in the earth because they think only of their ease and pleasure and do not want to undergo any troubles—as we see in many who are devoted to themselves and their own private convenience and evade all the duties of love and have no regard for the common edification. The head of the family is said on his return to have called his servants to a reckoning. This should make

288

the good more eager, since they know that their work is not at all wasted; and on the other hand it should greatly frighten the lazy and idle. We therefore learn that we should daily spur ourselves on, before the Lord come and enter into a reckoning with us.

Matt. 25.24. *Lord, I knew thee that thou art a hard man.* This hardness is not part of the essence of the parable, and they are philosophising irrelevantly who here dispute how God acts towards His people severely and strictly. Christ no more wanted to indicate such a rigorousness than to praise usury when He represented the head of the house as saying that the money should have been deposited in a bank so that it should at least have gained interest. Christ only means that there is no excuse for the slackness of those who both suppress God's gifts and consume their age in idleness. From this we also gather that no form of life is more praiseworthy before God than that which yields usefulness to human society.

Matt. 25.29-30. This sentence, *For unto everyone that hath shall be given,* has been expounded in chapter 13.

We have also said, in chapter 8, that *outer darkness* is the opposite of light in the house. In antiquity most feasts were held at night, by the light of many torches and lamps; so Christ says that those who are cast out of God's Kingdom are cast outside into darkness.

Luke 19.27. *Howbeit these mine enemies.* In this second part He seems to be rebuking the Jews in particular; yet He includes all who rise up in rebellion against their absent Lord. And Christ's intention was not only to frighten them with the threat of such horrifying vengeance, but also to keep His own in loyal submission. For it is no light temptation to see the Kingdom of God scattered by the treachery and rebellion of the many. Therefore, that we may remain quiet amid tumults, Christ tells us that He will come again and that at His coming He will avenge the ungodly rebellion.

*And when they drew nigh unto Jerusalem, and came unto Bethphage, unto the mount of Olives, then Jesus sent two disciples, saying unto them, Go into the village that is over against you, and straightway ye shall find an ass tied, and a colt with her: loose them, and bring them unto me. And if any man say aught unto you, ye shall say, The Lord hath need of them; and straightway he will send them. Now all this came to pass, that it might be fulfilled which was spoken by the prophet, saying, Tell ye the daughter of Zion, Behold thy King cometh unto thee, Meek, and sitting upon an ass, and upon a colt the foal of an ass. And the disciples went, and did even as Jesus appointed them, and brought the ass, and the colt, and put on them their garments; and He sat thereon. And the most part of the multitude spread their garments in the way; and others cut branches from the trees, and spread them in the way. And the multitudes that went before him, and that followed, cried, saying, Hosanna to the son of David: Blessed is he that cometh in the name of the Lord; Hosanna in the highest.* (Matt. 21.1-9)

*And when they draw nigh unto Jerusalem, unto Bethphage and Bethany, at the mount of Olives, he sendeth two of his disciples, and saith unto them, Go your way into the village that is over against you: and straightway as ye enter into it, ye shall find a colt tied, whereon no man ever yet sat; loose him, and bring him. And if any one say unto you, Why do ye this? say ye, The Lord hath need of him; and straightway he will send him back hither. And they went away, and found a colt tied at the door without in the open street; and they loose him. And certain of them that stood there said unto them, What do ye, loosing the colt? And they said unto them even as Jesus had said: and they let them go. And they bring the colt unto Jesus, and cast on him their garments; and he sat upon him. And many spread their garments upon the way; and others branches, which they had cut from the fields and spread them upon the way. And they that went before, and they that followed, cried, Hosanna; Blessed is he that cometh in the name of the Lord: Blessed is the kingdom that cometh in the name of the Lord, the kingdom of our father David: Hosanna in the highest.* (Mark 11.1-10)

*And it came to pass, when he drew nigh unto Bethphage and Bethany, at the mount that is called the mount of Olives, he sent two of the disciples, saying, Go your way into the village over against you; in the which as ye enter ye shall find a colt tied, whereon no man ever yet sat: loose him, and bring him. And if any one ask you, Why do ye loose him? thus shall ye say, The Lord hath need of him. And they that were sent went away, and found even as he had said unto them. And as they were loosing the colt, the owners thereof said unto them, Why loose ye the colt? And they said, The Lord hath need of him. And they brought him to Jesus: and they threw their garments upon the colt, and set Jesus thereon. And as he went, they spread their garments in the way. And as he was now drawing nigh, even at the descent of the mount of Olives, the whole multitude of the disciples began to rejoice and praise God with a loud voice for all the mighty works which they had seen; saying, Blessed is the King that cometh in the name of the Lord: peace in heaven, and glory in the highest.* (Luke 19.29-38)

It was not because He was tired from the journey that Christ sent His disciples for the ass but for a different purpose. The time of His death was drawing near and He wanted to show by a solemn ceremony the nature of His Kingdom. He had begun to do that from the time of His baptism, but He still had to give this example of it towards the end of His calling. For why had He hitherto refrained from using the title of king yet now openly professes that He is a king, save because He was not far from the end of His course? Therefore when His journey to heaven was near, He wished to inaugurate His Kingdom openly on earth. This display would have been ridiculous but that it corresponded to the prophecy of Zechariah. To claim royal honour, Christ entered Jerusalem riding on an ass. Magnificent splendour indeed! Add that the ass was borrowed for the occasion, and that because it lacked saddle and trappings the disciples had to throw their clothes across it—all this a sign of terrible and shameful poverty. I grant that a great crowd accompanied Him—but what were they? Those who had come thoughtlessly in from the villages. Shouts of praise resound. But from whom? From the poor, men of the despised masses. He might well seem, therefore, to be exposing Himself deliberately to the mockery of all men. But since there were two related activities that He had to perform in order to give proof of His Kingdom and to teach that it had nothing to do with earthly empires and was not set in the transient riches of this world, it was necessary for Him to take this way. Although it might perhaps have been meaningless to heathen men unless God had long before declared through His prophet that the King who would come to restore salvation to the people would be like this. Therefore lest Christ's lowly condition should be a hindrance to our seeing in this spectacle His spiritual Kingdom, let us keep before our eyes the heavenly oracle in which God adorned His Son more with the wretched appearance of a beggar than if He had gleamed with all the regalia of kings. The story would have no taste for us without this sauce. There is therefore great weight in Matthew's words when he says that the oracle of the prophet was fulfilled. For because it seemed hardly possible that men, who are given to over-opulence and display, should gain anything from this story by their own fleshly sense, he leads them from the mere sight of the event to the consideration of the prophecy.

Matt. 21.2. *Go into the village.* He was at Bethany, and therefore it was not to lighten the journey that he borrowed the ass, for He could easily have made the rest of the journey on foot. But as kings mount their chariots so as to be the more visible, so the Lord wanted to turn the eyes of the people to Himself and to confirm the acclamations of His followers by a certain sign, so that no-one should think that He was being called king against His own wishes. It is not clear where He told them to get the ass, although it can easily be deduced that it was a village near the city. It is ridiculous that some expound this allegorically of Jerusalem. Nor is the allegory any more pertinent which some have invented on the ass and the colt. They say the ass is a figure of the Jewish people which had long submitted to and borne the yoke of the Law, and the Gentiles are represented by the colt, which had never been ridden. Christ therefore first sat on the ass in that He owed His beginning to the Jews; afterwards He transferred to the colt in that He was in the second place set over the Gentiles. And Matthew seems to indicate that He rode on both. But synecdoches frequently occur in Scripture, and it is not surprising if two are named for one. From the other Evangelists, however, it is quite clear that Christ used only the ass. Zechariah removes all ambiguity, for he is, in the common usage of Hebrew, saying the same thing twice (9.9).

*And straightway ye shall find.* Lest the disciples should hesitate to do at once what He wished, the Lord answers their questions in advance. First He points out that He did not send them on the off-chance when He said that at the first entrance into the village they would find a young ass and its mother; and then that none would prevent them taking it away if they replied that there was need of it. And in this way He proved His deity. For to know what He cannot see and to turn men's hearts to assent, is for God alone. For although it could happen that the owner of the ass would be at home, whether it would then be convenient for him, whether he would trust unknown men, all this does not lie in the judgment of mortal man. But just as Christ confirms the disciples to obey readily, so we see how they on their side show themselves cheerfully obedient. And their success shows that this whole affair was divinely governed.

Matt. 21.5. *Tell ye the daughter of Zion.* These are not the *ipsissima verba* of Zechariah. But the Evangelist correctly applies to all godly teachers what God had bidden the prophet testify of one. For the single hope on which the children of God had to found and establish themselves was that at last the Redeemer would come. And this is why the prophet teaches that Christ's coming would bring believers full and real cause for joy. For since God is propitious to them only in the intervention of the Mediator and that Mediator is the one who frees His people from all evils, what can there be outside Him to rejoice men lost in their sins and overwhelmed with miseries? And just as we must needs be deeply stricken with sorrow by the absence of Christ, so the prophet reminds believers that they have real cause for rejoicing when the Redeemer is with them. And although Zechariah praises Christ with other titles—that He is righteous and furnished with a salvation—Matthew takes only one part and harmonizes it with his own purpose. This is, that He would come as a poor man or meek; in other words, unlike earthly kings who excel in the magnificence and wealth of their estate. Now he adds what marks Him out as poor, that He rides on an ass or the colt of an ass; for there is no doubt that he is contrasting the poor and common riding of an ass with regal pomp.

Matt. 21.6. *And the disciples went.* We have mentioned above that the disciples are praised here for their readiness to obey. For Christ's authority was not so great that His name by itself would be sufficient to move men unknown to Him. And they might also be afraid of being taken for thieves. This shows how much they deferred to the Master when they made no reply but simply hurried off to do what He had ordered relying on His commands and promise. Let us also learn by their example to advance through all difficulties and offer the Lord the obedience He demands from us. For He will take away the hindrances and find out a way and not let our efforts be in vain.

*And the most part of the multitude.* The Evangelists are here narrating that the people acknowledge Christ to be the King. The sight could well have been laughable—a rabble tearing down branches, strewing their clothes on the road, giving the empty name of King to Christ. But they were doing this in all seriousness, and their homage was paid sincerely; and Christ reckons them fit to be heralds of His Kingdom. We need not be surprised that it had such a beginning, when today, sitting at the right hand of the Father, He appoints from His heavenly throne obscure men to celebrate His majesty in their lowly manner. It seems improbable to me that (as some commentators conjecture) palm branches were cut down because of an ancient ritual act for that day. Rather it appears that this honour was shown to Christ from a sudden moving of the Spirit, and the disciples had no such intention, although they initiated it and the rest of the crowd followed them. This is what is inferred from Luke's words.

Matt. 21.9. *Hosanna to the Son of David.* This praise is taken from Psalm 118.25-26. Matthew deliberately recites the Hebrew words, so that we may know that the praises and prayers which the disciples were crying out were not given thoughtlessly to Christ, nor poured out without deliberation, but reverently followed a set form of prayer which the Holy Spirit had dictated to the whole Church by the mouth of the prophet. For although he was there treating of his own Kingdom, there can be no doubt that he himself was looking, and wanted others to look, at the eternal succession which the Lord had promised him. For he composed a perpetual law of praying for the Church, which would continue in use even when the welfare of the Kingdom had collapsed. And so the custom prevailed that prayers for the promised redemption took the form of these words. And, as

293

we have just said, Matthew's intention was to quote in Hebrew the well-known hymn and so teach that Christ was acknowledged as Redeemer by the crowd. The pronunciation of the words has changed a little, and it ought rather to be 'Hoshiana'—'I pray thee, save!' But we know that it is hardly possible to carry a word from one language to another without changing the sound of it to some degree.

Nor did the Spirit train only the ancient people to pray daily for the reign of Christ. The same rule is laid down for us nowadays. And indeed, God wishes to reign only by the hand of His Son; so that when we say, 'Thy kingdom come', we are saying the same thing that is expressed more clearly in the Psalms. Add that when we ask God to keep His Son as our King, we acknowledge that this Kingdom is not set up by men nor sustained by their power but stands invincible by heavenly help. He is said to come in the name of the Lord who does not intrude himself but takes up the Kingdom at God's command and appointment. This appears more definitely in Mark, when he adds another acclamation: 'Blessed is the kingdom of our father David, which cometh in the name of the Lord.' For they are speaking thus in regard to the promises; because the Lord had declared that He would at last be the Saviour of His people and signified in what way David's kingdom would be restored. Therefore we see that to Christ was ascribed the honour of Mediator, from whom the restoration of everything and of salvation was to be hoped. From the fact that the people who called Christ's Kingdom the kingdom of David were simple and uneducated we learn that this idea must have been very common although today it seems forced and hard to many, because they have not much knowledge of Scripture.

A few words are added in Luke: *peace in heaven, and glory in the highest.* There would be no obscurity in this, except that it does not correspond to the angels' song in chapter 2. There the angels give glory to God in heaven, but peace to men on earth. Here both peace and glory are referred to God. Yet there is no disagreement in meaning; for although the angels show more clearly the cause why they should sing glory to God (that is, because men in the world experience His mercy) yet the sense is the same that the crowd here proclaims, that there is peace in heaven, because we know that in the world unhappy souls find rest only when God reconciles Himself to them from heaven.

*And when he drew nigh, he saw the city and wept over it, saying, O, if thou hadst known in this day, even thou, the things which belong unto*

*thy peace! but now they are hid from thine eyes. For the days shall
come upon thee, that thine enemies shall cast up a bank about thee, and
compass thee round, and keep thee in on every side, and shall dash thee
to the ground, and thy children within thee; and they shall not leave in
thee one stone upon another; because thou knewest not the time of thy
visitation.* (Luke 19.41-44)

Luke 19.41. *He wept over it.* Since Christ desired nothing more than
to do the work appointed Him by the Father and knew that the purpose of His calling was to gather the lost sheep of the house of Israel,
He wished His coming to be the salvation of all. This was why He
was moved by compassion and wept over the approaching destruction
of Jerusalem. For when He considered that it had been divinely
chosen as the sacred abode, in which should dwell the covenant of
eternal salvation, the sanctuary from which salvation should come
forth for all the world, He could not help grieving bitterly over its
destruction. Nor is it any wonder that He could not hold back His
tears when He saw the people who had been adopted to the hope of
eternal life perishing wretchedly by their ingratitude and malice. Some
have the absurd idea that Christ was grieving over an evil which He
could have healed; but this problem is easily solved. For, just as He
descended from heaven to be the witness and minister of God's salvation in the human flesh that He put on, so He was truly endowed with
human feelings so far as concerned the office he had undertaken. And
it is always wise to observe the person that He bears when He speaks
or labours for men's salvation. Thus in this passage, to fulfil the
Father's command faithfully, He needed to desire that the fruit of
redemption should come to the whole body of the elect people.
Hence, in that He was given to this people for their salvation, He
bewailed their destruction for the sake of His office. I grant that He
was God; but as often as it behoved Him to fulfil the office of teacher,
His Deity rested and in a sense hid Itself, lest It should hinder Him as
Mediator. And by His tears He bore witness, not only that He had
a brotherly love for those for whose sake He became man but that also
there was poured into His human nature by God the spirit of fatherly
love.

Luke 19.42. *If thou hadst known.* This saying is broken by pathos.
For we know that when we are profoundly moved we can only speak
in half sentences. Add that two feelings are mixed together here:
Christ not only bemoans the destruction of the city, but also rebukes
the ungrateful people for their terrible crime in rejecting the salvation
offered to them and bringing on themselves the fearful judgment of
God. The conjunction 'even' is emphatic, in that Christ is tacitly

comparing Jerusalem to the other cities of Judaea, nay, of the whole world, in this sense: 'If even thou, who surpassest the whole world in the unique privilege you have been given; if thou shouldst at least know, who art a heavenly sanctuary on earth.'

There follows at once another amplification relating to the time. 'Although you have hitherto been wickedly and irreligiously obstinate against God, yet now at least is the time of repentance.' For He means that the day had already come which in God's eternal counsel had been fore-ordained for the salvation of Jerusalem and which had been foretold by the prophets. 'This is the acceptable time', says Isaiah, 'this is the day of salvation' (Isa. 49.8; II Cor. 6.2). 'Seek ye the Lord while he may be found; call ye upon him while he is near' (55.6).

By the word 'peace' he means, in the Hebrew usage, all the parts of happiness. He does not simply say that Jerusalem did not know its peace, but what belonged to its peace. For it often happens that men are very much aware of their happiness, but the way and the means, as they say, they do not know because they are blinded by their malice. Now, in that reproof is mingled with compassion, let us observe that the more excellent gifts with which men are endowed, the graver the punishment they deserve, in that sacrilegious profanation of heavenly grace is added to their other sins. Secondly, let us note that the nearer God comes to us and brings the light of sound doctrine, we are the less excusable if we neglect the opportunity. The gate of salvation is indeed always open, but because He is sometimes silent, it is an extraordinary blessing when He invites us to Himself familiarly and with clear voice. And therefore a more severe punishment awaits contempt of Him.

*But now they are hid.* This is not said to lessen the guilt of Jerusalem; rather their monstrous stupidity is remarked to make the disgrace plain when they had not perceived the presence of God. I grant that it is God alone who opens the eyes of blind minds; nor is anyone fit to perceive the mysteries of the Kingdom of heaven save he whom God enlightens inwardly by His Spirit. But those who perish from their own brutish blindness do not for that reason deserve pardon. Christ also wanted to remove the offence that might hinder some ignorant and weak people. For since the eyes of all were turned to that city, its example had a great influence, whether for ill or for good. Therefore, lest its unbelief and proud contempt of the Gospel should be a hindrance to anyone, He condemns its horrible blindness.

*Luke 19.43. The days shall come upon thee.* He now, so to say, takes up the role of judge and accuses Jerusalem more harshly. So also the prophets, although they wept over the destruction of those for whom

296

they were responsible, pulled themselves together to denounce them, for they knew that not only was the responsibility for men's salvation laid upon them but also they had been appointed heralds of the divine judgment. In this position He proclaims that horrifying punishments would be laid upon Jerusalem because it did not know the time of its visitation—that is, it despised the Redeemer who had been revealed to it and did not embrace His grace. Let the savagery of the punishments which that city endured terrify us, lest we extinguish the light of salvation by our slothfulness. Rather let us take care to receive God's grace, nay, run energetically to meet it.

# INDEX TO THE HARMONY

# INDEX OF NAMES

# GENERAL INDEX

Holy Spirit, 43., 45ff.
humility, 103f., 129., 213ff.

infant baptism, 252

James, 241, 270ff.
Jericho, 281
Jerusalem, 295ff.
Jews (passim)
Job, 142
John Baptist, 2ff., 5ff., 137f. 139ff., 204
John Evangelist, 239ff., 270ff.
Jonah, 58f., 178
Jordan, 183
justification, 127ff., 255
kindness of God, 221ff.
kingdom of Christ, 3f., 7. 15, 36, 91,
  106ff., 133f., 261ff., 270f., 291ff.
knowledge of God, 24

language, 48ff.
Law, 156ff., 254ff.
Lazarus (see parables)
Lebanon, 183

Macherus, 143
Magdala, 172
Martha, 62, 89f.
Marthaca, 140
Mary (mother of Jesus) 53ff.
Mary (sister of Martha), 89f.
Mary Magdalene, 62
marriage, 243ff., 248ff.
merits, 123f., 127ff., 257, 265f.
Meroë, 59
ministry, 17f.
miracles (see signs)
miracles
  blind man, 182
  blind men (and Bartimaeus), 278ff.
  daughter of Canaanite woman,
    166ff.
  deaf mute, 172ff.
  demoniac boy, 206ff.
  feeding of five thousand, 146ff.
  feeding of seven thousand, 174f.
  man with dropsy, 102.
  man with withered hand, 31ff.
  stilling storm, 151f.
  ten lepers, 131ff.
  woman with spirit of infirmity, 96ff.
Moses, 13, 43, 121, 198ff., 256.

Nazarenes, 135f.

newness of life, 109f.
Nile, 59.
Nineveh, 58f.

offences, 4f., 216ff.

parables, 66, 80f., 83
parables
  children at play, 10
  Dives and Lazarus, 116ff.
  draw net, 83ff.
  fig tree, 95f.
  hid treasure, 82f.
  importunate widow, 125ff.
  labourers in vineyard, 264ff.
  lost coin, 219f.
  lost sheep, 219f.
  marriage feast, 106ff.
  pearl of great price, 82f.
  Pharisee and publican, 127ff.
  places at table, 103f.
  ploughman, 122ff.
  prodigal son, 221ff.
  rich fool, 92ff.
  seed growing secretly, 79ff.
  sower, 63ff., 70ff.
  talents (and pounds), 285ff.
  tares, 74ff.
  unjust steward, 111ff.
  unmerciful servant, 233ff.
Paul, 22
Peter, 152ff., 165, 185ff., 192ff., 199ff.,
  233f., 237f.
Pharaoh, 43
Pharisees, 27ff., 32, 34, 46, 49, 57ff.,
  85ff., 98f., 100f., 103, 106, 114,
  127ff., 133f., 157f., 160, 162f.,
  175f., 179, 181 219, 243
Philip tetrarch, 140
Phoenicia, 172
Pilate, 95
power of keys, 187f., 230f.
prayer, 125f., 210
pride, 127ff.
prophets, 6ff.
publicans 127ff.

repentance, 16f., 25, 222f.
resurrection, 192
revelation, 21ff., 64ff., 200ff.
rigorism, 224f.

305

Printed in the United States
151328LV00015BA/78/A